GLOBAL MONITORING REPORT 2004

Policies and Actions for Achieving the Millennium Development Goals and Related Outcomes

1818 H Street, NW
Washington, DC 20433
Telephone: 202-473-1000
Internet: www.worldbank.org
E-mail: feedback@worldbank.org

1 2 3 4 07 06 05 04

This volume is a product of the staff of the World Bank and the International Monetary Fund. The findings, interpretations, and conclusions expressed herein do not necessarily reflect the views of the Board of Executive Directors of the World Bank, the Board of Executive Directors of the International Monetary Fund, or the governments they represent.

The World Bank and the International Monetary Fund do not guarantee the accuracy of the data included in this work. The boundaries, colors, denominations, and other information shown on any map in this work do not imply any judgment on the part of the World Bank or the International Monetary Fund concerning the legal status of any territory or the endorsement or acceptance of such boundaries.

ISBN 0-8213-5859-6

Contents

Boxes

Figures

Tables

Foreword

This *Global Monitoring Report* is the first in a planned series of annual reports assessing the implementation of policies and actions for achieving the Millennium Development Goals (MDGs) and related outcomes. These reports will underpin regular monitoring by the Development Committee, the joint Ministerial body of our two institutions, of progress on the policy agenda; and they will aid the Development Committee in setting priorities for action and defining the accountabilities of the key actors—developing and developed countries and multilateral institutions. The *Global Monitoring Report* is being published in order to disseminate its findings and messages more widely. We expect to publish these reports each year and to maintain the momentum toward achieving the MDGs by 2015.

This report has been prepared jointly by the staff of the World Bank and the International Monetary Fund, in close collaboration with partner agencies—other multilateral development banks, the United Nations, World Trade Organization, Organisation for Economic Co-operation and Development and its Development Assistance Committee, and the European Commission. It is particularly encouraging that we now have such a broad partnership supporting this effort. We hope that this first report will spur further interaction on policies and actions to meet the agreed development goals.

The findings of the report provide a sobering assessment of progress toward the MDGs, and of progress in meeting the commitments made at Monterrey. As the report makes clear, on current trends, most MDGs will not be met by most countries. This is not to downplay the impressive progress made in some countries, particularly large ones such as China and India. But there are many that are falling behind, especially in Sub-Saharan Africa. And we can do better even in countries where progress has been good. There is an urgent need to scale up actions, building on the foundations laid by past successes and lessons learned from past mistakes. The report identifies where the need for action is most critical.

The report provides a range of evidence on the improvement of policies and institutions in developing countries. We have seen evidence of this improvement directly, through our own visits and interactions with people in countries in all parts of the developing world. In Africa, for instance, the New Partnership for Africa's Development has asserted a new accountability, and there are now many countries that have taken credible steps to strengthen their policies and governance with a clear sense that there is now an unprecedented opportunity for accelerating progress on development results. More needs to be done to deepen and sustain reforms, but we believe that we have the basis for scaling up in many countries.

As the report shows, in contrast to the improving performance in many developing countries, the developed countries are falling behind on two critical fronts that are vital to accelerating progress and scaling up results—trade and aid. We cannot overemphasize the importance and urgency of reinvigorating the Doha Round, including agreement on improved market access for agriculture and labor-intensive manufactures that are so critical to the prospects of the poorest countries. The other area for priority attention is the quantity and quality of aid. There is a clear need to increase the volume of development assistance in support of countries implementing sound macroeconomic, structural, and institutional policies to accelerate progress toward the MDGs. In parallel, we need political commitment on the agenda to improve the quality of aid—to align aid better with country-owned priorities, to make it more predictable and flexible, to focus it on results, and to harmonize aid practices and procedures.

The report also highlights the need for continued attention to how international agencies, including our own, can strengthen their support at the country, regional, and global levels. There is clear recognition of the importance of strong results orientation in what we do individually and collectively. Refining and strengthening institutional roles in low-income countries, including deepening the process of preparation and implementation of Poverty Reduction Strategy Papers, is a priority area for attention. At the same time, we need to continue to adapt approaches and instruments to the evolving needs of middle-income countries.

In sum, this first *Global Monitoring Report* is, in our view, an important and credible step in putting in place a framework for results and accountability that will enhance the international development community's review of progress on and priorities for achieving global development goals.

James D. Wolfensohn
President
World Bank

Rodrigo de Rato
Managing Director
International Monetary Fund

Acknowledgments

This report has been prepared jointly by the staff of the World Bank and the International Monetary Fund. In preparing the report, staff have collaborated closely with partner institutions—other multilateral development banks, the United Nations, World Trade Organization, Organisation for Economic Co-operation and Development and its Development Assistance Committee, and the European Commission. The cooperation and support of staff of these institutions are gratefully acknowledged.

Zia Qureshi was the lead author and manager of the report. The work was carried out under the general guidance of Shengman Zhang, Managing Director, World Bank. The Bank team of contributors included Shaida Badiee, Gilles Bauche, Gordon Betcherman, Milan Brahmbhatt, Cecila Briceno-Garmendia, Barbara Bruns, Punam Chuhan, Mansoor Dailami, Anis Dani, Shantayanan Devarajan, Simeon Djankov, David Dollar, Mark Dorfman, William Dorotinsky, Poul Engberg-Pedersen, Antonio Estache, Manuel Felix, Deon Filmer, Lucia Fort, Engilbert Gudmundsson, Christopher Hall, Jonathan Halpern, Kirk Hamilton, James Hanson, Bernard Hoekman, Mary Hollifield, Philip Keefer, Steve Knack, Victoria Levin, Maureen Lewis, Pilar Maistera, Tamar Manuelyan Atinc, Roberto Martin-Hurtado, Caralee McLiesh, Aaditya Mattoo, Marcelo Olarreaga, John Panzer, Axel Peuker, Dilip Ratha, Vanessa Saldanha, Joanne Salop, Sudhir Shetty, Susan Stout, Eric Swanson, Caroline Van Den Berg, Dominique Van Der Mensbrugghe, and Linda Van Gelder.

Inputs from IMF staff were coordinated by James Boughton. Other Fund contributors included Charles Blitzer, Benedict Clements, Thomas Dorsey, Peter Fallon, Judith Gold, Sanjeev Gupta, Peter Heller, Timothy Lane, Hans Peter Lankes, James Morsink, David Robinson, Carlo Sdralevich, Mark Swinburne, Patrizia Tumbarello, and Kal Wajid.

Guidance received from the Executive Directors of the Bank and the Fund during discussions of the draft report is gratefully acknowledged. The report has also benefited from many useful comments and suggestions received from Bank and Fund management and staff in the course of the preparation and review of the report. The World Bank's Office of the Publisher coordinated book design, editing, and print production.

Abbreviations and Acronyms

AFD	Agence Française de Développement
AfDB	African Development Bank
AGOA	African Growth Opportunity Act
AMS	Aggregate measure of support
APRM	African Peer Review Mechanism
ARDE	Annual Review of Development Effectiveness
AROE	Annual Report on Operations Evaluation
AsDB	Asian Development Bank
ATC	Agreement on Textiles and Clothing
AVEs	Ad valorem equivalents
Bank	World Bank
BCP	Basel Core Principle
BEEPS	Business Environment and Enterprise Performance Surveys
BPO	Business process outsourcing
CAC	Collective action clauses
CAE	Country Assistance Evaluation
CAP	Common Agricultural Policy
CAS	Country Assistance Strategy
CBO	Community-based organization
CDF	Comprehensive Development Framework
CEDAW	Convention on Elimination of All Forms of Discrimination against Women
CGIAR	Consultative Group on International Agricultural Research
CIPE	Country Institutional and Policy Evaluation
CPA	Country Performance Assessment
CPIA	Country Policy and Institutional Assessment
DAC	Development Assistance Committee (OECD)
DATA	Data Accountability and Technical Assistance Project
DB	Doing Business Project
DEC	Development Economics Group (World Bank)
DHS	Demographic and Health Survey
EAP	East Asia and Pacific
EBA	Everything-but-Arms Initiative
EBRD	European Bank for Reconstruction and Development
ECA	Europe and Central Asia region
Educo	Education with the Participation of Communities Program
EFA-FTI	Education for All–Fast-Track Initiative
EIB	European Investment Bank
EPR	Environmental performance review

ESAF	Enhanced Structural Adjustment Facility (IMF)
ESW	Economic and sector work
EU	European Union
FDI	Foreign direct investment
FSAP	Financial Sector Assessment Program (IMF and World Bank)
FSLC	Financial Sector Liaison Committee
FSSAP	Female Secondary School Assistance Program (Bangladesh)
Fund	International Monetary Fund
GAC	Governance and Anti-Corruption Survey
GATS	General Agreement on Trade in Services
GDF	*Global Development Finance*
GDP	Gross domestic product
GEF	Global Environment Facility
GEP	*Global Economic Prospects*
GFATM	Global Fund to Fight AIDS, Tuberculosis, and Malaria
GFS	Government Finance Statistics
GNI	Gross national income
GPGs	Global public goods
GSP	Generalized System of Preferences
HIPC	Heavily indebted poor country
HIPC AAP	HIPC Assessment and Action Plan
HS	Harmonized System
IAP	Infrastructure Action Plan
IBRD	International Bank for Reconstruction and Development
ICA	Investment climate assessment
ICB/NCB	International Competitive Bidding/National Competitive Bidding
ICRG	International Country Risk Guide
IDA	International Development Association
IDB	Inter-American Development Bank
IEO	Independent Evaluation Office
IFC	International Finance Corporation
IFF	International Finance Facility
IFI	International financial institution
IFS	International Financial Statistics
IGR	Institutional and Governance Reviews
ILO	International Labour Organisation
IMF	International Monetary Fund
INFVP	Infrastructure Vice Presidency (World Bank)
IPP	Independent power producers
I-PRSP	Interim Poverty Reduction Strategy Paper
ITC	International Trade Center
ITU	International Telecommunication Union
JIC	Joint Implementation Committee
JSA	Joint Staff Assessment
KfW	Kreditanstalt fur Wiederaufbau
LAC	Latin America and Caribbean region
LDCs	Least developed countries
LICUS	Low-income countries under stress
MDB	Multilateral development bank
MDGs	Millennium Development Goals
MFA	Multifiber Arrangement
MFN	Most favored nation
MICs	Middle-income countries
MIGA	Multilateral Investment Guarantee Agency
MNA	Middle East and North Africa region
MoU	Memorandum of Understanding
MTEF	Medium-Term Expenditure Framework
NAFTA	North American Free Trade Agreement
NCA	New Capital Accord or Basel II
NEPAD	New Partnership for Africa's Development
NGO	Nongovernmental organization
NPV	Net present value

NTB	Nontariff barrier
O&M	Operation and maintenance
ODA	Official development assistance
OECD	Organisation for Economic Co-operation and Development
OED	Operations Evaluation Department (World Bank)
OTRI	Overall trade restrictiveness index
PARIS21	Partnership in Statistics for Development in the 21st Century
PEFA	Public Expenditure and Financial Accountability
PFM	Public financial management
PPP	Purchasing power parity
PREM	Poverty Reduction and Economic Management Group (World Bank)
PRGF	Poverty Reduction and Growth Facility
PRSP	Poverty Reduction Strategy Paper
PSE	Producer support estimate
QAG	Quality Assurance Group (World Bank)
ROSC	Reports on Observance of Standards and Codes
RPGs	Regional public goods
RTA	Regional trade agreement
SDT	Special and differential treatment
SME	Small and medium enterprises
SPA	Strategic Partnership with Africa
SSA	Sub-Saharan Africa region
SWAp	Sectorwide approach
TA	Technical assistance
TB	Tuberculosis
TI	Transition indicators
TRIPS	Trade-related aspects of intellectual property rights
TRQ	Tariff rate quota
TSE	Total support estimate
TUPE	Transfer of Undertakings and Protection of Employees
U.N.	United Nations
UNAIDS	Joint United Nations Programme on HIV/AIDS
UNCTAD	United Nations Conference for Trade and Development
UNDAF	United Nations Development Assistance Framework
UNDP	United Nations Development Programme
UNECA	United Nations Economic Commission for Africa
UNEP	United Nations Environment Programme
UNESCO	United Nations Educational, Scientific, and Cultural Organization
UNGASS	United Nations General Assembly Special Session on HIV/AIDS
UNICEF	United Nations Children's Fund
UNSD	United Nations Statistics Division
URAA	Uruguay Round Agreement on Agriculture (World Trade Organization)
USAID	United States Agency for International Development
VAT	Value-added tax
WBI	World Bank Institute
WBI GI	WBI Governance Indicators
WDR	*World Development Report*
WDI	*World Development Indicators*
WEO	*World Economic Outlook*
WHO	World Health Organization
WITS	World Integrated Trade Solution
WP-EFF	Working Party on Aid Effectiveness and Donor Practices
WSS	Water supply and sanitation
WTO	World Trade Organization

Executive Summary

MDG Prospects—Need to Scale Up Action, Significantly and Swiftly

On current trends, most Millennium Development Goals (MDGs) will not be met by most countries. The income poverty goal is likely to be achieved at the global level, but Africa will fall well short. For the human development goals, the risks are much more pervasive across the regions. Likely shortfalls are especially serious with respect to the health and related environmental goals—child and maternal mortality, access to safe drinking water and basic sanitation. Few, if any, regions will achieve the mortality goals.

The implication is clear. Achievement of the MDGs requires rising above current trends and substantially accelerating progress toward the goals. There is an urgent need for all parties to scale up action. The agenda has three essential elements:

- Accelerating reforms to achieve stronger economic growth—Africa will need to double its growth rate.
- Empowering and investing in poor people—scaling up and improving the delivery of human development and related key services.
- Speeding up the implementation of the Monterrey partnership, matching stronger reform efforts by developing countries with stronger support from developed countries and international agencies.

Priorities for Developing Countries

Policies in developing countries have improved, enhancing their capacity to make effective use of resources, domestic and external, for development. Performance varies widely, however, and reform needs to be accelerated and deepened in many countries, especially in Sub-Saharan Africa. The analysis suggests four areas for particular attention:

- *Improving the enabling climate for private sector activity,* by solidifying progress on macroeconomic stability, further reducing barriers to trade, and shifting emphasis from regulating business operations to strengthening market institutions. In macroeconomic policy, the main area for improvement is fiscal management. Strengthening property rights and the rule of law are the key areas for attention with respect to the institutional environment. An improved enabling economic climate is essential both for mobilizing domestic investment and attracting more foreign investment.
- *Strengthening capacity in the public sector and improving the quality of governance*

—the biggest challenge for many countries. The most serious shortcomings are in transparency, accountability, and control of corruption. Performance is better in general in public financial management—expenditure and revenue management—but needs to improve further. On average, low-income countries can increase tax revenue by at least 1 to 2 percent of GDP by eliminating tax exemptions and improving tax administration. The bulk of the financing needed to achieve the MDGs, however, will have to come from improving the efficiency of existing spending, economic growth, and external resources. In Africa, which has the weakest governance indicators, the New Partnership for Africa's Development (NEPAD) initiative provides a very promising foundation for reform to build on.

- *Scaling up investment in infrastructure and ensuring its effectiveness,* according priority to infrastructure services closely linked to the human development goals—water and sanitation, transport. Compared with the levels of the 1990s, infrastructure spending (investment plus operation and maintenance) will need to rise by 3.5 to 5 percent of GDP in low-income countries and by 2.5 to 4 percent of GDP in lower-middle-income countries, with the pace of the increase depending upon institutional capacity and macroeconomic conditions in the country concerned.
- *Enhancing the effectiveness of service delivery in human development,* by better targeting education, health, and social assistance services toward poor people, addressing governance-related impediments to service quality and effectiveness, increasing community participation, and scaling up on the basis of successful programs (for example, the Female Secondary School Assistance Program in Bangladesh, the Education with the Participation of Communities (*Educo*) program in El Salvador, and the Education, Health, and Nutrition (*Progresa*) program in Mexico). Implementation needs to be expedited on two key donor-supported programs—the Education for All-Fast Track Initiative (EFA-FTI) and the Global Fund to Fight AIDS, Tuberculosis, and Malaria (GFATM). As of January 2004, only $6 million had been disbursed under the EFA-FTI against initial commitments of $170 million (total external financing needs for primary education in low-income countries are estimated to rise to at least $3.7 billion by 2005–06, compared with actual assistance of about $1 billion in 2002). As of the same date, only $230 million had been disbursed under GFATM against $3.4 billion in pledges and $1.5 billion in commitments. Swifter action is needed on the part of both donors in providing funds and recipients in addressing implementation constraints.

Cutting across the policy agenda is the need to empower women, by removing barriers to their fuller participation in the development process, and the need to ensure environmental sustainability. These cross-cutting concerns should be fully integrated into policymaking.

Within the foregoing agenda, specific priorities and sequencing of actions of course vary across countries and must be determined at the country level in the context of coherent, country-owned development strategies, as reflected in the Poverty Reduction Strategy Papers (PRSPs) in the case of low-income countries and respective national strategy frameworks in the case of middle-income countries.

Priorities for Developed Countries

Overall, developed country actions to date have fallen well short of the Monterrey vision. Progress seriously lags commitments in most areas. This must change, and change quickly, to help accelerate progress toward the development goals. The vision of Monterrey needs to be translated rapidly into concrete actions. Priorities for developed countries relate to trade and aid policies. But also important are the broad conduct of macroeconomic and financial policies conducive to robust growth in the world economy and increased attention to key global public goods, including environmental sustainability.

- *Sustaining stable and strong growth in the global economy.* A key issue is the orderly resolution of fiscal and external imbalances, especially the large U.S. external current account deficit. An abrupt adjustment in the large economies could retard growth and leave global economic conditions vulnerable to shocks. Further work by developed countries—working with emerging market countries and international financial institutions—is needed to improve the international financial architecture to enhance prospects for stronger and more stable capital flows to developing countries and to reduce the likelihood and severity of financial crises. Rapid progress is being made in the use of collective action clauses, but substantial work remains to improve practices in sovereign debt restructuring.
- *Ensuring a successful, pro-development, and timely outcome to the Doha Round.* High-income countries, given their weight in the system, must lead by example. They should aim for reform targets that are sufficiently ambitious. These could include: complete elimination of tariffs on manufactured products; complete elimination of agricultural export subsidies and complete decoupling of domestic agricultural subsidies from production, and reduction of agricultural tariffs to, say, no more than 10 percent; and commitments to ensure free cross-border trade in services delivered over telecommunications links, complemented by actions to liberalize the temporary movement of workers. Developing countries also must seize the opportunity provided by the Round to further their own trade liberalization. For developing countries (especially the low-income ones) to take full advantage of improved market access, they will need support in dealing with the "behind-the-border" agenda. Some countries will also need assistance with adjustment costs associated with trade liberalization.
- *Providing more and better aid.* Aid flows need to rise well above current levels. Although donors have made post-Monterrey additional commitments of about $18.5 billion a year by 2006, estimates show that an initial increment of at least $30 billion annually can be effectively utilized by developing countries. As countries improve their policies and governance, the amount of additional aid that can be used effectively will rise into the range of $50 billion plus a year, which estimates suggest will be needed to support adequate progress toward the MDGs. ODA rose by $6 billion in nominal amount ($4 billion in real terms) in 2002, but the increase was almost wholly accounted for by special-purpose allocations—technical cooperation, debt relief, emergency and disaster relief. More aid will need to be provided in forms that can flexibly meet the incremental costs of achieving the MDGs, including providing a higher proportion directly to countries in the form of cash, supporting good policy performance with predictable and longer-term aid commitments, and allowing for the financing of recurrent costs where country circumstances warrant. There is also substantial scope for increasing the effectiveness of aid by improving the allocation of aid across countries, aligning aid with national development strategies and priorities (as expressed through PRSPs in the case of low-income countries), and harmonizing donor policies and practices around the recipient country's own systems. To ensure debt sustainability in heavily indebted poor countries that are pursuing good policies, a larger proportion of additional aid should be provided in the form of

grants. Timely and adequate assistance in the event of adverse exogenous shocks is especially important for these countries.

- *Improving policy coherence for development.* Increased aid and other actions need to be part of a coherent overall approach to supporting development. In many cases, there are contradictions in policies, with support provided in one area undercut by actions in another. Putting in place processes that enable an integrated assessment of the coherence of policies that affect development—trade, aid, foreign investment and other capital flows, migration, knowledge and technology transfer, environment—would help avoid such outcomes. Recent actions by Sweden to institute an "integrated global development policy," and by Denmark and other countries to prepare regular assessments of their contribution to the goal of establishing a global partnership for development, go in the right direction.

Priorities for International Financial Institutions

Review of how the international financial institutions are playing their role in contributing to the achievement of the MDGs and related outcomes shows that they have made progress in enhancing their development effectiveness. This is reflected in progress in country focus and ownership, results orientation of operations, transparency and accountability, and partnership. But there is much more to do. There are three key areas for action to deepen and build on the progress made:

- *Refining and strengthening institutional roles in low-income countries,* including by deepening the PRSP process and harmonizing operational programs and practices around national strategies and systems, while also continuing to adapt approaches and instruments to the evolving needs of middle-income countries.
- *Furthering progress on the results agenda,* including implementation of the action plan endorsed by the sponsoring agencies at the Marrakech Roundtable on Managing for Development Results held in February 2004.
- *Improving selectivity and coordination* of agency programs in line with comparative advantage and mandate to achieve greater systemic coherence and effectiveness.

Priorities for Strengthening the Monitoring Exercise

To carry this agenda forward, the World Bank and the International Monetary Fund plan to focus future Global Monitoring Reports on specific challenges—at the country, agency, and global levels—for meeting these priorities. This will require further work, especially in the following areas:

- Strengthening the underlying development statistics, including timely implementation of the action plan agreed among international statistical agencies at the Marrakech Roundtable.
- Conducting research on the determinants of the MDGs, on critical issues such as effectiveness of aid, and on development of more robust metrics for key policy areas such as governance and for the impact on developing countries of rich country policies.
- Deepening collaboration with partner agencies in this work, building on respective agency comparative advantage and ensuring that the approach to monitoring and evaluation is coherent across agencies.

Millennium Development Goals
Goals and Targets from the Millennium Declaration

GOAL 1	**ERADICATE EXTREME POVERTY AND HUNGER**
TARGET 1	Halve, between 1990 and 2015, the proportion of people whose income is less than $1 a day
TARGET 2	Halve, between 1990 and 2015, the proportion of people who suffer from hunger
GOAL 2	**ACHIEVE UNIVERSAL PRIMARY EDUCATION**
TARGET 3	Ensure that by 2015, children everywhere, boys and girls alike, will be able to complete a full course of primary schooling
GOAL 3	**PROMOTE GENDER EQUALITY AND EMPOWER WOMEN**
TARGET 4	Eliminate gender disparity in primary and secondary education, preferably by 2005, and at all levels of education no later than 2015
GOAL 4	**REDUCE CHILD MORTALITY**
TARGET 5	Reduce by two-thirds, between 1990 and 2015, the under-five mortality rate
GOAL 5	**IMPROVE MATERNAL HEALTH**
TARGET 6	Reduce by three-quarters, between 1990 and 2015, the maternal mortality ratio
GOAL 6	**COMBAT HIV/AIDS, MALARIA, AND OTHER DISEASES**
TARGET 7	Have halted by 2015 and begun to reverse the spread of HIV/AIDS
TARGET 8	Have halted by 2015 and begun to reverse the incidence of malaria and other major diseases
GOAL 7	**ENSURE ENVIRONMENTAL SUSTAINABILITY**
TARGET 9	Integrate the principles of sustainable development into country policies and programs and reverse the loss of environmental resources
TARGET 10	Halve by 2015 the proportion of people without sustainable access to safe drinking water and basic sanitation
TARGET 11	Have achieved a significant improvement by 2020 in the lives of at least 100 million slum dwellers
GOAL 8	**DEVELOP A GLOBAL PARTNERSHIP FOR DEVELOPMENT**
TARGET 12	Develop further an open, rule-based, predictable, nondiscriminatory trading and financial system (including a commitment to good governance, development, and poverty reduction, nationally and internationally)
TARGET 13	Address the special needs of the least developed countries (including tariff- and quota-free access for exports of the least developed countries; enhanced debt relief for heavily indebted poor countries and cancellation of official bilateral debt; and more generous official development assistance for countries committed to reducing poverty)
TARGET 14	Address the special needs of landlocked countries and small island developing states (through the Programme of Action for the Sustainable Development of Small Island Developing States and the outcome of the 22nd special session of the General Assembly)
TARGET 15	Deal comprehensively with the debt problems of developing countries through national and international measures to make debt sustainable in the long term
TARGET 16	In cooperation with developing countries, develop and implement strategies for decent and productive work for youth
TARGET 17	In cooperation with pharmaceutical companies, provide access to affordable, essential drugs in developing countries
TARGET 18	In cooperation with the private sector, make available the benefits of new technologies, especially information and communication

Note: The Millennium Development Goals and targets come from the Millennium Declaration signed by 189 countries, including 147 heads of state, in September 2000. The goals and targets are related and should be seen as a whole. They represent a partnership of countries determined, as the Declaration states, "to create an environment—at the national and global levels alike—which is conducive to development and the elimination of poverty."

Source: United Nations. 2000 (September 18). *Millennium Declaration.* A/RES/55/2. New York.

United Nations. 2001 (September 6). *Road Map towards the Implementation of the United Nations Millennium Declaration.* Report of the Secretary General. New York.

Overview

From Vision to Action

The turn of the century was marked by some significant and promising events for world development. The Millennium Declaration—signed by 189 countries in September 2000—led to the adoption of the Millennium Development Goals (MDGs). These goals set clear targets for eradicating poverty and other sources of human deprivation and for promoting sustainable development (see goals and targets, p. xxii). This was followed in 2001–02 by major international meetings in Doha, Monterrey, and Johannesburg that contributed to the emergence of a shared understanding of the broad development strategy and policies needed to attain the MDGs. The meeting in Monterrey in March 2002 ushered in a new compact between developing and developed countries. The Monterrey Consensus stressed mutual responsibilities in the quest for the MDGs. It called on the developing countries to improve their policies and governance. And it called on the developed countries to step up their support, especially by providing more and better aid and more open access to their markets.

With broad agreement on the goals and strategies to achieve them, the task now is implementation. It is time to translate vision into action; to strive for a better balance in the development effort so that all parties play their part. Implementation needs to happen within countries and at the global level. All parties must deliver on their part of the compact. This was the central message of the 2003 International Monetary Fund (IMF) and World Bank (Bank) Annual Meetings held in Dubai. But is implementation actually happening? What progress has been made? What constraints are blocking implementation? How are all parties doing in delivering on their commitments? What are the priorities in the agenda? This report attempts to answer those questions.

The themes of *implementation and accountability* constitute the fundamental motivation behind the global monitoring initiative, launched at the request of the Development Committee, the joint Ministerial body of the World Bank and the IMF. The annual global monitoring reports, of which this report is the first, will provide an assessment of progress on policies and actions for achieving the MDGs and related development outcomes. These reports will underpin the Development Committee's regular monitoring of progress on the policy agenda and reinforcement of the priorities for action and the accountabilities of the key actors—developing and developed countries as well as multilateral agencies.

Prospects for Meeting the MDGs: Reasons for Optimism, Grave Concerns

Income poverty goal: a mixed picture. At the global level, the world will likely meet the first goal of halving income poverty between 1990 and 2015, thanks to stronger economic growth spurred by improvements in policies—especially in China and India, the world's two most populous countries. With current trends, most regions will achieve or come close to achieving the goal. East Asia has already met it. However, Sub-Saharan Africa is seriously off track; just eight countries, representing about 15 percent of the regional population, will likely achieve the goal. Within other regions that will likely meet the goal at the aggregate level, a number of countries will not. Low-income countries under stress (LICUS), about half of which are in Africa, are especially at risk of falling far short. The trends are broadly similar with respect to the target of halving the proportion of people who suffer from hunger, also part of Goal 1. The target will likely be met at the global level, but Sub-Saharan Africa and a number of countries in other regions will likely fall short.

Human development and environmental goals: more serious concerns. The risks associated with the human development goals are more pervasive across the regions. While economic growth has a significant effect on education and health outcomes, just as it does on income poverty, the magnitude of the effect is typically smaller. Prospects for progress on the human development goals also depend importantly on the scale and effectiveness of development interventions directed specifically toward them. The determinants of these goals are multiple and cut across sectors.

The prospects are brighter in education than in health. With current trends, several regions will achieve or approach the goal of providing universal primary education. Again, shortfalls are likely in Sub-Saharan Africa, and possibly in South Asia and the Middle East and North Africa as well. Gender gaps in education are most serious in the same three regions. While the target for gender equality in primary and secondary education is to be achieved preferably by 2005, about a third of developing countries appear unlikely to achieve it even by 2015. Prospects for gender parity at all levels of education, including higher education, are even less comforting.

But the prospects are gravest in health. On current trends, the goals of reducing child and maternal mortality will not be attained in most regions. Only a small proportion of countries (15–20 percent) currently appear to be on track. The goal of halting and reversing the spread of HIV/AIDS (human immunodeficiency virus/acquired immunodeficiency syndrome) and other major diseases (malaria, tuberculosis) appears daunting. Their incidence continues to rise, further aggravating conditions affecting child and maternal mortality and entailing broad and serious economic and social consequences. The risks of failure to halt the spread of HIV/AIDS are especially high in Sub-Saharan Africa, but are substantial in many countries in other regions as well.

The health goals are rendered more difficult by the large gaps in access to safe drinking water and basic sanitation. The gaps are largest in Sub-Saharan Africa for water and in South Asia for sanitation. The goal of halving, by 2015, the proportion of population without access to safe water and sanitation means providing an additional 1.5 billion people with water and 2 billion with sanitation. With current rates of progress at about half what is needed, most regions will fall well short. At those rates, only about one-fifth of countries will achieve the target increase in access. Among low-income countries, only about one-tenth will make it.

Variation across countries. Global and regional trends hide considerable variation across countries. East Asia, with its rich diversity, provides a good example. At one end, the region has middle-income countries, such as China and Thailand, that have already met or will soon meet several of the MDGs; some of those countries are developing "MDG-plus" agendas. At the other end, low-income countries such as Cambodia and Papua New Guinea are seriously off track, as are many poor countries in Sub-Saharan Africa. There is also diversity within countries, especially large ones. Although China has already met the income-poverty MDG at the national level, progress has been much slower in some inland provinces that continue to have large concentrations of poverty.

In general, middle-income countries are much better positioned to achieve the MDGs than low-income countries. Many of them have already met the goals or are well on their way. Notwithstanding their progress on income poverty, those countries remain home to 280 million people living on less than $1 a day and 870 million people living on less than $2 a day. A number of them lag in relation to some of the non-income MDGs. For example, China, despite its spectacular performance in reducing income poverty, is not on track to meet the child mortality goal, based on current trends.

Daunting challenges, but grounds for hope. The MDGs present a difficult challenge, but past development successes give cause for hope. Globally, adult illiteracy fell by half over the past 30 years, while life expectancy at birth rose by 20 years over the past 40 years. Some countries have advanced particularly far, particularly fast. Vietnam, for example, a low-income country, reduced poverty from 51 to 14 percent from 1990 to 2002. Even in Sub-Saharan Africa, there have been encouraging stories of success. Botswana doubled the proportion of children in primary school in 15 years, nearly achieving universal primary education. Benin increased its primary enrollment rate and Mali its primary completion rate by more than 20 percentage points in the 1990s. Mauritania increased the ratio of girls to boys at school from 67 to 93 percent between 1990 and 1996. Uganda reduced HIV/AIDS infection rates for eight consecutive years in the 1990s. Zambia may soon become the second African country to slow the spread of this scourge. These achievements demonstrate that rapid progress is possible, given good policies and the support of partners.

Scaling Up on the Basis of the Monterrey Consensus

The implications of the foregoing assessment are clear. The achievement of the development goals will require rising above current trends and accelerating the pace of development, and doing so swiftly. In line with the principles and partnership established at Monterrey, all parties must scale up their action. The agenda has three essential elements:

- Accelerating and deepening reforms to achieve stronger economic growth
- Empowering and investing in poor people—stepping up action to improve the delivery of services affecting human development
- Speeding up the implementation of the Monterrey partnership, matching stronger developing country efforts to spur growth and improve service delivery to poor people with stronger support from developed countries and international agencies.

Acting on multiple fronts. The multidimensionality of the MDGs, the linkages among them, and their multisectoral determinants imply that the policy agenda for achieving the goals is similarly broad. Indeed, the agenda spans the gamut of development. There is no one-to-one link between the MDG relating to a sector and policies relating to that sector. The outcome in a given sector depends importantly on factors outside that sector. For child survival, for example, mother's education and access to safe water and sanitation may be more important than access to health facilities. Likewise, schools and health facilities may exist, but girls may be prevented from attending if they spend much of their time fetching water from distant sources or if adequate and safe means of transport are lacking. The agenda cuts across sectors, and across policies, investments, and institutions.

The scaling-up effort, therefore, will require concerted action on multiple fronts.

Promoting stronger economic growth. At the center of the strategy to achieve the MDGs and related development outcomes must be the promotion of stronger economic growth. Growth directly reduces income poverty and expands resources for use toward the non-income goals. So, first and foremost, economic growth in developing countries will need to be stronger than recently attained or currently projected. Sub-Saharan Africa will need to double its average GDP (gross domestic product) growth rate, to around 6 percent. This target is ambitious, of course, but some countries in the region achieved it in the 1990s: Cape Verde, Mauritius, Mozambique, and Uganda. What is needed is to accelerate policy and governance reforms to improve the enabling climate for growth: macroeconomic stability and openness, the regulatory and institutional environment for private sector activity, physical and financial infrastructure, and public sector governance.

Scaling up service delivery. Reaching the goals will also require policies and actions to enhance the capabilities of poor people—men and women—to participate in and benefit from growth. For their participation to be effective, the poor need to be empowered through improved delivery of education and health services, as well as related infrastructure services, such as water and sanitation and rural roads. Stepped-up investments in those services must be accompanied by reforms in sector policy and institutional frameworks that improve the effectiveness of delivery, including greater involvement of communities, especially poor people, in making decisions.

Enhancing the global development partnership. The developing countries are in the driver's seat in setting the agenda for achieving the development goals, but they will need help from development partners. Implementation will require increased cooperation at the global level. The developing countries need expanded access to markets in developed countries to increase exports and spur growth. And they need more aid to finance development programs that improve the delivery of human development and infrastructure services. This mutualism was clearly recognized and affirmed at Monterrey, but progress to date has been relatively slow. The spirit of Monterrey needs to be translated rapidly into action.

Priorities for Developing Countries

Policies improving, but much further to go. Indicators for the past five years show improvement in policies in all regions, although to varying degrees. On average, policy indicators remain the lowest in Sub-Saharan Africa, but even there show an encouraging improvement on most dimensions, suggesting that recent reforms are beginning to take hold. The improvement in policies is creating conditions that enhance countries' capacity to make effective use of resources for development, domestic and external. While some improvement has occurred across all policy areas, progress is especially notable in macroeconomic management and trade policy. Average inflation and tariff rates have been cut in half in the past decade. The improved policy environment has contributed to a pick-up in economic growth. Indeed, average per capita GDP growth in low-income developing countries in the past five years was higher than during any other five-year period in the past two decades. Better policies pay off.

Despite this improvement, however, growth in many countries—most of them in Sub-Saharan Africa—remains below the level needed to achieve the MDGs. During 1998–2002, nearly 60 percent of low-income countries (with a combined population of 950 million) experienced per capita growth of less than 2 percent, while 32 percent (with a combined population of 555 million) experienced negative per capita growth. Factors such as adverse political and external circumstances have played a role, including the limited availability of aid resources and impediments to access to export markets in developed countries, but the growth response to improvements in the macroeconomic and trade policy environment has been dampened by slower progress on structural and institutional reforms that are essential to improving the enabling climate for private sector activity. Stronger growth in the future will depend crucially on more vigorous and consistent efforts to speed up reforms in these areas.

In the delivery of services—human development, infrastructure—the picture is broadly similar. Some areas show encouraging progress; others require stronger action. Resource allocation has improved somewhat, as evidenced by the increased investment in human capital. Public education and health spending increased over the 1990s from 6.9 to 7.4 percent of GDP in those low-income countries for which data are available. Successful innovations in service delivery to the poor are encouraging. These include the Education with the Participation of Communities (EDUCO) program in El Salvador; the *Progresa* program of conditional cash transfers to the poor linked to school and clinic attendance in Mexico; and the Female Secondary School Assistance Program in Bangladesh, which employs targeted financial incentives and community engagement to increase girls' enrollment in schools. Key ideas from these innovations are now being applied in other countries, including most recently Nepal. In many countries, however, the quality and effectiveness of service delivery show major deficiencies. These gaps point to the need to accelerate improvements in the underlying policy and institutional framework to raise the yield of increased spending on services.

The core of the reform agenda: institutional reform. Cutting across the policy agenda is the need to improve governance. Public sector governance, while improving, remains the weakest area of the reform agenda in most countries. Institutional dimensions of reform are also paramount in the improvement of the private sector business climate and the performance of the service delivery sectors. In macroeconomic management as well, performance is strongly correlated with the quality of institutions responsible for policy implementation. And in most developing countries, improved management of the environment requires building up fledgling environmental institutions. Responding to these challenges, governments in more and more developing countries have launched governance and institutional reforms. An important example is the New Partnership for Africa's Development (NEPAD), an initiative owned and led by African countries that places improvement in governance at the center of the reform agenda.

Country focus and ownership: central to success. The primary determinant of the prospects for achieving the MDGs is developing countries' own policies. Overall, progress has been encouraging, but reforms need to be accelerated and deepened. The review conducted for this report points to five areas needing particular attention, as discussed below. Within these broad areas, policy priorities for individual countries must be determined at the country level, in the context of coherent country development strategies. Country ownership and leadership of the development strategy are crucial to effective implementation and achievement of results.

For low-income countries, the Poverty Reduction Strategy Papers (PRSPs) are the primary avenue of expression of a country-owned and -led development strategy. In middle-income countries, the policy integration and prioritization role is performed within respective national strategy frameworks. By the end of March 2004, 37 countries had prepared and were implementing full PRSPs; 16 more had prepared Interim PRSPs (I-PRSPs). Countries are increasingly reflecting the MDGs in their PRSPs. The PRSP process itself is being deepened along various dimensions, including participatory process, growth strategies, public expenditure management, and poverty and social impact analysis. Continued strengthening of the PRSP process, and deepening of the links with the MDGs, will ground the agenda for achieving the development goals in country-owned strategies. Countries can spell out their commitments to policy and institutional reforms in these strategies, which in turn enables donors to commit support in a coherent and consistent way.

Solidifying Macroeconomic Stability

Fiscal management: the main area for improvement. Macroeconomic management has improved in all regions. Yet progress has been uneven and remains fragile in many countries, especially in Sub-Saharan Africa. Fiscal management is the area of most concern. Performance is much better on monetary and exchange rate management. Fiscal policy, as it relates to the sustainability of public debt and containment of fiscally derived macroeconomic imbalances, remains unsatisfactory in about a third of low-income countries. The deficiencies in structural aspects of fiscal policy are even more serious, with nearly half of low-income countries assessed as having an unsatisfactory composition of public expenditures. For these countries, therefore, a strengthening of macroeconomic policies, especially fiscal management, remains necessary. Even in countries with better performance, maintaining and building on macroeconomic stability—an essential foundation for sustained growth—will be a continuing challenge.

In middle-income countries, macroeconomic policy indicators are better, on average, than in low-income countries. Because middle-income countries typically are more integrated into international capital markets, maintaining sound macroeconomic policies is especially important for reducing vulnerability to crises—which can wash away hard-won gains in reducing poverty. In the past two decades, average output loss in developing countries from currency crises is estimated at about 7.5 percent of pre-crisis GDP. Although vulnerability indicators have improved in the past few years, the reduction of public debt, especially external debt, relative to GDP remains a key area for improvement in several countries. Governance of financial and corporate sectors also needs to be strengthened to prevent the build-up of balance-sheet vulnerabilities.

Improving Private Sector Enabling Environment

Extending progress toward outward-oriented strategies. Despite significant liberalization, there is substantial scope for further reductions in trade barriers, especially in regions where they remain high. In South Asia, for example, despite sharp declines since the late 1980s, the average tariff remains around 20 percent. Taking into account nontariff barriers (excluding technical product regulations), South Asia's average tariff equivalent was an estimated 32 percent in 2001, the highest among developing regions. Developing countries should take advantage of the Doha Round to make further strides toward trade openness. Countries that derive a sizable part of government revenue from trade taxes may need assistance in adjusting to a regime of lower trade tariffs. In addition to reducing trade barriers, countries should move vigorously on the "behind-the-border" agenda, to enable the private sector to exploit the opportunities created by lower trade barriers. The agenda includes the efficient supply of services closely related to trade—customs, transport, and telecommunications, financial services—and improvement of the broader enabling environment for entrepreneurship and private investment. Evidence suggests that full liberalization and regulatory reform in services trade could add significantly to economic growth.

Reducing regulation, strengthening institutions—especially property rights, rule of law. While improving, the regulatory and institutional environment for private sector activity still needs significant reform in many countries. Regulation typically is much heavier and more complex in low-income countries, notwithstanding their more limited implementation capacities, raising the cost of starting and operating a business and creating opportunities for corruption. Starting a business in high-income countries typically takes 30 days and costs less than 10 percent of per capita income; in low-income countries, it takes 74 days and costs two times per capita income. While regulation is heavy, the essential institutions underpinning markets are weak. The most serious shortcomings are in property rights and rules-based governance, an area assessed as less than satisfactory in almost four-fifths of low-income countries. Such an environment deters investors, both domestic and foreign. Weak creditor rights and contract enforcement also inhibit the growth and deepening of the financial system.

Countries need to shift emphasis from regulating business operations to building institutions that facilitate business by supporting efficient and fair functioning of markets. A key area of reform is the strengthening of property rights and of institutions that establish and enforce the rule of law, including legal and judicial reform and the reduction of bureaucratic harassment. Continued strengthening of the institutions of corporate governance, especially in middle-income countries, is also important.

Upgrading Public Sector Governance

Accelerating governance reform. The need to accelerate reform is greatest in public sector governance. The quality of public sector governance has improved, especially in Europe and Central Asia and South Asia. But the reform agenda calls for more vigorous action in many countries. In three-fourths of low-income countries, overall public sector governance is assessed to be less than satisfactory, making it the weakest area of performance. The weaknesses are most pervasive precisely in those countries where stronger institutional capacities are needed to manage development interventions that will spur progress toward the MDGs—low-income countries in Sub-Saharan Africa. They are especially acute in the low-income countries under stress. Governance ratings are higher in middle-income countries, but those ratings still are lower than their ratings in other policy areas. These findings highlight governance and institution-building reforms as an area for particular attention, as poor governance and weak institutions can seriously undermine the effectiveness of policies and programs throughout an economy. Initiatives such as the NEPAD, therefore, are especially valuable and timely.

Controlling corruption. The most serious shortcomings are in transparency, accountability, and control of corruption. Reform is complex in these areas, which are less amenable to "technocratic" solutions. Progress will depend on a careful nurturing of reform ownership and of needed changes in bureaucratic culture. Political will is key, as are political processes that allow broad participation, build in checks on executive authority, and enable citizens to hold administrations accountable.

Building on progress in public financial management. Performance is better in public financial management, on average. A greater focus on public expenditure and budget management in the preparation of the PRSPs and in the initiative to help heavily indebted poor countries (HIPCs) has contributed to progress in these areas, which must be sustained and deepened. The importance of improved management of public resources is underscored by the need to create fiscal space for increased spending on key infrastructure and human development services (see below) within sustainable overall fiscal positions. In many countries, the scope for reallocating spending toward development remains substantial. On the revenue side, analysis shows that on average low-income countries can increase their tax-to-GDP ratio by 1 to 2 percentage points by eliminating tax exemptions and improving tax administration. Doing so would help mobilize resources, although the bulk of the financing needed to achieve the MDGs will have to come from improving the efficiency of existing spending, economic growth, and external resources.

Decentralized governance can improve the delivery of services at the local level. Decentralization is especially important for large middle-income countries like Brazil and China that need to tackle major concentrations of poverty at the subnational level. To be effective, decentralization must be underpinned by sound intergovernmental fiscal systems and local institutional capacities.

Strengthening Infrastructure

Substantial scaling up of investment needed. Infrastructure plays a dual role in the effort to achieve the MDGs. It is an important part of the enabling environment for economic growth, and it also delivers services that are key to meeting the human development and gender equality goals. Gaps in the availability and quality of key infrastructure are large, especially in low-income countries and in rural areas within countries. Narrowing those gaps will require sizable increases in investment and associated spending on operation and maintenance. Average spending on infrastructure (investment plus operation and maintenance) in low-income and lower-middle-income countries may have to almost double from the levels of the 1990s (when such spending fell by 2 to 4 percent of GDP). This implies increases in infrastructure spending (covering power, transport, telecommunications, and water and sanitation) on the order of 3.5 to 5 percent of GDP in low-income countries and 2.5 to 4 percent of GDP in lower-middle-income countries relative to the low levels of the 1990s. The pace of the increase will depend upon the institutional capacity and macroeconomic conditions in the country concerned.

Financing this spending will be a major challenge. Private investment in infrastructure has increased, but not as much as expected. Efforts must continue to improve the regulatory and institutional environment for such investment. Innovative instruments for risk mitigation could also help leverage more private financing. At the same time, the decade-long decline in public spending on infrastructure needs to be reversed. That will require stronger mobilization of domestic resources, including improved cost-recovery and reallocation of spending, and increased external assistance. Especially in the low-income countries, external assistance must provide a larger share of total infrastructure spending than the roughly 10 percent it provided in the 1990s. Infrastructure requirements relating to water and sanitation warrant special attention in public spending and foreign assistance programs, given their close links to the health and gender goals, and the fact that this sector traditionally attracts less private financing than other infrastructure sectors such as power and telecommunications.

Increased investment: not the sole answer. To ensure its effectiveness and sustainability, investment must be underpinned by improvements in the policy and governance framework, especially the capacity of key institutions. With more and more responsibilities in infrastructure falling on local governments, strengthening administrative and financial capacities at the local level, including developing and facilitating the use of appropriate subsovereign financing instruments, is increasingly important.

Accelerating Human Development

More resources complemented by more effective use. Encouraging progress has been made in human development. More investment is being made in education and health and more attention is being paid to the effectiveness of service delivery. But progress needs to be accelerated and broadened if the human development goals are to be achieved. The deficiencies in service delivery are most serious in Sub-Saharan Africa and South Asia, although even in these regions, individual countries are making progress, such as Ghana on child mortality, and Ethiopia and Rwanda on primary completion.

In most low-income countries, the targets in education and health require the commitment of more resources to these services. However, in a number of these countries, there is substantial scope for increasing the impact of existing spending by correcting poor targeting of subsidies, lax resource management, low efficiency and quality of service, and information failures. Examples abound. In Guinea, the share of public spending on education and health accruing to the richest quintile was found to be seven times that accruing to the poorest. In Uganda, 87 percent of nonwage resources intended for schools was diverted to other uses before the problem was discovered and corrective action taken. Teacher salaries absorbed more than 90 percent of the recurrent education budget in Kenya. Teacher absenteeism is 39 percent in Bihar, India. Among doctors in primary health facilities in Bangladesh, absenteeism is 73 percent. Despite free immunization, 60 percent of children are not immunized in India, because mothers are unaware of the benefit. Many of these problems can be traced to weaknesses in governance and institutional capacities.

Main elements of the agenda. Concerted action is needed on several fronts: scaling up investment in human capital in low-income countries while maximizing the impact of existing public spending by improving the targeting of public services in education, health, and social assistance; paying attention to intersectoral linkages when developing and implementing programs (it is hard to reduce child mortality when only 10 percent of the poor households have access to an improved water source, as in Ethiopia); addressing governance-related impediments to service quality and effectiveness; and piloting and evaluating empowerment options to strengthen the involvement of stakeholders, especially poor people, in the design and delivery of services (and scaling up on the basis of successful programs, such as *Educo* and *Progresa*).

Community involvement is particularly important to the goal of reducing gender disparities in education. Since the success of interventions to educate girls is fundamentally embedded in the sociocultural context, community involvement can help ensure that interventions are responsive to needs. Effective improvement of female access to education—and to other key services—requires that the design of services reflects gender concerns. Indeed, the goal of empowerment of women calls for gender concerns to be fully integrated into policymaking more broadly.

Donor support: EFA-FTI and GFATM. The scaling up of human development in low-income countries will require that more donor support come in forms that promote broad sector reform, encompassing the policy and institutional dimensions of the sector and moving away from past practices focused more on earmarked expenditures or vertical programs that delivered a narrow package of interventions. The Education for All–Fast Track Initiative (EFA-FTI) is helping to support a shift in that direction. Disbursements under the program, slow to take off because of agency programming and budgeting cycles, need to be expedited. As of January 2004, only $6 million of the first $170 million committed to the initial group of countries had been disbursed. World Bank projections suggest that as the FTI scales up to all low-income countries, at least $3.7 billion per year will be needed in external financing for primary education by 2005–06, compared with about $1 billion in 2002. Implementation has also been slow under the Global Fund for AIDS, Tuberculosis and Malaria (GFATM). As of January 2004, out of $3.4 billion in pledges, $1.5 billion had been committed but only $230 million had been disbursed. Expediting progress in this priority area requires better donor coordination and the alleviation of institutional capacity constraints in recipient countries.

Priorities for Developed Countries

Actions well short of the Monterrey vision. As agreed in Monterrey, if the MDGs are to be achieved, stronger reform actions by developing countries must meet with stronger support from developed countries in an enhanced global development partnership. Priorities for developed countries relate to trade and aid policies. Also important is the broad conduct of macroeconomic and financial policies in a way that is conducive to strong global economic growth and stable private capital flows. Attention to key global public goods is also needed. How well are developed countries doing in living up to their commitments? The assessment carried out for this report shows that actions seriously lag commitments in most areas. Accelerating progress toward the MDGs requires much stronger actions of support from the developed world than witnessed so far. As for developing countries, the agenda can be grouped under five heads.

Fostering a Robust Global Economic Recovery

Through their impact on trade and capital flows, global economic conditions exercise a major influence on prospects for growth and poverty reduction in developing countries. Growth in the developing countries cannot thrive in the absence of strong and sustainable growth in the advanced economies. Although the prospects for recovery in world economic growth appear to be reasonably bright over the near term, sustaining a strong global economy will require the major countries to address some outstanding issues and imbalances.

Orderly resolution of imbalances. Disorderly adjustment in the largest economies could retard growth or leave global economic conditions vulnerable to shocks. Most notably, the United States is running a large external current account deficit. Such large external imbalances, financed increasingly with debt instruments, are difficult to sustain for a long period. As economic growth in the United States gathers steam, a gradual tightening of fiscal and monetary policies could help bring about an orderly adjustment. In Europe, the central challenge is to implement needed structural reforms, especially in labor markets and social security systems, to return economic growth to a sustainable 2 to 3 percent range over the medium term. In Japan, economic policy needs to continue to focus on countering deflationary tendencies, stabilizing public sector debt, and addressing the accumulation of imbalances in the financial and corporate sectors. A common, longer-term structural challenge is to address the fiscal impact of the demographic changes building up in these countries.

The ongoing global economic recovery, buttressed by low interest rates in the advanced economies, is reflected also in some recovery in private capital flows to developing countries in 2003. The outlook for sustaining these flows in the longer term would improve if the large fiscal and external imbalances in the advanced economies were reduced, freeing up financing for developing countries, and the recipient countries continued to improve their policy and institutional environment to make sound and sustainable use of external financing. Prospects for private capital flows would also benefit from improvements in the international financial architecture to make those flows more stable and reduce the likelihood and severity of financial crises, including more extensive use of collective action clauses and improved practices in sovereign debt restructuring.

Moving Forcefully on the Doha Development Agenda

Trade barriers: a major impediment to development. Improving market access for developing country exports would provide a major boost to economic growth and accelerate progress toward reducing poverty and meeting other MDGs. At present, trade barriers in developed countries effectively discriminate against developing countries in many cases. They are highest on products of major export interest to developing countries. Protection in agriculture is a multiple of that in manufacturing. Taking into account both tariff and non-tariff barriers—including domestic subsidies but excluding technical product regulations—average protection in agriculture in high-income OECD (Organisation for Economic Co-operation and Development) countries in 2001 was 25.6 percent, compared to 3.6 percent in manufacturing. Both border barriers (tariffs) and domestic subsidies contribute significantly to the high protection in agriculture, but the former have a much larger impact. Protection is particularly high on key individual products. OECD countries' protection rates for sugar are frequently above 200 percent, and their support to sugar producers of $6.4 billion a year roughly equals developing country exports. In the European Union, producer support for beef is as high as 84 percent of the value of domestic production. U.S. subsidies to cotton growers totaled $3.6 billion in 2001–02, twice as much as all U.S. foreign aid to Africa, and cost West African cotton growers an estimated $250 million by depressing prices.

Within manufacturing, while average protection is low, tariff peaks and escalation discriminate against developing country exports and efforts to move up the value chain. In clothing, for example, tariff peaks average 16 to 17 percent in Canada, Japan, and the United States. More than 60 percent of imports subject to tariff peaks originate in developing countries. The incidence of contingent protection—antidumping actions—also is higher against developing countries, on average.

Trade policy reform: source of large gains. Gains from a significant removal of these trade barriers would be substantial, both for developing and developed countries. Stronger growth resulting from a pro-development outcome of the Doha Round could increase real income in developing countries by $350 billion by 2015 (roughly equivalent to the entire GDP of Sub-Saharan Africa), and lift an additional 140 million people out of poverty by that year (a decline of 8 percent). The bulk of these potential income gains—as much as 70 percent—would arise from liberalization in agriculture.

Liberalization of services trade, including migration: source of substantial additional gains. Gains from liberalization of trade in services, especially the temporary movement of workers, could be a multiple of those from liberalization of merchandise trade, according to some estimates. Services overall are the fastest growing component of developing country exports. Services provided over telecommunications links and through migrant workers show particular dynamism. Workers' remittances, estimated at $93 billion in 2003, are now the second-largest source of private external funding for developing countries, behind foreign direct investment. Against this background, the recent build-up of protectionist pressure against services imports in some developed countries is a cause for concern. This build-up is exemplified by new legal norms in the European Union (EU) and pending legislation in the United States that could limit outsourcing of government contracts, for example.

Timely and pro-development outcome of the Doha Round: a critical need. Putting the Doha Round back on track must be accorded the highest priority. Developed countries, because of their weight in the system, need to lead by example. Bilateral or regional agreements are a poor alternative to a forward movement on the multilateral front. Agreement on some focal points or targets for trade policy reform would provide a needed impetus. Such focal points could include complete elimination by high-income countries of tariffs on manufactured products by a target date; complete elimination of agricultural export subsidies and complete decoupling of all domestic agricultural subsidies from production, and reduction of agricultural tariffs to, say, no more than 10 percent, by a target date; and commitments to ensure free cross-border trade in services delivered through telecommunications networks, complemented by actions to liberalize the temporary movement of service providers. At the same time, reform should aim to achieve greater transparency and predictability in trade policy, by limiting the use of less transparent instruments such as specific tariffs, simplifying regulatory requirements, and imposing greater discipline on the use of contingent protection.

Any incorporation of rules relating to domestic regulations such as competition and investment policies (the so-called Singapore issues) into World Trade Organization (WTO) trade agreements needs to ensure that the rules support development and take into account the different implementation capacities of developing countries. A flexible approach is warranted. An example of such flexibility is the agreement reached in 2003 to clarify the Trade-Related Intellectual Property Rights (TRIPS) Agreement to expand poor countries' access to essential drugs at low cost. Relatedly, support to developing countries should be stepped up to build their institutional capacities to deal with the trade-related agenda and take advantage of better market access opportunities. The Integrated Framework for Trade-Related Technical Assistance is a useful initiative in that context. "Aid for trade," and complementary measures to facilitate technology transfers to developing countries, can have high impact, and will be needed to enable poor countries to realize the potential gains from global trade reforms discussed above. Some of these countries will also need assistance in adjusting to a reduction in trade preferences following further nondiscriminatory trade liberalization, and to the potential effects of a significant increase in world food prices—should that materialize.

Providing More and Better Aid

Need for a substantial increase in ODA. Official development assistance (ODA) needs to rise well beyond current commitments. At current levels of ODA, there is a large gap between the development ambitions of the international community and the resources provided. An increase in aid is critical for low-income countries, to support their reforms and enhance their prospects for achieving the development goals. Aid also plays an important role in middle-income countries by reinforcing domestic efforts to tackle concentrations of poverty and countering negative shocks. Against this background, it is encouraging to see aid volumes begin to reverse the decline of the past decade. ODA rose in 2002 and, according to preliminary estimates, again in 2003. Indications of increased assistance from the donor community in follow-up to Monterrey, if realized, would raise ODA by about $18.5 billion by 2006 from the 2002 level of $58 billion. This would increase total net ODA to 0.29 percent of donors' gross national income (GNI), up from the 2002 level of 0.23 percent. This is indeed welcome, but well short of what is needed as part of the global compact to achieve the MDGs.

Country-level analysis conducted recently by the World Bank indicates that, as a conservative estimate, an initial increment of at least $30 billion could be used effectively. Early commitment of this additional sum would help create a virtuous circle by encouraging developing countries to undertake and sustain deeper reforms, which would make aid still more productive. As countries improve their policies and governance and upgrade their capacities, the amount of additional aid that can be used effectively would rise into the range of $50 billion plus a year that estimates suggest is likely to be necessary to support adequate progress toward the MDGs. Ongoing work to examine the merits of various options, such as an international financing facility, to mobilize the substantial additional resources that are needed and can be effectively used to achieve development results is therefore important and timely.

It is useful to view these numbers in context. An additional $50 billion would raise ODA relative to donors' projected GNI in the latter half of the 2000s to roughly the same level as at the turn of the 1990s (levels in earlier decades were still higher). Since then, conditions for effective use of aid in developing countries on average have improved, thanks to better policies. Donors' income levels have also risen. Ironically, as aid has become more productive and donors' capacity to give has grown, aid amounts have declined sharply. This does not mean that all donors have reduced their assistance. The aid effort varies widely across members of the OECD Development Assistance Committee (DAC), ranging from a high of 0.96 percent of GNI in the case of Denmark to a low of 0.13 percent in the case of the United States in 2002 (however, the United States has more recently increased its aid commitments, which would raise its net ODA in 2006 by about 50 percent over the 2002 level).

While aid volumes are rising again, there is some concern that much of the increase may be dominated by strategic considerations—the war on terrorism, conflict and reconstruction in Afghanistan and Iraq. Large amounts have recently been committed for these purposes, but it is unclear whether all of these commitments represent an increase in total aid or are in part a reallocation of aid from other countries. In the period ahead, it will be important to ensure that development aid is not crowded out by aid influenced by such strategic objectives.

Improving the allocation of aid. Most donors today are more selective than they were about a decade ago; they are allocating more aid to countries with better policies and more poverty. However, there is considerable variation among donors. On average, multilateral institutions are more than three times as selective as bilateral donors, based on a newly developed index that measures both policy and poverty selectivity in aid allocation. Multilateral assistance is much more sharply targeted to good policies and to poverty, with the International Development Association (IDA) being the most selective. About two-thirds of total ODA is bilateral aid. Among bilateral donors, the Nordic countries, the Netherlands, and the United Kingdom are the most selective (with Denmark the highest). The index shows that some of the largest donors in absolute size, such as France and the United States, have not been particularly selective along either the policy or poverty dimension. Japan is selective on policy but not on poverty, reducing the overall selectivity of its aid. Thus while the typical donor has improved its aid quality in terms of targeting more funds to poor countries with better policies and governance, this cannot be said for the typical aid dollar, as the largest donors in absolute amount are less selective. Looking ahead, actions now being taken by some of these donors, such as the establishment of the Millennium Challenge Account (MCA) in the United States, are expected to contribute to further improvements in aid allocation. The MCA aims to improve aid effectiveness by tying increased assistance to performance.

Efforts to target aid better need to take account of the special needs of conflict-affected and other low-income countries under stress. The challenge is to balance issues of weak policies and institutions with the need to maintain critical engagement. Appropriately timed and directed aid, sensitive to local efforts to rebuild and the institutional capacity constraints, can play a very useful role in these situations. Well-timed aid can also be quite productive following adverse exogenous shocks, helping to limit the diversion of development resources into short-term relief efforts.

Increasing the effectiveness of aid through improved alignment and harmonization. Related to better allocation of aid across countries, the effectiveness of aid depends crucially on its alignment with national development priorities within country programs and on harmonization and coordination of donor policies and procedures around the recipient country's own systems. In low-income countries, the PRSP provides the framework for strategic alignment with country-owned and -led priorities and for achieving better coherence and coordination in donor support activities. The country-led alignment and harmonization efforts in Tanzania and Vietnam, centered on the PRSP, provide good examples. Aid alignment and harmonization efforts were given an impetus by the High-Level Forum on Harmonization held in Rome in February 2003. Important follow-up work is now being carried out by the donor community jointly under the auspices of the DAC Working Party on Aid Effectiveness and Donor Practices (WP-EFF), including elaboration of a set of indicators of progress. Results from this work will be important to widening the application of good practices and better monitoring progress.

Providing aid in forms that are responsive to country circumstances and needs. As countries build a track record of policy performance, their efforts should be supported with timely, predictable, and longer-term aid commitments. Such commitments would enable them to embark upon sustained reforms and investments necessary to meet the MDGs, with assurance that needed support would be forthcoming. Aid should be provided in forms that can flexibly meet countries' needs for incremental financing. Currently, only about a third of bilateral ODA is available for program and project expenditures in recipient countries. The rest is allocated to special purposes such as technical cooperation, debt relief, emergency and disaster relief, food aid, and costs of aid administration. These special-purpose grants accounted for almost all of the $6 billion nominal increase in ODA in 2002. (In real terms, the increase was about $4 billion.)

Going forward, a much higher proportion of additional aid will need to be provided directly to countries in the form of cash so that it can be deployed in accordance with country priorities to finance the costs of meeting the MDGs. Where country circumstances warrant, and budget frameworks are sound, more aid could be provided in forms that allow for the financing of recurrent costs, either through budget or sectorwide support, or through targeted assistance to well-designed sectoral programs. Many activities in education and health that are crucial to progress toward the MDGs involve in major part an expansion of recurrent spending. To ensure debt sustainability in heavily indebted countries that are pursuing good policies, consideration should be given to providing a larger share of additional aid in the form of grants.

Debt relief and debt sustainability. Much progress has been made under the HIPC Initiative in reducing heavily indebted poor countries' debt and debt service burden and creating fiscal space for much-needed increases in poverty-reducing spending. While most acute in the case of the HIPCs, the issue of achieving and maintaining debt sustainability is of broader concern to low-income countries. Work is under way at the IMF and World Bank on a debt sustainability framework that is intended to provide guidance on issues relating to financing strategies for low-income countries, including the range of indicators for assessing debt sustainability, the role of policies in determining appropriate debt thresholds, the importance of including domestic debt in such assessments, and the appropriate mix of grants and new credits. These issues are becoming increasingly important in the light of the need for large increases in external financing to meet the MDGs and implications for country debt sustainability. Debt sustainability is not only a resource flow issue, however; it also depends crucially on increasing growth, expanding and diversifying exports, improving access to global markets, and mitigating the effects of exogenous shocks.

Stepping Up Action on Key Global Public Goods

As globalization has advanced, and awareness has grown of the international spillovers of local actions and conditions, there has been a welcome increase in attention to areas for global collective action. Reference has been made in the foregoing to several such areas—control of infectious diseases, promotion of education and dissemination of knowledge, opening up of the international trade regime, promotion of a more stable international financial system. In all of these areas, there is progress to report, but, as noted, there is also need to step up action.

Stronger resolve needed to address environmental concerns. One key area for global collective action, and directly related to the MDGs, is environmental sustainability. Developed countries bear much of the responsibility for the preservation of the global environmental commons, as they are the largest contributors to the degradation of the commons and possess the financial and technical resources needed for prevention and mitigation. Developing countries must also play their part by improving their environmental management, including by increasing regional cooperation among themselves that donors could support. While there has been good progress on protecting the ozone layer, thanks to implementation of the Montreal Protocol, much less progress has been made in most other areas—greenhouse gas emissions, biodiversity, fisheries. Aid to developing countries to support improved environmental practices, both bilaterally and through multilateral vehicles, has declined after a short-lived increase following the 1992 Rio Convention. Not all advanced countries have shown weak resolve in addressing the environmental challenges; there are good global citizens such as Sweden and Switzerland. Looking ahead, priorities include stronger and more concerted action on greenhouse gas emissions and increasing aid to developing countries in support of environmental sustainability, including through the Global Environment Facility (GEF).

Improving Policy Coherence for Development

Cutting across the policy areas is the need to improve the overall coherence of policies in high-income countries in terms of their development impact. All too often, there are contradictions in policies, with support to development provided in one area defeated by actions in others. There are both collective and individual country examples: $58 billion in ODA by the OECD countries is undermined by five times as much protection to domestic agricultural producers; advocacy of and support for private sector development and export diversification in developing countries are blunted by systematic escalation of tariffs on higher-value imports from those countries; Norway's stellar performance as an aid donor coexists with the most restrictive agricultural trade policy regime among the OECD countries; a similar contradiction between aid and trade policies applies to the European Union; the African Growth and Opportunity Act of the United States was undercut by its 2002 Farm Bill and its higher protection against imports from low-income and least-developed countries than from the rest of the world.

Institutionalizing policy coherence. The realization that development policy extends well beyond aid and specific trade preferences is leading to welcome indications that the developed countries are willing to look broadly at the policy areas that affect development—trade, aid, foreign investment and other capital flows, migration, knowledge and technology transfer, environment—and to put in place institutional arrangements that would help ensure coherence. A noteworthy development in this context is the passing into law of an "integrated global development policy" in Sweden in January 2004 that calls for the country's aid, trade, agriculture, environment, migration, security, and other policies to be aligned with the objective of reducing poverty and promoting sustainable development. Another notable development has been the issuance by Denmark of the first in a planned series of reports on how it is contributing to the goal of establishing a global partnership for development (the aim of MDG 8). Preparation of similar reports is being considered by some other OECD members, including

Belgium, Canada, Finland, Germany, the Netherlands, Norway, and Sweden.

Two related ongoing initiatives at the OECD are a "Horizontal Project" on policy coherence for development that looks at the impact on developing countries of a broad range of developed-country policies, and increased attention in DAC peer reviews to issues of policy coherence. Work on these issues is also being undertaken by private think tanks and civil society, among them the Center for Global Development and the World Economic Forum. These encouraging efforts would prove very valuable if they were instrumental in bringing about more systematic attention to issues of development impact and coherence in policymaking in rich countries.

Priorities for International Financial Institutions

How are the international financial institutions (IFIs) contributing to the achievement of the MDGs and related outcomes? This report assesses the IFI contribution along four dimensions: country programs, global programs, partnership, and results. Applying the framework across the IFIs suggests that there has been progress in recent years, especially since Monterrey. But the evidence is inconclusive on the critical questions of comparative performance and whether the whole of the IFI contribution is larger (or smaller) than the sum of the individual IFI contributions. Going forward, greater availability and comparability of evaluation data will facilitate monitoring, and in turn improve the quality of reporting to the taxpaying public in all countries. The joint work program on results endorsed by the multilateral development banks (MDBs) in February 2004 at the Marrakech Roundtable on Managing for Development Results should provide a key vehicle for progress. Future assessments of the IFI role will also benefit from greater use of external evaluations.

Individual IFIs. Within each of the institutions, the evidence points to enhanced attention to client focus and country ownership, transparency, results, and accountabilities. Naturally, the degree of progress varies across institutions and areas. Highlights include the strong start of the IMF's Independent Evaluation Office—whose creation means that all the IFIs now have independent evaluation offices reporting directly to their executive boards—and its reviews of prolonged use of Fund resources, the Fund's role in capital-account crises, and fiscal adjustment in Fund-supported programs; the World Bank's commitment to the results agenda and its focus on actions and implementation in countries, with partners and within the Bank; and the regional development banks' respective commitments to enhanced operational quality, development effectiveness, and results, as demonstrated recently in Marrakech. But there is clearly no room for complacency. The recent progress needs to continue and be deepened.

- *IMF.* For the Fund, the priority is to continue to refine its role in assisting low-income countries, in several ways: by adapting its instruments of financial and technical support to enable its low-income members to catalyze other donor assistance, deal with postconflict situations, respond to exogenous shocks, absorb the cost of adjustment to multilateral trade liberalization, and establish institutions that will enable them to gain access to private financing. The Fund's work agenda also aims at strengthening the design of Fund-supported economic programs in low-income countries, while enhancing alignment with the PRSP. A third element of the Fund's ongoing work, together with the World Bank, is to develop an effective and flexible framework for assessing debt sustainability in low-income countries.
- *World Bank.* The Bank's country support priorities are to continue to work with countries and partner agencies to deepen the PRSP process as a basis for the design of its assistance strategies in low-income countries; to adapt approaches and instruments to the evolving needs of middle-

income countries; and to complete the major agenda the Bank has set out on results, harmonization, and simplification. Supporting and complementing the deepening of country-led approaches in the Bank's assistance strategies is the strengthening of its analytic, knowledge, and advocacy work. A priority for Bank-supported global and sectoral programs is the implementation of an effective framework for appraisal, statistics, monitoring, and evaluation that is every bit as strong as the framework for country programs.

- *Regional Development Banks.* The other MDBs also have large agendas before them—in their country programs and in their support for regional public goods. All need to complete their ongoing reforms associated with the results agenda, as they set out at the Marrakech Roundtable. In addition, like the World Bank, they need to apply greater efforts to strengthen the overall governance and accountability framework for their regional and sectoral programs.

Systemic coherence. Looking across the IFIs, the evidence also points to progress collectively—both institutionally and in day-to-day work at the country level. Bank-Fund collaboration and coordination among the MDBs are smoother and more productive than five years ago. In tandem with the increase in partnership and coordination, there also is a healthy movement toward greater specialization in line with institutional comparative advantage. This reverses the trend of the early 1990s when overlaps in IFIs' and other agencies' capacities increased, as the consensus on the comprehensiveness of the development paradigm was beginning to grow. But the "gains from trade" between and among IFIs have not all been harvested yet. Opportunities include increased selectivity of agency programs in line with comparative advantage, harmonization of agency practices around national poverty reduction strategies and systems, and joint evaluations of their support.

Progress is needed also in the ongoing work related to IFI governance. Strengthening the voice and participation of developing countries in the IFIs is part of the Monterrey compact.

Priorities for Strengthening the Monitoring Exercise

Fully developing the potential of the global monitoring exercise will require a strong focus on specific challenges at the country, agency, and global levels for meeting the priorities set out above. This will in turn require continuing work to strengthen the statistical and analytic foundations of the exercise and to deepen collaboration with partner agencies. Three areas for further work are particularly important:

- *Data.* Timely statistics on the desired development outcomes and good metrics for the key policy drivers are critical for effective monitoring. At present, there are major gaps in data, especially with respect to human development and infrastructure services and outcomes in developing countries. The World Bank and its partner agencies in the U.N. system, working together and in consultation with client countries, have developed a time-bound and costed action plan to strengthen a broad range of data in developing countries and build their statistical capacities. Presented and agreed at the Marrakech Roundtable, the plan will need timely and coordinated donor support for its objectives to be realized.
- *Research.* More research is needed to strengthen the analytic underpinnings of the monitoring framework, especially the links between policies and outcomes. While there is a broad consensus on the main policy and institutional determinants of growth, poverty reduction, and the other MDGs, less is known about the precise transmission mechanisms and the relative weights of the various determinants and interrelationships among them.

Collaborative research is under way at the World Bank, the IMF, and the U.N. Millennium Project to better model and quantify some of these relationships, especially through in-depth work at the country level. More research is also needed on critical issues such as aid effectiveness and on development of more robust metrics for key policy areas such as governance and for the impact on developing countries of rich country policies.

- *Partnership.* In these and other areas, collaboration developed with partner agencies—the United Nations, other MDBs, the WTO, OECD, the European Commisson—in the preparation of this first global monitoring report will be deepened further, building on respective agency mandates and comparative advantage and ensuring that the approach to monitoring is coherent across agencies. This could include broadening the framework for reflecting the contribution of the multilateral agencies, currently focused on the IFIs, to encompass other agencies as well, even as efforts are made to strengthen the evaluation of the IFI contribution, including through better harmonizing the self- and independent-evaluation criteria used by the IFIs. Collaboration will also be expanded with civil society, which has become increasingly involved in monitoring activities.

I

Framework

1

Monitoring Framework

The purpose of the *Global Monitoring Report* is to assess progress on the policies and actions needed to achieve the Millennium Development Goals and related outcomes. Covering developing and developed countries as well as multilateral agencies, the assessment aims to facilitate the Development Committee's monitoring of the accountabilities of the entities jointly responsible for reaching the development goals.[1] It also aims to inform the international community more broadly on progress on the development policy agenda and the priorities for action.

The report is organized as follows. Part I sets out the context and analytic framework for monitoring progress on the policy agenda for achieving the MDGs. It also assesses prospects for attaining the goals based on current trends. That assessment informs the subsequent presentation of the need to scale up policies and actions. Part II moves on to evaluate policies in developing countries. The focus is on low-income countries, where the challenge to achieve the development goals is greatest, but the discussion also covers issues important to middle-income countries—among them reducing economic volatility and promoting sustainable growth, and addressing concentrations of poverty and deprivation at the subnational level. Part III assesses the policies of developed countries, suggesting actions they need to take to fulfill their commitments in support of the development goals. Part IV looks at the role of multilateral agencies, asking how they are supporting countries' progress toward the development goals, both individually and collectively.

Background on Global Monitoring

Discussions at major international meetings at the beginning of the new millennium produced a broad consensus on key development goals and on the strategies and partnerships needed to achieve them. The 2000 U.N. Millennium Summit led to the adoption of the Millennium Declaration and the Millennium Development Goals, 8 clear goals and 18 targets (p. xxii) by which the international community could measure progress on key dimensions of development.[2] Since their adoption, the MDGs have rallied public support for development. Reinforcing the agreement on the development goals, meetings in Doha, Monterrey, and Johannesburg in 2001 and 2002 contributed to the emergence of a shared understanding of the broad development strategy and policies needed to attain the goals, as well as of the roles of the different development partners.[3] The meeting in

Monterrey ushered in a new compact between developing and developed countries—the Monterrey Consensus—that stressed their mutual responsibilities and accountabilities in the development effort.

With broad agreement on the goals and strategies, attention soon focused on implementation, to convert the ideas and shared approaches into concrete actions and to monitor progress on the delivery of commitments under the compact. It was against this background that the Development Committee, at its meeting in September 2002, expressed its intent to regularly monitor progress on the policies and actions needed to achieve the MDGs and related development outcomes. To reinforce the accountabilities of the key actors—developing countries, developed countries, and multilateral agencies—the Committee asked the World Bank and the International Monetary Fund to prepare proposals for monitoring MDG-related policies, while recognizing the role of the United Nations in monitoring the MDGs.[4]

In response to the request, the staffs of the Bank and Fund proposed a monitoring framework that the Development Committee discussed at its April 2003 meeting.[5] A progress report on implementation of the monitoring framework, including issues related to the measurement and assessment of relevant policies and actions and collaboration with partner agencies, was presented to the Development Committee at its September 2003 meeting.[6] The framework envisages an annual *Global Monitoring Report*—to be prepared jointly by Bank and Fund staff in advance of the Committee's spring meeting—supplemented by interim reports on selected issues.

This first annual report is part of a broad architecture of monitoring and reporting that has emerged since the Millennium Declaration and the Monterrey Consensus. Individual international agencies lead the monitoring work in the areas of their respective mandates and expertise, while supporting and complementing the work of partner agencies. With its focus on policies and actions, the *Global Monitoring Report* complements the United Nations' monitoring of the MDG targets and indicators. The latter includes an annual report by the Secretary General to the General Assembly on the implementation of the Millennium Declaration and an annual report with a biennial comprehensive review by the Secretary General to the General Assembly on the implementation of the agreements reached at the International Conference on Financing for Development in Monterrey.[7] Complementing these reports, the U.N. Millennium Project is a three-year research project—to which the Bank and the Fund are also contributing—designed to identify approaches for achieving the MDGs. The Millennium Campaign is aimed at mobilizing public support for the MDGs and fostering country ownership.

In preparing this report, Bank and Fund staff have worked closely with the United Nations and other partner agencies, including the other multilateral development banks (MDBs), the World Trade Organization (WTO), the Organisation for Economic Cooperation and Development (OECD), and the European Commission (EC). The collaboration has spanned the initial design of the monitoring framework and the subsequent assembling of the supporting data and analysis. All of the partner agencies participated in an Inter-Agency Workshop on Global Monitoring organized by the Bank and the Fund in Washington in June 2003.[8] Going forward, collaboration will be deepened further, building on respective agency strengths and ensuring that the approach to monitoring is coherent across agencies. Collaboration also will be expanded with civil society organizations that have become increasingly involved in monitoring activities.[9]

To establish a baseline for future assessments, this report covers policies and actions for achieving the MDGs and related outcomes in a comprehensive manner. Future reports may be more selective and thematic, focusing on identified priorities and major changes from the baseline established here.

Timely statistics on desired outcomes and good metrics for key policies are critical for effective monitoring. But there are important gaps in both areas, especially in countries most at risk of not meeting the MDGs. Filling in those gaps calls for systematic investment in more robust and timely data and more precise indicators of the relevant policies and their impact. Research to strengthen the analytical underpinnings of the monitoring framework is also needed—especially into the links between policies and outcomes. In particular, while there is broad consensus on the main policy and institutional determinants of growth, poverty reduction, and the other MDGs, as described in the next section, less is known about the precise transmission mechanisms, interrelationships among the determinants, and their relative weights and elasticities with respect to the development goals.

The Bank and the Fund are working with their partners on initiatives to address these gaps.[10] Progress has been made in developing a time-bound and costed action plan for international support for strengthening a broad range of data in developing countries and building their statistical capacities (box 1.1). Progress and needed follow-up work in measuring specific policies and their impact and supporting research are noted in the respective sections of the report. The ongoing work will strengthen the statistical and analytic foundation for monitoring. However, results will take time to materialize. The global monitoring exercise, therefore, should be seen as a phased process, the full potential of which will appear only in the medium term. With more timely and reliable underlying data, better metrics for key policies, and more clarity on the links between policies and outcomes, the findings and recommendations reported to the Development Committee will become increasingly specific and quantified.

Complementing the annual monitoring reports to the Development Committee, an open information platform accessible through the Development Gateway will present the data underlying the reports for monitoring by the broader international community on an ongoing basis.[11]

Framework Linking Policies to Development Goals

The MDGs reflect the multidimensional nature of development. They span income and important non-income dimensions of development, which are interlinked. Higher incomes and less poverty mean better human development outcomes. Better health and education contribute to increased productivity and higher incomes.[12] There are important linkages among the human development goals. Perhaps the strongest determinant of child mortality, for example, is the mother's education.[13] Health and nutritional status affect the probability that a child will enroll and succeed in school.[14] And the human development outcomes are affected greatly by conditions in other sectors. Child mortality is closely linked to access to safe water and basic sanitation.[15] Roads and other transport facilitate access to education and health facilities, electrification of those facilities improves the quality and effectiveness of the services they provide, and refrigeration networks help preserve vaccines.[16]

The multidimensionality of the MDGs, interlinkages among them, and their multisectoral determinants imply that the policy agenda for the achievement of these goals is similarly broad. Indeed, it spans the gamut of development. The central element of the agenda is promotion of stronger economic growth. Growth directly reduces income poverty and expands resources available for progress toward the other MDGs. No country has made rapid progress toward these development goals without robust growth. In most low-income countries, reaching the goals will require improvements in policies and governance to achieve stronger economic growth than recently attained or currently projected. It will also require policies specifically targeted to enhancing the capabilities of poor people to participate in growth, especially through improved access to education, health, and related key services. While economic growth has a significant effect on education and health outcomes, the magnitude of

BOX 1.1 An action plan for improving development statistics

The focus on measurable development goals, as embodied in the MDGs, and clear accountability for policy, as reflected in the Monterrey Consensus, implies the need for more and better statistics to inform policy and monitor progress. But the new demands placed on national statistical systems exceed the capacity of many countries. External support has helped, but often progress has not been sustained. Today many national statistical systems underperform, in part because they receive inadequate domestic funding and uncertain, sometimes conflicting, donor support.

Recognizing the need for action, the statistics community is responding, at both the national and international levels. Learning from experience, the new initiatives emphasize responsiveness to country needs and priorities and country-level capacity building. Most encouraging are national efforts embedded in broader national development strategies, such as the PRSP. Notable initiatives at the international level include the PARIS21 (Partnership in Statistics for Development in the 21st Century) consortium that brings together users and producers of data, the U.N. MDG Indicators Expert Group to pool agencies' data and expertise, improved international data standards, and trust funds and lending facilities to support investment needs in national statistical capacity building.

Building on these initiatives, and reflecting collaborative work across agencies, a global action plan was discussed and agreed at the second Roundtable on Managing for Development Results held in Marrakech on February 4–5, 2004. The plan recommends six short- and medium-term sets of actions aimed at achieving tangible and sustainable improvements in national and international statistical capacity.

The first set of actions addresses *national* needs:

- Action 1. Mainstream strategic planning of statistical systems and prepare national statistical development strategies for all low-income countries by 2006
- Action 2. Begin preparations for the 2010 census round
- Action 3. Increase financing for country-level statistical capacity building.

The second set addresses *international* responsibilities:

- Action 4. Set up an international Household Survey Network
- Action 5. Undertake urgent improvements needed for MDG monitoring by 2005
- Action 6. Increase the accountability of the international statistical system.

Cost estimates have been prepared for the implementation of the action plan in 2004–06. The annual incremental cost of improvements to *national* statistical systems is estimated at $115 million to $120 million. These costs are extrapolated from a limited number of countries based on recent experience or expert opinions. For many of the poor countries, external financing will be necessary. Additional spending by development agencies for improvements in the international system is estimated at $24 million to $28 million a year.

There is need for a clear and strong commitment on the part of the international community to a shared work program over the next three to five years for improving development data and building statistical capacity in developing countries. The tasks specified in the action plan are not exhaustive, nor are they intended to preclude other initiatives. But they do require commitment on the part of the international community to work together, to share resources, and to keep the needs and priorities of developing countries at the forefront. In keeping with the spirit of the Monterrey compact, countries that set realistic goals for improvements in their statistical systems and make a reasonable commitment of their own resources should receive commensurate assistance from the international community.

Source: A full description of the action plan is available at:
http://www.managingfordevelopmentresults.org/Agenda-Seminar2.html.

the effect is typically smaller than on income poverty. Prospects for progress on the human development goals also depend on the scale and effectiveness of development interventions targeted directly toward these goals.[17] And policies and programs need to take into account implications for environmental sustainability. Although the developing countries themselves are in the driver's seat, implementing this agenda will require increased cooperation at the global level, in which stronger reform efforts by developing countries are matched with enhanced support from developed countries and international institutions.

The consensus forged at Monterrey in March 2002 was based on a recognition that a strong global development partnership was needed to achieve the MDGs. It called on developing countries to improve their policies and governance and on developed countries to step up their support, noting that the goals called for scaling up actions to accelerate development on the part of both of these groups. Are the parties to the consensus delivering on their commitments? It is the purpose of this report to provide an answer. Anchored in the Monterrey Consensus, the global monitoring framework translates the agenda for achieving the MDGs and related development outcomes into a set of policies and actions, or accountabilities, of developing and developed countries, and a corresponding set of responsibilities of international agencies, that will be monitored on a regular basis.

The analytic framework underpinning the global monitoring exercise is outlined in figure 1.1. It depicts the results chain leading to the MDGs, running from the inputs of policies and actions of developing and developed countries and international agencies to the intermediate outcomes of economic growth and delivery of human development and related key services to poor people and on to the final outcomes—the MDGs themselves. The main elements of the framework, and the policies and actions to be monitored, are discussed below.

FIGURE 1.1 Framework linking policies and actions with development outcomes

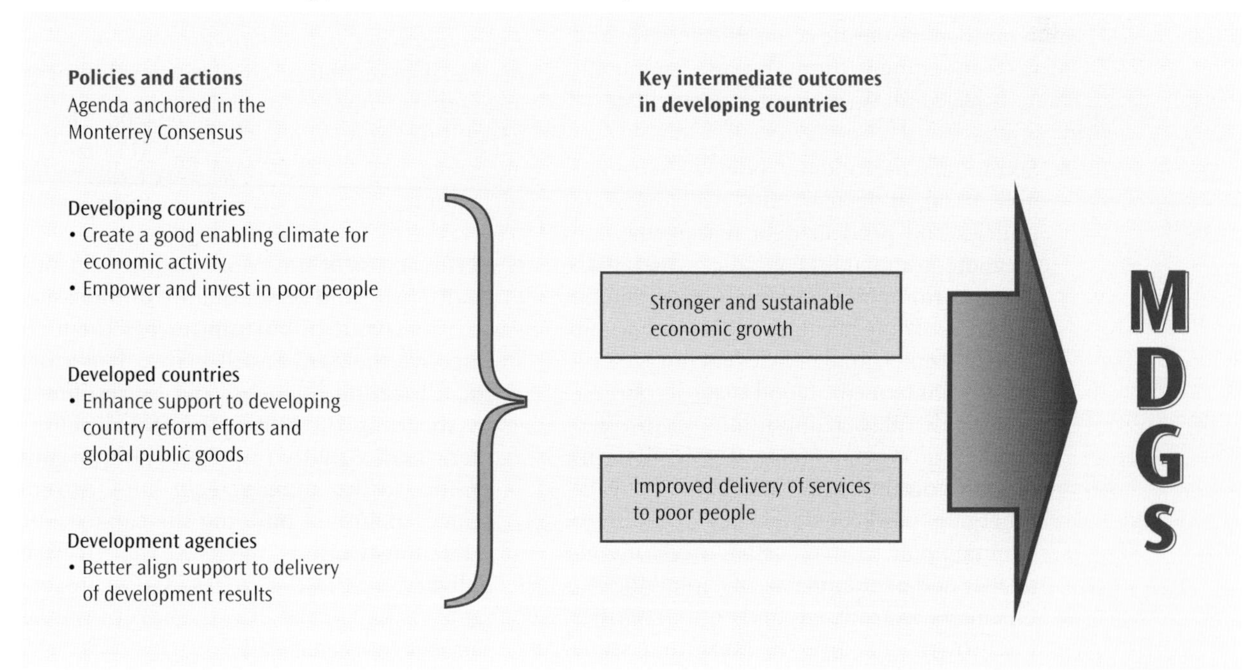

Developing Countries

Research and experience have led to a broad consensus on an effective strategy for development, one that is country owned and country led, promotes economic growth, and ensures that poor people participate in it and benefit from it—and that produces maximum progress toward the MDGs. The strategy has two interlinked and mutually reinforcing pillars. The first is an enabling climate for economic activity that encourages private firms and farms to invest, create jobs, and increase productivity. The second is empowerment of and investment in poor people. Improvements in the economic climate spur growth but also expand opportunities for the poor. Empowerment of poor men and women through improved access to education and health fosters social inclusion but also promotes growth as these groups increase their participation in economic activity.

Enabling climate for economic activity. The first pillar focuses on the process of the growth. Entrepreneurship, investment, and innovation by the private sector drive economic growth. But they will not occur without the right environment. A good economic climate spurs domestic economic activity and attracts investment from abroad. Such a climate is based on several policy elements:

- Sound macroeconomic policies—sustainable fiscal, monetary, and exchange-rate policies and prudent debt management—promote sustainable economic growth with low inflation and instill confidence among investors. By fostering a stable economic environment, sound policies encourage saving and investment. Good macroeconomic policies also play an important role in averting the high costs of financial crises in terms of lost output and increased poverty. Emerging markets in particular need to maintain policies that sustain investor confidence and avoid the risk of capital flight.
- Openness to trade expands opportunities for growth and diversification and spurs innovation. Development success has generally been associated with an outward orientation with respect to trade policies, with trade acting as a crucial engine of growth.[18]
- Good governance and institutions are essential to competitive and efficient functioning of markets, providing a level playing field and predictability and enforceability of contracts. This is especially important for smaller firms, which are less able than large firms to finance the costs of dealing with excessive and arbitrary regulations.
- Stronger and deeper financial markets channel savings to productive uses and broaden access to finance. A sound financial sector complements good macroeconomic management in maintaining economic stability and strengthening an economy's resilience to shocks.
- Investment and productivity also depend on the availability of key physical infrastructure—transport, power, telecommunications. In addition to facilitating growth, infrastructure services contribute directly to the development goals, as when access to safe water and sanitation reduces child mortality.

Empowerment of and investment in poor people. The second pillar of the development strategy is concerned with increasing the capabilities of poor people, by widening their access to key services and fostering social inclusion:

- Better access of the poor to education and health care, and better quality of these services, expand opportunities for them to improve their own well-being. This calls for allocating adequate public resources to spending on human capital development and, equally important, improving public sector management and governance, including building the capacity of related institutions, to ensure the effective delivery of these services. Good governance is key to the effectiveness of public services more generally.

- Also important is the poor's access to social protection—well-targeted safety nets that protect poor and vulnerable people from unforeseen shocks and dislocations occasioned by necessary reforms.
- The effectiveness of any strategy to empower and invest in the poor will depend to an important degree on mechanisms that foster their participation in decisions that affect them. Enabling the poor to have an increased voice needs to be an integral element of the strategy.
- Cutting across this agenda is the empowerment of women by removing barriers to their fuller participation in the development process. Promoting gender equality is not only an important social goal itself, but is also essential for the achievement of the development goals more broadly.[19]

Environmental sustainability. Both the enabling economic climate and empowerment of the poor have environmental dimensions. The principles of sustainable development must be fully integrated in economic policies. Environmental concerns are addressed through an agenda similar to that outlined above, spanning policies that generate the right incentives for private agents (using and creating markets, through instruments such as taxes, user charges, concessions, and tradable permits), regulations (particularly for toxic substances or where market-based instruments are impractical), capable institutions, and engagement of the public. The important linkages between environmental and other development outcomes, such as poverty alleviation and human development, should inform policymaking. Proper management of natural resources protects rural incomes, just as access to water and sanitation reduces child mortality.

It is clear from the foregoing that attainment of the MDGs will depend on progress in developing countries across a broad range of policies and institutions. The framework for monitoring developing-country policies classifies the policy agenda into four clusters: economic and financial policies; public sector governance; human development; and policies for environmental sustainability. These are represented by the four facets of the developing-country "policy diamond" in figure 1.2.

Developed Countries

In calling for a global partnership for development (MDG 8), the international community recognized that attaining the agreed development outcomes would require, in addition to redoubled reform by developing countries, enhanced support from the developed world. Developed countries help by maintaining macroeconomic and financial policies that promote stability and growth in the world economy. But the Monterrey Consensus also envisages increased support in two key areas that affect outcomes in the developing world more directly—trade and aid. In addition, developed-country policies greatly affect outcomes in areas of global collective action, such as the preservation of the global environmental commons. The global monitoring framework focuses on these key

FIGURE 1.2 Monitoring: dimensions of developing-country policies

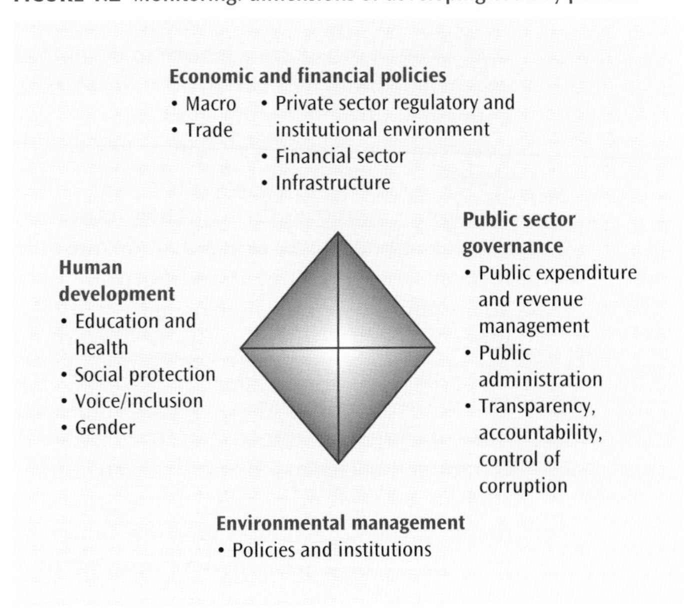

FIGURE 1.3 Monitoring: dimensions of developed-country policies

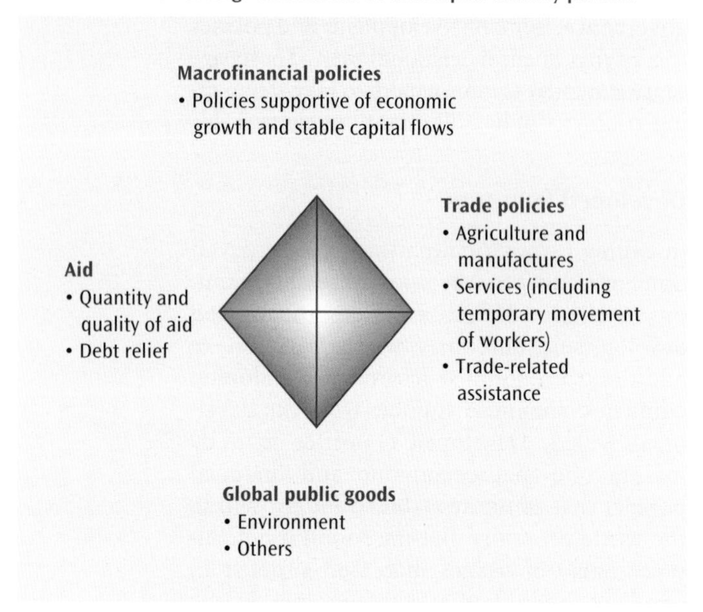

aspects of developed-country policies, as depicted by the developed-country "policy diamond" in figure 1.3.

Macroeconomic policies. Macroeconomic policies and outlook in developed countries exert a major influence on developing countries' growth prospects. Growth in developed countries stimulates activity in developing countries through trade and creates the potential for raising aid flows. Macroeconomic policies and outcomes also affect developing countries through their impact on private capital flows, which include not only foreign direct investment and portfolio debt and equity flows but, increasingly, workers' remittances. Fluctuations in real GDP in developing countries tend to be synchronized and positively associated with GDP fluctuations in large developed countries. Macroeconomic policies in advanced countries that support a stable and growing world economy, therefore, make an important contribution to progress toward desired development outcomes in developing countries.[20]

Trade policies. Better access to developed-country markets is crucial to the development of poor countries. Many developing countries that have opened their trade regimes are prevented from reaping the benefits because of barriers maintained by developed countries, especially in agriculture, textiles, and clothing—labor-intensive sectors where developing countries typically have a comparative advantage. Reducing trade protection can yield large benefits for developing and developed countries alike.[21] Liberalizing trade in services, including through the so-called Mode 4 trade (temporary migration of workers), also promises large potential gains.

The Doha Development Agenda provides an opportunity for major progress on market access for developing-country exports, as well as for further liberalization by developing countries themselves. Liberalization must be supported by increased trade-related financial and technical assistance to help developing countries with the "behind-the-border" investments they need to make to take advantage of wider market access and to enhance their institutional capacity to make and implement effective trade policy.

Aid. The parties to the Monterrey Consensus agreed that more and better aid would be necessary to meet the MDGs. Various estimates prepared in the past year indicate that the additional aid requirements are sizable. A major factor determining whether aid is effective is of course the recipient country's own policies; hence the focus on developing-country actions, including sound macroeconomic management, structural reform, and improved institutions and governance. Such policies not only enhance the effectiveness of aid, but also help alleviate the macroeconomic instability that can result from a large influx of aid. Recent and ongoing reforms in many developing countries have improved the setting for effective use of aid.[22] A recent study of better-performing developing countries showed that, as a conservative estimate, additional assistance of $30 billion or more can be productively absorbed.[23] The effectiveness of aid also depends importantly on the policies of donors. As underscored at the High Level Forum on Harmonization held in Rome in February 2003, and in the follow-up work of the Development Assistance Committee Working Party on Aid Effectiveness and Donor Practices, there is large scope for increasing the impact of aid through a stronger focus on selectivity in aid allocation, tighter alignment of aid with national poverty reduction strategies and priorities, provision of aid in forms that are responsive to recipients' needs, and closer harmonization of donor policies and practices.[24] What is needed now is consistent implementation of that consensus and concerted monitoring.

Heavily indebted poor countries need debt relief to create the fiscal space to allocate more resources to social spending and other programs to reduce poverty and accelerate growth. That need underscores the importance of continued progress on the Heavily Indebted Poor Country (HIPC) Initiative. If heavily indebted countries are to avoid slipping back into unsustainable debt positions, they will have to continue to strengthen their policies to promote increased efficiency in resource use and stronger economic growth, and new external assistance will have to be provided on appropriately concessional terms. Stronger export growth is especially important to such countries, underscoring the need for better market access and improved trade-related infrastructure.

Global public goods. Developed countries also need to step up action in support of key global public goods and areas for global collective action. In some areas, notably the prevention and treatment of infectious and communicable diseases, especially HIV/AIDS, investment in global public goods will provide essential support for national programs. Major issues relating to the global environmental commons—mitigation of global warming (tropical countries are particularly vulnerable to climate change and environmental degradation) and preservation of biodiversity—also call for stepped-up efforts at the global level. Developed countries have a special contribution to make to protecting the global environment, as they dominate energy use, consume the most natural resources, and produce the most pollutants. Of course, developing countries also need to play their part, including through increased regional cooperation among themselves that aid donors should support. International financial stability, another important global public good, can be enhanced by strengthening the international financial architecture to improve crisis prevention and resolution and avoid the spread of contagion between countries.

International Financial Institutions

The international financial institutions (IFIs) have an important role to play in helping countries achieve the MDGs and related development outcomes. How are they playing their part? The monitoring framework for assessing their contribution is focused on four key dimensions: country programs—strategic alignment with country-owned and country-led strategies for poverty reduction and other MDGs, and design of programs and instruments that support those priorities; global programs—support for global public goods such as international financial stability, health, environmental sustainability, an open trade system, and spread of knowledge; partnership—effectiveness in working together, through harmonization of policies and practices, strategic selectivity in country support programs, and coordination; and results—orientation to quality and results in operations and transparency in evaluation and reporting. These four monitoring dimensions are represented in the IFI "policy diamond" in figure 1.4. The assessment also looks across individual agencies and addresses issues of systemic performance and coherence—whether the overall effectiveness of the multilateral agencies is larger or smaller than the sum of individual agency contributions.

FIGURE 1.4 Monitoring: dimensions of development agency support

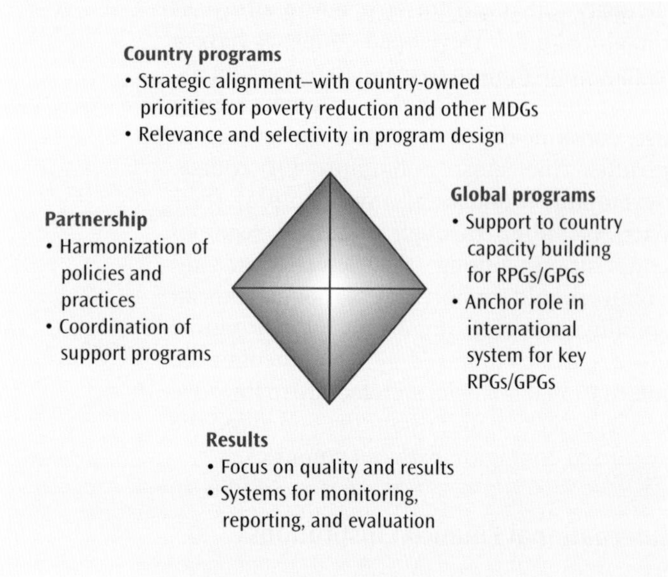

Country programs
- Strategic alignment–with country-owned priorities for poverty reduction and other MDGs
- Relevance and selectivity in program design

Partnership
- Harmonization of policies and practices
- Coordination of support programs

Global programs
- Support to country capacity building for RPGs/GPGs
- Anchor role in international system for key RPGs/GPGs

Results
- Focus on quality and results
- Systems for monitoring, reporting, and evaluation

Country Focus and Ownership

The elements of the global compact and the implied policy agenda for achieving the MDGs must come together at the country level within coherent country development strategies that respond to local conditions and priorities and are nationally owned. Policy priorities vary across countries and time, and policies also vary in terms of the relative weights they carry with respect to the different development goals. It is in the process of articulating and integrating a country development strategy that priorities are identified and coherence achieved. Country ownership and leadership of the development strategy are crucial to effective implementation.

For low-income countries, the Poverty Reduction Strategy Papers (PRSPs) are the primary avenue of expression of such a country-

Box 1.2 Strengthening the links between PRSPs and the MDGs

The MDGs are global, but their implementation must occur at the country level, through country-owned and -led development strategies. In low-income countries, the Poverty Reduction Strategy Paper is the vehicle through which country policies and programs and resource requirements are linked to the MDGs.

Although there is no required set of indicators or goals that must be included in PRSPs, the targets specified are expected to be framed against the backdrop of the Millennium Development Goals. They also need to take account of initial conditions and national priorities so that they set out credible policies and programs for making progress toward the goals. As they prepare PRSPs, therefore, countries need to balance their long-term aspirations linked to the MDGs with the need to formulate concrete measures that can be feasibly implemented in the context of their annual planning cycles. Thus, for example, Vietnam's PRSP (called the Growth and Poverty Reduction Strategy) articulates the government's commitment to the MDGs but specifies goals and targets (the Vietnam Development Goals) that reflect extensive work to adapt progress toward the MDGs to local conditions.

Overall, most PRSPs do reflect fairly good coverage of the MDG topics, and that coverage has improved over time. All PRSPs completed by July 2003 included targets related to poverty headcount, school enrollment, and maternal health. Over 90 percent of the strategies covered child mortality and water access. On the other hand, coverage of the MDG indicators for women's voice, income distribution, biodiversity, and housing was only around 20 percent. Moreover, while the indicators chosen in PRSPs are often consistent with the MDGs, they frequently differ from the specific indicators chosen to track the MDG targets.

Data limitations and methodological issues associated with the time spans covered by PRSPs (three to five years) and the MDGs (up to 2015) make it difficult to compare the respective targets. However, a recent review by World Bank staff suggests that in some areas (malnutrition, access to water) targets set out in full PRSPs tend to be at least as ambitious as the MDG targets. On the other hand, for child and maternal mortality targets, PRSPs often set less ambitious targets than the MDG targets. At the same time, PRSP targets are generally quite ambitious compared to historical trends.

owned and -led development strategy. In middle-income countries, the policy integration and prioritization role is performed within respective national strategy frameworks. By the end of March 2004, 37 countries had prepared and were implementing full PRSPs; 16 more had prepared Interim PRSPs. Increasingly the MDGs are being incorporated in national PRSPs, and the PRSP process itself is being deepened along various dimensions—participatory processes, growth strategies, public expenditure management, poverty and social impact analysis. Continued strengthening of the PRSP process, and deepening of the links with the MDGs, will be key to the grounding of the policy agenda for the achievement of the development goals at the country level, in country-owned strategies in which countries spell out their commitments to policy and institutional reforms and which donors can commit to support in a coherent and consistent way (box 1.2).

Notes

1. The Development Committee is the Joint Ministerial Committee of the Boards of Governors of the World Bank and the International Monetary Fund on the Transfer of Real Resources to Developing Countries.
2. United Nations 2000, 2001.
3. WTO 2001; United Nations 2002a, 2002b.
4. Development Committee 2002.
5. Development Committee 2003a, 2003b, 2003c.
6. Development Committee 2003f, 2003g.
7. United Nations 2003.

For poverty, malnutrition, immunization, child mortality, and access to water, most countries for which data are available have set PRSP targets at levels that entail a substantial acceleration of improvement relative to current rates of progress.

Looking ahead, it is important that low-income countries (with support from their development partners) continue to strengthen the links between their PRSPs and the MDG targets. One way of doing this, suggested in the 2003 PRSP Progress Report, is for countries to develop alternative scenarios that illustrate how improved policies and governance and more and better aid would help them in accelerating progress toward the MDGs.

Linking the PRSP approach more closely to the MDGs will require work on several fronts, and countries will need support from external partners in the process. First, PRSPs will need to reflect medium-term goals that are linked to the MDG targets for 2015. These goals should be sufficiently ambitious, relevant to country circumstances, and based on national consultations undertaken as part of the PRSP process. Second, the goals should be related to a medium-term program of policy, institutional, and financing requirements that will include, in addition to the normal growth agenda, necessary infrastructure investments, service-delivery improvements, capacity upgrades, and market-access enhancements. Third, the medium-term program will need to be linked to a medium-term budget, including a public expenditure program and financing requirements. Fiscal constraints will need to be considered, together with options for increasing aid volumes and changes in aid modalities. Fourth, donors will need to be willing to make upfront commitments to close the medium-term financing gap in ways that are consistent with a realistic assessment of the country's spending priorities and debt sustainability. As long as the country's implementation of its PRSP remained on track, its program would be supported by higher and more predictable aid flows provided in ways appropriate to meeting the MDGs.

An enhanced approach along these lines could initially be applied in a group of focus countries based on their relative readiness. The experience in implementing the approach would provide lessons, which could then be used to extend the approach to other countries.

Sources: Development Committee 2003d; Harrison, Swanson, and Klugman 2003.

8. For the proceedings of this workshop, see the World Bank's global monitoring Web site at http://www.worldbank.org/.

9. See the papers submitted to the March 2003 and September 2003 Development Committee meetings (Development Committee 2003a, 2003b, 2003f) for a fuller account of the related monitoring activities of the partner agencies and collaboration with them, as well as the relevant activities of the civil society.

10. Details of this work were set out in the global monitoring implementation report provided to the September 2003 Development Committee meeting (Development Committee 2003f).

11. Development Gateway Web site: www.developmentgateway.org.

12. Ends in themselves, better education and health also are means to stronger economic growth because they raise workers' productivity. One study estimated that a 10 percent improvement in life expectancy at birth can raise the per capita income growth rate by 0.4 percentage point (WHO 2001). Barro (2001) estimated that an additional year of schooling can raise the growth rate by about 0.5 percentage point.

13. A large part of this effect might not be general education but specific health knowledge, but this is usually acquired using literacy and numeracy skills learned in school, as a study in Morocco found (Glewwe 1999).

14. A study in the Philippines found that a one–standard deviation increase in early-age child health increased subsequent test scores by about one-third of a standard deviation (Glewwe and King 2001). An evaluation of school-based mass treatment for deworming in rural Kenya found that student absenteeism fell by one-fourth (Miguel and Kremer 2001).

15. An eight-country study found that going from no improved water to "optimal" water access was associated with a 6-percentage-point reduction in the prevalence of diarrhea in children under three years of age (Asrey 1996). Lack of access to water supply and sanitation kills an estimated 2.1 million to 3.5 million children a year (WHO 2002).

16. The interlinked nature of the MDGs and their multisectoral determinants are illustrated by a recent study of child mortality, which found that, holding other factors constant, child mortality declines by 3 to 4 percent if access to drinking water improves by 10 percent, by 3 percent if years of schooling among women rise by 10 percent, by 0.8 to 1.5 percent if government health spending rises by 10 percent, by 1 to 1.5 percent if the density of paved roads rises by 10 percent, and by 2 to 3 percent if per capita income growth rises by 10 percent (Wagstaff 2003).

17. The growth elasticity of income poverty is typically between 1 and 2, whereas that of child mortality and primary enrollment is around 0.5 (Filmer and Pritchett 1999; Pritchett and Summers 1996; Schultz 1987). These elasticities of course are not fixed; they can be higher with better policies and governance.

18. For a recent review of evidence on the role of trade in growth and poverty reduction, see Berg and Krueger (2003).

19. Studies find that gender equality contributes to better education and health outcomes (see, for example, Behrman and others 1999). Research on Sub-Saharan Africa shows that greater gender equality in farm inputs could increase farm output by up to 20 percent (Udry 1996). More recent cross-country research has found that gender inequalities in education impede economic growth (Klasen 2002).

20. It is estimated that a 1 percent increase in output growth in G-7 countries has on average been associated with a 0.4 percent increase in developing country growth (IMF 2001).

21. Results from modeling of a pro-development outcome of the Doha Round show that stronger growth associated with the removal of significant impediments to merchandise trade and slashing of tariff peaks could mean as many as 140 million fewer people living in dire poverty in 2015—a decline of 8 percent. Agricultural subsidies also have a huge cost for the developed countries. It is estimated that these subsidies cost the average working family in the European Union, Japan, and the United States more than $1,000 a year (World Bank 2003).

22. For evidence on increased productivity of aid in developing countries, see Goldin, Rogers, and Stern (2002).

23. Development Committee 2003e. See chapter 11 for more discussion of additional aid requirements.

24. See Rome Declaration on Harmonization, February 25, 2003, at http://www1.worldbank.org/harmonization/romehlf.

2

MDG Prospects

Reasons for Optimism, Grave Concerns

Past the halfway mark to the 2015 target date, prospects for achieving the Millennium Development Goals raise both optimism and grave concerns. Based on current trends and growth forecasts, the goal of halving extreme poverty and hunger will be achieved—although Sub-Saharan Africa remains highly vulnerable. A few countries, notably China, already have reached the goal; some others, including India, are on track to meet it. But progress has stalled in some countries, and others are at severe risk of falling short of the goal. In Sub-Saharan Africa, on current trends, only eight countries are projected to halve extreme poverty by 2015.

Progress on non-income poverty goals has been considerably slower.[1] The least progress has been made in child and maternal mortality and in providing access to safe water and sanitation. In hardly any region are those goals likely to be met by the target date of 2015. Only 16 percent of countries, home to 22 percent of the developing world's population, are on track to meet the under-five mortality target.

Prospects for reaching the goal of universal primary education are better, but the goal remains a challenge. The East Asia and Pacific region has nearly met the goal; Europe and Central Asia and Latin America and the Caribbean are on target to achieve it. The Education for All Fast Track Initiative is likely to accelerate progress toward universal primary school completion, but shortfalls are still likely in Sub-Saharan Africa. While there has been global progress toward gender parity in education, particularly at the primary level, the 2005 goal of parity in primary and secondary education may not be met in about a third of developing countries even by 2015.

Accelerating economic growth is central to achieving the MDGs. The link between economic growth and income poverty is particularly strong, but growth is also an important determinant of human development outcomes. For faster growth, developing countries will need to implement substantial policy and institutional reforms. Particularly important will be actions to improve the regulatory and institutional framework for private sector activity, strengthen infrastructure, and enhance the quality of governance.

Making progress on the human development goals will also require efforts directed at improving the delivery of key services—health, education, and water and sanitation—especially to poor people. Investment in human development will need to be scaled up, together with reforms in public sector governance and capacity building to improve service delivery.

The effectiveness of interventions will also depend on taking into account cross-effects among goals. Health and nutritional status, for example, directly affect a child's probability of school enrollment, and access to safe water and sanitation is critical for child survival. The existence of such cross-effects means that improvements in one goal depend also on progress on other goals. Interlinkages are also evident across sectors. Sectoral interlinkages imply that isolated interventions may do little to achieve goals if bottlenecks remain in other sectors. Progress on the goal of universal primary education, for example, may depend importantly on better transportation, as well as increased spending on schools. Accordingly, national reform programs must be built on multisectoral analysis and anchored in coherent country development strategies.

As envisioned in the Monterrey Consensus, national efforts will need to receive stronger support from external partners. Priority areas of support are more open access to export markets and more and better aid.

The human development goals present a daunting challenge, but they are not unreachable. Past successes, such as halving adult illiteracy in the last 30 years and extending life expectancy by 20 years over the last 40 years, suggest that much can be achieved.[2]

Growth and Prospects for Achieving the MDGs

Economic growth is central to achieving the MDGs, particularly the goal of reducing income poverty. Economic growth reduces poverty because average incomes of the poor typically tend to rise proportionately with the average income of the population.[3] This result is robust over time and across countries and regions.

Higher national income contributes to human development goals as well. At the macro level, growth generates increased public resources to improve the quantity and quality of education, health, water supply, sanitation, and other services. At the household level, as growth reduces income poverty, demand for schooling, health care, and other services rises. Thus income, health, and education reinforce one another. More income leads to better human development outcomes, while better health and education can lead to increased productivity and higher incomes.[4]

Growth Outlook

The outlook for growth over the next decade is promising—although with continuing wide disparities across regions.[5] Should the current favorable trend in growth continue, most regions will see an acceleration in per capita income growth—some substantial (figure 2.1). East Asia is likely to continue its strong growth in the medium term, with an eventual moderation in growth as some countries in the region begin to approach the level of income of OECD countries. The robust turnaround in Europe and Central Asia should continue—although at a more moderate pace than that of the last five years—with the accession of several countries of the region to the European Union and also as the transition from planned economies advances.

There is some evidence that countries in Sub-Saharan Africa have turned the corner. Between 1997 and 2002, 24 of 46 countries in Sub-Saharan Africa—representing 53 percent of the region's population—experienced positive per capita income growth.[6] Reforms undertaken over the last few years, and a shift toward more manufacturing exports, should benefit African economies—although continued conflict and the HIV/AIDS epidemic will weigh on their prospects. To achieve the MDGs, growth in the region will have to accelerate much further (see below).

The other regions also will benefit from past and ongoing reforms—a more stable macroeconomic environment and greater openness—to boost their long-term growth rates, with South Asia leading the pack. Latin America is the only developing region to have faltered in the late 1990s and early 2000s—mostly weighed down by the lengthy crisis in Argentina, with related contagion to the rest of the region. A hopeful sign is that popula-

FIGURE 2.1 Growth prospects improve, but not enough
Real per capita growth by region, 1990–2015

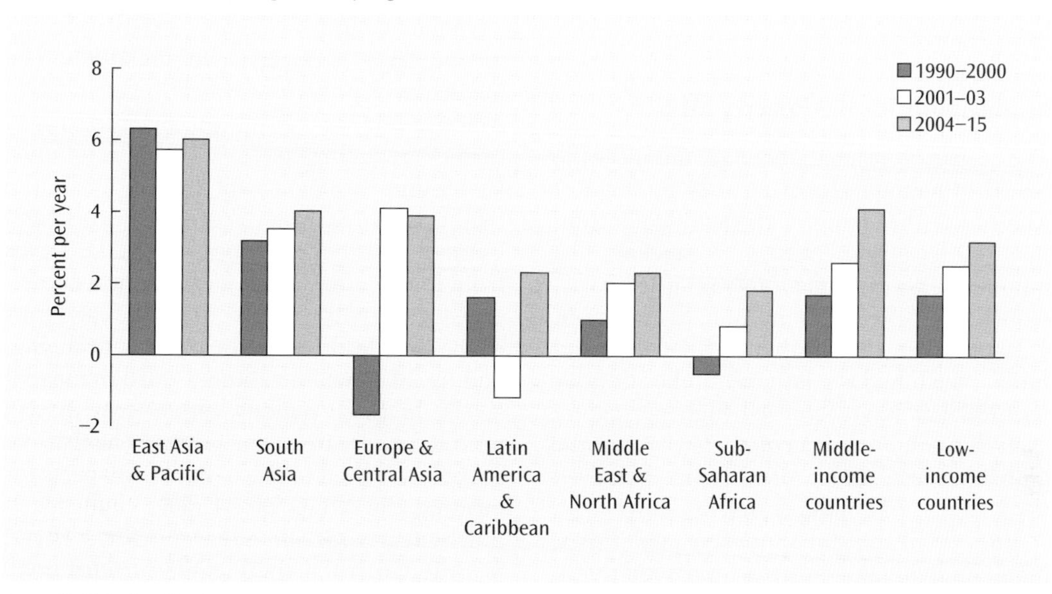

Source: World Bank staff estimates.

tion growth is slowing in the developing world: average growth is expected to be about 1.1 percent over the next decade (2005–15), below the 1.4 percent rate of the 1990s.

Drivers of growth. Underlying the growth scenario are structural shifts—first from subsistence agriculture to low-skilled manufacturing and later, as investment accelerates and skills are upgraded, to intermediate and finished goods of increasing technical sophistication.[7] A dramatic decrease in barriers to trade and cross-border investment in recent decades has made these structural transformations possible.[8] Greater openness has been accompanied by improvements in investment climate. Inflation has dropped dramatically across the world as policymakers have come to understand the negative impacts of high inflation. Government balances have improved, contributing to both macroeconomic stability and more effective use of public resources in support of development. Workers have become better educated and healthier; infrastructure has grown; and institutions have improved.

The contribution of productivity to growth will become more important in the future. First, millions of low-productivity agricultural workers—particularly in Asia and Africa—constitute a labor reserve for industrial and tertiary activities. Second, productivity in most developing countries lags far behind that in industrial countries—a significant opportunity for convergence as global trade and investment linkages convey the knowledge and technologies needed for greater productivity.

The scenario presented above is useful primarily as a reference point. Hypothetical deviations from it provide insights into the potential range of outcomes—particularly those driven by changes in specific policies. For example, full global merchandise trade reform has the potential to boost the average growth rate in developing countries by up to half of a percentage point—depending on how trade reforms deal with the factors that affect productivity.[9] But the converse is also true. Numerous factors could lead to slower growth than that assumed in the reference scenario—either on a cyclical or sustained basis, and with a global, regional, or more localized impact. Examples include a rise in protection, failure to address long-term structural imbalances, regional conflicts, and financial crises.

Implications for the Poverty MDG

The scenario outlined above would meet the MDG of halving global poverty by 2015.[10] The poverty headcount index would fall from its 1990 level of 27.9 to 12.5 percent. The number of poor people (on a $1-a-day basis) would fall below 735 million, from about 1.22 billion in 1990 (table 2.1).[11] China and India, which had the largest number of poor in 1990 but have achieved high per capita growth rates, would account for most of the global success. China already has achieved the poverty goal; India is well on its way.

But even if the global poverty goal is met, many individual countries, particularly in Sub-Saharan Africa, will fail to achieve the target (figure 2.2). Even in regions with strong overall performance, some countries are seriously off track. It is also likely that some countries that meet the income poverty target at the national level may leave some areas or groups behind. Special effort will need to be made to address the situation facing vulnerable groups (box 2.1).

The Sub-Saharan Africa region is the least likely to achieve the income poverty MDG, having made little or no progress on reducing the incidence of poverty over the 1990s. The incidence of poverty is much lower in Latin America and the Caribbean, but progress in further reducing poverty has been slow. Faster improvement will be needed if the region is to reach its target. In Europe and Central Asia, poverty rates rose in the 1990s from low average levels as the region experienced a sharp drop in income in the early part of the decade. These rates are now declining, and by 2015 will be about a third of current levels. In these regions, either growth will need to accelerate or the poverty elasticity of growth will need to rise to boost prospects for meeting the MDG target. The challenge is much greater for Sub-Saharan Africa. There, in order to reach the income poverty goal, GDP growth will have to double relative to the base scenario, or the poverty elasticity of growth will have to rise by a large factor.

Sub-Saharan Africa faces low per capita growth and a relatively low poverty elasticity. Of the 43 countries in the regional sample, 28, representing two-thirds of the region's population in 2000, had per capita growth rates of 2 percent or less (table 2.2). On cur-

TABLE 2.1 Growth rates and decline in poverty by region, through 2015

	Annual average growth rates (2004–15)		Population living under $1 per day					
	Scenario		Headcount (percent)			Number of persons (millions)		
Region	Per capita GDP	GDP	1990	2001	2015	1990	2001	2015
East Asia and Pacific	6.0	6.3	29.6	15.6	2.3	472	284	44
China	6.4	7.0	33.0	16.6	3.0	377	212	41
Europe and Central Asia	3.9	3.8	0.5	3.7	1.3	2	18	6
Latin America and Caribbean	2.3	3.7	11.3	9.5	7.6	49	50	46
Middle East and North Africa	2.3	4.1	2.3	2.4	1.2	6	7	4
South Asia	4.0	5.3	41.3	31.1	16.4	462	428	268
Sub-Saharan Africa	1.8	3.8	44.6	46.5	42.3	227	314	366
Total	3.7	4.7	27.9	21.3	12.5	1,219	1,101	734
Excluding China	3.0	4.1	26.1	22.8	15.4	841	888	692

Source: World Bank staff estimates.

FIGURE 2.2 **Most regions will reach the goal of halving poverty by 2015, but Sub-Saharan Africa is seriously off track**
Actual and projected decline in number of people living on less than $1 a day by region, 1990–2015

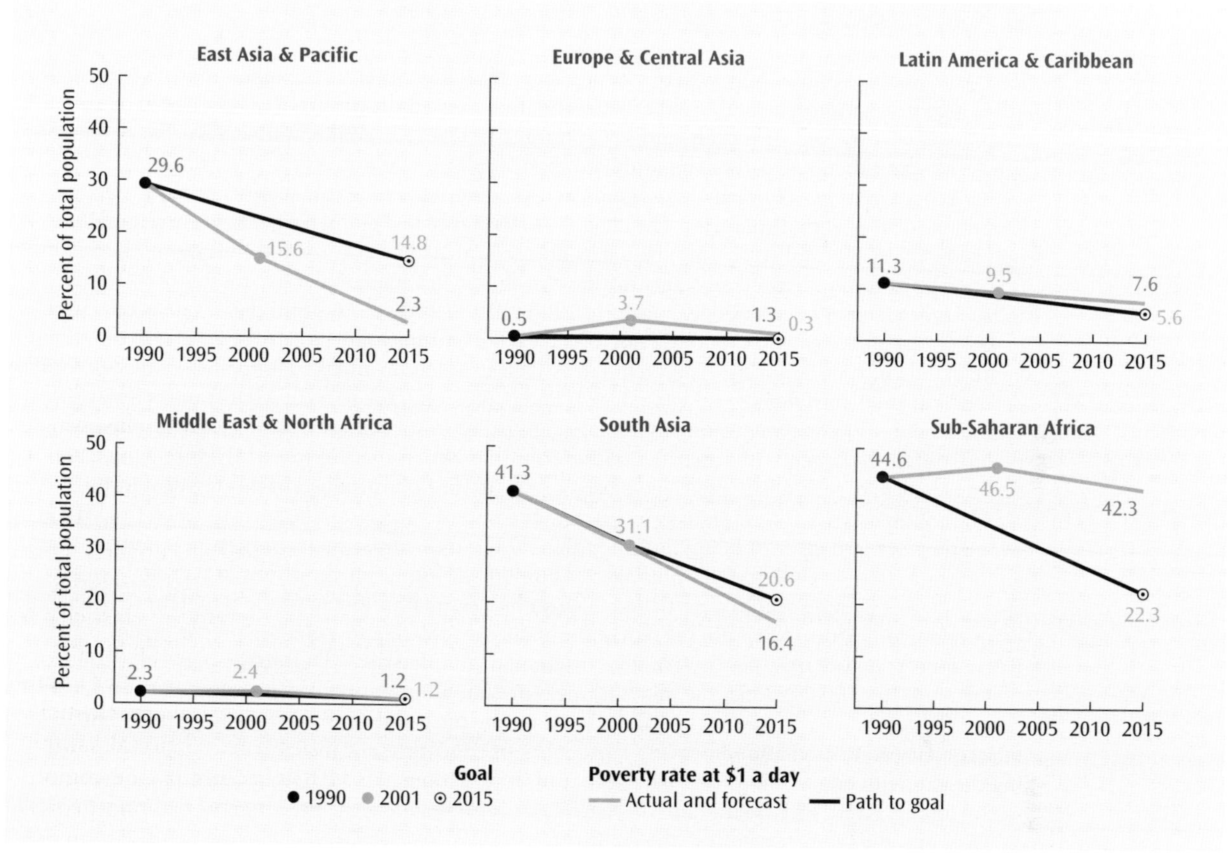

Source: World Bank staff estimates.

rent trends, only four countries—with some 16 percent of the region's population—are likely to see per capita growth of more than 3 percent. Mirroring the growth figures, only two countries in the region are expected to see an improvement in the headcount index of 50 percent or more between 2000 and 2015,[12] with six more countries achieving an improvement between 30 and 50 percent. Together, these eight countries represent somewhat less than 15 percent of the 2000 population.

The two countries with the best poverty performance have relatively modest per capita growth rates (between 2 and 3 percent), but have a relatively high poverty elasticity. Both also have the more equal income distribution, with Gini coefficients under 0.2.[13] Pro-growth policies would help the region, but pro-growth policies that favor the poor would have a much greater impact on the incidence of poverty.

Why some countries and regions have succeeded in reducing poverty while others have lagged was the subject of a major conference on scaling up poverty reduction held in May 2004 in Shanghai. The review of a number of country experiences, based on case studies, provided new insights into what works and what doesn't and what countries can learn from the experience of others. The main purpose of the conference, cohosted by the Government of China and the World Bank, was to encourage South-South learning about scaling up poverty reduction. Many of the

BOX 2.1 East Asia and Pacific: Despite solid performance on MDGs, challenges remain

East Asia has done remarkably well in meeting several MDGs. Seven of the nine countries for which adequate information is available either have already achieved the poverty reduction goal or are on track to achieve it. East Asia is also broadly on track to meet the goal on universal primary education, with enrollments already comparable to many high-income countries.

But progress has been uneven: across goals, across countries, and across socioeconomic groups and geographical areas within countries. The region's performance on health, particularly child immunization and maternal mortality, does not match its progress on income poverty and education. The region is not on track to cut the child mortality rate by two-thirds. In China, under-five mortality is estimated to have fallen from 49 per 1,000 live births in 1990 to 39 in 2001; however, if there is no acceleration in this pace of improvement, China will not meet the child mortality target of 16 for 2015. On the other hand, middle-income Southeast Asian economies such as Malaysia and the Philippines saw significant decreases in child mortality over the last decade and appear on track to meet MDG targets for 2015.

The region's low-income countries are lagging behind in several dimensions (see accompanying table). And the persistence of disparities *within* countries with respect to most MDGs remains a continuing challenge, even where goals have been or are about to be attained in the aggregate.

The region needs a differentiated approach that combines accelerated efforts to reach the MDGs where they are in danger of being missed with a will to exceed particular targets in countries that are on track. The so-called MDG-plus agenda could focus on faster reduction of national poverty, specify targets with respect to a particular geographic region or segment of the population, or specify different indicators to capture the remaining challenges relating to a goal. In preparing its Poverty Reduction Strategy Paper, the Government of Vietnam adapted the MDGs to the particular context of Vietnam. In many respects, the adaptations represent an ambitious agenda, including reducing poverty faster than envisaged in the MDGs, eliminating the gender gap not only in primary but also in secondary education and improving the quality of education not just access to it, and eliminating the gap with ethnic minorities. Thailand, too, is developing an MDG-plus agenda for incorporation into its Ninth Five-Year Plan. This agenda calls for reaching the poverty goal in the northeast of Thailand, the poorest region in the country.

Prospects for reaching the MDGs in East Asia

Country	Poverty	Child malnutrition	Primary school completion	Gender equality in school	Child mortality	Births attended	Immmunization for measles	Access to safe water
Cambodia	Off track	* *	Off track	* *	Seriously off track	Seriously off track	Off track	Off track
China	Achieved	On track	Achieved	Achieved	Off track	Achieved	Achieved	Off track
Fiji	* *	* *	* *	* *	Off track	On track	Achieved	* *
Indonesia	Achieved	On track	Off track	Achieved	On track	Seriously off track	Achieved	Off track
Lao PDR	On track	Off track	Off track	Seriously off track	On track	Seriously off track	Seriously off track	Off track
Malaysia	Achieved	* *	* *	Achieved	On track	Achieved	Achieved	* *
Mongolia	* *	Seriously off track	* *	Achieved	Off track	Achieved	Achieved	Off track
Papua New Guinea	Seriously off track	* *	* *	On track	Seriously off track	Seriously off track	Seriously off track	Seriously off track
Philippines	Achieved	Seriously off track	On track	Achieved	On track	Seriously off track	Seriously off track	Seriously off track
Thailand	Achieved	* *	Off track	Off track	Off track	Achieved	Achieved	Off track
Vietnam	Achieved	Off track	Achieved	* *	Off track	Seriously off track	Achieved	Off track

Seriously off track	Off track	On track	Achieved	Insufficient data
				* *

Note: Prospects in the above table are assessments based on the current levels of these indicators and recent progress toward the targets. Outcomes in the future could change markedly from past trends.
Source: UNESCAP/UNDP 2003; World Bank 2003a and 2003b.

TABLE 2.2 Projected per capita growth and improvement in poverty in Sub-Saharan Africa, 2000–2015

Projected growth of consumption per capita, 2000–2015	Number of countries	2000 Population (millions)	2000 Population share (percent)
<1	12	233	37.2
1–2	16	190	30.3
2–3	11	103	16.4
3–4	4	101	16.1
>4	0	0	0.0

Percent improvement in headcount index, 2000–2015	Number of countries	2000 Population (millions)	2000 Population share (percent)
<10	9	223	35.6
10–20	16	244	38.9
20–30	10	69	11.0
30–50	6	48	7.7
>50	2	43	6.8

Source: World Bank staff estimates.

basic ingredients of a successful poverty reduction strategy are relatively well known. How countries and communities have applied them and with what results differs widely, however. There is no one size that fits all, and the point of the conference was to enable practitioners to learn about successful cases and draw their own conclusions about what may or may not be transferable to their own unique situation.[14]

Hunger. Halving the proportion of the world's people who suffer from hunger is part of Goal 1. The target of halving the proportion of underweight children under five years of age between 1990 and 2015, the key measure of progress toward the goal, requires an average annual reduction of 2.7 percent. Available data show that, as for income poverty, the target is achievable at the global level, but Sub-Saharan Africa is seriously off track, as are a number of countries in other regions. In Sub-Saharan Africa, on current trends, only 17 percent of countries expect to reach the target.[15] In some countries, notably in Europe and Central Asia, slippages are occurring, resulting in rising malnutrition, particularly in the former Soviet Union.[16]

Prospects for Other MDGs

Economic growth has a significant effect on non-income development goals—education, health—just as it does on income poverty. However, the magnitude of the effect on the former is typically smaller than on the latter. Prospects for progress on the human development goals also depend importantly on the scale and effectiveness of development interventions specifically directed toward them, such as policies that improve the delivery of key services. And the determinants of these goals are multisectoral. Compared to the typical estimate of the elasticity between growth and income poverty of 1 to 2, the typical estimate of the elasticity between growth and the primary completion rate or under-five mortality is around 0.5. However, these elasticities are not fixed and can be higher with policies and institutions that are better able to translate growth into improved human development outcomes.[17]

Another reason that gives some cause for optimism is that over time, education and health outcomes have been improving for the same income level, reflecting advances in knowledge and technology, such as break-

FIGURE 2.3 Mortality at a given level of national income has been declining
Changes in the association between GDP per capita and child mortality, 1990 to 2000

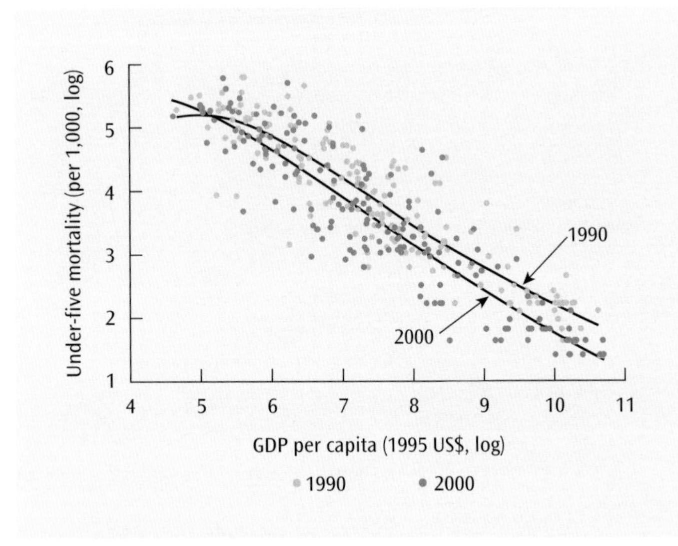

Note: Lines show outcome as predicted by a nonlinear function of GDP per capita.
Source: GDP per capita data from *World Development Indicators* database. Under-five mortality from UNICEF (2002).

throughs in immunizations against infectious diseases (figure 2.3). The changes are significant, even among poorer countries. For example, at a national income of $600 per capita, predicted child mortality fell from 100 per 1,000 births to 80 between 1990 and 2000—a full 20 percent.[18]

In the discussion that follows, the prospects for the achievement of non-income poverty goals are reviewed, based on the growth outlook described in the preceding section and current assessments with respect to the status of other determinants of these goals—relevant polices and institutions, multisectoral linkages.

Primary education. The target for completing primary school is 100 percent by 2015. While a few regions are close to the target, as measured by a new database on primary completion rates jointly developed by the World Bank and the United Nations Educational, Scientific, and Cultural Organization (UNESCO), others are at risk of falling short if current trends persist. East Asia and Pacific and Europe and Central Asia were fairly close to the target in 2000, with population-weighted completion rates of 97 and 93 percent, respectively (figure 2.4). Although both regions would need to accelerate progress slightly over the trend observed in the 1990s, the required pace appears achievable.

Of the other four regions, Latin America has registered the fastest progress and is on track toward the goal. In South Asia and the Middle East and North Africa, however, progress on primary completion rates is slower than one would expect from the regions' average per capita GDP growth. A sharp acceleration over recent trends will be needed to meet the goal. Sub-Saharan Africa could miss the target by a wide margin. Because the annual improvement in completion rates was just 0.2 percent in the 1990s, an annual improvement of more than 4.5 percent will be needed for the period 2000–15 to achieve the target (table 2.3). Even if the economic growth rate doubles, other mechanisms and policies will be needed to achieve the education target in the region. The Education for All Fast Track Initiative specifically addresses the reform and financial needs of countries that are struggling to move toward the education goals.

Gender equality. The third MDG seeks to promote gender equality and empower women. The targets include achieving gender parity in primary and secondary education preferably by 2005 and at all levels of education by 2015. Progress at the primary level has been relatively good, with the ratio of girls to boys enrolled improving from 88 to 94 percent between 1990 and 2000. Girls' enrollments have increased faster than boys' in all regions, and in the three regions where gender inequalities are greatest—Sub-Saharan Africa, the Middle East, and South and West Asia—disparities have eased. Nonetheless, the target of gender parity in primary and secondary education by 2005 will not be met. Moderate to serious gender disparities against girls at the primary level in about 35 percent of developing

FIGURE 2.4 A few regions are close to the target on primary education; others are off track
Primary education completion rates by region, 1990–2015

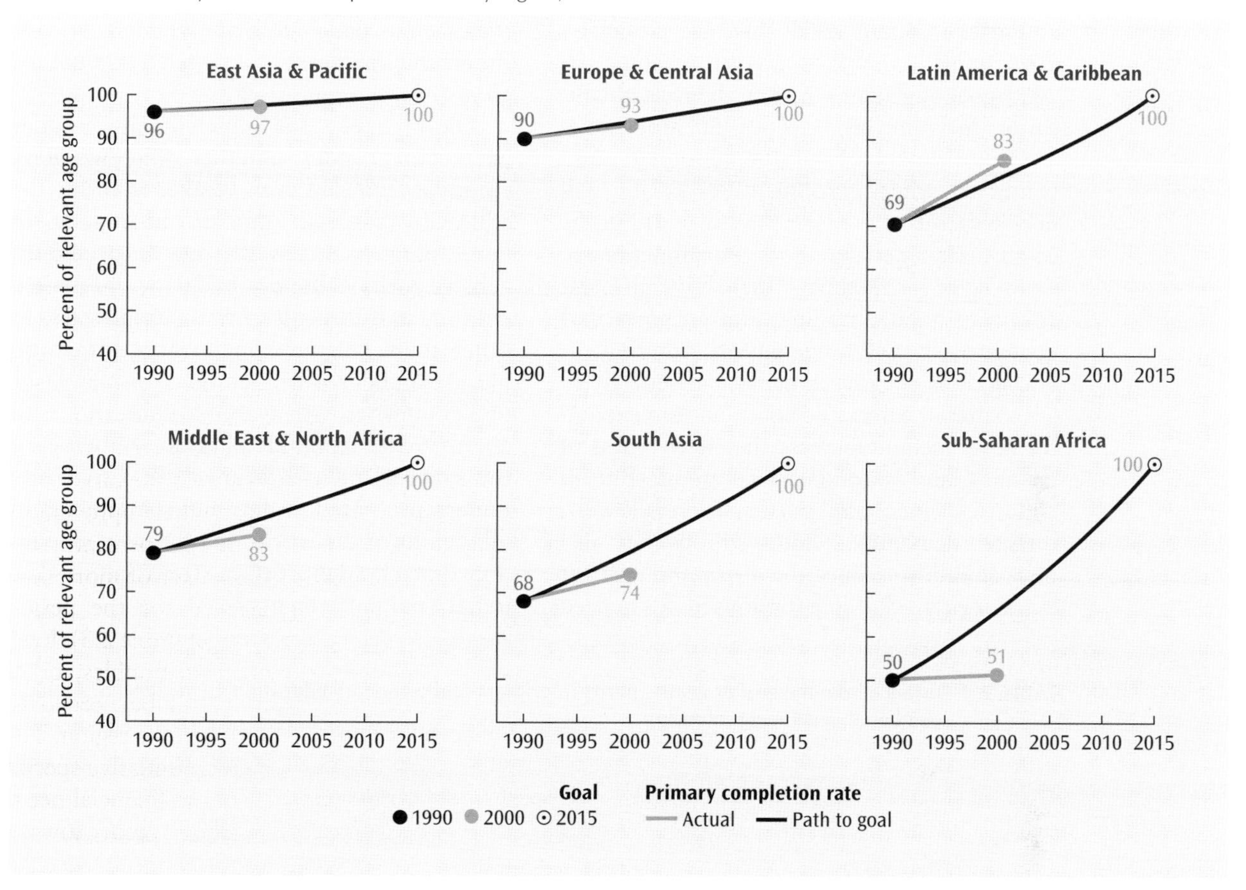

Source: United Nations; World Bank staff estimates.

TABLE 2.3 Primary education completion rates, progress needed by region (percent)

	Annual improvement		
Regions	Required 1990–2015	Observed 1990–2000	Required 2000–15
East Asia and Pacific	0.16	0.10	0.20
Europe and Central Asia	0.42	0.33	0.48
Latin America and Caribbean	1.50	1.86	1.25
Middle East and North Africa	0.95	0.50	1.25
South Asia	1.55	0.85	2.03
Sub-Saharan Africa	2.81	0.20	4.59

Source: United Nations; World Bank staff estimates.

countries and at the secondary level in about 43 percent of countries suggest that a number of countries may not reach this target even by 2015 (table 2.4).[19] Prospects for reaching the 2015 goal of gender parity at all levels of education, including higher education, are remote.

Girls' primary school completion rates and secondary-school enrollments, especially, will need to grow even faster than they did in the 1990s. The fact that girls' enrollments are growing at a faster pace than boys' in most countries is encouraging, and suggests that gender parity will hinge importantly on general actions by governments, particularly in Sub-Saharan Africa and South Asia, to expand the coverage and increase the effectiveness of primary and secondary schooling. But in countries where girls' participation is lowest, targeted demand-side interventions may also be required, to reduce the direct and indirect costs of girls' schooling for households in need of girls' labor or concerned about their safety, particularly where schools are far away. Countries such as Bangladesh and Guatemala have shown the effectiveness of targeted stipends for girls.

The prospects for achieving the broader MDG on gender equality and women's empowerment are even weaker than for the education targets. Almost one-quarter of developing countries are not expected to achieve parity in literacy by 2015, and limited data make it difficult to evaluate progress in other areas. Unemployment rates, for example, are higher for women than for men in 21 of 37 countries with available data, and in no country with available data do women earn the same as men.[20] Women are also vastly underrepresented in national parliaments in all regions of the world. In only 14 countries do women hold more than 30 percent of seats in national parliaments.[21]

TABLE 2.4 Distance from the goal of gender parity in primary and secondary education, by region, circa 2000 (number of developing countries)

Region	Have achieved GPI between 0.97 & 1	Close to goal GPI between 0.95 & 0.96	Medium position GPI between 0.80 & 0.94	Far from goal GPI < 0.80	Total number of countries
Primary education					
East Asia and Pacific	11	2	4		17
Europe and Central Asia	18	2	2		22
Latin America and Caribbean	19	4	2		25
Middle East and North Africa	4	4	5	2	15
South Asia	2		2	1	5
Sub-Saharan Africa	10	5	14	12	41
Subtotal	64	17	29	15	125
Secondary education					
East Asia and Pacific	2	2	8	4	16
Europe and Central Asia	17	2	2	1	22
Latin America and Caribbean	4	4	13	2	23
Middle East and North Africa	2	1	8	2	13
South Asia		1	1	3	5
Sub-Saharan Africa	3		16	17	36
Subtotal	28	10	48	29	115

Note: The Gender Parity Index (GPI) is the ratio of the gross enrollment ratio (GER) for girls divided by that for boys. The GER is the number of pupils enrolled in a given level of education, regardless of age, expressed as a percentage of the population in the relevant official age group. For this table, in cases where girls' GER exceeds that of boys (which would produce a GPI greater than 1), the inverse of GPI was used in order to allow GPI values to be compared on a scale with a maximum value of unity. Thus, this table registers gender gaps against boys as well as against girls. While at the primary level, all of the moderate to serious gender disparities are against girls, this is not true at the secondary level, where gender gaps are observed in both directions.
Source: Adapted from UNESCO 2003.

Child mortality. Progress on child mortality has been particularly weak, and prospects for reaching the under-five child mortality goal are dim (figure 2.5). For developing countries on average, under-five child mortality was measured at roughly 80 deaths per 1,000 in 1990. The goal is to lower this by two-thirds by 2015. Progress is highly uneven across regions and countries, as well as within countries, often reflecting differences in income. As of 2000, only 16 percent of developing countries, with 22 percent of the developing world's population, were on track to meet the target.[22] At the regional level, only one region—Latin America and the Caribbean—is on track. The target is unlikely to be reached in other regions, including East Asia, which will comfortably attain the income poverty target. Progress has been particularly slow in Sub-Saharan Africa, where conflict and the HIV/AIDS epidemic have driven up rates of infant and child mortality in several countries. Not a single country in this region is on track to meet the child mortality target.

Meeting the child mortality target calls for an average annual mortality reduction of 4.3 percent during 1990–2015. Because improvements in this indicator have been slow, a reduction of this magnitude will be challenging in the best of environments.[23]

In some countries the gap in child mortality is widening between the poor and the better-off. Results on the disparities between rich and poor (comparing the bottom and

FIGURE 2.5 Prospects for reaching the child mortality goal are dim
Mortality rate for children under age five by region

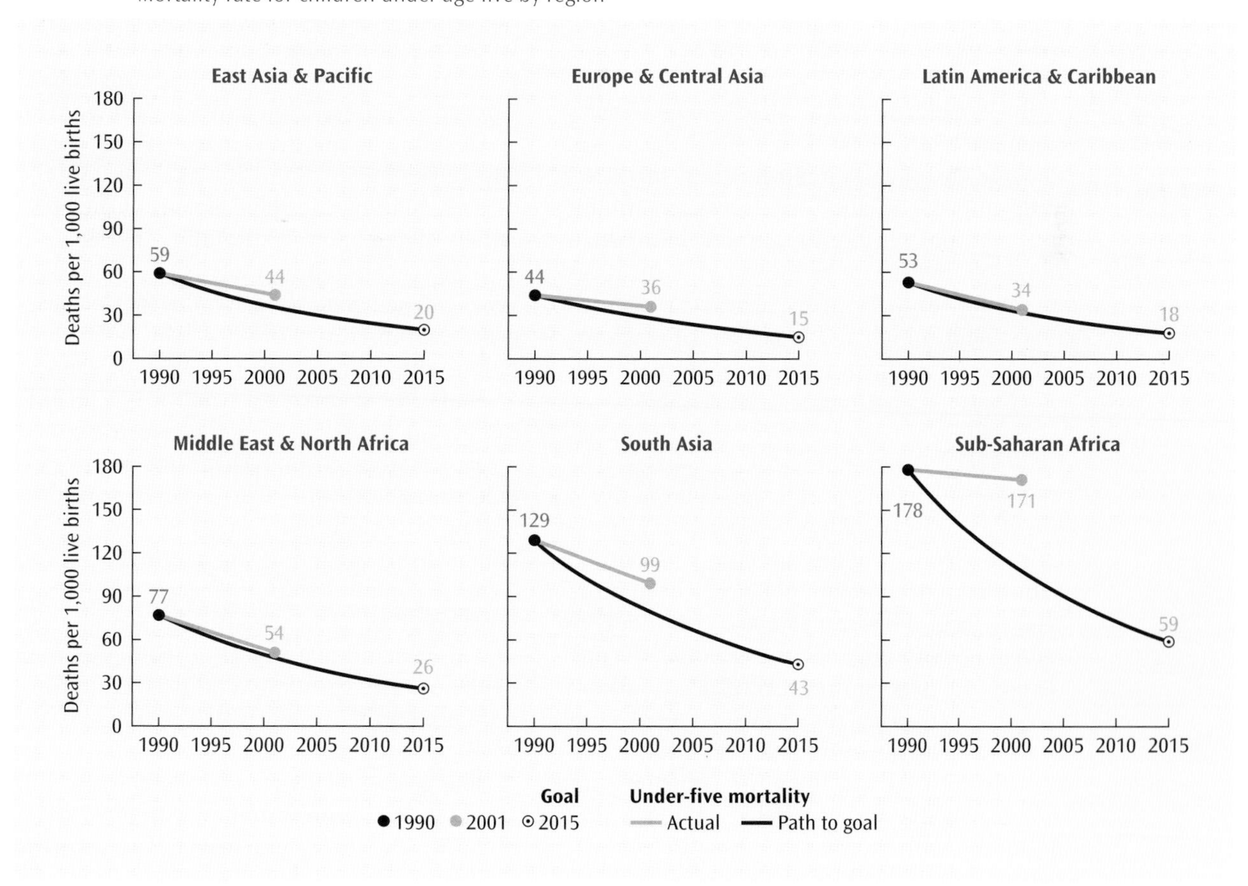

Source: United Nations; World Bank staff estimates.

top quintiles) for both infant and child mortality for four countries—Armenia, Bolivia, Cambodia, and Central African Republic—suggest that poverty underlies much of the lack of progress in improving the health status of children.[24] Low incomes, ignorance, and limited access to effective services contribute to the problem. Advances on intermediate factors that affect well-being (immunization coverage, availability of effective diagnosis and treatment, water availability, responsive provider behaviors) will be required to make a serious dent in child mortality.

Maternal health. Progress on reducing maternal mortality has been insufficient, and prospects are rather bleak. The MDGs call for a full three-quarters reduction in maternal mortality between 1990 and 2015, equivalent to an annual reduction of 5.4 percent. With an average annual decline of 3.2 percent in the 1990s, the developing world as a whole is off target.[25] Only 17 percent of countries, with 32 percent of the developing world's population, are on track to achieve the target. Poverty, distance, limited hospital facilities, and uneven quality of services inhibit progress and require investment in a broad range of areas to make meaningful advances in saving mothers' lives. The cost of such investment is high and likely out of reach for the poorest countries, where maternal mortality rates are highest.

HIV/AIDS, malaria, and other diseases. The most prevalent and problematic communicable diseases—HIV/AIDS, malaria, and tuberculosis—have proven difficult to contain; achieving a decline in incidence is even more challenging. HIV prevalence continues to increase—with but a few exceptions. The epidemic remains most severe in Southern Africa, where pregnant women 15 to 24 years of age display infection rates of 18 to 39 percent. In East Africa, there are some encouraging signs that the prevalence of infection is declining, with the rate dropping in Uganda, for example, from nearly 30 percent in 1990 to 9 percent in 2002. In West and Central Africa, prevalence remains low (1 to 3 percent), although Cameroon reports a prevalence of 12 percent.

Although the risks of failure to halt the spread of HIV/AIDS are especially high in Sub-Saharan Africa, they are substantial in many countries in other regions as well. Even though current estimates suggest overall low prevalence rates in India and China, the absolute number of cases is estimated at more than 4 million in India and is approaching 1 million in China. In Latin America and the Caribbean, where the epidemic is well established, 12 countries report HIV prevalence of 1 percent or more among pregnant women. The highest rates of increase in HIV/AIDS infection are found in Europe and Central Asia, where the absolute number of reported cases is about 1.5 million. Denial, stigma, and the institutional challenges of providing services to marginalized and vulnerable subpopulations, such as injecting drug users, jeopardize progress in combating HIV/AIDS.

Declines in the prevalence of HIV/AIDS lag considerably behind efforts to contain the disease, making the achievement of the HIV/AIDS-related goal especially challenging. Those newly diagnosed were infected 8 to 10 years earlier. The long latency period suggests the imperative of mass education campaigns and other early preventive measures.

Malaria has proven a stubbornly endemic disease in many parts of the world. Failed efforts to stop mosquito breeding with pesticides have left limited intervention options, among them the use of treated bed nets in endemic areas and drug prophylaxis and treatment. Behavioral and economic factors limit progress, since the affordability and use of bed nets and pharmaceuticals require new behaviors and spending on the part of households and public and private providers of services and goods.

The global incidence of tuberculosis (TB) is on the rise, with 9 million estimated cases in 2001. The increase is most affected by the HIV epidemic in Sub-Saharan Africa. TB infection and disease are especially prevalent among those with impaired immune systems and poor nutrition. There has been a major expansion in the application of the approach for TB control recommended by the World Health Organization (WHO), which was adopted by more than 155 countries with an average cure rate of 82 percent in 2001. It is estimated that only one-third of TB cases were reported in 2001. The interim target is 70 percent reporting for 2005, suggesting that the goals for TB will be difficult to achieve. Progress in Sub-Saharan Africa is slowest, but there are encouraging signs of progress elsewhere, even in low-income countries.

Water and sanitation. The MDGs call for halving the proportion of the world's population without access to safe drinking water and sanitation between 1990 and 2015. To meet that target, 1.5 billion additional people (1 billion in urban areas and 0.5 billion in rural areas) will have to be provided with sustainable access to safe water and about 2 billion more with access to basic sanitation (1.1 billion in urban areas and 0.9 billion in rural areas) in the period from 2000 to 2015. At current rates of service expansion, about 20 percent of countries are on track, but fewer than 10 percent of low-income countries appear to be on track. Much faster access rates will be required if countries are to achieve the water and sanitation goals. Only one region—Latin America and the Caribbean—currently appears likely to attain the MDG for drinking water. Water access rates will need to grow much faster, especially in Sub-Saharan Africa—from a current pace of 0.43 percent a year to 2.53 percent.[26]

Accelerating Progress toward the Development Goals

The implication of the foregoing assessment is clear. The achievement of the development goals will require rising above current trends and accelerating the pace of development, and doing so swiftly. In line with the principles and partnership established at Monterrey, all parties must scale up their action. The agenda has three essential elements:

- Accelerating and deepening reforms to achieve stronger economic growth than recently experienced or currently projected
- Stepping up action on the delivery of human development and related key services—education, health, water and sanitation
- Speeding up the implementation of the Monterrey partnership, matching stronger developing country efforts to spur growth and improve service delivery to poor people with stronger support from developed countries and international agencies.

Substantial reforms of domestic policy and institutions will be necessary to boost growth. Particularly important are reforms to improve the enabling environment for private sector activity—by extending progress on macroeconomic stability, improving the regulatory and institutional framework governing markets, and strengthening basic infrastructure. Also key are reforms to enhance the quality of governance and the capacity of the public sector. Such reforms will improve the effectiveness of existing resources and help mobilize more domestic resources. Moreover, they will allow increases in aid to be productively utilized.

Policy and institutional reforms will also boost MDG prospects by improving the delivery of key services, especially to the poor. Investment in services such as education, health, and water and sanitation needs to be scaled up, in many cases substantially. But the effectiveness of the delivery of these services will depend on improvements in the underlying policy and governance framework. Too often, basic services fail to reach poor people.[27] Since societies often view basic services such as education and health as largely the responsibility of governments, reforms that strengthen public sector institutions—making them more responsive to the poor, more accountable, and less corrupt—will be critical to improving access to and quality of services.

The acceleration and deepening of reforms in developing countries must be complemented by increased support from developed country partners. Priorities include improving market access to developing country exports and providing more and better aid. Also important is the broad conduct of macroeconomic and financial policies in a way that is conducive to strong global economic growth and stable capital flows.

A recent World Bank study of 18 low-income countries with relatively good policies found that reforms that substantially strengthen policies and institutions, supported by additional external resources, can be a very powerful combination.[28] It showed that if better policies and institutions were combined with more aid, the number of countries in the sample that would achieve MDGs 1 to 7 would at least double—with all of them achieving the poverty goal (figure 2.6).

The rest of this report assesses the various elements of this powerful combination: how developing countries are doing on improving policies and governance (Part II); how developed countries are fulfilling their commitments (Part III); and how the international financial institutions are contributing to the development effort (Part IV).

Notes

1. United Nations 2003.
2. World Bank 2002.
3. Dollar and Kraay 2002; Adams 2002. Income inequality, conversely, changes more slowly (Ravallion 1995, 2001; Adams 2002). All these studies used household survey data to examine how growth affects inequality. The studies concluded that income distributions are rather stable over time, and that economic growth does not affect inequality.

FIGURE 2.6 Reform combined with stronger partner support can substantially boost prospects for achieving the MDGs

Results for 18 low-income countries undertaking reforms

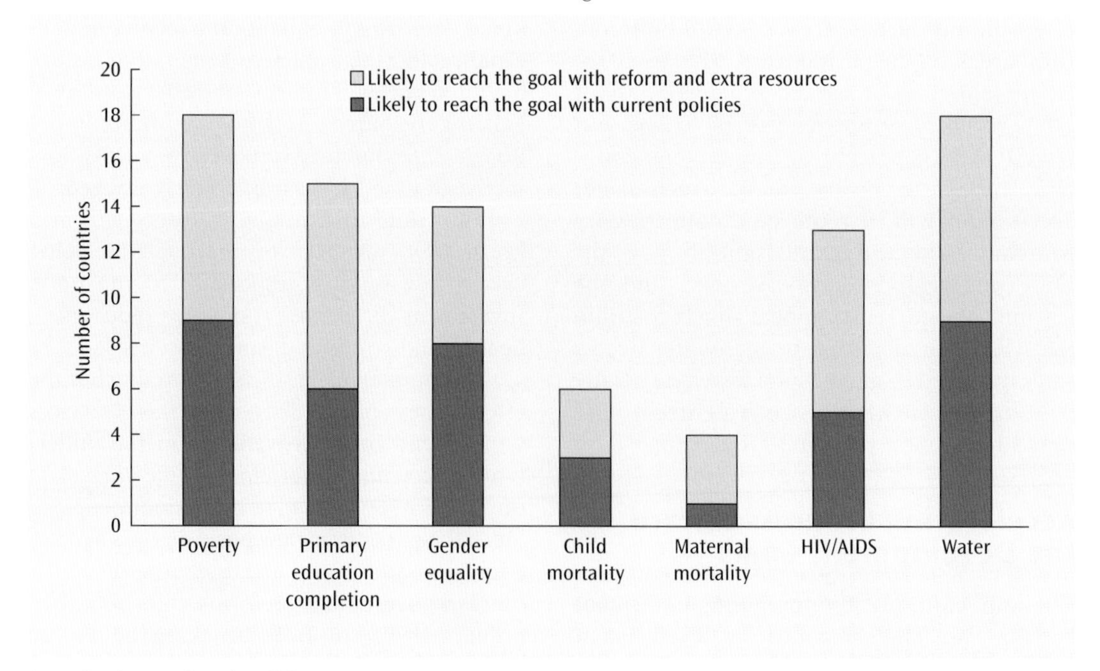

Source: Development Committee 2003.

4. Studies that have tried to disentangle these relationships typically have found income to be a robust and strong determinant of outcomes.

5. A word of caution regarding the economic scenarios described here. The key word is scenario. Unlike short- and medium-term forecasts—such as those presented regularly in the World Bank's annual *Global Economic Prospects* or the IMF's *World Economic Outlook*—long-term forecasts are predicated on informed assumptions, particularly as regards supply-side factors. In this sense, the scenarios are more akin to growth-accounting exercises, where more attention is paid to underlying growth fundamentals—employment, productivity, savings, investment, and capital accumulation. These scenarios also try to deduce long-term structural changes, such as the rising share of services in economic output, increasing urbanization, and terms-of-trade impacts, particularly as they affect commodity-dependent exporters and importers. Some of these structural changes can also be used to deduce potential impacts on achieving the nonmonetary MDGs. For example, increasing urbanization may make it easier to provide health and educational services. Unlike the short- and medium-term forecasts, long-term outlooks typically are not linked to econometrically validated economic relations with standard confidence intervals. While this may be perceived as a weakness, the purpose of scenario analysis is different from the short- and medium-term forecasting exercise, and providing confidence intervals would be either imparting a false sense of certainty or producing such a wide band as to make the intervals meaningless.

6. Nigeria almost eked out positive growth, losing 0.1 percent per capita over the five-year span. The addition of Nigeria to the list of countries with positive growth would have increased the proportion of the region's population experiencing positive growth to nearly 75 percent.

7. One of the most striking outcomes of this structural transformation is the change in the composition of developing-country exports since the 1970s. Three decades ago, exports of primary products (including processed foods), accounted for three-fourths of total developing-country exports. Manufactured products now account for the same percentage, or more, and trade growth has been phenomenal over a broad range of sectors. Though there are regional variations, this picture holds broadly over all developing countries, including Sub-Saharan Africa, even though in the latter region manufacturing exports are still a small share because of the initial starting point.

8. Three factors have driven the decline in barriers. First, successive rounds of multilateral trade negotiations have simultaneously lowered barriers across a broad set of countries. Since the end of World War II, eight multilateral rounds have been concluded, with the ninth, the Doha Round, scheduled to be concluded by the end of 2004. The second factor has been the creation of several large regional free-trade areas—for example, the European Union, North American Free Trade Agreement (NAFTA), and Southern Cone Common Market (Mercosur). The third factor has been the wave of unilateral liberalization following the debt crisis of the early 1980s—affecting mostly countries in Latin America. Freer trade enabled producers to purchase technology embodied in imported inputs and capital goods, contributing to productivity.

9. World Bank 2001b, 2003c.

10. The poverty forecast for most countries is based on an estimated functional form for the Lorenz curve. The parameters of the Lorenz curve are estimated from the latest available household surveys, which are available for over 80 developing countries. For most regions, distribution neutrality is assumed. In technical terms, this means that the shape of the Lorenz curve is assumed to be constant between 2000 and 2015. The two exceptions are China and India, where some specific assumptions are made regarding change in the pattern of regional income disparities. Typical values of the elasticity of the headcount index relative to growth are between –1 and –2. The elasticity approach has limitations as a tool for making projections over very long periods since the elasticity (assuming distribution neutrality) increases over time (in absolute terms).

11. While the income poverty MDG is defined in terms of proportion of people living on less than $1 per day, that definition underestimates the extent of poverty in regions where the true poverty line would be higher, such as in Europe and Central Asia. Numbers in table 2.1 should be interpreted with that caveat in mind.

12. The MDG is a 50 percent improvement between 1990 and 2015, not 2000 and 2015. At this time, the 1990 headcount by country is not available.

13. Only 8 countries in the sample of 43 have poverty elasticities above 1.25, 22 have elasticities between 1 and 1.25, and the remainder are under 1. Four countries have poverty elasticities under 0.5. The average Gini coefficient is around 0.5, lower than in Latin America but significantly higher than in most of Asia.

14. For more information on the conference, see http://www.worldbank.org/wbi/reducingpoverty/index.html.

15. World Bank 2004.

16. Rokx, Galloway, and Brown 2002.

17. The World Bank and its partner institutions are conducting research into a framework that will allow a better modeling of the relationship between growth, other determinants, and the MDGs. A two-track approach has been laid. The first track involves pilot studies (initially in Ghana and Ethiopia). Researchers will develop a framework for forecasting the MDGs at the country level, with the intention of extending the approach to other countries. The second track will focus on global analysis, using the findings of the pilot studies to inform regional and global level assessments. Preliminary results will be available for discussion by Spring 2005.

18. Preston 1980.

19. Seventy-seven countries have moderate to serious gender gaps at the secondary level. In 49 of these countries the gender disparity is against girls and in 28 the disparity is against boys.

20. United Nations Millennium Project Task Force on Education and Gender Equality 2004.

21. Based on data from Inter-Parliamentary Union (IPU) 2004: www.ipu.org. Also see World Bank 2001a.

22. World Bank 2004.

23. Monitoring health goals is challenging because quality data are difficult to obtain. This is partly due to the large element of judgment needed to classify causes of death, as well as constraints to data collection by public and private providers. The Partnership in Statistics for Development in the 21st Century works with DAC members and other donors to strengthen statistical capacity building in developing countries. See OECD 2004.

24. World Bank 2003d.

25. World Bank 2004.

26. World Bank 2004.

27. World Bank 2003d.

28. Development Committee 2003.

II

Developing-Country Policies

3

Overall Picture

As discussed in Part I, achieving the MDGs will require stronger economic growth in developing countries than recently attained or currently projected. It will also require actions to empower poor people and enhance their capabilities to participate in growth, through improved delivery of key services to them. Progress on this agenda calls for improvements in policies and governance in developing countries and stronger support to these reforms from developed countries and international agencies, as recognized in the Monterrey Consensus. To achieve the goals, each of these three groups of actors must scale up their efforts. Against this background, how are their policies and actions actually evolving? The rest of this report attempts to provide an assessment.

As the quest for better development outcomes must begin with developing countries themselves—their policies and institutions—this assessment likewise begins there. How the developed countries and international agencies are playing their part is reviewed in Parts III and IV, respectively. This chapter provides an overview of progress on reform in developing countries, drawing on broad country policy assessments prepared by the various international agencies that cover country policies and institutions in a relatively comprehensive manner. The following chapters in Part II then focus on specific policy areas, using a host of indicators and data specific to those policy areas and drawn from a multiplicity of sources.

Overall, there is an improving trend in developing-country policies. This progress is reflected in the World Bank's Country Policy and Institutional Assessment (CPIA) ratings, which have improved on average over the past five years (figure 3.1). This is true for both low- and middle-income countries. Average ratings have improved in all regions. And in most regions they have improved across the four policy clusters that are assessed in the CPIA: economic management (comprising macroeconomic policies); structural policies (broadly covering trade, financial sector, and regulatory policies that determine the enabling climate for the private sector, as well as policies for environmental sustainability); policies for social inclusion and equity (covering policies for human resource development, gender, social protection, and equity of resource use); and public sector management and institutions (comprising public financial management, quality of public administration, control of corruption, and rules-based governance).[1]

While the ratings have improved, the change in general has been relatively modest, though encouraging nonetheless. Going forward, the scope for improvement remains

FIGURE 3.1 Developing countries' policies have improved; governance and institutions lag
Trends in developing-country policies and institutions, 1999–2003

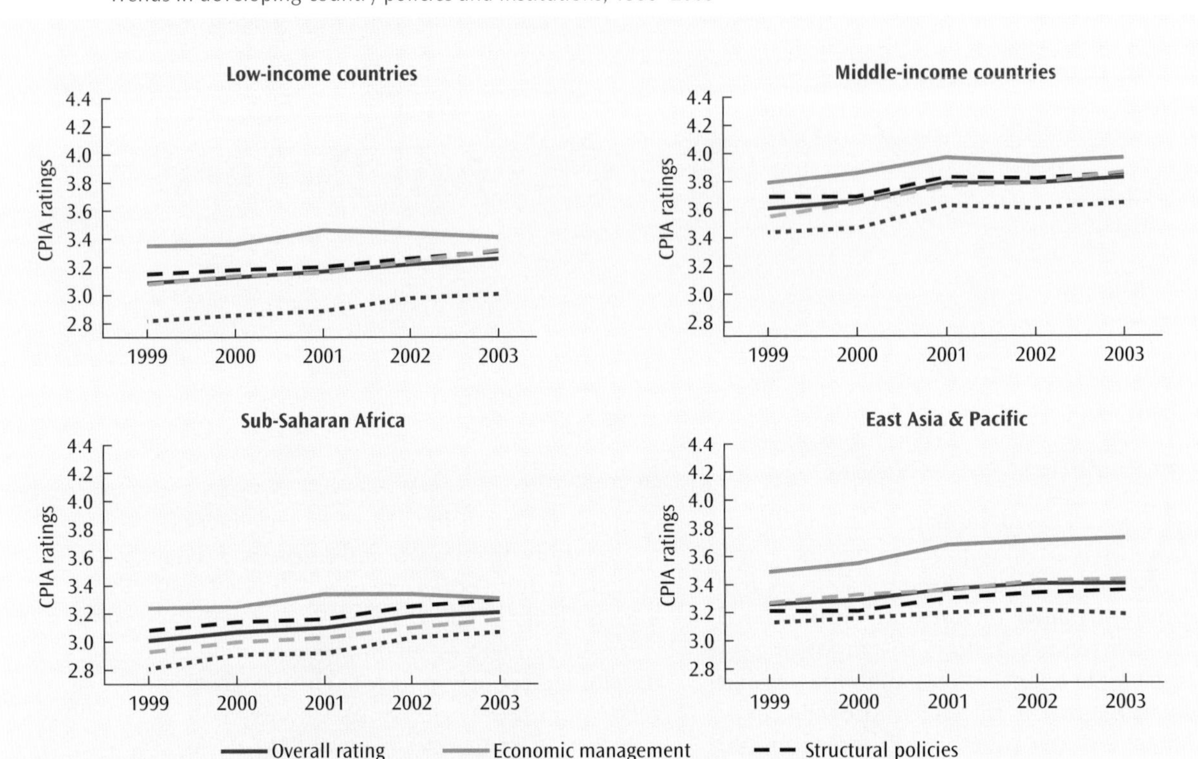

large. Notwithstanding the rise in the ratings, average ratings remain in the 3 to 4 range, on a scale of 1 (low) to 6 (high). Ratings for low-income countries on average are appreciably lower than those for middle-income countries. And, across regions, average ratings remain the lowest in Sub-Saharan Africa, though improving. The regional averages of course also hide large differences among countries within a region.

Across country groups, there is a fairly consistent pattern in terms of policy relativities. Ratings are highest for macroeconomic management; those for structural and social policies are in the middle; and those for public sector governance are the lowest. This is true across regions and across income categories. This pattern provides part of the explanation of the developing countries' growth performance reviewed in chapter 2. While macroeconomic management has improved, providing a more stable enabling economic climate, this progress has not been equally reflected in an improved growth performance. Part of the explanation is that progress on structural and governance reforms has been slower, limiting private sector response.

The low ratings for public sector governance are also reflected in the relative weakness of the more institutional dimensions of policy in other areas. Within the nexus of structural policies affecting private business environment, the weakest area is property rights. Within social sector policies, again the

FIGURE 3.1 (continued)

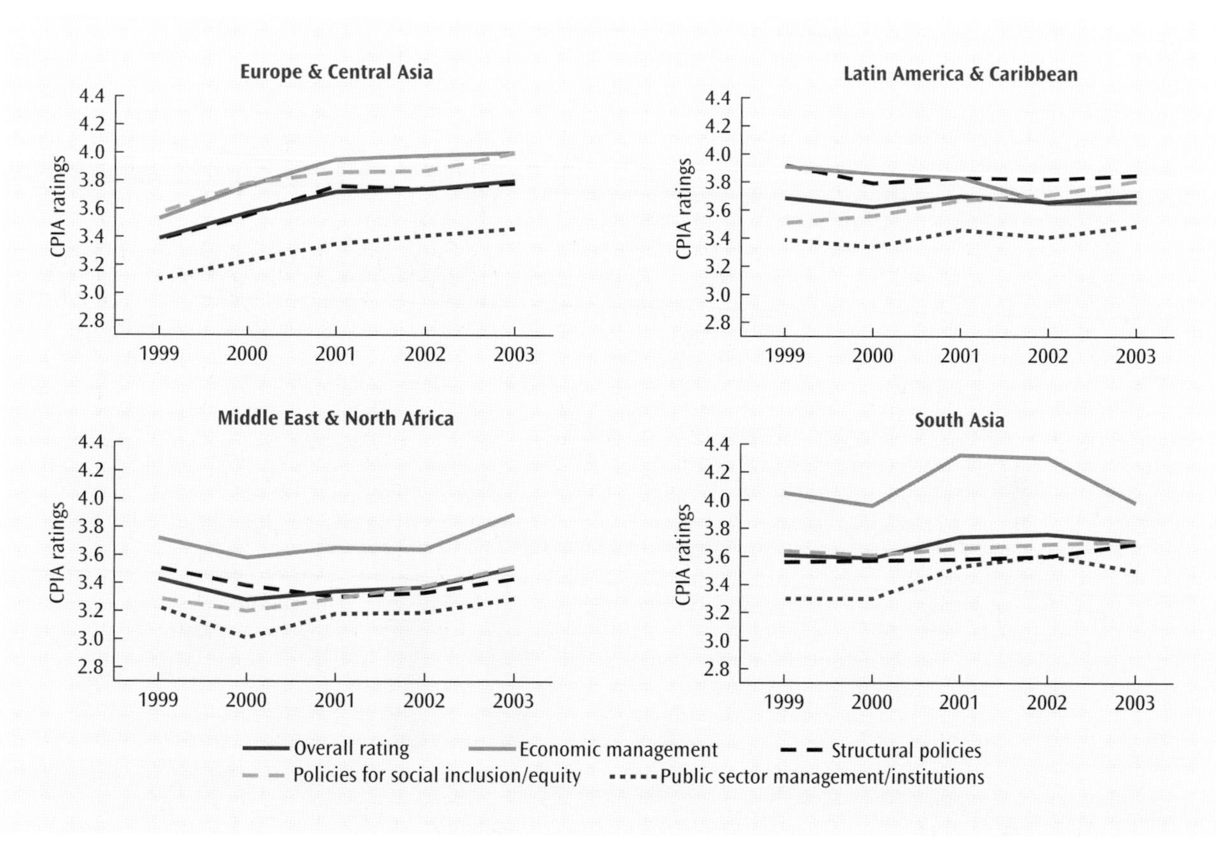

Note: World Bank CPIA ratings range from a low of 1 to a high of 6, with an increase denoting improvement.
Source: World Bank CPIA database.

weakest link in most cases is the quality and capacity of the underlying institutional framework. These findings serve to focus attention on governance and institution-building reforms as an area for particular attention, as poor governance and weak institutions can seriously undermine the effectiveness of policy initiatives throughout an economy. Fortunately, developing-country governments recognize this, and more and more of them have launched governance and institutional reforms. This is reflected in the improving ratings for governance, but the pace of reform needs to be accelerated.

These trends and findings are corroborated by similar country policy assessments conducted by other multilateral development banks for their respective regions. The assessments conducted by the African Development Bank (AfDB), also called Country Policy and Institutional Assessment, and the Asian Development Bank (AsDB), called the Country Performance Assessment (CPA), are quite similar to the World Bank's CPIA in terms of the policy criteria and clusters. Their country policy ratings for recent years show broadly the same trend and pattern. There is a gradual improving trend in policies across policy areas. In terms of policy relativities, governance and institutions are the weakest area (figure 3.2).

In the context of its concessional resource allocation system, the Inter-American Development Bank (IDB) also initiated in 2002 a

FIGURE 3.2 Other ratings corroborate that developing-country policies have improved but that governance and institutions lag

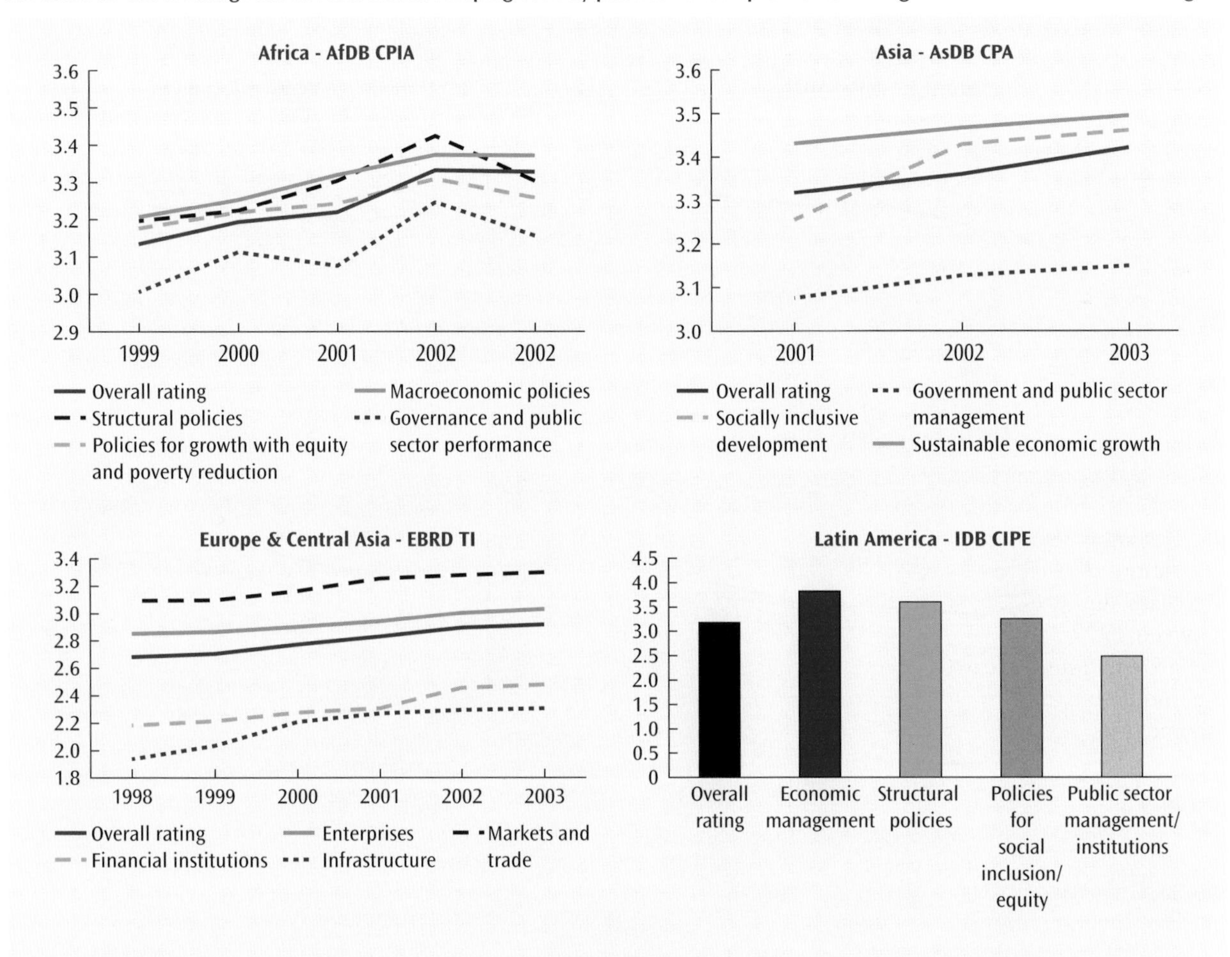

Note: AsDB and IDB ratings cover member countries eligible for concessional borrowing. AfDB and EBRD ratings cover all of their developing-country members. IDB ratings shown relate to 2002. AfDB, AsDB, and IDB ratings range from 1 to 6 and EBRD ratings from 1 to 4+. An increase denotes improvement in all cases.
Source: For Africa, African Development Bank; for Asia, Asian Development Bank; for Europe and Central Asia, European Bank for Reconstruction and Development; for Latin America, Inter-American Development Bank.

Country Institutional and Policy Evaluation (CIPE) exercise for the 12 eligible countries. The CIPE does not as yet provide a time series on the ratings, but the pattern indicated by the 2002 CIPE is consistent with that of the other MDB ratings. The strongest policy area is macroeconomic management and the weakest is public sector management and institutions.

The European Bank for Reconstruction and Development (EBRD) uses Transition Indicators (TI), which focus on policies related to transition to a market-based economy. These indicators show sustained progress in the transition process in Europe and Central Asia, with the ratings on average higher for market liberalization measures than for institutions underpinning markets: financial institutions; and the regulatory and institutional framework for the provision of infrastructure.[2]

Progress on transition is also indicated by the results of surveys of regional enterprises in Europe and Central Asia jointly conducted by the EBRD and the World Bank in 1999 and 2002 (Business Environment and Enterprise Performance Surveys, or BEEPS). These surveys aim to provide more in-depth assessment of key elements of the business environment and governance. Comparison between the 1999 and 2002 surveys shows broad progress. Areas where obstacles to business are perceived to be greater are those involving firm-state interactions and the judicial system (figure 3.3).

Figure 3.4 maps the World Bank's CPIA ratings into the four policy clusters identified for assessing progress on developing-country policies as part of the global monitoring framework set out in chapter 1: economic and financial polices; public sector governance; human development; and policies and institutions for environmental sustainability. As the policies improve and the ratings rise, the "policy diamond" defined by these four clusters increases in size. In the five-year period between 1999 and 2003, the policy diamond has grown. The increase has been greater in the middle-income countries than in the low-income ones. It is also clear that the diamond,

FIGURE 3.3 The transition countries are making broad progress in removing obstacles to business
Index of progress for 26 transition countries in Europe and Central Asia

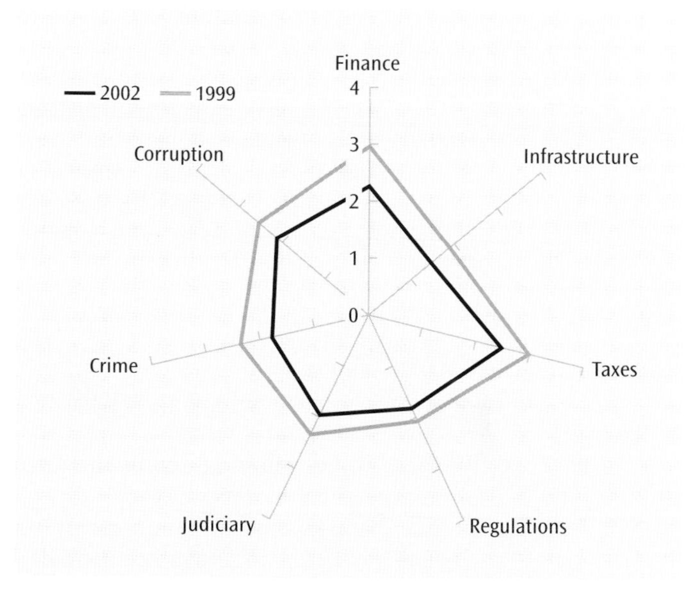

Note: Numerals refer to scores on the BEEPS survey, where 1 indicates low obstacles to business and 4 indicates high obstacles, so a decrease denotes improvement.
Source: EBRD and World Bank Business Environment and Enterprise Performance Surveys.

FIGURE 3.4 The developing-country policy diamond shows progress, but much more is needed
Progress in developing countries, 1999–2003

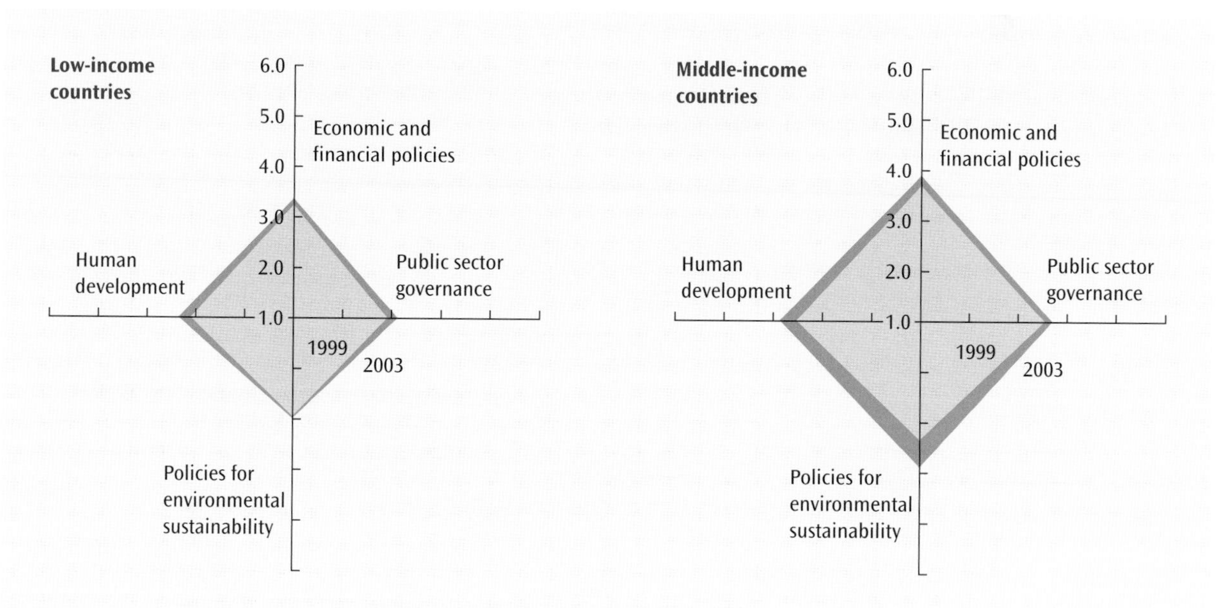

Note: The diamond corresponds to the global monitoring policy diamond for developing countries (see figure 1.2). The scale is based on World Bank CPIA ratings, ranging from a low of 1 to a high of 6, with an increase denoting improvement.
Source: World Bank CPIA database.

especially in low-income countries, is still small relative to the boundary defined by best practice (a rating of 6). The shape of the diamond, as outlined by the four facets, shows the policy relativities. These reflect the picture discussed earlier, with performance stronger in economic and financial policies and weaker in public sector governance. Policies and institutions for environmental sustainability also are a relatively weak area.[3] These have shown some improvement, however, especially in middle-income countries.

In summary, a review of assessments of developing-country policies conducted by the World Bank and other development agencies leads to the following main conclusions:

- Policies in developing countries are improving and creating a more conducive environment for development, including more effective use of assistance provided by partners.
- While this is encouraging, the pace of reform will have to be accelerated if the development goals are to be achieved, especially in the low-income countries and in Sub-Saharan Africa.
- The core of the reform agenda is institutional—reform of public sector governance and the building of institutions underpinning private sector activity.

Notes

1. There are 20 policy and institutional criteria in all, divided into these four clusters, that capture the different dimensions of an effective growth and poverty reduction strategy and that are rated annually on the basis of staff assessments. The individual criteria are assigned equal weights in averaging them. The CPIA methodology is periodically reviewed as part of a continuing effort to increase its robustness, for example, through improving the documentation of the evidence and indicators on which the assessments are based. Increased disclosure of the CPIA ratings for IDA-eligible countries is currently under consideration. For a more detailed description of the CPIA, see http://siteresources.worldbank.org/IDA/Resources/FinaltextIDA13Report.pdf.

2. Comparison between the ratings of other MDBs and World Bank CPIA ratings for the respective regions shows broad consistency. While there inevitably are some differences at the level of detailed ratings for individual policy criteria or countries, the overall correlation is high. For example, the estimated correlation coefficients between the AfDB and the World Bank CPIA ratings for 2003 and between the EBRD TI and the World Bank CPIA for the same year exceed 0.9. The high correlation serves to enhance confidence in the robustness of these ratings.

3. These are included among structural policies in the CPIA but shown separately in the global monitoring policy clusters.

4

Improving Enabling Climate for Growth

Economic and Financial Policies

The preceding chapter makes clear that economic growth in developing countries needs to accelerate if the Millennium Development Goals are to be achieved. Strong growth requires an economic climate that is conducive to investment, job creation, and higher productivity. Key elements of such an enabling economic climate are macroeconomic policies that help maintain economic and financial stability; openness to trade that promotes access to world markets for goods, services, and knowledge; a regulatory and institutional environment for private sector activity that facilitates rather than impedes entrepreneurship and competition; and a financial sector that efficiently and sustainably mobilizes resources and channels them to their most productive uses. How are the developing countries doing with respect to these determinants of growth?

In general, there has been a notable improvement in macroeconomic and trade policies, which needs to be consolidated and deepened. There is also an improving trend in removing regulatory impediments to private activity and strengthening supporting legal frameworks, and in placing financial systems on a more solid footing and building their capacity to play their role in contributing to development. Progress on these more structural and institutional dimensions of reform, however, has been less in many countries. This has acted to limit economies' supply response to the improvement in the macroeconomic and trade policy environment. Going forward, stronger growth will depend crucially on more vigorous and consistent efforts to ease the burden of regulation of private enterprise and build supportive institutions.

Macroeconomic Policies

Sound macroeconomic policies are an essential foundation for sustained growth. The impact of macroeconomic policies on poverty reduction works largely through growth: policies that contribute to macroeconomic stability help sustain growth, and growth is typically associated with lower poverty. Policies that impede the attainment of macroeconomic stability, such as expansionary monetary policies that encourage high inflation and lax fiscal policies that produce large budget deficits, can hurt growth by reducing investment and the rate of increase in productivity.

Low-Income Countries

Macroeconomic policies in low-income countries have improved over the past decade. Better macroeconomic management in turn has contributed to the recent improvement in these countries' growth performance and outlook, as reviewed in chapter 3. Inflation has

TABLE 4.1 Macroeconomic indicators for low-income countries, by region, 1983–2008 (annual averages)

Region	1983–87	1988–92	1993–97	1998–2002	2003 (estimated)	2004–08 (projected)
Inflation (median annual %)						
East Asia and Pacific	6.9	9.7	8.0	7.1	6.6	3.4
Europe and Central Asia	1.3	196.2	453.5	11.1	4.8	4.0
Latin America and Caribbean	5.2	11.7	7.4	3.7	3.3	3.2
Middle East and North Africa	13.7	17.8	26.3	6.4	6.4	4.6
South Asia	7.7	10.5	8.8	4.7	4.7	4.3
Sub-Saharan Africa	10.8	10.3	13.5	4.7	6.6	3.8
All low-income	7.1	10.0	12.4	5.1	5.0	3.8
Current account balance (% of GDP)						
East Asia and Pacific	–1.3	–6.3	–2.2	–1.0	–3.1	–3.7
Europe and Central Asia	–0.7	–5.6	–13.2	–8.4	–8.3	–5.2
Latin America and Caribbean	–10.6	–14.2	–14.0	–13.0	–13.1	–11.1
Middle East and North Africa	–7.4	–5.3	–2.2	0.3	–2.8	–9.8
South Asia	–8.8	–5.4	–6.9	–2.0	–2.0	–1.9
Sub-Saharan Africa	–7.0	–8.8	–9.3	–9.5	–9.1	–8.5
All low-income	–6.0	–8.3	–8.7	–7.4	–7.6	–7.0
Debt service (% exports of goods/services)						
East Asia and Pacific	22.2	14.2	12.9	13.4	10.9	9.4
Europe and Central Asia	0.0	2.0	8.5	14.3	14.5	11.7
Latin America and Caribbean	18.5	39.4	37.6	12.3	11.5	9.2
Middle East and North Africa	6.7	18.8	25.3	7.2	3.8	4.3
South Asia	20.4	19.5	20.8	15.9	13.2	11.2
Sub-Saharan Africa	17.5	21.4	21.2	24.5	17.7	16.6
All low-income	16.5	20.1	20.5	18.8	14.7	13.2
Fiscal balance (% of GDP)						
East Asia and Pacific	–8.7	–6.7	–4.4	–4.3	–4.5	–3.5
Europe and Central Asia	–1.3	–6.8	–11.1	–4.4	–1.8	–1.2
Latin America and Caribbean	–8.5	–6.0	–2.4	–4.5	–5.7	–3.7
Middle East and North Africa	–17.6	–11.8	–8.1	–0.5	–1.8	–1.9
South Asia	–6.1	–5.1	–4.8	–5.9	–5.5	–4.5
Sub-Saharan Africa	–6.2	–6.9	–5.8	–5.7	–4.8	–2.6
All low-income	–6.6	–6.7	–5.7	–5.0	–4.4	–2.9
Memo Item: Real GDP per capita growth (%)						
All low-income	0.7	–0.8	0.7	1.2	1.7	3.1

Note: Averages are calculated as unweighted means of country values. Median inflation is calculated from the annual medians and then averaged over five-year periods.
Source: IMF *World Economic Outlook* database, staff calculations.

slowed on average to half the rate of a decade ago. Other indicators also show improvements, though less spectacular. Fiscal and external current account deficits have narrowed, and external debt service ratios typically have improved. Looking ahead, this trend is expected broadly to continue (table 4.1).

While all regions show some improvement in the macroeconomic policy indicators, progress has been uneven and remains fragile in many countries, especially in Sub-Saharan Africa. In these countries, therefore, the need remains for a broad strengthening of macroeconomic policies. Even in countries with better performance, maintaining and building on progress on macroeconomic stability, especially in the face of possible shocks, will be a continuing challenge.

To get a better perspective on the quality of macroeconomic policies in low-income countries, IMF staff have assessed recent country experience with a view to evaluating and categorizing them on several key policy dimensions.[1] The results show that there are substantial differences in the quality of policies across the different policy areas (figure 4.1). Broadly, fiscal areas seem to be of the most concern. Overall fiscal management, in relation to the goals of public debt sustainability and containment of fiscally derived inflationary pressures, remains unsatisfactory in about one-third of low-income countries. The deficiencies are more serious with respect to structural aspects of fiscal policy: almost half of low-income countries are assessed to have unsatisfactory composition of public expenditures. In contrast, there are serious concerns in only a relatively small proportion of countries in monetary areas—monetary policy, foreign exchange regime. Looking at the consistency of macroeconomic policy as a whole, the picture is unsatisfactory in about one-fifth of the countries.

Staff assessments suggest that faster-growing low-income countries typically have better macroeconomic policies (see figure 4.1). While this result does not reveal the direction of causality, it is consistent with studies that suggest that better policies are good for growth.[2] Faster-growing countries

FIGURE 4.1 **Faster growing countries typically have better macroeconomic policies**
Growth performance and quality of macroeconomic policies, low-income countries

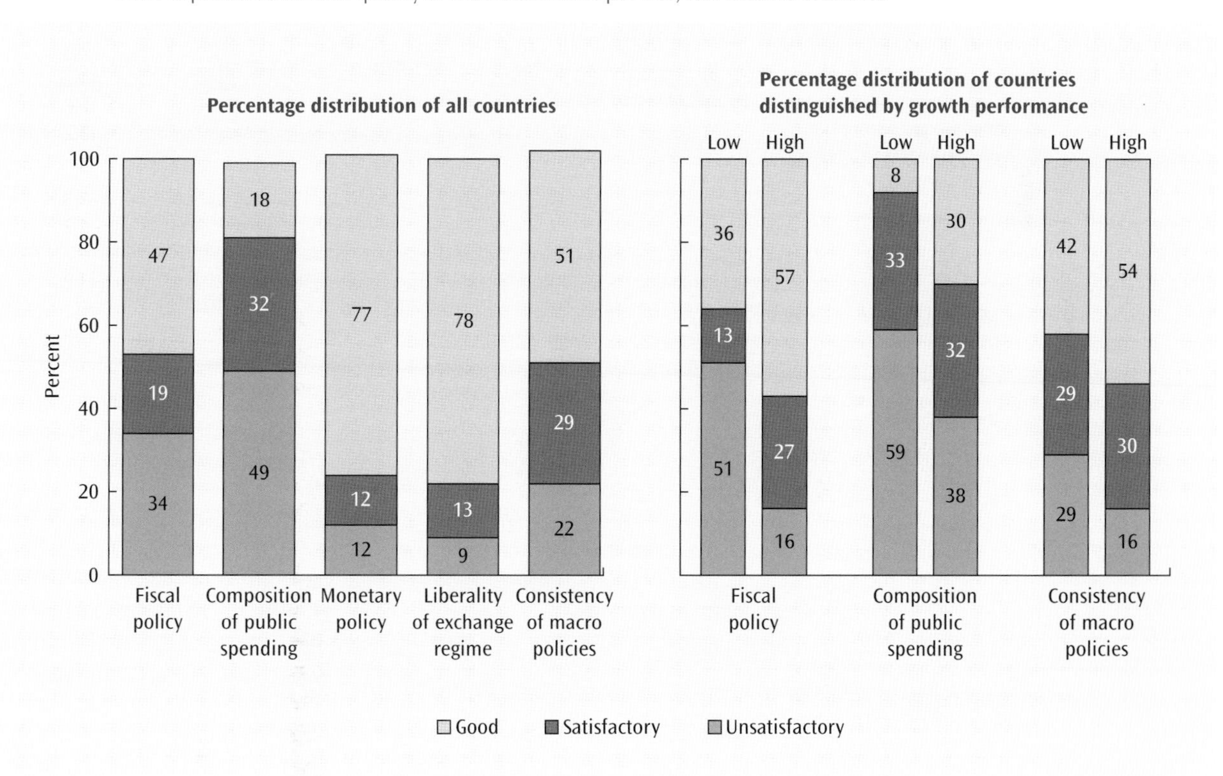

Note: Low and high refer to countries with GDP growth below or above the median rate for the whole group. Some numbers do not add up to 100 because of rounding.
Source: IMF staff assessments.

appear to have markedly better fiscal policies, as well as public sector spending compositions that are more consistent with growth and poverty reduction. They also have superior consistency in their overall macroeconomic frameworks. Differences in monetary policy areas are less pronounced.

Analysis of the factors in terms of different country characteristics that underlie the variation in the quality of macroeconomic policies shows some interesting patterns (table 4.2). The quality of fiscal policy is typically higher in countries with a higher general level of economic development (proxied by per capita income). The association is much stronger with respect to government effectiveness (quality of institutions for policy implementation), as suggested by World Bank governance indicators. The quality of the composition of public expenditures and the overall consistency of macroeconomic policies are particularly strongly correlated with government effectiveness (for example, over two-thirds of countries with low government effectiveness have unsatisfactory public expenditure compositions compared with half of all low-income countries).

Countries with undiversified commodity exports generally have significantly weaker policy performance.[3] Differences in policy performance associated with the degree of export diversification are broadly similar to those linked to government effectiveness. This finding is consistent with the view that reliance on just a few exports tends to be associated with weak governance, resulting from

TABLE 4.2 Quality of macroeconomic policies for low-income countries, by country characteristics (percent of countries)

Country characteristic	Fiscal policy	Composition of public spending	Monetary policy	Liberality of exchange regime	Consistency of macro policies
Income per capita					
Below median					
Unsatisfactory	41	51	16	16	24
Good	43	22	68	73	43
Above median					
Unsatisfactory	28	48	8	3	21
Good	49	38	85	82	54
Exports					
Undiversified					
Unsatisfactory	45	66	17	17	24
Good	31	21	69	66	31
Diversified					
Unsatisfactory	27	40	10	4	21
Good	56	17	81	85	60
Government effectiveness					
Below median					
Unsatisfactory	48	69	18	13	34
Good	34	8	68	68	32
Above median					
Unsatisfactory	23	31	5	5	11
Good	59	28	85	87	66
All low-income countries					
Unsatisfactory	34	49	12	9	22
Good	47	18	77	78	51

Note: Policies are assessed good, satisfactory, or unsatisfactory. Percentages in the table do not add up as the intermediate category—satisfactory—is not shown.
Source: IMF staff assessments.

nontransparency of payment of revenues. Lack of export diversification also renders countries more prone to shocks that can adversely affect fiscal revenues and macroeconomic performance. Small economies and low-income countries are particularly vulnerable to natural disasters and terms-of-trade shocks. IMF staff calculations show that losses per large natural disaster averaged more than 6 percent of the GDP of the affected low-income countries from 1997 to 2000. Losses from terms-of-trade shocks averaged more than 4 percent of the GDP of the affected low-income countries during the same period.

Broadly, governance factors seem to be important in determining the quality of fiscal policy and public expenditure management and the consistency of policies. The quality of monetary policy and the liberality of the exchange regime also vary with these country characteristics, but proportionally less. Variations in these policy areas can be as readily explained by the general level of economic development.

Middle-Income Countries

Middle-income countries have enjoyed consistently higher average growth than low-income countries since the late 1970s; the indicators suggest that such growth has been supported by better macroeconomic policies (table 4.3). This advantage, however, has been blunted by the risk of financial crisis. These countries are typically more integrated with international capital markets, and financial globalization has increased the vulnerability to fluctuations in these markets.[4] The consequent risk of economic volatility has also made sustained reductions in poverty more difficult. The 1990s have witnessed several financial crises, of which the East Asian crisis is perhaps the best known. In East Asia, poverty increased markedly (table 4.4) as real wages fell and unemployment rose.

A number of measures are needed to make the economies of middle-income countries, and particularly those of emerging market countries, more resilient to economic shocks. First, reducing public debt, and particularly external debt, relative to GDP is a central item on the agenda as high debt levels increase the likelihood of debt crises. Increased flexibility in exchange rates can also help, both by dampening destabilizing capital flows and by facilitating adjustments between tradable and nontradable sectors. Other structural reforms are also important, particularly in the financial and corporate sectors, to prevent the build-up of balance-sheet vulnerabilities. Several of these countries also need to improve their social protection systems to cushion the impact of shocks and economic adjustments on the poor and vulnerable.

TABLE 4.3 Macroeconomic indicators for middle-income countries, 1983–2008 (annual averages)

Indicator	1983–87	1988-92	1993-97	1998-2002	2003 (estimated)	2004–08 (projected)
Inflation (median annual %)	7.9	14.4	11.5	5.0	4.5	3.6
Fiscal balance (% of GDP)	–4.4	–2.7	–2.7	–3.6	–3.0	–1.4
Current account balance (% of GDP)	–2.6	–1.2	–4.1	–3.4	–1.5	–1.3
Debt service (% exports of goods/services)	25.4	22.5	19.0	21.7	20.1	18.0
External debt (% of GDP)	44.0	43.5	42.1	44.8	44.4	38.1
Broad money (% of GDP)	52.8	54.2	46.3	51.9	55.9	57.0
Real GDP per capita growth (%)	1.4	0.0	1.7	2.1	2.8	3.3

Note: Averages are calculated as unweighted means of country values. Mean inflation is calculated from the annual medians and then averaged over five-year periods.
Source: IMF *World Economic Outlook* database and staff calculations.

TABLE 4.4 Impact of financial crises on poverty, East Asia, 1997–98

		Poverty headcount index (percent)		
Country	Crisis year	Overall	Urban	Rural
Indonesia	1997	11.0	9.2	12.4
	1998	19.9	15.8	23.0
Korea	1997	2.6	7.5	—
	1998	7.3	10.0	—
Malaysia	1997	8.2	—	—
	1998	10.4	—	—
Thailand	1997	9.8	1.2	11.8
	1998	12.9	1.5	17.2

— Not available.
Source: Fallon and Lucas 2002.

Some progress has been made in all of these areas. On average for middle-income countries, fiscal deficits and debt and debt service ratios have fallen since the late 1990s. There has also been a clear shift among emerging market economies toward more flexible exchange rate regimes. For example, in 2001, half of these economies had floating regimes, compared with only 17 percent in 1990. Even within emerging market economies that maintain exchange rate regimes that are intermediate between hard pegs and floating regimes, there has been a shift toward greater flexibility. As a cushion against volatility, foreign reserve positions have in general been appreciably strengthened. As discussed later in this chapter, the financial soundness of banks in developing countries has also improved, and reforms have been initiated to improve corporate governance. And some countries have taken steps to strengthen their social protection systems, while taking care to ensure their sustainability.

Trade Policy

Complementing sound macroeconomic policies, openness to international trade contributes to an environment fostering growth, by giving firms and households access to world markets for goods, services, and knowledge and encouraging investments in areas where countries have a comparative advantage. The primary determinant of the benefits from trade is a country's own policies, though, as discussed in chapter 10, restrictions imposed by trading partners can significantly limit the possibilities for trade. Progress in trade reform by developing countries in the past several years has been encouraging. However, while many developing countries have done well in using trade as part of a growth strategy, several others have not. Thus, the benefits of trade are distributed asymmetrically across (and within) countries.

Merchandise Trade Liberalization

The average nominal tariff in developing countries was cut by half during the past decade, dropping to 13.5 percent (table 4.5). Particularly notable progress has been made in reducing nontariff barriers (NTBs). The prevalence of core NTBs (quotas on trade, nonautomatic licensing, minimum prices, and similar policies), as measured by the number of tariff lines covered, has fallen dramatically in almost all regions during the past decade, dropping from over 50 percent in some regions (South Asia) to the 2 to 15 percent range (table 4.6). Currently, core NTBs cover some 11 percent of imports in developing countries. Despite this significant liberalization, trade policies continue to generate significant anti-export bias in some regions; for example, even after the significant decline, the average tariff in South Asia remains around 20 percent.

The above picture is confirmed by the IMF's trade restrictiveness index. The average rating for low-income countries was 3.8 (relatively open) in 2003, down from 5.4 (moderately restrictive) in 1997. Trade liberalization has contributed to a rise in developing countries' share of world trade, which rose from 17 percent in 1995 to 22 percent in 2002. The share of low-income countries also rose, though in absolute terms it remains small, at around 3 percent.

While traditional trade policy barriers have been lowered, there has been a tendency for technical product regulations (mandatory health and safety standards) to rise. Although not generally protectionist in intent, they are increasingly becoming a factor in international trade and have been argued to be an impediment for low-income countries to penetrate export markets.[5] The incidence of such standards is four times higher in middle-income countries than in low-income countries. Countries in Latin America and in the Middle East and North Africa subject around 20 percent of all imports to product standards, compared with less than 5 percent in the least developed countries.

In a number of (mostly) middle-income countries, there has also been an increase in the use of contingent protection—antidumping and safeguard actions. Measured on a "per dollar of imports affected" basis, many of the largest developing countries are now more intensive users of antidumping than the advanced countries (table 4.7). Although it is often argued that such "safeguard" instruments are needed to allow countries to pursue trade liberalization, the country incidence of these actions is biased against other developing countries; it also imposes substantial costs on the economies invoking such protection.

The spread of bilateral and regional trade agreements (RTAs), of both South-South and North-South types, has continued. Many countries are involved in both bilateral and regional trade negotiations with different partners at the same time. As of March 2003, only four WTO members—Macao SAR; Mongolia; Taiwan, China; and Hong Kong, China—were not members of any RTA. The question has often been posed whether regionalism is a building block toward multilateral liberalization or whether it is more likely to be a stumbling block. There is no clear consensus on this issue. Much depends on the specifics of the agreements. Overall, however, discrimination can be costly; it not

TABLE 4.5 Decline in tariffs in developing countries, late 1980s to 2003 (simple averages of MFN tariffs, percent)

Region	Late 1980s	2003
East Asia and Pacific	18.8	10.4
Europe and Central Asia	10.2	8.9
Latin America and Caribbean	22.4	12.0
Middle East and North Africa	17.3	14.8
South Asia	68.9	19.8
Sub-Saharan Africa	25.1	17.6
All developing countries	25.4	13.5
Least developed	28.4	16.4
Low income	31.7	15.8
Middle income	21.8	12.7

Source: World Bank, *World Development Indicators*, various years; IMF tariff data.

TABLE 4.6 Decline in core nontariff barriers in developing countries, 1989–94 to 2000 (percent of tariff lines affected)

Region	1989–94	2000
Latin America and Caribbean (13, 17)	18.3	15.3
Europe and Central Asia (11)	N.A.	3.4
East Asia and Pacific (7, 9)	30.1	5.5
Sub-Saharan Africa (12, 17)	26.0	2.3
Middle East and North Africa (4, 8)	43.8	8.5
South Asia (4, 3)	57.0	13.3

Note: Numbers in parentheses indicate the number of countries for which data are available for 1989–94 and 2000, respectively. Due to differences in country coverage, data are not strictly comparable across years by region.
Source: World Bank.

TABLE 4.7 Major users of antidumping, developing countries, 1995–2002

	Against all economies	
Country initiating	Number of antidumping initiations	Initiations per US dollar of imports Index (USA=100)
Argentina	176	2,549
Brazil	98	580
India	273	2,197
Indonesia	39	90
Korea	48	126
Malaysia	22	106
Mexico	56	144
South Africa	157	2,006

Source: World Bank staff based on notifications to the WTO.

TABLE 4.8 Overall trade restrictiveness of developing-country groups, 2001 (in percent)

Region	Overall OTRI	OTRI toward low-income countries	OTRI toward LDCs
East Asia and Pacific	12.1	12.6	11.4
Europe and Central Asia	11.6	12.0	12.1
Latin America and Caribbean	16.8	16.5	18.3
Middle East and North Africa	17.7	14.0	12.4
South Asia	32.2	26.4	29.9
Sub-Saharan Africa	10.7	13.1	11.8
All developing countries	15.1	14.8	16.6
Least developed	18.2	14.4	11.6
Low income	23.3	20.0	24.2
Middle income	14.2	13.5	12.7

Source: World Bank staff estimates.

only hurts those excluded but also imposes costs on those included. By reducing trade barriers on a subset of partners, countries generally increase the real cost of their imports, reduce the flow of technology from nonmember countries, and increase dependence on particular export markets. If liberalization proceeds on a discriminatory basis, there is a danger of stronger pressure against further opening up of the regional market through the WTO. Finally, given the limited administrative resources of poor countries, diverting these away from multilateral negotiations can entail a substantial opportunity cost.

The policy indicators reviewed above—tariffs, core NTBs, technical standards, and preferential arrangements—cannot be readily compared across countries. To enable a comparison that encompasses tariffs and different types of NTBs, an index has recently been developed at the World Bank that measures the overall policy restrictiveness implied by these barriers. It measures the uniform tariff equivalent of the actual structure of tariffs and NTBs that would generate imports at the observed levels in a given year.[6] The index, called the Overall Trade Restrictiveness Index (OTRI), has been estimated for some 100 developing and developed countries for which underlying data are currently available.

The average OTRI across all developing countries in the sample was 15.1 percent in 2001 (table 4.8). The most restrictive region is South Asia. On average, trade barriers against low-income countries imposed by middle-income countries are somewhat lower than the average restriction on overall trade, and barriers against the least developed countries (LDCs) are somewhat lower still (12.7 percent). However, low-income countries as a group impose higher barriers against LDCs than against low-income countries. LDCs impose, on average, lower barriers against trade with other LDCs than on trade with the rest of the world. As is often the case, the regional and income-based aggregations hide considerable variance across countries.

OTRIs are negatively correlated with per capita income, indicating that richer countries tend on average to have less restrictive trade regimes (figure 4.2).[7] Developing countries with the highest OTRIs include India, Tunisia, Jordan, Morocco, Bangladesh, Algeria, and Lebanon (OTRIs above 20 percent). India is the most restrictive country in the sample, with an OTRI of 36 percent. Countries in the Middle East and North Africa tend to have more restrictive trade regimes: of the 10 most restrictive countries in the sample, 5 are in that region—Tunisia, Jordan, Morocco, Algeria, and Lebanon. In Latin America, Mexico and Argentina have the most restrictive trade regimes. Among Sub-

Saharan African countries, Nigeria and Mauritius have the highest OTRIs. China and Thailand are the most protective countries in East Asia, and Romania and Poland in Europe and Central Asia. Developing or transition economies with the lowest OTRIs include the Baltic states, Costa Rica, Guatemala, Indonesia, Philippines, South Africa, Trinidad and Tobago, Ukraine, and the low-income countries of Sudan, Madagascar, and Uganda (with OTRIs below 7.5 percent).

Services Liberalization and "Behind-the-Border" Agenda

Developing countries' services trade has been rising more rapidly than merchandise trade, fueled by falling communications and transport costs and the associated rise in global outsourcing. The share of services in total developing-country exports rose from 20 percent in 1990 to 26 percent in 2000. India is a well-known example of a country that has greatly expanded distance business services exports, but several other countries also have increased such exports. Business service exports from Brazil, Dominica, India, and Mauritius grew at rates around or above 20 percent per year from 1995 to 2000. The potential for further growth of services exports from developing countries is substantial.

The benefits of services trade extend beyond services exports and can generate substantial gains on the import side as well. Services, such as customs clearance, logistics relating to product labeling and standards, transport and telecommunications, and financial services, are an important input into the production process and affect the competitiveness of an economy more broadly. Progress on this "behind-the-border" agenda is crucial for countries to take full advantage of the increased market access resulting from reduction in border barriers (tariffs, NTBs). The availability of these services at low cost is becoming increasingly important as international competition becomes sharper and efficient and just-in-time supply chain management more crucial. A more open services trade regime can contribute to the lowering of such key behind-the-border costs. It can also generate broader spillover benefits arising from increased competition and new technology and know-how brought by foreign service providers.

FIGURE 4.2 Better-off countries tend to restrict trade less
Overall Trade Restrictiveness Index and GDP per capita, 2001

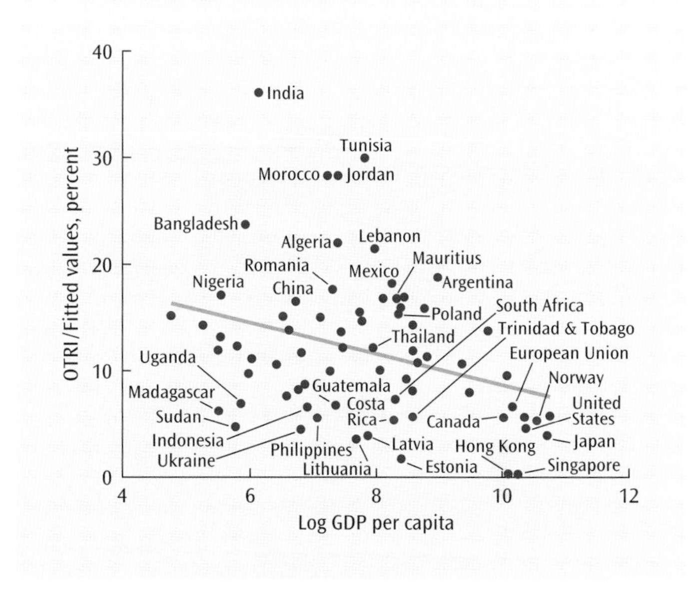

Source: World Bank staff.

Research provides supporting evidence that openness to services trade contributes to better longer-term growth performance. A study finds that, controlling for other determinants of growth, countries that fully reformed the financial services sector grew, on average, about 1 percentage point faster than other countries. An even greater impetus to growth was found to come from fully reforming both the telecommunications and the financial services sectors, with countries that fully liberalized both sectors achieving average growth of about 1.5 percentage or higher than others.[8] While these estimates are only suggestive, they do indicate the scope for substantial gains from liberalizing key service sectors.

Developing countries have made progress on liberalization, but policy remains relatively restrictive in many of them. Services tend to be less tradable across borders than goods, implying the need to open up to foreign direct

FIGURE 4.3 Overall policy on trade in services remains more restrictive in developing countries
Liberalization indices for financial services and telecommunications, most recent years

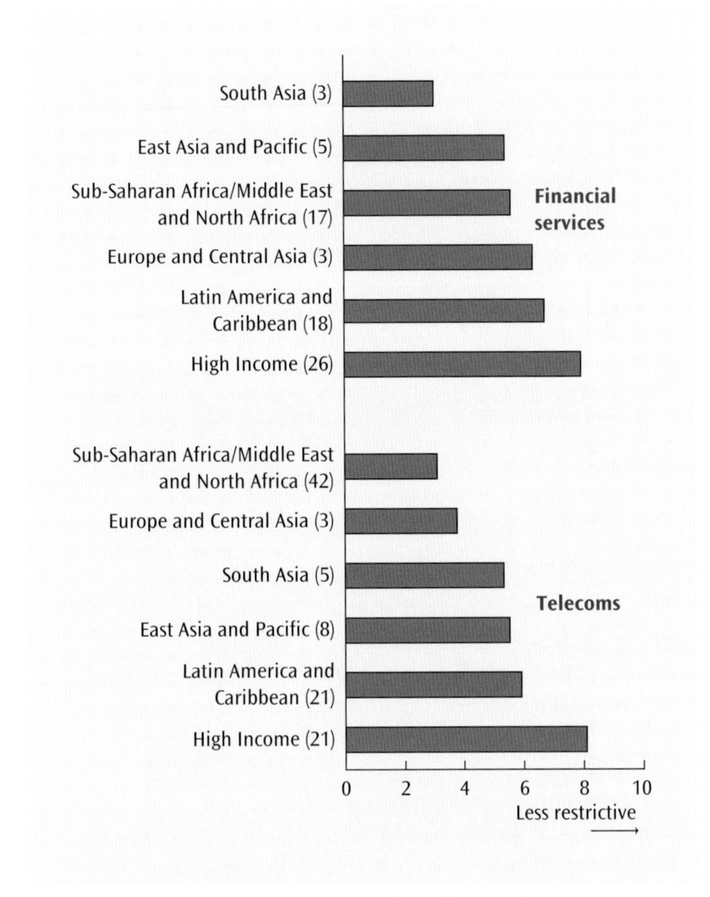

Note: Numbers in parentheses show the number of countries covered.
Source: Mattoo, Rathindran, and Subramaniam (2001).

investment. Many countries restrict trade in services through barriers to labor movement or to entry of foreign-owned firms. With respect to financial services and telecommunications, for example, the picture varies substantially across regions. While some regions have made appreciable progress, overall policy remains significantly more restrictive than in developed countries (figure 4.3).

Successful reform of trade policy in services requires more than lowering entry barriers. They need to be underpinned by complementary changes in domestic regulation. Badly designed reform can seriously undercut the benefits of liberalization. For example, if liberalization of financial services is not supported by strengthening of the regulatory and institutional framework for prudential regulation and supervision, the soundness of the financial system could be placed at risk. If privatization of state-owned service monopolies is conducted without attention to creating conditions for competition and appropriate regulatory oversight, the result may largely be transfers of monopoly rents to private owners—perhaps foreign ones. Also, if policies to ensure broad access are not put in place, liberalization may not improve access to essential services for smaller businesses and the poor. Getting the elements and sequencing right, therefore, is important to the realization of benefits.

Private Sector Regulatory and Institutional Environment

A vibrant private sector requires a favorable regulatory environment. But in many countries, especially low-income ones, businesses are hampered by bureaucratic regulations and weak protection of property rights. The result is slower development. The more time entrepreneurs spend dealing with red tape or defending property rights, the less time they spend building their business. A host of evidence shows that heavy regulation of business is associated with poor economic outcomes—less investment (both domestic and foreign), employment, and productivity (figure 4.4).[9] The ultimate effect is slower growth and more poverty.

As an example, compare China and South Asia. Recent studies show that a sizable part of the gap between their economic performance is the result of differences in investment climates.[10] Similarly, by improving infrastructure and regulatory conditions to the levels of Shanghai, studies show that firms in Dhaka could increase productivity by 43 percent; those in Calcutta, 78 percent; and those in Karachi, 81 percent. Even cities within China would experience dramatic gains by emulating Shanghai. For instance, if Chengdu could attain investment climate indicators identical to those of Shanghai, pro-

FIGURE 4.4 **Heavy regulation is associated with lower productivity**
Ease of starting a business and labor productivity

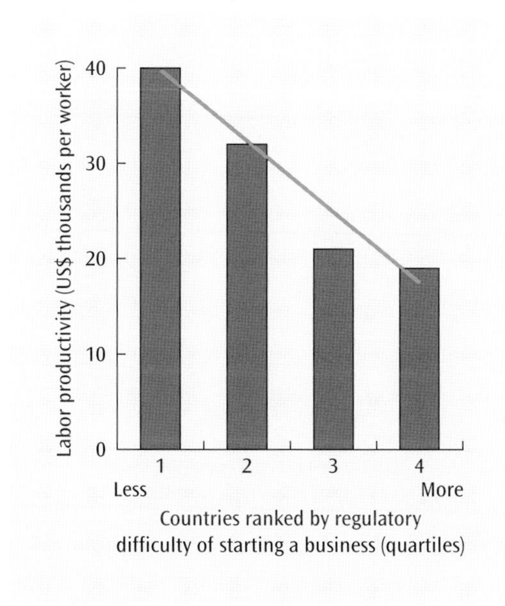

Source: World Bank Doing Business database 2003.

ductivity of its firms could be increased by about 30 percent, their investment rate from 14 percent to 19 percent, and their average sales growth by up to one-half.[11]

The cost of poor business regulation is not just economic. Heavy business regulations hurt the very people they are supposed to protect. Faced with burdensome rules and little benefit from registering officially, many entrepreneurs tend to operate in the informal sector (figure 4.5). There, there are no worker safety or product standards, there is no social security, access to credit and use of the courts is more difficult, and firms do not contribute to government and social services by paying taxes. This is the case for well over half of business activity in many developing countries. Another social cost is corruption, a regressive tax that hits poor people the hardest. Without checks and balances, complex rules breed discretion. Each encounter between a bureaucrat and an entrepreneur becomes an opportunity to extract a bribe. Not surprisingly then, more bureaucratic procedures are associated with higher levels of corruption (figure 4.5).

Burdensome regulation excludes vulnerable groups from the opportunity to participate in markets. The wealthy and connected can find ways around cumbersome rules. They may even be protected by them. But new entrants and the disadvantaged are shut out. For example, rigid employment regulation is associated with higher female and youth unemployment. There is no evidence that countries with stronger employment protection have more equal income distributions. If anything, the rigidity of employment laws may be associated with more inequality (figure 4.6). Relatedly, poor credit laws particularly hurt small firms' access to credit.[12]

Complex and rigid business regulation thus brings both poor economic and social outcomes. But this does not of course suggest that all regulation is harmful. All countries regulate business activity. The most successful ones do so in a simple and transparent manner. Rather than intervene heavily in business operations, successful governments channel their resources into regulations and institutions that protect property rights and ensure an even playing field for firms. Doing so encourages investment, facilitates trade beyond a narrow circle of established business networks, and enhances access to credit. As one example, protection of creditor rights and efficient enforcement of contracts through courts is associated with deeper credit markets (figure 4.7).

Current Picture and Agenda

The countries that most need a vibrant private sector—low-income countries—are the very ones that place the most obstacles in front of entrepreneurs. Indicators developed under the World Bank's Doing Business Project (DB) show that on average it takes 30 days and costs less than 10 percent of income per capita to start a business in high-income countries.[13] In low-income countries, it takes 74 days and costs twice income per capita—prohibitive for the ordinary person. Among low-income

FIGURE 4.5 Heavier regulation contributes to the informal economy and corruption

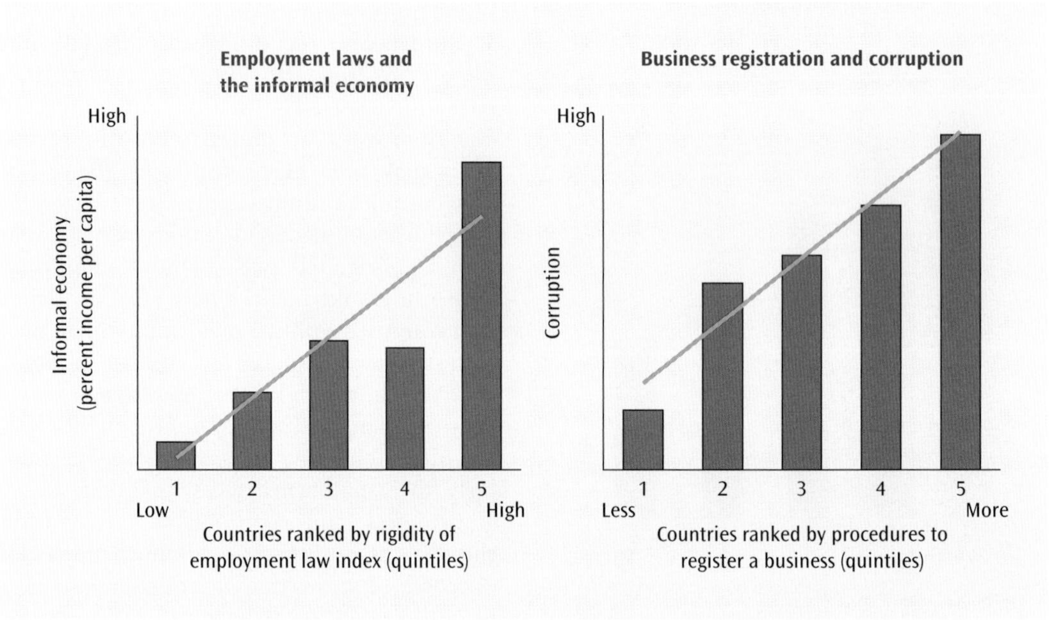

Employment laws and the informal economy

High

Informal economy (percent income per capita)

1 2 3 4 5

Low High

Countries ranked by rigidity of employment law index (quintiles)

Business registration and corruption

High

Corruption

1 2 3 4 5

Less More

Countries ranked by procedures to register a business (quintiles)

Source: World Bank *Doing Business* database 2003.

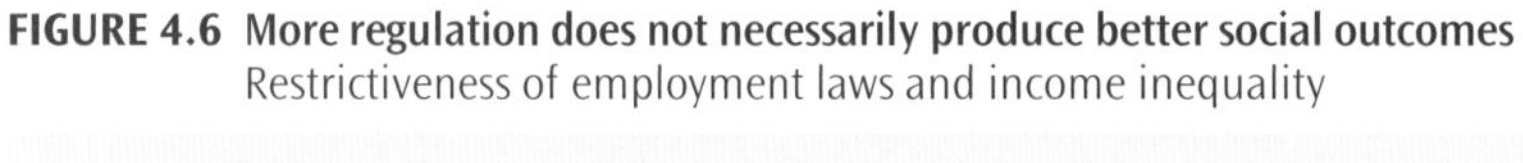

FIGURE 4.6 More regulation does not necessarily produce better social outcomes
Restrictiveness of employment laws and income inequality

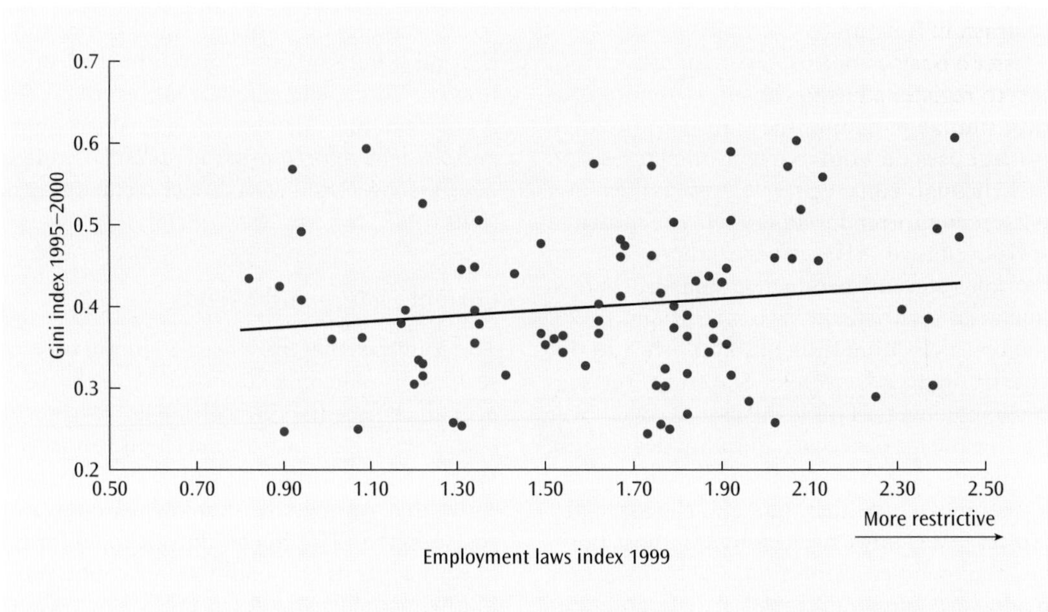

Source: World Bank staff estimates.

FIGURE 4.7 Protecting property rights is associated with more credit

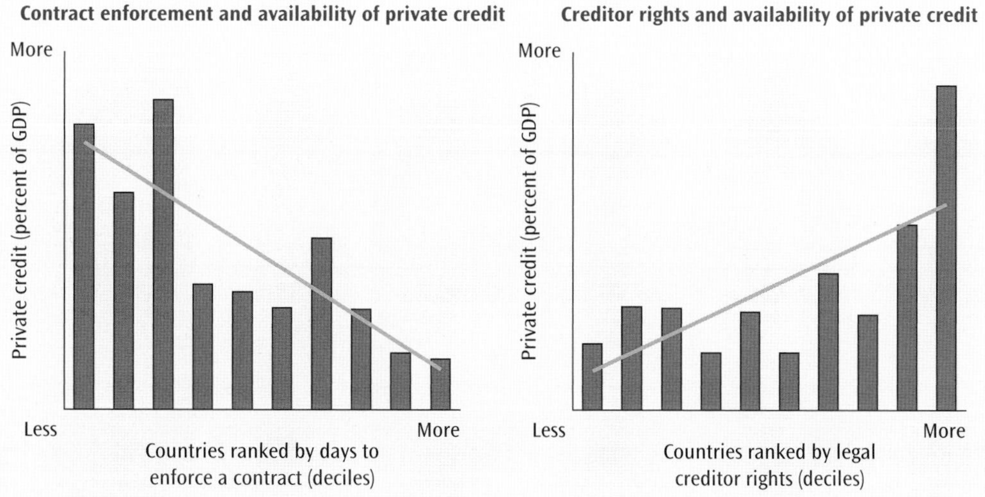

Source: World Bank *Doing Business* database 2003.

countries, the time varies from 22 days in Pakistan to 215 days in the Democratic Republic of Congo, and the cost ranges from 9 percent of income per capita in Armenia to as much as 10 times income per capita in Sierra Leone. By contrast, in Australia it takes only two days to register a business and in Denmark there is no cost to register a business.

A similar picture emerges when an entrepreneur uses the courts to resolve disputes, or goes through bankruptcy procedures. Delays are much shorter in high-income countries. For example, insolvency procedures on average take around four years in low-income countries, compared with two in high-income countries. It costs on average 8 percent of income per capita to enforce contracts through courts in the latter but 64 percent in the former. In Cambodia, Indonesia, Kyrgyz Republic, and Malawi, for example, fees could amount to more than twice income per capita. Faced with such high fees, most businesses avoid the courts and opt for informal means of enforcement, and limit trade to only a narrow circle of known partners.

Regulation typically is heavier and more complex in low-income countries than in high-income countries, contrary to what one would expect given the greater enforcement capacity and more developed regulatory regimes for protecting workers, consumers, and the environment in the latter (figure 4.8). Most strikingly, in low-income countries, it takes on average 30 procedures to enforce a contract through the court. By contrast, it takes only 18 procedures in the high-income countries. Similarly, an entrepreneur must undergo an average of 11 procedures to start a business in low-income countries, compared with only 7 in high-income countries. Indexes of the rigidity of employment law and court involvement in bankruptcy are over 20 percent greater in low-income countries.

In which areas do lower-income countries lag the most? The costs to start a business and enforce a contract are areas where there appear to be large opportunities for reform. Average costs of business in these respects are a large multiple of those in best-practice countries (figure 4.9).

FIGURE 4.8 Poor countries regulate the most
Degree of regulation, developed and developing countries, 2003

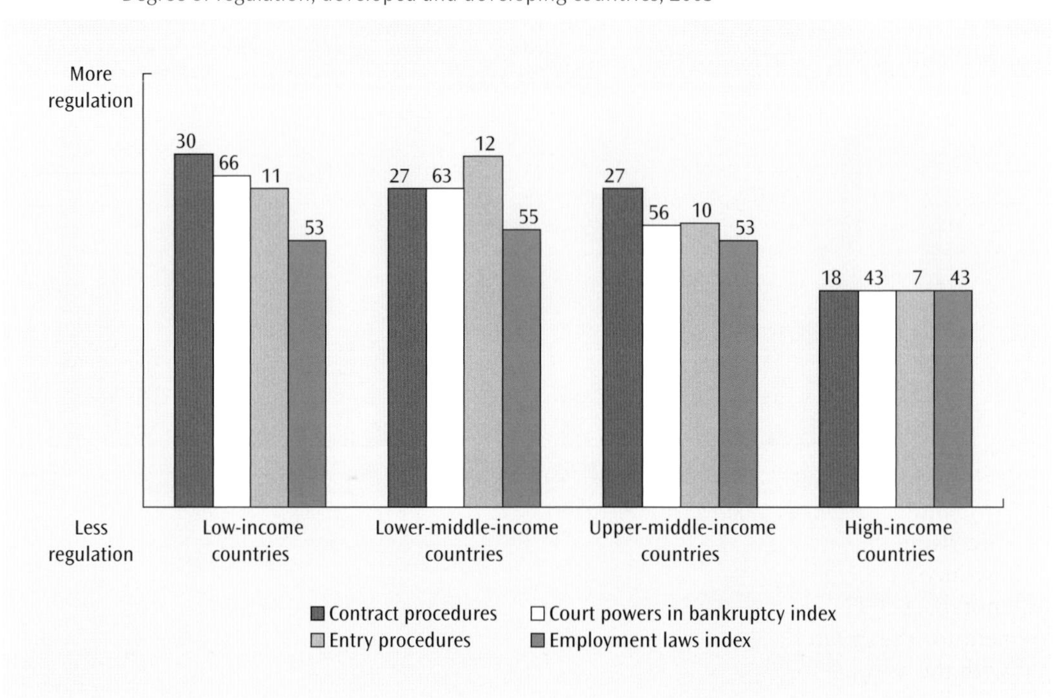

Note: The indicators for high-income countries are used as benchmarks. The average value of the indicator is shown above each column.
Source: World Bank *Doing Business* database 2003.

These findings are corroborated by evidence gathered through the World Bank's investment climate assessments (ICAs).[14] These studies find bureaucratic harassment to be a major constraint to business. For example, customs clearance typically takes much longer in low-income countries. Firms in these countries in general also experience greater production losses from power failures and have less access to credit (table 4.9). Related research finds that these deficiencies in investment climate tend to offset the low-wage advantages of the low-income countries and make it much harder for them to compete with better-off middle-income countries.[15] Economic growth will have greater impact on reducing poverty if countries do not have to rely on low-wage strategies to make up for investment climate deficiencies.

A similar picture emerges from the World Bank's Country Policy and Institutional Assessment ratings (figure 4.10). Average ratings for low-income countries are lower than those for higher-income countries for all dimensions of private sector regulatory and institutional environment covered by these ratings. The area of property rights and rules-based governance emerges as the weakest element of the business environment. This is an area of relative weakness for all developing countries, low or middle income, but the ratings are particularly low for the former.

Although the developing countries regulate more heavily on average, the picture varies appreciably across countries and even within the same country across different types of business regulation. This is encouraging, as it suggests that good practices do exist in developing countries and that partial reforms are possible as a step toward more comprehensive, longer-term reform. Over the past decade, countries such as Jamaica, Latvia, Pakistan, Serbia and Montenegro, Slovakia,

South Africa, Thailand, Tunisia, and Vietnam have greatly improved certain aspects of business regulation. Following reforms to its judicial procedures in 1996, Tunisia is now among the most efficient countries in resolving commercial disputes. The 1999 Thai bankruptcy reforms have achieved great success, as have revisions to collateral law in Slovakia. And recent streamlining of business registration in Latvia, Pakistan, Serbia and Montenegro, and Vietnam has significantly reduced the regulatory requirements to start a business. Although time-series data on business regulations are scant, evidence from the CPIA suggests a trend toward improvement. While average CPIA ratings for business environment remain relatively low (on a scale of 1 to 6), indicating continuing weaknesses, they are rising (figure 4.11).

Low-income countries are making particularly notable progress in the competitive environment for the private sector, narrowing the gap with the average for all developing countries (including middle-income ones). Less progress has been made in property rights and rules-based governance, although the overall trend in this respect also is positive.

Reforms are also taking place in the area of corporate governance. This is a particularly important area of reform in middle-income countries; weak corporate governance contributed to the corporate financial vulnerabilities that underlay the East Asian crisis in the late 1990s. But it is also relevant to low-income countries seeking to attract capital for growth. For the past three years, the World Bank has been conducting assessments of corporate governance in client countries, and by the middle of 2004, 38 such assessments (known as Reports on Observance of Standards and Codes, or ROSCs) will have been completed.[16] In almost all of the countries surveyed, there is now a wide acceptance of importance of corporate governance reform. However, reforms are only just beginning to penetrate the business cultures in most countries. Table 4.10 summarizes some of the lessons learned from the corporate governance ROSC assessments.

FIGURE 4.9 Low-income countries lag far behind best practice in promoting business

Low-income country average relative to the 10 best-practice countries

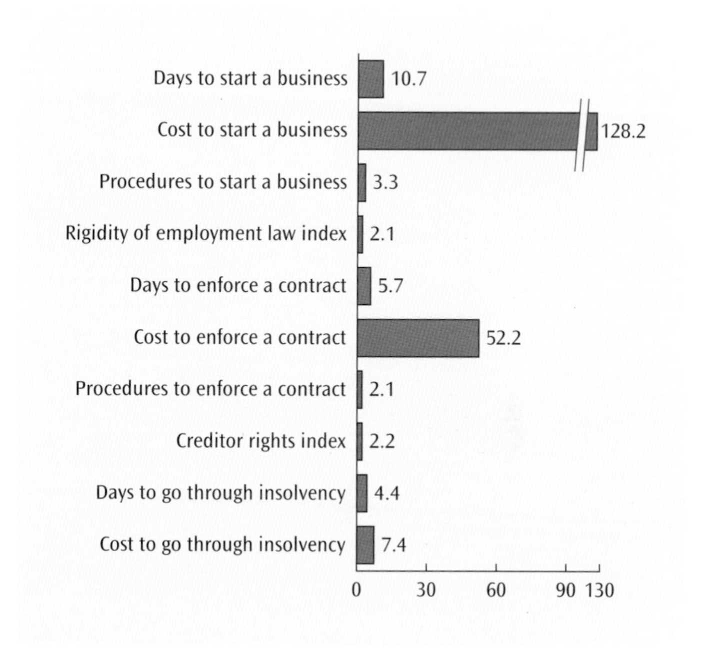

Note: Numbers denote multiples by which low-income country indicators fall short of those in the top 10 countries.
Source: World Bank *Doing Business* database 2003.

The foregoing assessment suggests two broad themes for the reform of the private sector regulatory and institutional environment. First, countries need to simplify regulations related to the start and conduct of business. Eliminating unnecessary procedures and simplifying those that are necessary will reduce business costs, minimize chances of corruption, and boost firms' competitiveness—while reducing costs for government. Second, emphasis should shift from regulating business operations to strengthening institutions that facilitate business by supporting the efficient and fair functioning of markets. A key area is strengthening property rights and the legal and judicial system underpinning contract enforcement. Another priority, especially in middle-income countries, is the continued building of the institutions of corporate governance.

TABLE 4.9 Investment climate, selected low- and middle-income countries, 2002

Country	Avg. days to clear customs (exports)	% of production lost from power loss	Have own generator (%)	Firms with overdraft or line of credit (%)	Firms with a loan from a bank or financial institution (%)
Middle-income countries					
Algeria	8.6	5.3	29.5	38.6	50.4
Brazil	8.4	2.5	17.0	74.4	34.7
China	5.5	1.8	17.0	26.6	57.0
Ecuador	7.1	5.7	33.8	71.5	72.8
Honduras	1.9	5.2	33.3	43.1	51.6
Malaysia	2.6	—	22.6	71.7	87.1
Morocco[a]	1.7	—	16.7	78.9	45.1
Peru	5.2	3.3	27.6	47.7	44.6
Mean	**5.1**	**4.0**	**24.7**	**56.6**	**55.4**
Low-income countries					
Bangladesh	8.8	3.3	71.5	66.2	58.8
Eritrea	3.2	5.5	43.0	47.4	44.9
India	5.1	6.5	68.5	57.4	11.6
Mozambique	17.0	5.1	23.3	12.1	29.0
Nicaragua	2.0	6.5	18.4	29.5	44.0
Pakistan	9.2	5.4	41.8	22.8	19.5
Mean	**7.6**	**5.4**	**44.4**	**39.2**	**34.6**

— Not available.
a. Data from a year 2000 survey.
Source: World Bank investment climate assessment surveys.

FIGURE 4.10 Low-income countries lag the most in property rights and rule of law
Property rights, rule of law, and competitive environment, developing countries

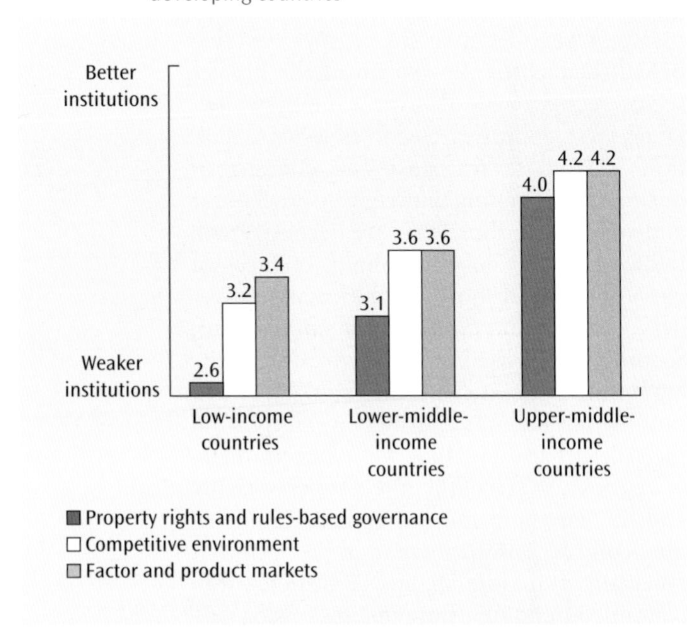

Source: World Bank CPIA ratings 2003.

Financial Sector Policies

An effective financial system promotes economic growth and reduction of poverty by mobilizing savings and allocating them to productive uses. It can also reduce poverty directly: it protects savings, allows migrants to remit funds, and provides small entrepreneurs access to credit, including women through microfinance programs responsive to their needs. Higher incomes and financial assets feed back into gains on the non-income poverty MDGs as well, such as education and health. A sound financial system also strengthens an economy's resilience to shocks, thereby protecting growth and the hard-won gains in reducing poverty.

Financial Deepening

For most of the last decade, banking sector penetration, as measured by the ratio of bank deposits to GDP, has been on the rise for developing countries as a whole. The ratio rose from 27 percent in 1990 to 34 percent in 2002 (figure 4.12). The aggregate indicators, however, mask wide differences between groups of countries both across income levels and across regions. Looking across income levels, countries with higher income have higher banking sector penetration, with the ratio ranging from 21 percent of GDP in low-income countries to 42 percent in middle-income countries in 2002 (49 percent in upper-middle-income countries).

The overall trends in banking penetration also mask considerable inter- and intra-regional differences. The process has progressed most in emerging market countries in Southeast Asia, and recently in the developing and transition countries in Europe and Central Asia. In Latin America, penetration rates were on the rise during most of the 1990s, reflecting economic reform and price stability, but have receded since 2000, following the ebbing of capital flows and a wave of financial crises. In Sub-Saharan Africa, bank penetration continues to be low, owing to long-standing legal, judicial, and institutional weaknesses.

Bank credit to the private sector has also grown, but more slowly than deposits. For developing countries as a whole, bank credit to the private sector increased from 24 percent of GDP in 1990 to 27 percent in 2002. As for deposits, there are large variations across income levels, with the ratio ranging from 13 percent for low-income countries to 35 percent for middle-income countries in 2002 (40 percent for upper-middle-income countries). Private credit to GDP ratios in general stagnated during this period for low-income countries, and rose only marginally for lower-middle-income countries, while displaying a more dynamic trend in upper-middle-income countries.[17]

In many countries, the slower growth in private sector credit reflects increases in net credit to government arising from restructurings of banking systems and fiscal deficits, and in central bank debt related to the conduct of monetary policy. A rise in banks' own holdings of foreign assets (in part to hedge their foreign liabilities) also has contributed to the outcome (figure 4.13). Analysis of a sample of 14 developing countries with relatively large financial systems and 10 African countries shows that, in most cases, relatively little of the growth in deposits was reflected in an increase in credit to the private sector. In the case of the African countries in the sample, in aggregate, none of the deposit growth was translated into growth in private credit.

FIGURE 4.11 **Countries are improving their private business environment**
Business environment indicators, developing countries

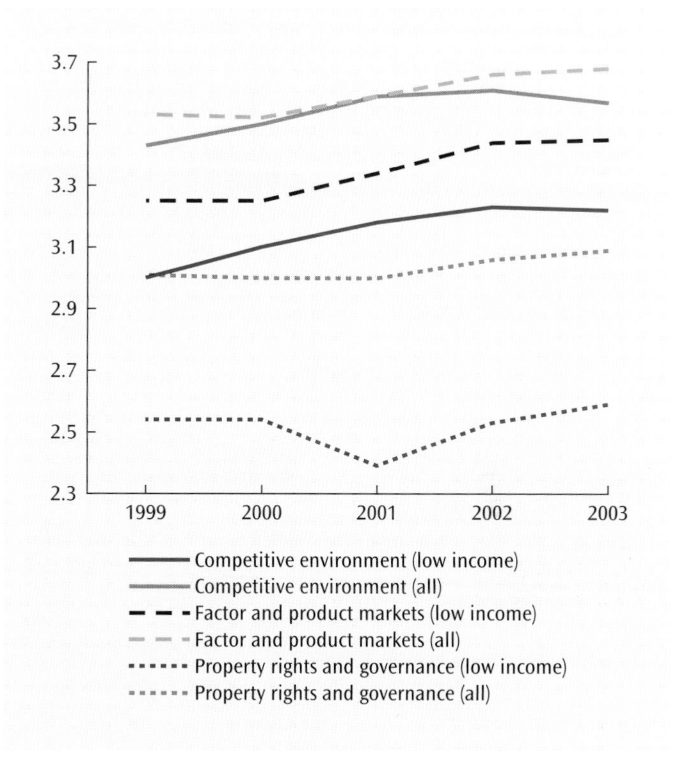

Source: World Bank CPIA ratings 2003.

Access to credit remains a difficult issue in most developing countries, reflecting not only crowding-out by public sector credit, but also weaknesses in the informational and legal and judicial frameworks. Attempts simply to channel low-cost funds to small borrowers to overcome these and other obstacles are likely to undermine sustainable finance for rural and other small and medium enterprises (SMEs), as occurred in the era of repressed finance. A sustainable improvement in access

TABLE 4.10 Summary of lessons learned from corporate governance assessments

Successes	Improvements needed
Basic shareholder rights	
• Improving shareholder record-keeping infrastructure • Improved shareholder meeting mechanics • Powers of board and shareholders being clarified	• Several items of interest to international investors remain unresolved in many countries (such as share blocking, shareholder meeting notification period) • In some countries fundamental decisions can be taken by board (not shareholders)
Ownership and related party transaction disclosure	
• Basic rules in place in many countries	• Compliance with ownership and related party transaction disclosure is still spotty in many countries • Understanding ownership remains difficult
Financial and nonfinancial disclosure	
• Greatly improved rules, standards, and formats • Gradual progress on accounting and auditing reform • Audit committee introduced in many countries • Electronic information dissemination now standard	• Compliance with new rules is growing more slowly • Quality of financial reporting is still mixed in many countries
Duties of board of directors	
• Board role being strengthened and clarified • Duties better described in law • Idea of "independence" introduced in many countries • Many efforts at improving director training	• True independence remains rare • Most director training is in early stages
Shareholder redress and enforcement	
• Lowered thresholds for shareholder action • More active regulators and exchanges	• Results in basic legal reform are limited • Implementation of new laws is lacking • Enforcement remains key challenge

Source: Corporate Governance ROSCs, World Bank.

to credit requires improvement of credit information and strengthening of creditors' rights, to increase incentives for sound lending to small borrowers. Attempts are under way in many countries to improve information on borrowers. For example, 23 developing countries have established public credit bureaus since 1994. In several other countries the functioning of existing public and private credit bureaus is being improved.[18]

The legal and judicial framework, particularly with regard to execution of collateral but also bankruptcy, is important to credit access. In many countries, the legal system favors debtors, making collateral execution almost impossible. Furthermore, even if the legal system provides for creditors' rights in theory, weaknesses in the judicial system may make collateral execution difficult in practice. Many countries are now reforming their laws with respect to collateral execution and bankruptcy, but, unless accompanied by a stronger judicial system, enforcement will remain weak. Another key area for improvement is titling, particularly for small mortgages and land.

There are institutions in developing countries that have successfully sustained credit access to small borrowers and that provide good examples. Microbanking institutions are of all sizes, ranging from Bank Rakyat, Indonesia's *unit desa* program (with a small-loan portfolio of $2.5 billion) to Bangladesh's Grameen Bank ($275 million), Peru's MiBanco ($100 million), Ecuador's CrediFe ($35 million), India's SEWA ($10 million), and Uganda's FOCCAS ($1 million). Whether large or small, successful institutions follow a few key principles: collect on loans; charge

FIGURE 4.12 **The financial sector is deepening in the developing world, but at a varying pace**
Trends in financial intermediation in developing countries, 1990–2002

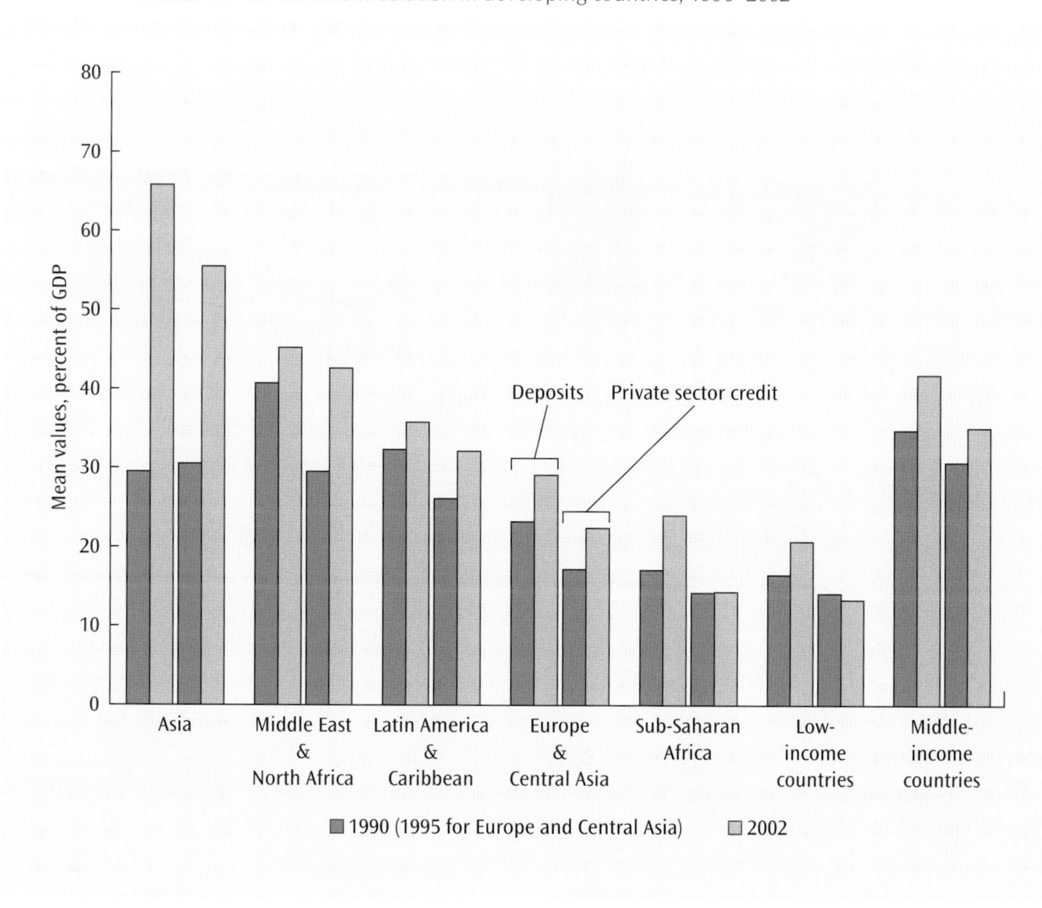

Source: IMF, International Financial Statistics.

enough to cover costs; contain costs and select borrowers well; mobilize deposits and reduce dependence on donors; and provide transparent information on accounts, clientele, and any subsidies.[19]

Systemic Soundness and Stability

A sound financial system is essential for macroeconomic stability. Crises in financial systems during the 1990s spilled over into slower economic growth and led to a costly overhang of debt. Some improvements have occurred, notably an increased role of reputable international banks in Eastern European and Latin American banking systems. Yet much remains to be done to reduce the risk of crises. The variation in the health of the banking systems across developing countries is reflected in key indicators of financial soundness, such as the return on assets, the ratio of nonperforming loans to total loans, and the ratio of capital to assets (table 4.11). A key indicator of financial soundness, the average ratio of performing loans to total loans, does show some improvement in most regions recently. However, improper loan classification and regulatory forbearance mean that the figures likely understate the size of problem loans. The average capital to asset ratios, on the other hand, have not increased much.

FIGURE 4.13 **Deposit growth has not been equally reflected in growth in private sector credit**
Changes in ratios of bank assets and liabilities plus capital to GDP in the 1990s

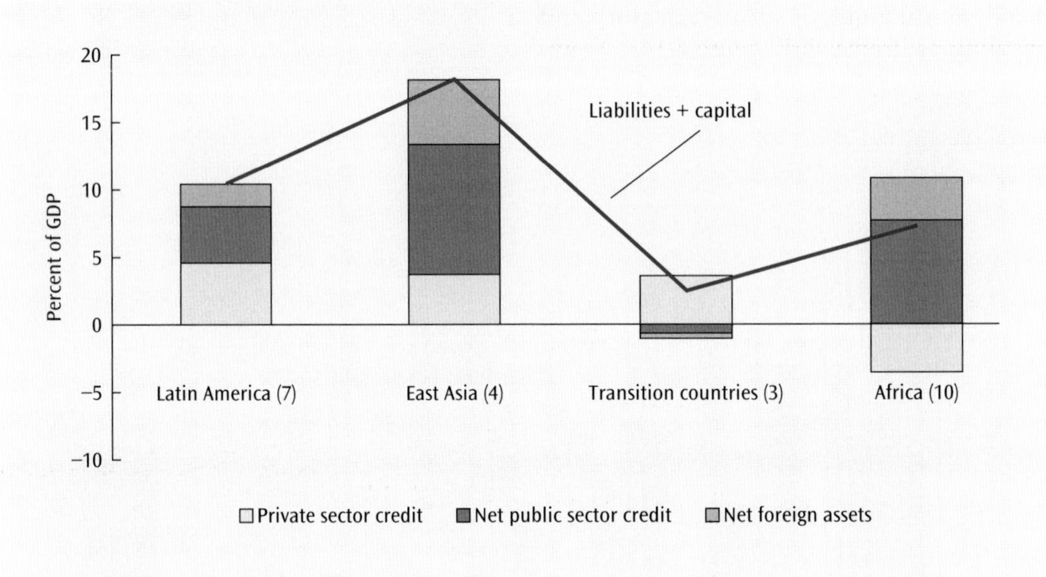

Source: IMF, International Financial Statistics.

TABLE 4.11 **Evolution of selected financial soundness indicators, 1998–2002 (percent)**

Region	Return on assets			Nonperforming loans to total loans			Capital to assets		
	1998	2000	2002	1998	2000	2002	1998	2000	2002
Latin America									
Mean	1.2	0.3	0.7	7.2	10.3	9.5	11.9	11.0	10.3
Standard deviation	2.0	1.5	2.3	3.1	7.1	5.3	4.2	2.5	4.7
Eastern and Central Europe[a]									
Mean	–0.5	1.0	1.3	11.6	10.4	8.9	11.2	10.6	10.5
Standard deviation	1.8	0.9	0.5	8.3	7.6	6.7	5.1	3.7	2.4
Asia[b]									
Mean	–2.7	0.3	0.8	20.9	14.8	12.9	5.0	6.6	7.4
Standard deviation	6.8	0.9	0.4	15.2	5.8	8.5	7.1	3.4	3.8
Middle East and North Africa									
Mean	1.4	1.1	1.1	10.5	13.7	16.3	8.8	9.6	9.3
Standard deviation	0.6	0.5	0.6	3.7	5.6	8.2	1.9	2.7	2.5
Sub-Saharan Africa									
Mean	2.6	3.9	3.2	20.4	18.9	16.5	9.7	9.8	9.9
Standard deviation	1.8	2.3	1.5	10.5	11.4	14.0	1.8	1.9	1.8

a. Includes Israel and Turkey.
b. Excludes Japan.
Source: National authorities, EDSS, Bankscope, Moody's, IMF staff estimates.

Evidence shows that the financial strength of a country's banking system goes hand in hand with the quality of its regulatory and institutional framework (figure 4.14). A simple comparison of indices of financial strength and compliance with Basel Core Principles for Effective Banking Supervision (BCPs) shows a close association between the two indexes (the simple correlation is 0.65).[20] It also shows that the financial strength of institutions is generally lower in developing countries. By and large, this is associated with weaker compliance with BCPs—although in some countries, institutions remain financially weak despite a higher degree of compliance.

A more detailed comparison of individual BCPs across developing countries reveals patterns that suggest areas for particular attention. In banking, close to half of the countries for which supervisory assessments have been completed have weak arrangements for managing credit risks (credit policies, connected lending, loan classification and provisioning) and market risks. Similarly, half of the countries assessed have weak supervisory independence, including the adequacy of resources to conduct a proper supervision, and institutional arrangements for consolidated supervision are weak in 70 percent of the countries assessed. Weak accounting and auditing, limited availability of corporate financial information, and widespread government guarantees limit market discipline.

Efforts are under way in many countries to remedy these deficiencies. An important focus of these efforts is to strengthen the regulatory and supervisory framework. Measures are also being taken to improve market discipline. Both the IMF and the World Bank are providing technical assistance to countries in these areas. Looking ahead, the New Capital Accord (Basel II, or NCA), which proposes to improve the risk sensitivity of capital requirements, is a particularly important initiative, even though some of its elements have proved controversial, including the concern that it may not be appropriate to the less sophisticated banking systems in many developing countries.

FIGURE 4.14 Financial system strength is typically positively correlated with compliance with Basel Core Principles
Correlation between financial strength and compliance with Basel Core Principles

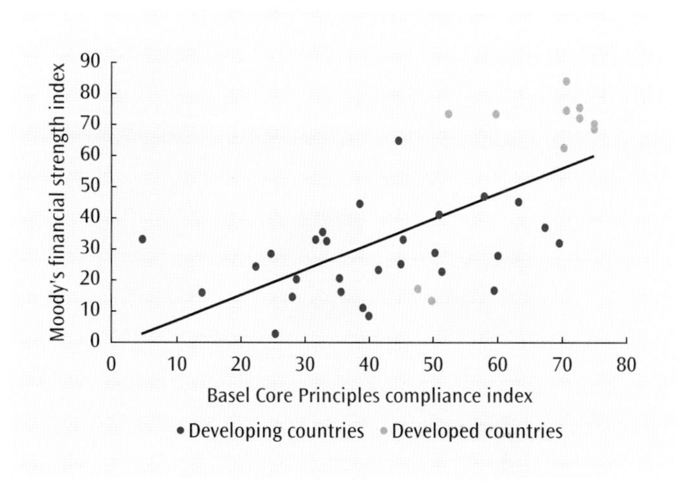

Sources: Moody's and IMF Basel Core Principle Assessment, staff calculations.

An area important to both financial sector deepening and stability is the development and sound functioning of domestic capital markets. In most cases, secondary markets in developing countries are shallow and illiquid. This prevents the diversification of risks away from the banking system and limits the means available to entrepreneurs to raise finance for investment (figure 4.15). As a precondition for the development of domestic capital markets, countries need to improve their corporate governance regimes, regulatory framework for financial information and reporting, and clearance and settlement infrastructure.

Notes

1. For this purpose, IMF staff assessed each low-income country according to a common set of criteria. For example, a country with an unsustainable level of public debt and a large fiscal deficit would be judged to have an unsatisfactory fiscal policy.

2. See, for example, Barro 1997 and Berg and Krueger 2003.

3. For the definition of export diversity, see IMF 2003, p. 188.

FIGURE 4.15 **Capital markets are shallow in low-income countries**
Stock market capitalization, 2002

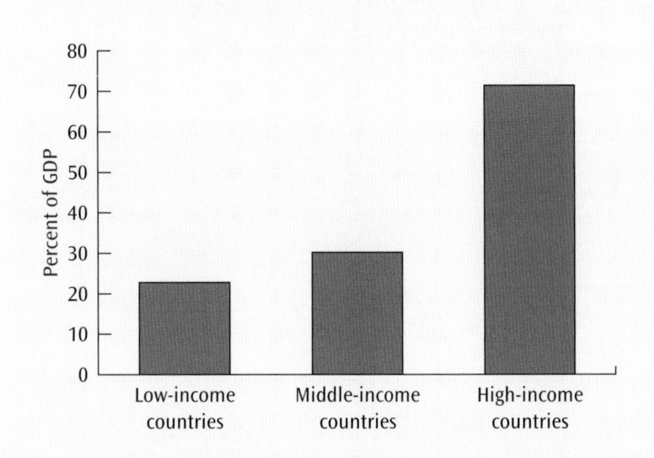

Source: Standard & Poor's 2003; World Bank.

4. One recent study, focusing on currency crises in 30 developing countries and 20 advanced countries over 1975–97, found that the developing countries experienced an average of one crisis per country every five years—roughly twice the average for advanced economies (Aziz, Caramazza, and Salgado 2000).

5. Maskus and Wilson 2002; Wilson 2002.

6. The measure calculated is a variant of the trade restrictiveness index developed by Anderson and Neary (2003). The index is a theoretically well-grounded measure of protection that allows for consistent comparisons of the level of restrictiveness of trade policy across countries and time. The OTRI does not suffer from the well-known drawbacks of simple or import-weighted tariff averages and allows the impact of both tariffs and NTBs to be estimated. The methodology used for the measure comprises four steps. First, import demand elasticities by country and by product were estimated at the 6-digit level of the Harmonized System of commodity classification (HS) (some 4,200 product categories). Second, an estimate was made of the impact on imports, again at the 6-digit HS level, of core NTBs (such as quotas, nonautomatic licensing, and minimum prices) and domestic support granted to agriculture. Third, using these demand elasticity and impact estimates, the product-level ad valorem equivalent (AVE) of the two types of NTBs (core NTBs and domestic agricultural support) was calculated for each country in the sample. Finally, tariffs (ad valorem and AVEs of specific tariffs) and AVEs of NTBs at the product level were aggregated to produce an overall measure of trade restrictiveness. The index is calculated bilaterally for every country and its partners. Data on technical product regulations (such as labeling and testing requirements, product requirements to protect human and animal health) were not used in the estimation of the OTRIs, because of incomplete reporting by countries. However, estimates of the AVEs of such measures are available on request and can be found in the background document (Kee, Nicita, and Olarreaga 2004).

7. The simple correlation coefficient between OTRI and GDP per capita is –0.32, and is statistically significant at the 1 percent level.

8. Mattoo, Rathindran, and Subramaniam 2001. The measure of reform included not just liberalization but also regulatory improvements.

9. World Bank 2003; Alesina and others 2003; Scarpetta and others 2002; Dollar and others 2003; Batra 2003.

10. Dollar and others 2003.

11. Dollar, Hallward-Dreimeier, and Mengistae 2003; Hallward-Dreimeier, Wallsten, and Xu 2003.

12. World Bank 2003.

13. These indicators of business regulation cover more than 130 countries and are based on data gathered through study and assessment of laws and regulations in force, with input and verification by local experts. For more on the Doing Business Project, see http://www.worldbank.org/doingbusiness.

14. Country investment climate assessments are based on standardized firm surveys that cover a range of potential constraints to business operations. For more details on the ICAs, see http://www.worldbank.org/privatesector/ic.

15. For example, Dollar, Hallward-Dreimeier, and Mengistae (2003) find that despite low wages, low productivity resulting from a poorer investment climate makes it hard for Cambodian garment firms to compete in open markets with those in China, India, and Pakistan.

16. The corporate governance ROSCs are benchmarked against OECD Principles of Corporate Governance. For more on these assessments, see http://www.worldbank.org/ifa/rosc_cg.html.

17. Even these figures may overstate the growth of private sector credit. Many countries, such as China, report all nongovernment credit, including public enterprise credit, as private sector credit.

18. World Bank Doing Business Project database.

19. Yaron, Benjamin, and Piprek, 1997.

20. The first index is the Moody's indicator of financial strength, with a scale of 0 to 100. It is a composite of the financial strength of individual banks measured by key financial ratios. The second index is based on the qualitative assessments of compliance with BCPs. (Since 2001, almost 60 country assessments have been conducted in Financial Sector Assessment Programs, or FSAPs), of which 41 have been for developing countries.) The index is constructed by mapping the qualitative assessment of each of the 25 BCPs on a scale from 0 to 100 and taking the average across BCPs for each country.

5

Upgrading Public Sector Governance

Public sector governance is related to the Millennium Development Goals in two critical ways. First, alongside the economic and financial policies reviewed in chapter 4, governance is a key element of the enabling environment for economic growth. Better governance produces better growth outcomes.[1] Growth, in turn, contributes to the reduction of income poverty and to other MDGs.[2] Higher incomes increase citizens' effective demand for health and education, as well as resources with which to satisfy that demand.

Second, better governance contributes to more efficient and effective delivery of education, health, and other services that are key to the achievement of non-income MDGs. Indeed, it is a critical element in ensuring that public spending translates into quality services that reach target groups. Where corruption is prevalent, funds may be diverted from programs that would benefit the poor toward activities that benefit well-connected people or public officials themselves. Resources are wasted if procurement contracts or jobs are allocated on the basis of connections, rather than on merit.[3]

Governance consists of the manner in which the state acquires and exercises the authority to provide and manage public goods and services.[4] Its two pillars—capacity and accountability—are anchored on sets of rules called governance institutions. Those institutions interact to shape the incentives of state actors and thus the quality of governance—the extent to which high-quality public goods and services are provided to the citizenry and the business community. Capacity means that the state has appropriately skilled personnel, sufficient financial resources, and adequate supporting processes, such as a working budget system. Accountability means that the state is responsible to citizens for delivering public goods and services; its stewards (politicians, policymakers, bureaucrats, judges) are prepared to explain and face the consequences of failures occurring within their jurisdiction. Weak capacity and low accountability—poor governance—translate into inefficient and inadequate provision of public goods and services.

Progress in improving public financial management—expenditure management, revenue mobilization—in developing countries is assessed in the next section. There is slow but steady improvement in developing countries on these dimensions of public sector governance, but reforms need to go much further. Transparency, accountability, and control of corruption in government are assessed in the subsequent section. Progress is more modest in these areas than in those more amenable to "technocratic" reforms—public financial management—and serious weaknesses persist in many countries.

The analysis underscores the need to accelerate governance reform and capacity building in the public sector, with special attention to improving the quality of governance—reduction of corruption, enhancement of accountability. As compared to other policy areas, performance in developing countries is in general weakest in public sector governance. And within public sector governance, it is weakest with respect to transparency, accountability, and control of corruption. The weaknesses are most pervasive precisely in countries where stronger institutional capacities are needed to manage development interventions that will spur progress toward the MDGs—poor countries. Governance reform is of crosscutting significance, since poor governance and weak institutions can seriously undermine the effectiveness of policies and programs throughout an economy.

Fortunately, recognizing the centrality of good governance, governments in more and more developing countries are stepping up reform efforts. The New Partnership for Africa's Development initiative is a particularly encouraging development, especially as it manifests clear and strong African ownership of the governance reform agenda.

Measuring the quality of public sector governance is difficult. While recent years have seen much progress in this area, more work is needed. Efforts to improve the indicators of the quality of governance are reviewed in the last section.

TABLE 5.1 Improvement in public financial management in developing countries, 1999–2003 (average CPIA ratings)

	Quality of budgetary and financial management		Efficiency of revenue mobilization	
Income category	1999	2003	1999	2003
All developing countries	3.21	3.43	3.27	3.56
LICUS	2.05	2.30	2.50	2.73
Low income	2.95	3.18	3.09	3.32
Middle income	3.54	3.73	3.27	3.56

Note: Table entries are mean values for indicated country groups. Ratings are on a rising scale of 1 to 6.
Source: World Bank CPIA database.

Public Financial Management

The importance of improved public resource mobilization and use is underscored by the need to support stronger programs in infrastructure and human development as part of the effort to achieve the MDGs, as discussed in chapters 6 and 7. While increased external assistance will help, more resources will also have to be found domestically to support these priorities—through raising more revenues and improving expenditure allocation and management.

Public Expenditure and Budget Management

Developing countries' performance in public financial management improved slowly from 1999 to 2003, according to the World Bank's Country Policy and Institutional Assessment (table 5.1). Not surprisingly, average ratings are lower for low-income countries, and are lower still for low-income countries under stress.

Improved expenditure tracking and management is an important element of reform in the heavily indebted poor countries covered by the HIPC initiative. The HIPC Assessment and Action Plan (AAP) assesses the quality and capacity of public expenditure systems in these countries and formulates action plans to strengthen those systems. The assessment focuses on government capacity to manage priority public spending as defined in each country's PRSP. It covers a minimum of 15 measures indicative of the quality of a country's public expenditure management system (table 5.2).

The first major assessment under the AAP was completed in 2002, based on field assessments carried out during 2001–02. Covering 24 countries, the assessment concluded that public financial systems of 15 countries needed substantial upgrading; those of the 9 other countries also needed some improvement. Twenty-one countries had inactive or

TABLE 5.2 Public financial management benchmarks used in HIPC assessments

	Budget management	Benchmark description
Formulation	**Comprehensiveness**	
	1. Composition of the budget entity	Meets GFS definition of general government
	2. Limitations to use of off-budget transactions	Extra- (or off-) budget expenditure is not substantial
	3. Reliability of budget as guide to outturn	Level and composition of outturn is "quite close" to budget
	4. Data on donor financing	Both capital and current donor-funded expenditures included
	Classification	
	5. Classification of budget transactions	Functional and/or program information provided
	6. Identification of poverty-reducing expenditure	Identified through use of classification system (such as a virtual poverty fund)
	Projection	
	7. Quality of multiyear expenditure projections	Projections are integrated into budget formulation
Execution	**Internal control**	
	8. Level of payment arrears	Low level of arrears accumulated
	9. Quality of internal audit	Internal audit function (whether effective or not)
	10. Use of tracking surveys	Tracking use on regular basis
	Reconciliation	
	11. Quality of fiscal/banking data reconciliation	Reconciliation of fiscal and monetary data carried out on routine basis
Reporting	**Reporting**	
	12. Timeliness of internal budget reports	Monthly expenditure reports provided within four weeks of end of month
	13. Classification used for budget tracking	Timely functional reporting derived from classification system
	Final Audited Accounts	
	14. Timeliness of accounts closure	Accounts closed within two months of year end
	15. Timeliness of final audited accounts	Audited accounts presented to legislature within one year

Source: IMF–World Bank 2002.

ineffective audit arrangements, and 20 lacked a medium-term perspective integrated into their budget formulation process. On the brighter side, in 16 of the countries it was possible to establish a broad mapping of budget data to the poverty-reducing spending categories defined in final or interim PRSPs. Fifteen of the 24 countries had conducted public expenditure tracking surveys to monitor whether budget allocations were reaching the intended service providers.

A 2003 update on the assessment indicated that most countries were making progress in implementing action plans that were developed to address the weaknesses identified in the earlier assessment. More than three-fourths of the measures described in the action plans had been implemented or were under implementation. An increasing number of countries were able to report on poverty-reducing spending—and to report that such spending was rising in relation to GDP and total expenditures.[5]

The 2004 HIPC AAP reassessment will yield results for 28 countries in mid-2004, although fewer than seven assessments had been completed as of February 2004. Preliminary results suggest mixed progress, with some countries improving and others falling in the number of benchmarks met. The former, unsurprisingly, were the ones that the 2003 update found as more active in implementing their action plans.

The IMF prepares Reports on the Observance of Standards and Codes that have been agreed upon for fiscal transparency. The reports examine transparency practices in relationships between levels of government, adequacy of budget preparation, execution and reporting, and strength of oversight. The

BOX 5.1 Improving fiscal transparency through ROSCs

As of the end of April 2004, fiscal reports on standards and codes (ROSCs) had been completed for 46 developing countries; 41 are published on the IMF Web site. Analysis of the completed ROSCs points to a number of common areas for attention.

- Reporting and dissemination of fiscal information tend to be incomplete and subject to considerable lags. Many developing countries do not meet adequate standards of timeliness or reliability in reporting. Coverage of general government expenses is weak in many countries because of inadequate subnational data. Moreover, a wide range of governments resort to off-budget fiscal activity, such as quasi-fiscal activities and unreported contingent liabilities (for example, Malawi, Mali, Poland, Romania, and Tanzania).
- Unrealistic budgeting is a widespread phenomenon. Because of the absence of clear legal and regulatory provisions governing the budget (for example, in Azerbaijan, Mali, and the Philippines) or weak compliance with such provisions (such as in Bangladesh and Papua New Guinea), actual spending often differs substantially from the budget. This, together with poor reporting of expenditures, limits the usefulness of the budget as an indicator of fiscal policy.
- Many of the above issues arise because government activities are not clearly distinguished from those of nongovernmental public sector agencies. This factor is often the genesis of excessive quasi-fiscal activity (for example, in Bangladesh, Iran, and Malawi). In addition, the roles and responsibilities of the different levels and branches of government are not yet clearly defined in some transition countries (such as Azerbaijan and the Kyrgyz Republic).
- Widespread tax exemptions, excessive discretion in tax administration, and inadequate enforcement are also common in many developing countries (such as Bangladesh, the Kyrgyz Republic, and Malawi).
- External audit mechanisms are weak in a number of countries (Azerbaijan, Benin, Honduras, and Mauritania, for example).

Many countries participating in fiscal ROSCs have since undertaken or are undertaking significant fiscal reforms that will lead to improved fiscal transparency practices. These reforms include strengthening budget execution and reporting (Cameroon, Honduras, Papua New Guinea, Zambia), implementing program budgeting (Brazil, Mexico, South Africa), developing modern budget laws (Brazil, the Czech Republic, Hungary, Poland, South Africa), and reducing the scope of quasi-fiscal activities through privatization and price liberalization (Benin, Burkina Faso, Mozambique, Nicaragua, Tunisia, Uganda, Zambia).

Source: IMF Fiscal Affairs Department.

reports find that there has been progress in these areas, but much remains to be done in a number of countries (box 5.1).

Building on the assessment work under the HIPC AAP, efforts are under way at the IMF and the World Bank—working with the multidonor Public Expenditure and Financial Accountability Program (PEFA)[6] and in cooperation with the OECD-DAC Joint Venture on Public Financial Management—to develop a broader public financial management performance measurement framework that could be used in a wider group of client countries. The HIPC AAP indicators are the foundation of this system, but it will include some additional indicators as well, for example, those relating to fiscal risk management, government procurement, external audit, and parliamentary scrutiny. The proposed framework will be a central element of an integrated diagnostic assessment of public financial management, undertaken increasingly in the context of country-owned and -led development strategies. The approach going forward is anchored on the following key principles: government articulation of a public expenditure reform strategy in the PRSP or other country-owned document; an integrated and well-sequenced program of diagnostic work by development partners; well-coordinated technical and financial support from development partners for implementation of the countries' public expenditure reform strategies; and periodic reporting by countries of performance in public expenditure policy, financial management, and procurement.[7]

Revenue Mobilization

Excessive taxation can impede private sector development, but in most developing countries the problem is collecting enough revenue to provide essential public infrastructure and human development services. Tax revenue in low-income countries as a share of GDP is about 14 percent, compared with about 19 percent in lower-middle-income countries and 23 percent in upper-middle-income countries (table 5.3). The ratios, however, conceal large variations across and within regions. Overall, it appears that there is scope in many countries for raising additional revenues.

Policies to enhance domestic revenue mobilization need to focus on a few taxes that can generate significant revenues at relatively low cost. In view of the high share of agriculture and informal economic activity in many countries, corporate and personal income taxes are unlikely to be a major source of domestic revenues in the short to medium term. The value-added tax (VAT) perhaps offers the greatest potential. To maximize revenues from a VAT, countries need to ensure that the tax base is as broad as possible and the rate structure is simple. Excise taxes also have significant potential, although care needs to be taken in their design, as some of them can be regressive. Currently, excise revenues amount to less than 2 percent of GDP in low-income countries, compared with about 3 percent in high-income countries. Levied on products such as alcohol, tobacco, petroleum products, vehicles, and spare parts, this tax has a potentially buoyant base and can be administered at a low cost.

Reducing tax exemptions and tax incentives can generate substantial revenues. In many developing countries, tax incentives

TABLE 5.3 Central government tax revenue, 1990–2001 (percent of GDP)

Countries/regions	Total tax revenue	Taxes on international trade	Excises	General sales tax	Social security
Low income (21)	14.1	4.2	1.8	3.1	1.8
Lower middle (26)	18.5	3.4	2.3	4.9	3.7
Upper middle (20)	23.1	3.1	2.5	5.9	6.4
High income (31)	26.7	1.4	2.7	6.0	7.4
Asia (12)	13.4	3.7	2.1	2.6	0.3
Latin America and Caribbean (16)	17.0	2.0	2.4	4.7	2.6
Middle East and North Africa (6)	17.9	4.5	2.3	3.3	1.7
Sub-Saharan Africa (12)	16.6	6.8	1.4	3.1	0.5
Europe and Central Asia (20)	23.9	1.6	2.6	6.4	7.7
OECD (23)	29.1	0.6	3.0	6.0	8.4

Note: Figures are unweighted averages over the indicated period. Some taxes are omitted; hence, columns may not add to the total. Numbers in parentheses represent the maximum number of countries in each group for which data are available. Because of data availability, sample size varies across taxes.
Source: IMF Government Finance Statistics; IMF *World Economic Outlook*, various years.

and exemptions are a major source of revenue loss. They not only shrink the tax base but also complicate tax administration. Tax incentives are often used to attract investment. But studies have shown that investment decisions depend on a host of other factors that can be more important than tax incentives.[8] Once established, tax incentives and exemptions are difficult to abolish. In addition, their budgetary cost is not made explicit. Eliminating or reducing tax incentives and exemptions can enhance the efficiency of the tax system by enlarging the tax base and simplifying tax administration.

Efforts to mobilize tax revenues should include steps to strengthen tax administration. Policies should focus on strengthening the technical capacity and organization of revenue authorities through computerization and improved operating procedures. Stricter enforcement mechanisms and improved tax audits and inspections could increase taxpayer compliance. Countries could increase their tax-to-GDP ratio by an estimated 1 to 2 percentage points through elimination of tax incentives and exemptions and better administration.[9]

But the potential for generating additional revenues is almost certainly less than what is needed to achieve the MDGs in most developing countries. The bulk of the financing will have to come from improving the efficiency of existing spending, economic growth, and external resources.

TABLE 5.4 Quality of public sector governance, 1999–2003 (average CPIA rating)

	Quality of public administration		Transparency, accountability, control of corruption in public sector	
Income category	2001	2003	1999	2003
All developing countries	3.13	3.19	2.92	3.18
LICUS	2.03	2.25	2.05	2.23
Low income	2.87	2.95	2.73	2.97
Middle income	3.33	3.49	3.16	3.44

Note: Table entries are mean values. Ratings are on a rising scale of 1 to 6. For the quality of public administration, the base year shown is 2001 rather than 1999, because the CPIA definition of that criterion was revised significantly in 2001.
Source: World Bank CPIA database.

Quality of Public Administration and Control of Corruption

Policy ratings for developing countries on the quality of governance—quality of public administration, transparency, accountability, and control of corruption—are lower on average than their ratings for public financial management (table 5.4). This is not altogether surprising. Changing public expenditure or revenue management or budget processes, where technocratic improvements can bring quick returns, is likely to be easier than changing the culture of public bureaucracies and strengthening accountability. There may be powerful interests with a stake in blocking reform in any policy area. However, opposition to reforms that embrace known international best practices is more easily exposed as self-interested. Best practice is clearer in budget management and tax policy than in other areas, where accountability mechanisms are weak. Less is known about how to change the culture of dysfunctional public bureaucracies, or how to implement the checks on executive power necessary to ensure an open and accountable administration. Progress in these areas depends on a careful understanding of the underlying context and behavior and fostering of reform ownership.

Although public sector governance ratings are low on average compared to the ratings for other policy areas—making it the weakest policy area—there is a trend toward improvement. All developing country regions showed some improvement in the quality of governance from 1999 to 2003, as measured by the World Bank CPIA (figure 5.1). The largest improvement was in Europe and Central Asia, followed by South Asia. The lowest average ratings are in Sub-Saharan Africa, but there is evidence that increased attention to governance issues is beginning to pay off, as reviewed in the next section.

The patterns and trends in governance revealed by CPIA assessments are corroborated by similar assessment exercises undertaken by the regional development banks. As reviewed in chapter 3, country ratings by the African Development Bank, Asian Development Bank, and Inter-American Development Bank show public sector governance to be the weakest policy area on average across countries. Where ratings are available across years—as in the AfDB and ADB assessments—they also show that governance is improving, albeit gradually. The particularly notable improvement in governance in Europe and Central Asia is confirmed by the results of the Business Environment and Enterprise Performance Surveys (BEEPs), conducted jointly by European Bank for Reconstruction and Development and the World Bank. For example, the BEEPS surveys found that in a majority of the developing and transition countries in the region, the incidence of payment of bribes by firms fell substantially between 1999 and 2002.[10]

The worldwide governance indicators compiled by the World Bank Institute (WBI) and the Bank's Development Economics Group (DEC) are an important source of cross-country assessments of the quality of governance. They take the form of indices of various aspects of the quality of governance, aggregated from several sources.[11] Consistent with the CPIA results, average ratings on the WBI/DEC indicators are lower for low-income countries than for all developing countries, and lowest for the LICUS group (table 5.5). The gaps relative to the indicators for advanced countries are large. However, there is no clear trend over time in country group ratings relative to those of other groups. The indicated changes between 1998 and 2002 are too small to be statistically significant.

FIGURE 5.1 The quality of governance is weak but improving in developing countries
Scores for overall quality of governance by region, 1999–2003

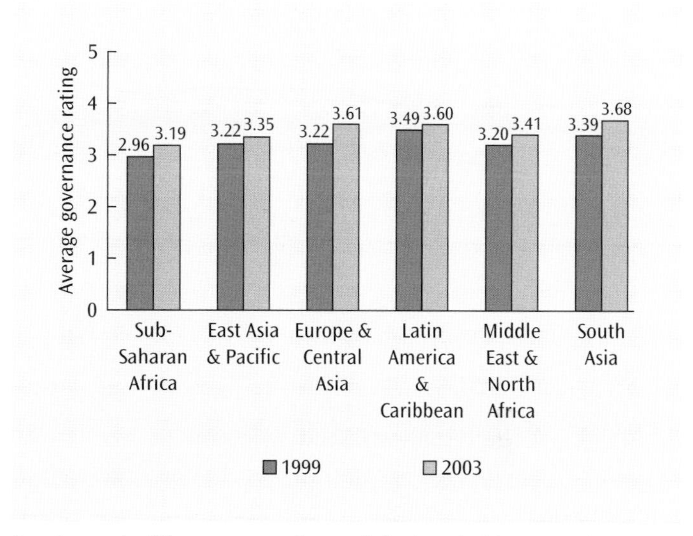

Note: Because the differences across regions are similar for each of the CPIA public sector governance criteria, ratings for criteria 4, 17, 18, and 20 are averaged in this figure. Criterion 19 was omitted because comparable data are available beginning only in 2001. In all, CPIA has 20 criteria, of which these 5 are more directly related to public sector governance.
Source: World Bank CPIA database.

TABLE 5.5 Worldwide governance indicators, 1998–2002

	Control of corruption		Voice and accountability		Government effectiveness	
Income category	1998	2002	1998	2002	1998	2002
All developing countries	–0.44	–0.48	–0.19	–0.24	–0.34	–0.39
LICUS	–0.93	–1.10	–0.95	–1.08	–1.16	–1.24
Low income	–0.72	–0.80	–0.40	–0.49	–0.54	–0.65
Middle income	0.44	0.41	0.27	0.31	0.39	0.44
OECD DAC members	2.02	1.77	1.35	1.43	1.81	1.71

Note: Table entries are mean values for country groups. Values represent the number of standard deviations above or below (indicated by a minus sign) the overall mean value (of 0). The approximate range of values for each index is +2 to –2.
Source: World Bank, WBI/DEC governance database.

FIGURE 5.2 **Civil liberties are gradually improving in developing countries**
Trend in civil liberties in developing countries, 1995–2002

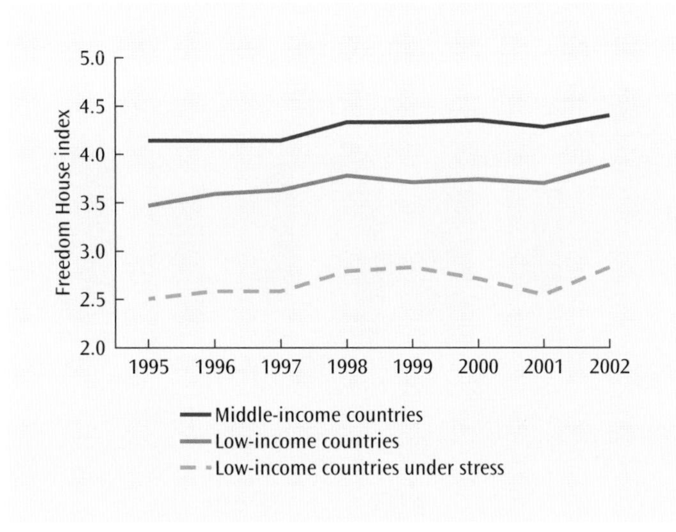

Source: Freedom House.

FIGURE 5.3 **Participatory processes are also improving in developing countries**
Percentage of country leaders elected in multiparty elections with less than 75 percent of the vote

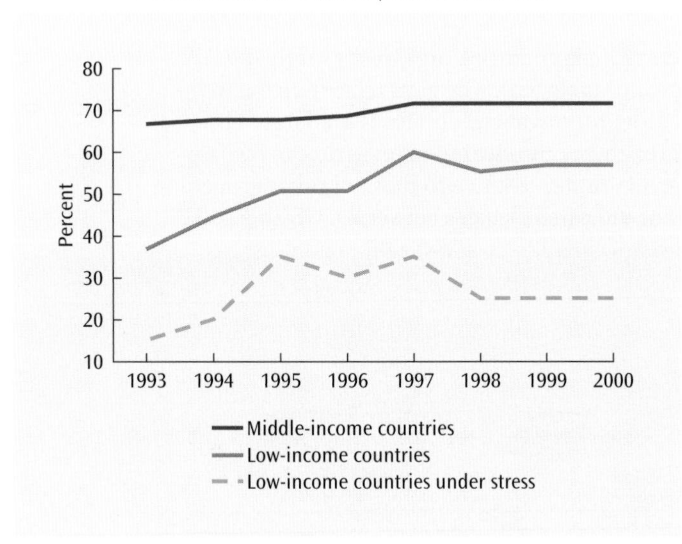

Source: Beck and others (2000).

Some of the data sources used in the WBI/DEC governance indicators provide a good basis for a comparison of the level of ratings over time.[12] The Freedom House indicators of civil liberties, for example, have been published since the mid-1970s and have used a fixed methodology since 1990. The indicators show a gradually improving trend in civil liberties in developing countries (figure 5.2).[13]

Objective indicators corroborate the trend in Freedom House indicators. Over time, there has been an increase in the number of chief executives in developing countries who have been elected rather than appointed by other means. Moreover, the number of chief executives who have been elected in contests featuring candidates from multiple parties has increased. There is some indication of increasing fairness and integrity in electoral procedures. For example, the percentage of chief executives who have been chosen in multiparty elections in which the winner received less than 75 percent of the official vote has increased since 1993 (figure 5.3).[14] The data on executive elections, together with the Freedom House data, indicate a trend toward broader participatory processes by which citizens can influence policymaking and hold their leaders accountable.

Increased Focus on Governance in Africa

Good governance is an increasingly important topic in Sub-Saharan Africa, which historically has been a weak performer in this area. A powerful consensus is evolving across Africa on the critical role of good governance as a precondition for Africa to meet its development challenges. The MDGs are being instrumental in focusing the attention of policymakers on the need to accelerate reforms to deal with governance-related impediments to the achievement of poverty reduction and other development goals. The PRSP process is helping to integrate these reforms into overall country development strategies.

A key manifestation of the strengthened resolve in the region to come to grips with the governance agenda is the New Partnership for Africa's Development (NEPAD). Launched in 2002, this initiative, owned and led by African countries, places improvement of governance at the center of the reform agenda. To give

BOX 5.2 The African Peer Review Mechanism: self-assessing governance

The New Partnership for Africa's Development (NEPAD), an organization of African leaders who have pledged to place their countries on a path of sustainable growth and development, has launched the African Peer Review Mechanism (APRM) "to foster the adoption of policies, standards, and practices that lead to political stability, high economic growth, sustainable development, and accelerated subregional and continental economic integration through sharing of experiences and reinforcement of successful and best practice, including identifying deficiencies and assessing the needs of capacity building."

The APRM addresses all dimensions of governance, organized under four headings: democracy and political governance; economic governance and management; corporate governance; and socio-economic development. By the end of 2003, 16 countries had formally joined the APRM: Algeria, Burkina Faso, Cameroon, Republic of Congo, Ethiopia, Gabon, Ghana, Kenya, Mali, Mauritius, Mozambique, Nigeria, Rwanda, Senegal, South Africa, and Uganda. An independent panel of seven eminent Africans, working with the countries, is responsible for producing country reviews to be submitted to NEPAD and the African Union. The first reviews are scheduled to begin in April 2004.

In March 2003, NEPAD agreed on a set of objectives, standards, criteria, and indicators to be applied in each country review. The set includes 25 broad governance and development objectives and 76 African and international standards. Among the objectives are the following:

- An objective on constitutional democracy, political competition, and the rule of law that takes as its standard the African Charter on Human and Peoples' Rights
- An objective on transparent, predictable, and credible economic policies that includes international accounting and auditing standards and codes of good practices
- An objective on accountable, efficient, and effective public office holders and civil servants that refers to the African Union's Convention on Preventing and Combating Corruption.

The APRM process will build upon in-country self-assessments that involve extensive consultations with all branches of government, civil society, and the private sector. The challenge is to build upon existing processes, such as the PRSPs, and add value with governance assessments made by African stakeholders, their governments, and eminent independent opinion leaders from the region. Expanding the APRM to all NEPAD member countries and ensuring wide discussion of its findings will be important to the success of the APRM initiative.

Source: NEPAD 2003a, 2003b.

concreteness to its reform focus and objectives, NEPAD is putting in place an African Peer Review Mechanism that aims to improve governance policy and practice through mutual learning from national governance assessments prepared by the African countries themselves (box 5.2).

An increased focus on governance is also reflected in the work of regional development agencies. An example is a major new report on governance in Africa prepared by the United Nations Economic Commission for Africa (UNECA). The report, which draws on detailed individual country studies, indicates that while the reform agenda is huge, African countries are making progress toward good governance. It emphasizes African achievements but recognizes the occurrence of setbacks and the depth of the challenges ahead (box 5.3).

Improving the Monitoring of Governance

The centrality of good governance to development effectiveness underscores the importance of reliable measures of the various dimensions of the quality of governance.

BOX 5.3 Governance in Africa—progress on a difficult agenda

The United Nations Economic Commission for Africa (UNECA) has launched a multiyear project to monitor progress toward good governance in Africa. Twenty-eight country studies have been undertaken, each based on a household survey, a survey of national experts, and a desk-study with a range of governance indicators. The project explores three components of good governance: political representativeness, institutional effectiveness and capacities, and economic governance and management. Summarizing the country reports, UNECA's *African Governance Report* (forthcoming) finds that:

- African countries have made significant strides toward political representation. The political system has been liberalized, more political parties are being allowed to operate, civil society has gained a place in social and political bargaining, elections form the basis of political leadership, and the integrity of the political system is on the rise in many countries. Most countries have embarked upon the process of constitutional review, to promote a culture of constitutionalism with adherence to the rule of law, due process, and political accountability. The issue of leadership succession and change through the electoral process constitutes a significant step in the process of democratic renewal and a new culture of governance in Africa.
- Despite progress on social inclusiveness in the elected organs of government, drawbacks remain in two major areas: domination of the political process by an urban-based political elite, and unfair treatment of minority groups. Although the political regime is becoming more inclusive through more robust public participation achieved by the media, civil society, and high voting rates, political parties remain weak.
- Democracy, good political governance, effective economic governance, and prudent public financial management are intertwined. Management weaknesses persist, especially in public procurement, and in equity in resource mobilization and public expenditure. Several African countries are using the Medium-Term Expenditure Framework (MTEF) to improve macroeconomic stability, resource allocation, and prioritization of public expenditures, leading to greater accountability for the outcomes of public expenditures.
- Dominance of the executive branch is gradually decreasing. Laws, rules, and regulations proposed by the executive are debated in standing or select committees of the legislature and subsequently enacted. Other emerging checks and balances are the laws and regulations managing the ways in which a government conducts its business: conflict of interest laws, codes of conduct for elected and appointed officials, and asset declarations by politicians. The judiciary remains in a formative stage, as many African governments are still defining judicial independence. In many countries, an overburdened court system denies poor and disadvantaged citizens access to justice, encourages corruption, and undermines the rule of law.
- African governments are making headway in terms of institutional capacity, accountability, transparency, and policy coherence, whereas service delivery is still inadequate. In many countries, criteria other than merit still take precedence in recruitment, promotion, and discipline of public servants. While government business is often shrouded in official secrecy, some countries have passed legislation on administrative justice and access to information. Although the state bureaucracy exercises growing institutional and professional competence in policy design and implementation, there is considerable variation among African countries in the adequacy, quality, and efficiency of basic public services.

Source: UNECA forthcoming.

More and better measures of governance are available today than was the case about a decade ago. But work continues to improve the indicators to enhance their robustness.

Effective monitoring of governance must ideally meet the following requirements: agreement on a set of *international benchmarks* for good governance; identification of *specific governance measures* that indicate change toward or away from the agreed benchmark; and formulation of indicators that are *cost-effective* and *replicable* and that can be *applied* and *managed* by the countries themselves. Especially difficult challenges attend the search for robust indicators in areas of governance not related to the public budget—accountability, corruption—where agreed international benchmarks and good quantitative measures are lacking in comparison.

At the World Bank, efforts include both improving indicators that allow cross-country comparisons to be made (for example, improving the quality of the CPIA governance indicators by underpinning them with more detailed and specific assessment criteria) and deepening the analysis of governance issues at the individual country level, for example, through in-depth Institutional and Governance Reviews (IGRs)[15] and Governance and Anti-Corruption (GAC) Diagnostic Surveys.[16]

Several partner institutions also are involved in similar efforts, individually as well as with others. The work being carried out in the framework of PEFA and by NEPAD APRM and UNECA, as noted above, are examples. The Africa work is especially promising in view of its strong ownership and leadership by the countries themselves, and its use of self-assessment and peer review mechanisms. Governance is also an area where private think tanks and civil society are active. Their measures provide a useful supplement to those developed by official entities.

Future assessments of governance will benefit from an increased emphasis on the need to ground governance measures as much as possible in objective, quantifiable indicators.[17] Nonetheless, qualitative assessment will remain an inevitable element of these measures, given the difficulty of quantifying behavioral aspects of governance. There is also an increasing use of citizen surveys, which would complement—and provide a check against—assessments based on expert opinion.

Another area of emphasis in the future work on public sector governance is the development of better information at the subnational level of governance. In an effort to improve service delivery at the local level, many governments in developing countries are devolving more responsibilities to local governments. Effective public resource management and adequate institutional capacities at the local level will become increasingly important to development effectiveness and to the effort to achieve the MDGs. Monitoring at the subnational level is at present hampered by major data gaps relating to subnational finances and administrative arrangements. Filling these gaps should receive more attention in the work ahead.

Notes

1. Mauro 1995; Knack and Keefer 1995; Evans and Rauch 1999; IMF 2003. Knack and Keefer found that each 10-point increase in a 50-point index of the quality of governance was associated with a 1-percentage-point increase in growth of per capita income. The Spring 2003 IMF *World Economic Outlook* found that an improvement in Sub-Saharan Africa's level of institutional development from its current average to the mean of developing Asia would imply an 80 percent increase in the region's per capita income.

2. Dollar and Kraay 2002; Bruno, Ravallion, and Squire 1998. Pritchett and Summers (1996) showed that each 10 percent increase in income reduces infant and child mortality in developing countries by between 2 and 4 percent.

3. Kaufmann, Kraay, and Zoido-Lobaton (1999) showed that countries with better governance—as measured by measures of corruption, voice, and accountability—have lower infant mortality and higher literacy rates. They found that an improvement of 1 standard deviation in the quality of governance produces an increase of 15 to 25 percentage points in literacy. Much of this effect is indirect,

through the impact of governance on income levels; but part of it is attributable to the direct effect of better governance on more accountable and effective delivery of public services. The quality of governance has also been linked to volatility in income growth (IMF 2003), which can affect service delivery quality by increasing the unpredictability of both revenues and demand for services.

4. World Bank 2003.

5. World Bank 2003.

6. The Public Expenditure and Financial Accountability Program was established in 2001. PEFA is a partnership of U.K. Department for International Development, the European Commission, France, Norway, SECO (Switzerland), the Strategic Partnership with Africa, and the IMF and World Bank. PEFA supports integrated and harmonized approaches to assessment and reform of public expenditure, procurement, and financial accountability systems. See http://www.pefa.org. PEFA cooperates with the OECD-DAC Joint Venture on Public Financial Management, for which the establishment of a means to monitor public financial management performance in partner countries is a priority objective.

7. IMF–World Bank 2003.

8. OECD 1994; Tanzi and Zee 2000.

9. World Health Organization 2002.

10. Not all data sources, however, show the same large improvements in Europe and Central Asia as shown by the CPIA and BEEPS.

11. The advantage of aggregating indicators from different sources is that it reduces the impact of measurement error in any single source, producing more accurate comparisons at a point in time. However, index values for each country are defined relative to the mean for all countries in a given year, so the indexes are not designed to track change over time on an absolute scale (Kaufmann, Kraay, and Mastruzzi 2003).

12. The benefit of disaggregated indexes comes at the potential cost of increased measurement error, which results from relying on a smaller number of sources. However, because the purpose here is to describe the performance of large groups of countries, errors in measuring the performance of individual countries are of less relevance.

13. Freedom House assigns a rating of 1 for countries with the most civil liberties and 7 for those with the least. For figure 5.2, the index was reversed so that higher values indicate more civil liberties.

14. These data are from the Database on Political Institutions (Beck and others 2000). The 75 percent threshold used is meant to capture competitive elections with candidates from multiple parties; a greater than 75 percent vote share often is associated with questions about the fairness of the election.

15. Fifteen Institutional and Governance Reviews were completed during 2001–03, and a similar number is planned for 2004. More information on the IGRs is available at: http://www.worldbank.org/prem/PREMNotes/premnote 75.pdf.

16. The Governance and Anti-Corruption Surveys cover citizens, firms, and public officials, and are used to diagnose areas of particular strengths and weaknesses in governance, such as the incidence of corruption across government agencies or public services. Surveys have been completed or are under way in 25 countries, about half of them in Europe and Central Asia.

17. These are sometimes referred to as "second generation governance indicators." See Knack, Kugler, and Manning 2003.

6

Strengthening Infrastructure

Infrastructure plays a dual role in the effort to achieve the MDGs. It is an important element of the enabling environment for economic growth—energy to power industry, transport to support commerce. Reducing poverty by promoting growth is one channel through which infrastructure contributes to the achievement of the MDGs. But the availability of reliable and affordable infrastructure also contributes more directly to the attainment of the MDGs by providing or supporting the delivery of key services. Some MDGs relate to particular infrastructure services, such as those that aim to reduce the proportion of people without sustainable access to safe drinking water and basic sanitation, and to make housing and shelter more accessible. The MDGs related to human development (education, health, empowerment of women) rely on services whose effective delivery depends greatly on supportive infrastructure: improved water and sanitation to prevent disease and free up women's time from daily chores; electricity to serve schools and health clinics; and roads to access them.

But there are large gaps in the availability and quality of the key infrastructure services in developing countries. Although particularly great in low-income developing countries, those gaps remain sizable in most middle-income countries. Within countries, coverage rates are typically much lower in rural areas, where the majority of the poor population lives; but coverage in urban areas also is under pressure from rapid rural-to-urban migration in many countries.

Narrowing gaps in access and quality will require sizable increases in investment and in associated spending on operation and maintenance (O&M). Efforts must continue to improve the enabling environment for private investment, which has increased but not as much as expected. At the same time, public investment in infrastructure will need to reverse the decline of the past decade. This will require stronger domestic resource mobilization, as well as increased foreign assistance.

Increased investment alone, however, is not the answer. Investment must be underpinned by improvements in policy and governance to ensure effectiveness and sustainability. Many countries have made progress in this respect by implementing policy and regulatory reform. Progress has been uneven across regions and income groups. Africa and low-income countries have tended to lag behind other groups, although not on all dimensions. Progress has also been uneven across sectors. In general, telecommunications is well ahead of the curve; electricity, transport, and housing are at intermediate stages of reform; and water and sanitation lag behind.

Assessment of policies and needs in infrastructure is seriously constrained by gaps in data. A better information base is needed, not only for effective monitoring but also to inform policymaking. Filling the data gaps should be a priority area for donor support.

Infrastructure and the Millennium Development Goals

A growing body of evidence, across and within countries, supports the importance of infrastructure in facilitating growth, reducing poverty, and achieving related development goals.[1] In a sample of 102 studies conducted over the last 15 years, few report a negative effect of infrastructure investment on productivity or growth (table 6.1). The sample includes 30 multicountry studies (including developing countries); 41 studies on the United States; 19 on Spain; and 12 on specific developing countries (Argentina, Brazil, Colombia, India, and the Philippines).

Studies of the United States and of multiple countries offer mixed results: the effect of infrastructure investment does not appear to be significant in about half of the cases. The results for the United States reflect the effects of differences in infrastructure endowments in a mature economy. Findings of negative effects often can be explained by saturation of some types of infrastructure or by negative externalities. For example, a new transport project in a specific state may facilitate an exodus of workers or industries from other states, hence slowing down growth in those states. Similar conclusions emerge from the cross-country data sets.

TABLE 6.1 Distribution of studies according to their findings on impact of infrastructure investment on productivity or growth

		Percent of studies showing		
Country/group	Number of studies	Positive effect	No significant effect	Negative effect
Multiple countries	30	40	50	10
United States	41	41	54	5
Spain	19	74	26	0
Developing countries	12	100	0	0
Total	102	53	42	5

Source: De la Fuente and Estache 2004.

The studies of Spain make a much stronger case for investment in infrastructure. In the Spanish context, infrastructure has generally been found to be a major determinant of growth and productivity convergence across regions. Studies of developing countries confirm the role of infrastructure in reducing disparities between rich and poor regions. Research on Argentina, Brazil, Colombia, India, and the Philippines demonstrates the significant impact on growth and productivity of various types of infrastructure. Taken jointly, the results suggest that the returns on investment in infrastructure are probably high in the early stages of development, when infrastructure is scarce and basic networks have not been completed. Returns on infrastructure investment tend to fall, sometimes sharply, as economies reach maturity.

Measuring the elasticity of output to improvements in infrastructure quantity or quality gives a more concrete sense of the potential impact of infrastructure investment and associated policies. Depending on the sector, country (or country groups), and the period covered, the elasticity estimates range from 0.14 to 1.12, but the lower bound is not as small as it may seem. Consider the case of Latin America. In the 1990s, the elasticities estimated for that region imply that a 10 percent increase in infrastructure stocks would have enabled an increase of 1.4 to 1.6 percent in output—quite significant, since a rise of 1 percentage point in per capita income would reduce the share of people living in poverty by half a percentage point.[2] Another recent study of Latin America estimated that lack of investment in infrastructure during the 1990s reduced long-term growth by 1 to 3 percentage points, depending on the country.[3] This assessment suggests that infrastructure insufficiencies account for about one-third of the difference in output per worker between Latin America and East Asia.

The story for Africa is similar. One of the most extensive multicountry studies suggests that if Africa had enjoyed growth rates in telecommunications and power generation infrastructure comparable to those observed in East Asia in the 1980s and 1990s, its annual growth rate would have been about 1.3 percent higher.[4] The authors' overall conclusion is that for developing and transition economies, the quantity and quality of infrastructure are critical components of the growth equation, even if the relative importance of each subsector may vary by country and over time.

A more limited body of literature looks at the direct impact of improvements in infrastructure on the poor. Datt and Ravallion found that rural poverty rankings of Indian states in 1990 were very different from those of 1960.[5] States starting with better infrastructure and human resources saw significantly higher long-term rates of poverty reduction. Deininger and Okidi obtained similar results in exploring factors underlying growth and poverty reduction in Uganda during the 1990s.[6] In their work, the importance of improving access to basic education and health care emerges clearly, but benefits also depend on complementary investments in electricity and other infrastructure. A study by Fan, Zhang, and Zhang documents the critical role of infrastructure development, particularly roads and telecommunications, in reducing rural poverty in China between 1978 and 1997.[7] The authors show that the reduction in poverty is due to growth in rural nonfarm employment following expansion of infrastructure.

Access to infrastructure can have little effect, however, if the service is not affordable.[8] Governments must bear this in mind when setting tariffs, particularly in cases where average tariffs must cover average costs to support private sector participation. Two main solutions are being pursued. A large body of experience across regions—particularly with water supply and sanitation, rural electrification, and secondary roads—demonstrates the effectiveness of offering households (and businesses) a range of service levels at a range of costs, allowing them to choose according to their preferences and ability to pay.[9] A second solution is to design tariff structures that include an explicit, well-targeted subsidy to ensure that the share of their income users spend on infrastructure services stays within reasonable boundaries. A common rule of thumb is that expenditures on utilities and transport should not exceed 15 percent of a poor individual's income.[10]

Other recent research emphasizes the importance of core infrastructure inputs for the achievement of the MDGs. Leipziger, Fay, and Yepes, for example, estimated from a sample of 43 countries that differences in access to water explained about a quarter of the difference in infant mortality between the poorest and richest quintiles and 37 percent of the difference in child mortality. Similarly, the difference in access to sanitation accounts for 20 percent and 10 percent, respectively, of the difference between the poorest and richest quintiles in the prevalence of malnutrition. In rural India, Jalan and Ravallion found that the prevalence and duration of diarrhea among children under five were significantly lower on average for families with piped water than for those without it.[11]

Supply Gaps and Policies in Infrastructure Services: The Current Picture

The preceding section gave a sense of the implicit demand for infrastructure; this section provides an assessment of supply. The monetary value of the world's infrastructure stock, at best-practice average prices and excluding housing, is approximately $15 trillion.[12] Of the total, about 60 percent is found in high-income countries (16 percent of total population), 28 percent in middle-income countries (45 percent of total population), and 13 percent in low-income countries (39 percent of total population). Electricity and roads account for about 80 percent of the total asset value.

The assessment of the current status of infrastructure services in developing countries in terms of access to and quality of services and progress on sector policy reform is constrained by major gaps in data. Indeed, obtaining better infrastructure data should be among donors' priorities for improving developing-country data. The World Bank, in collaboration with partner agencies in the United Nations system and elsewhere, has initiated an infrastructure indicators project that aims to develop a more systematic database of core infrastructure indicators.[13] The most serious data gaps are found in the transport sector, where the poorest spend half of the resources they allocate to public services. For lack of an appropriate international database, it is not possible to monitor access rates to transport services on a regular basis.

Access to Infrastructure Services

City dwellers in low-income countries have far less access to infrastructure services of all types than do urban residents of middle-income countries (table 6.2). This means that any effort to catch up will require major investments. Rural populations, which make up more than 60 percent of the population of low- and middle-income countries, have significantly lower rates of access than do urban populations—roughly 30 percent lower (table 6.2). The discrepancy does not mean that investment requirements are significantly larger for rural areas than for urban areas, however, because costs are lower in rural areas.

Similar differences can be seen in access to housing. The percentages of the population with authorized housing are 36, 73, and 91 for low-, lower-middle-, and upper-middle-income countries, respectively.[14] Behind these overall figures lie major disparities within countries between low-income slums and better-off areas. For example, whereas 33 percent of households in Mysore, India, have water connections, only 8 percent of those in informal settlements do. The result of such disparities is evident in health outcomes: whereas the under-five mortality rate in urban Kenya averages 84 (and 62 in Nairobi), in the two largest slums it averages 187 (Kibera) and 254 (Embakasi).[15]

Quality of Infrastructure Services

Although data on access are more meaningful when combined with data on service quality, most current access data are not "quality

TABLE 6.2 Access of population to infrastructure services

Country income category	Electricity (1997–2001)[a]	Water (2000)[a]	Sanitation (2000)[a]	Telecoms (1999–2002)[b]	Transport (1994–2001)[c]
			Urban		
Low	62.4 (24)	76.9 (56)	74.6 (55)	4.6 (65)	90 (7)
Lower middle	95.1 (8)	90.8 (40)	90.5 (37)	22.0 (52)	—
Upper middle	—	92.3 (23)	92.5 (22)	53.9 (36)	—
			Rural		
Low	20.3 (24)	52.7 (54)	41.8 (52)	1.7 (55)	61 (21)
Lower middle	67.3 (8)	75.0 (40)	59.8 (37)	8.7 (43)	—
Upper middle	—	76.4 (23)	81.3 (22)	22.5 (24)	—

— Not available.

Note: Figures in parentheses indicate the number of countries for which data are available.

a. Percent of population

b. For urban populations: telephone subscribers per 100 people; for rural populations: main lines per 100 people

c. For urban populations: percent of population within 20 minutes of public transport; for rural populations: percent of population within 2 km of an all-season road

Source: USAID, Demographic and Health Surveys; World Bank, *World Development Indicators*, various years; International Telecommunications Union; Roberts 2003.

adjusted." Access data usually include individuals with all-day access, as well as individuals with access for just a few hours a day. But quality matters. A recent study covering seven Latin American countries suggests that the effectiveness of public infrastructure in that region is only about 74 percent of that in industrialized countries because of poor quality.[16] According to the same study, the long-run cost of this underperformance is equivalent to about 40 percent of real GDP per capita. Raising infrastructure effectiveness to industrialized-country levels would reduce the per capita income difference between Latin America and the United States from tenfold to about sevenfold.

Despite growing recognition of the economic and social significance of service quality, there is currently no indicator of the combined dimensions of quality. So in the short run, the only option is to rely on partial indicators. In some cases, for example, quality must be inferred from associated health indicators. While this is clearly not satisfactory, analysis based on partial indicators provides a global sense, for each sector and each country group, of the importance of objective quality indicators.

The amount of information available on *technical quality* varies widely across sectors (table 6.3). Reasonable technical indicators are widely available for electricity and telecommunications. The usual approximation for transport, the ratio of paved roads to total roads, is useful, but it may be somewhat misleading, since paving roads is not necessarily a priority for the poorest countries. Most worrisome is the water supply and sanitation sector, which does not systematically generate indicators such as water losses, number of hours of service per day, water quality, or volume and quality of treated sewage.

The available data suggest that the correlation between income levels and technical quality is extremely high. The main practical consequence of that correlation is that the difference in investment requirements across income groups is probably much more significant than the access data alone would suggest. Not only must access be improved, but major rehabilitation efforts and capacity building are probably also needed to address weak technical performance.

With new investment, policy changes are required to ensure that service quality is improved and maintained at a reasonable level—and that assets are effectively operated and systematically maintained. Preventive maintenance translates into lower operating costs, reduced adverse external impacts, and

TABLE 6.3 Technical quality of infrastructure services

	Electricity	Water	Telecoms	Transport	Housing
Country income category	Transmission and distribution losses as percent of total output (1999)	Percentage of urban households with water access that get water from piped or well water source (1997–2001)	Reported phone faults per 100 main lines (1997–2000)	Percentage of total roads paved (1997–2000)	Permanent structures: percentage of structures built to last 20 years (1994–2000)
Low	24.1 (33)	89.4 (48)	77 (48)	28.6 (59)	76
Lower middle	16.2 (31)	84.5 (18)	42.9 (38)	46.9 (46)	94
Upper middle	13.6 (23)	—	25.3 (27)	55.1 (33)	97
Best practice in OECD	8–12	100	<5	>80	100

— Not available.
Note: Figures in parentheses indicate the number of countries for which data are available. No information was available on sanitation as measured by volume and quality of treated wastewater.
Source: USAID, Demographic and Health Surveys; World Bank, *World Development Indicators*; International Telecommunications Union. Housing estimates are from Angel 2000.

TABLE 6.4 Quality of infrastructure services as perceived by commercial users (ratings scaled 1 to 7, with 7 indicating highest quality)

	Quality of delivered services		Quality of water pollution regulation	Quality of telephone infrastructure	Quality of delivered services			
Country income category	Electricity (2001–02)	Water (2001–02)	Sanitation (2001–02)	Telecoms (2001–02)	Roads (2000)	Railroads (2001–02)	Ports (2001–02)	Airports (2001–02)
Low	2.6 (9)	4.0 (27)	2.3 (9)	3.4 (9)	3.4 (27)	2.7 (9)	2.6 (9)	3.6 (9)
Lower middle	4.2 (25)	4.8 (24)	3.1 (25)	4.9 (25)	4.2 (24)	2.6 (25)	3.5 (25)	4.2 (25)
Upper middle	5.1 (20)	5.0 (18)	4.0 (20)	5.6 (20)	4.1 (18)	2.9 (26)	3.8 (20)	4.5 (20)

Note: Figures in parentheses indicate the number of countries for which data are available.
Source: World Economic Forum 2003; World Bank 2000.

extended asset life—savings that are generally underestimated when maintenance budgets are cut to meet specific fiscal targets.

Available data on the *perceived quality* of infrastructure services reflect commercial and industrial perspectives (table 6.4). There is no systematic effort to collect comparable data from residential users—a clear information gap.

The available evidence suggests three conclusions:

- Perceived quality is higher in all sectors in countries with higher income levels, except for roads.
- Even for upper-middle-income countries, perceived quality is lower than best practice.
- In all country groups, the water sector is perceived by commercial users to be the most effective. The favorable perception of the water sector illustrates the bias introduced by the use of indicators collected from the business community. Water is not a major issue for many businesses, many of which have their own water supplies and do not depend on urban utilities for their supply.

Progress on Policy Reform

Reliable data on infrastructure policies are no easier to come by than data on infrastructure outcomes. A review of available indicators, however, shows that the policy and regulatory environment for infrastructure has been improving—although much remains to be done. The picture varies appreciably across regions, countries, and sectors.

A 1998 scorecard on the electricity sector in 115 countries consisted of questions on commercialization, restructuring, regulation, legal reform, and private investment in the sector.[17] At the time, less than half the steps identified as necessary for fully effective reform had been taken in the energy sectors of the countries studied. Reforms have progressed significantly since then, as the forthcoming update of the scorecard is expected to show. Updated results on the scorecard indicators are available for a selected number of low-income countries (table 6.5). Expert respondents in each sampled country were asked whether a variety of reforms had been completed and to grade reforms in progress on a scale of 1 to 5 (from low to high progress). All but one of the countries in the sample have a new electricity law; all but three have or will soon have an independent regulator. Progress on corporatization and restructuring is less uniform. Even more disparate is the presence of the private sector, except perhaps in the form of independent power producers (IPPs) in the generation subsector.

A survey of urban water issues showed that 65 percent of countries had achieved a

TABLE 6.5 Electricity reform in selected countries, 2003

Country	Commercialized/ corporatized	Law	Independent regulator	IPPs	Restructured[a]	Private generation	Private distribution
Albania	Y	Y	Y	N	IP-1	N	N
Bangladesh	Y	Y	IP-4	Y	IP-2	N	N
Benin	N	Y	N	N	Y	N	N
Bolivia	Y	Y	Y	Y	Y	Y	IP-4
Burkina Faso	N	Y	N	N	N	N	N
Ethiopia	IP-3	Y	Y	N	N	N	N
Honduras	N	Y	Y	Y	N	N	N
India[b]	N	Y	Y	Y	Y	N	N
Indonesia	Y[c]	Y	IP-4	Y	Y	Y	N
Kyrgyz Republic	Y	Y	Y	Y	Y	N[d]	N
Madagascar	IP-4[e]	Y	IP-5	Y	N	N	N
Mali	N	Y	Y	IP-1	IP-4	Y	Y
Mauritania	N	Y	Y	N	N	N	N
Mozambique	Y	Y	IP-2	Y	IP-2	N	IP-1
Pakistan	Y	Y	Y	Y	Y	IP-3	IP-3
Tanzania	IP-4	IP-3	IP-4	Y	IP-3	N	IP-4
Uganda	Y	Y	Y	Y	Y	Y	IP-4
Vietnam	Y	N	N	Y	IP-3	N	N

Note: Y and N stand for yes and no, respectively, to the question about whether significant reform has been completed. Reforms in progress are indicated by IP, where IP-1 indicates an early stage of implementation and IP-5 indicates that implementation is nearing completion.
a. A state-owned utility is deemed to have been restructured if it has successfully completed accounting separation.
b. Some of India's states have done much more than others.
c. The state utility, PLN, is a limited liability company.
d. The government does not intend to privatize existing strategic generation assets but is seeking private investment in small hydro schemes.
e. Moving toward a management contract.
Source: World Bank, Infrastructure Vice Presidency.

degree of separation between operator and government, whereas only 17 percent had a functioning regulatory body in place.[18] An increasing number of countries were using more appropriate policies, governance, and management arrangements. But the challenge remains formidable, especially in low-income countries. Out of a maximum score of 7, low-income countries averaged 1.8, compared to 3.1 for lower-middle-income countries and 3.9 for upper-middle-income countries. These results show that although progress has been made in the past decade, most countries have a long way to go in establishing an environment that will stimulate increased investment.

According to the International Telecommunications Union, by the end of 2002 more than half the countries of the world had fully or partly privatized their telecommunication operators. A further quarter (24 percent) of countries—although retaining state-owned incumbents—had introduced private sector participation through licensing of new fixed, international, or mobile operators. Today, fewer than one-fifth of countries have no form of private participation in their telecommunications sector. Most are low-income countries.

The introduction of competition has been uneven, with a majority of countries retaining monopolies in fixed-line services such as local and long-distance telephony. An overwhelming majority of countries, however, now allow competition in the mobile and Internet access markets. International long-distance market competition also grew dramatically throughout the 1990s. By mid-2003, 73 countries were allowing users a choice of more than one facility-based operator for international telephone calls—up from just 8 countries in 1992.

There has been progress in regulation as well. The number of telecommunications regulatory agencies has increased dramatically over the last decade. In 1990, only 12 countries had regulatory agencies that functioned separately from telecom operators. The number had increased to 123 by mid-2003. A further 28 countries have indicated their intention to establish a separate regulator in the coming years. In Latin America and Sub-Saharan Africa, more than three-quarters of countries have regulatory agencies. South Asia and Europe and Central Asia follow closely with more than 60 percent. The East Asia and Pacific Region remains behind, with only 18 percent of countries having a separate regulator.[19]

The Agenda Ahead

Addressing the large gaps in access and quality identified in the preceding section will require action across a broad front. Substantial new investment will be needed. But that is only part of the challenge. Policy and governance regimes must continue to improve, building on past gains, to ensure that new investments translate into improved infrastructure services for underserved segments of the population and economy.

Gauging the Need for New Investment

Estimating the amount of investment needed to fill gaps in access and quality is difficult. The estimate should reflect the needs of both the household sector and businesses—in agriculture, commerce, and industry. This means that requirements need to be related to the broad growth prospects of the economy. One set of estimates developed on this basis shows that the investment requirements are large. For the first decade of the new millennium, preliminary estimates of new investment needs vary from a high of 3.2 percent of GDP for low-income countries to a low of 0.4 percent of GDP for upper-middle-income countries, with an average of 2.7 percent for all developing countries.[20]

Operation and maintenance requirements follow a similar pattern. Total resources needed, for both investment and maintenance, are estimated at roughly 6.9 percent of GDP in low-income countries and 5.1 percent in lower-middle-income countries, with an average of about 5.5 percent of GDP for all developing countries (table 6.6). In terms of sectoral allocation, three sectors (electricity, telecommunications, and roads) account for four-fifths of the total new investment.

The needed investments and maintenance expenditures amount to roughly $465 billion a year for the years between 2005 and 2010. Most are related to telecommunications (about $185 billion), followed by power generation (about $140 billion), roads (about $90 billion), and water and sanitation (about $30 billion).

The numbers presented in table 6.6 underestimate the actual investment requirements because they do not take into account the needs in transmission and distribution.

TABLE 6.6 Expected annual needs for new investment and maintenance in infrastructure, 2005–10

	New investment		Maintenance		Total	
Country income category	Billions of dollars	Percent of GDP	Billions of dollars	Percent of GDP	Billions of dollars	Percent of GDP
Low	50.0	3.18	58.6	3.73	108.6	6.92
Lower middle	183.2	2.64	173.0	2.50	356.2	5.14
Upper middle	136.0	0.42	248.0	0.76	384.0	1.18
All developing countries	233.1	2.74	231.7	2.73	464.8	5.47

Note: These estimates exclude the needs in electricity transmission and distribution as well as in ports and airports.
Source: World Bank staff estimates.

Including these two business lines could roughly double the estimates of the needs for energy and add, for low-income countries, up to 3 percent of GDP to the estimates of the investment needs in the table. Another exclusion from these estimates is investment in ports and airports. However, as these types of infrastructure represent a relatively small proportion of the total, it is unlikely that including them would change the estimates greatly, especially for poor countries.[21]

While there are no formal international statistics on past investment levels in infrastructure, investment estimates can be generated from past changes in stocks. Five-year averages of past investment levels can be very roughly approximated by pricing changes in stocks (at a constant price). Doing so yields a monetary value that can then be normalized to GDP.[22] Such a rough approximation based on the evolution of stocks suggests that investments in the past 5 to 10 years were about 4 percent of GDP in low-income countries, 2.9 percent in lower-middle-income countries, and 2.6 percent in upper-middle-income countries—a decline of 2 to 4 percentage points from previous decades.[23]

Comparing the past investment and O&M rates to the projected requirements, and allowing for efficiency improvements, the gap could be 3.5 to 5 percent of GDP for low-income countries and 2.5 to 4 percent for lower-middle-income countries (figure 6.1). The gap is likely to be less than 0.5 percent of GDP for upper-middle-income countries—most of it ascribable to O&M and major rehabilitation. This suggests that sizable increases in investment from recent levels are needed. In water and sanitation, for example, investment would need to double from historical levels.

Traditionally, most investment in infrastructure has been publicly funded. According to a recent estimate, 70 percent of all infrastructure spending in developing countries in the 1990s was financed by governments or public utilities' own resources. The private sector contributed 20 to 25 percent, while official development assistance financed 5 to 10 percent.[24] These proportions of course vary across sectors, with telecommunications, for example, attracting more private investment and relying less on official assistance than water and sanitation.

Private sector commitments to infrastructure in developing countries during the 1990s amounted to some $805 billion (table 6.7). The bulk of investments went into energy and telecommunications in Latin America, East Asia, and, to a lesser extent, Eastern Europe. The commitments increased sharply during the 1990s before declining rapidly after 1997, affected by the series of major crises starting in East Asia and ending in Argentina in 2001. Indeed, as uncertainty grew in emerging markets, the cost of capital shot past the point where most new projects could generate adequate rates of return. In 2002, private investments totaled $46.7 billion, the lowest level of investment since 1994.

During the 1990s the public sector in many developing economies reduced its participation

FIGURE 6.1 Gaps in infrastructure call for significantly increased spending, which must be managed well for effectiveness
Annual spending on infrastructure services, actual vs. needed

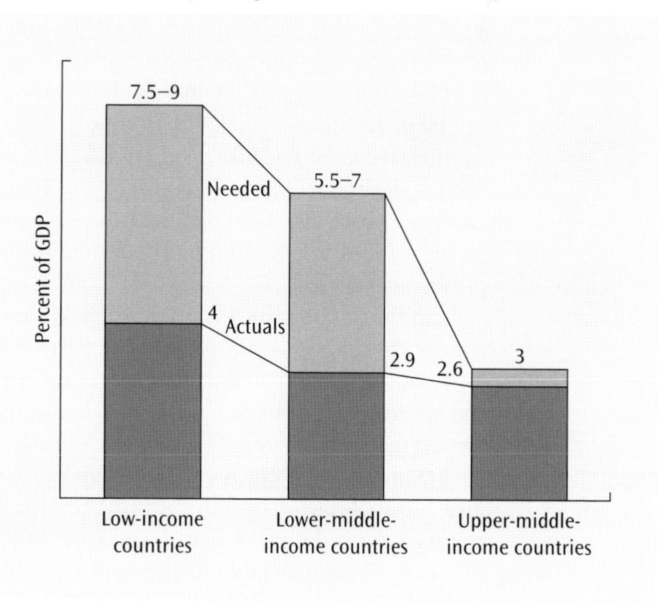

Note: Actual = levels in the 1990s. Needed = estimated requirements for 2005–10. Annual spending includes investment plus spending on operations and maintenance.
Source: World Bank staff estimates (work in progress).

TABLE 6.7 Private commitments for infrastructure, 1990–2002 (US$ billions)

Region	Telecoms	Electricity	Natural gas	Airports	Railways	Seaports	Toll roads	W & S	Total
East Asia and Pacific	56.2	68.3	6.8	2.8	10.3	10.3	26.8	17.0	198.4
Europe and Central Asia	68.1	21.1	11.3	1.5	0.3	0.7	2.6	3.5	109.0
Latin America and Caribbean	182.9	100.4	19.5	7.5	18.3	6.9	40.6	21.3	397.4
Middle East and North Africa	10.6	8.4	3.9	0.9	0.2	1.2	—	1.3	26.5
South Asia	19.7	22.6	0.2	0.2	—	2.1	0.8	0.2	45.8
Sub-Saharan Africa	18.5	5.0	1.3	0.4	0.3	0.1	2.0	0.2	27.8
Total	355.9	225.7	43.0	13.2	29.4	21.2	72.8	43.6	804.9

— Not available.
Source: World Bank, Private Participation in Infrastructure Database.

in infrastructure. This unexpected development was the result of anticipated increases in private sector participation and fiscal adjustment programs. There is growing evidence that fiscal retrenchment usually leads to a disproportionate reduction in public capital expenditures, particularly in infrastructure. Easterly and Servén found that during the 1990s, reductions in public infrastructure investment in Latin America made up a sizable share of fiscal adjustment in the region—ranging from 31.5 percent in Mexico to 174.3 percent in Brazil.[25] But the problem is more generalized. In India, total investment in infrastructure was 5.4 percent of GDP in 1990, including 4 percent of public sector money. By 1998, total investment in infrastructure had dropped to 4.6 percent, with a decline in public investment of 1 percentage point of GDP. Private investment increased, but not enough to offset the drop in public investment.

That most urban infrastructure (secondary roads, drainage, sanitation) is the responsibility of local governments has contributed to the decline in public investment. Local governments are increasingly dependent on local taxation since, with fiscal decentralization and consolidation, many countries have reduced central government fiscal transfers.

Evidence suggests that changes in ODA also may have contributed to the decline. For example, the level of commitment to infrastructure of the multilateral development banks has declined since 1995, reaching a low of $13.5 billion in 1999 before rebounding to $16 billion in 2002. Even at their peak, commitments were small in relation to needs.

The Conditions for Increased Investment

If developing countries are to reach investment levels consistent with their needs in a context of fiscal constraints and limited private investment, external assistance to infrastructure will need to increase. This is particularly true for low-income countries, but foreign assistance plays an important catalytic role in middle-income countries as well. The impact of aid can be enhanced through reallocations that reflect the relative effectiveness of the various forms and uses of support. Moreover, with innovation and coordination efforts across the development community, ODA could be used to better leverage private and local public resources. Better coordination between bilateral and multilateral donors would help maximize leverage of funding from all sources, including the private sector.

The use of resources, both foreign and domestic, needs to be guided by clear priorities at the country level. Access and quality deficiencies are typically much more serious in rural areas, implying the need for a special focus on the needs of rural and underserved areas. At the same time, the rapid increase in urbanization will require attention to the infrastructure needs of the migrating population. Better planning of investment in infrastructure networks (secondary roads, sanitation, drainage) and protection of green spaces can help ensure economic, social, and environmental sustainability in the context of urban expansion.

Cutting across the various infrastructure sectors is the need to emphasize quality and to make adequate provisions for O&M in the allocation of resources. It is not uncommon to find underinvestment in O&M because the incentive structure is such that it is easier to raise resources to finance new investment or major rehabilitation than to design tariffs to recover O&M expenses. Such a bias in incentives must be corrected, as the impact and productivity of investment depend crucially on its quality and upkeep.

Affordability is a key determinant of the effective access of the poor to infrastructure services. It is important to consider the extent to which the pricing of services and the quality options offered to consumers are consistent with ability to pay. Without affordability, expanded access is of only limited use to the poorest. As illustrated in the recent debate on public utilities in Argentina, the many indirect taxes levied on infrastructure services, many of which are regressive, must be documented. While such taxes may reflect fiscal concerns, governments need to recognize that they may thwart the desired improvement in the poor's access to public services.

Institutional capacity building is a key cross-cutting element of the reform agenda. The problems of quality deficiencies, the declining interest of potential private investors, misallocations of resources, and excessive costs observed in many countries often can be traced to insufficient institutional capacity. Capacity constraints can be especially acute at the local level. With urban growth and fiscal decentralization, public sector responsibilities for infrastructure planning, financing, and management are increasingly falling to local governments, many of which lack the requisite capacity. Effective delivery of infrastructure services at the local level calls for adequate intergovernmental arrangements for sharing the investment costs of local public-good infrastructure, enhanced resource mobilization by local governments, and stronger efforts at local capacity building.

Increased private sector participation in infrastructure requires an adequate regulatory framework, including competent regulatory agencies. Such agencies now exist in many countries but often lack adequate capacity. Coordinated efforts by governments and donors to provide the necessary technical assistance for capacity building would have a high payoff. Governments and donors can also bring pressure to bear on the private sector to contribute to the effort to improve governance—for example, by adopting a code of ethics to commit to due process in regulatory interactions. Increasing the transparency of decisionmaking processes can minimize the risk of corruption.

To better assess and monitor infrastructure needs and policies along these and related dimensions, the availability of information will need to improve markedly. The monitoring of service quality, affordability, fiscal cost, and governance quality is handicapped by major information gaps, and data are lacking even on basic access to some key infrastructure, especially transport. The international community should commit to supporting a systematic effort to develop a better information base, including statistical capacity building in developing countries.

Countries, supported by their development partners, are responding to these challenges. Declining public investment in infrastructure and overoptimistic expectations of private sector participation, combined with growing appreciation of infrastructure as a foundation for achievement of the MDGs, have forced the international development community to begin reassessing its priorities. At the World Bank, this reassessment has resulted in the Infrastructure Action Plan (IAP).[26] The IAP is designed to respond to client-country demand for infrastructure with a broad menu of options for public and private infrastructure

BOX 6.1 Water supply and sanitation in the MDGs

The MDG for water supply and sanitation aims to halve by 2015 the proportion of people who lack access to safe drinking water and adequate sanitation. Currently, one in five people in the developing world lacks access to clean water; one in two has inadequate sanitation. For four out of five—4 billion people—wastewater disposal is inadequate. Every day, 25,000 people die from diseases associated with poor water supply, sanitation, and hygiene. Morbidity is even higher.[a]

Improving water supply and sanitation is known to reduce child mortality and protect health, while promoting gender equality, educational opportunity, and environmental sustainability. Yet at current rates of service expansion, only about 20 percent of countries are on track to meet the goal, and fewer than 10 percent of the low-income countries are on track. The actual number may well be lower, due to huge gaps in data on access.

To meet the goal, about 1.5 billion people (1 billion in urban areas, and 0.5 billion in rural areas) will have to be provided with sustainable access to safe water, and about 2 billion to basic sanitation (1.1 billion in urban areas and 0.9 billion in rural areas). Various analyses suggest that investment will need to double, from $15 billion to $30 billion annually.[b] Existing assets must be properly operated and maintained, and new investments will have to be efficient. Additional investment will be needed for wastewater treatment, rehabilitation of existing infrastructure, and infrastructure for water storage and conveyance to deal with urbanization and growing climatic variability.

The bulk of the financing needed will have to come from the public sector and official external assistance, even if efforts succeed in mobilizing increased private participation in the sector. In the past decade, 43 percent of the funding for water supply and sanitation came from government budgets and about 28 percent from external assistance. Another 17 percent was funded by small-scale providers, communities, and households. Internal cash generation from utilities provided only 7 percent, in part reflecting inappropriate pricing policies. The international private sector contributed 5 percent.[c]

Focusing solely on investment will not generate sustainable service improvements, however, as the experience of the International Drinking Water Decade has shown. Success in achieving the millennium goal requires a combination of sound policies, improved governance, capable institutions, increased investment and financing, and more effective financing modalities.

A rapid water sector survey carried out in 2002 showed that while 65 percent of the countries had achieved a degree of separation between operator and government, only 17 percent had a functioning regulatory body in place. And 13 percent of the countries still had to embark on any form of urban sector reform.[d] A recent survey of 246 water utilities in 51 countries showed that overall quality was unacceptable, although with significant exceptions.[e] That 25 percent of the operators were performing well shows that efficient service delivery is possible where sound policies and governance are in place.

Access to water and sanitation by region, 2000

	Percentage of population with access					
	To improved water supply			To improved sanitation		
Region	Urban	Rural	Total	Urban	Rural	Total
East Asia and Pacific	93	67	76	73	35	48
Europe and Central Asia	95	82	91	97	81	91
Latin America and Caribbean	94	66	86	86	52	77
Middle East and North Africa	95	77	87	93	70	83
South Asia	94	80	85	67	22	34
Sub-Saharan Africa	83	44	57	73	43	53
Developing countries	95	71	82	77	35	52
Least developed countries	82	55	62	71	35	44

Source: JMP 2000.

An increasing number of countries are now using more appropriate policies and institutional arrangements, but the challenge ahead is still formidable, especially in low-income countries. Effectively managing existing assets and sizable new investments will require stronger efforts at policy reform and institutional upgrading, supported by increased international assistance. A broad consensus on the main elements of the policy agenda at the country level, and of international support, is beginning to emerge. These are:

Investment in water and sanitation will need to double
Historical and required MDG investment levels

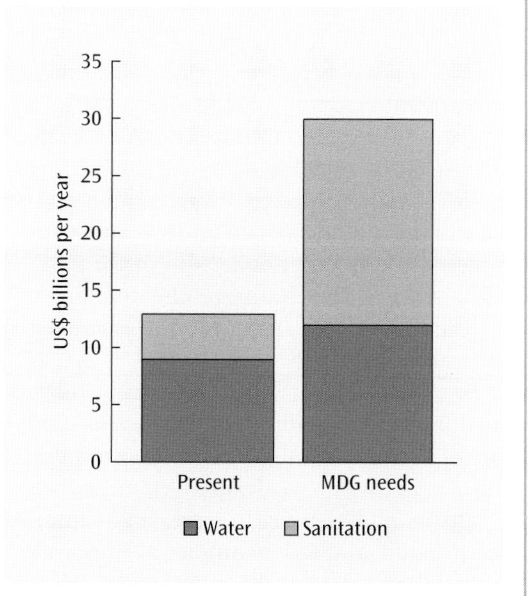

Source: Global Water Partnership 2000 and World Bank.

- Providing incentives to invest and operate efficiently and promoting sustainable access for the poor. Existing capacity must be optimally used to meet demand through tariffs that recover costs while taking into account the ability of consumers to pay; and policies that emphasize managerial autonomy and accountability.
- Strengthening the capacity of local institutions to scale up activities. Efforts need to focus more on building the financial and administrative capacities of subnational institutions responsible for service delivery. This should be accompanied by institutional reforms that enable stakeholders, especially poor people, to monitor and discipline service providers.
- Creating and disseminating knowledge needed to set priorities and improve resource use. Policymakers and stakeholders need reliable information to make good decisions, to use resources efficiently, and to hold providers accountable for the quality of service they deliver.
- Mobilizing financing for investments to expand access and improve service quality. Appropriate cost-recovery policies and practices are a prerequisite for raising the large amounts of investment financing needed in the sector. Increased domestic resource mobilization should be supported by increased external assistance.
- Enhancing the range and reliability of financial instruments. Most IFIs provide contractual and regulatory risk coverage, credit risk coverage, and foreign exchange risk coverage. Yet demand for risk mitigation instruments is low because few international investors are willing to invest in water supply and sanitation in developing countries. Only a few IFIs provide subsovereign lending on a significant scale. The IFIs are now stepping up the deployment of risk mitigation instruments and considering how to increase financial and technical support to subsovereigns, as proposed by the Camdessus Panel in 2003.[f]
- Aligning development assistance programs with country priorities and capacities, pooling aid at the country level, and ensuring continuity of support. Toward these ends, several consultative meetings have been held in the past year to increase donor coordination—among them an informal consultative meeting between bilateral donors and the World Bank in May 2003 and a February 2004 consultative meeting of IFIs and bilateral donors to coordinate support for millennium goals in water supply and sanitation.

In the Water Action Plan adopted at the Evian Summit in June 2003, the G-8 governments requested the World Bank and other IFIs to study and recommend measures to facilitate subsovereign lending and improve risk mitigation. A comparative review of IFIs showed that only EBRD and the Islamic Development Bank presently have a sizable subsovereign lending program; others reported legal or policy constraints on subsovereign lending. Four more IFIs (AfDB, EIB, IDB, and IFC) are planning to increase this type of financial support; IFC and IBRD are piloting a municipal fund to enable such lending.

Notes: (a) JMP 2000. (b) Global Water Partnership 2000; Winpenny 2003; United Nations Millennium Project Task Force on Water and Sanitation 2003. (c) Development Committee 2003. (d) World Bank 2002. (e) Kingdom and Tynan 2002. (f) Camdessus 2003.

provision and a scaling up of the project pipeline, with a better integration of infrastructure into country assistance strategies and poverty reduction strategy papers. The IAP also aims at rebuilding the knowledge base for infrastructure by strengthening analytic work to support policy reforms and instituting more systematic collection of data.

The scale of the challenge ahead is huge. The response needs to span all the elements of the agenda outlined above. And it needs increased international support—from bilateral donors and multilateral agencies—and more effective coordination of that support. Efforts under way to scale up investment, policy reform, and support in water and sanitation provide a good example of the way forward (box 6.1). But these efforts are still at an early stage, and success will require sustained commitment to the goals.

Notes

1. The 1994 *World Development Report* on infrastructure (World Bank 1994) highlighted an emerging debate on the relationship between access to infrastructure, productivity, and growth.
2. Estache, Foster, and Wodon 2002.
3. Caldéron, Easterly, and Sérven 2003.
4. Ramirez and Esfahani 2000.
5. Datt and Ravallion 1998.
6. Deininger and Okidi 2003.
7. Fan, Zhang, and Zhang 2002.
8. Estache, Foster, and Wodon 2002.
9. Estache, Foster, and Wodon 2002.
10. Households in Guatemala spend around 10 percent of their household budget on water, energy, and telecommunications services (Foster and Tre 2000). More than half is spent on energy for cooking and heating, and more than 25 percent on energy for lighting and powering appliances. Barely 0.5 percent of income is spent on water services. The overall budget share is relatively constant across consumption quintiles, although the composition of the budget shifts away from cooking fuels and toward telecommunications for richer households. Although only a tiny fraction of the poorest households have access to telephones, those that do so spend as much as 5 percent of their income on the service. Such breakdowns, however useful for designing tariff structures to ensure affordability, are seldom available.
11. Jalan and Ravallion 2001; Jayasuriya and Wodon 2003; Leipziger, Fay, and Yepes 2003; Development Committee 2003.
12. Fay and Yepes 2003.
13. The project is part of the Bank's Infrastructure Action Plan, which is described later in this chapter.
14. Angel 2000.
15. APHRC 2002.
16. Roja 2003.
17. Bacon 1999.
18. World Bank 2002.
19. Qiang 2004.
20. These estimates are calculated with an econometric model estimating the elasticity of demand with respect to GDP growth. For details, see Fay and Yepes (2003). This type of approach is much better suited to producing aggregate results, which usually provide reasonable ballpark estimates, than it is to producing individual country predictions. Also, it cannot adequately capture the impacts of improvements in efficiency, differentiation in service levels, and cross-sectoral linkages between infrastructure sectors.
21. Extending the forecast to 2015—the MDG horizon—requires much more analysis of the sensitivity of various determinants of investment demand and would be much less robust. Simulations for 2010–15 imply that for low-income countries, annual investment needs would be roughly the same as for the previous period with a margin of +/–0.5 percent of GDP. They could be as much as 1 percent lower for middle-income countries.
22. This is clearly a rough approximation, since it ignores the effects of technological changes on prices. This effect is particularly important, for example, for telecommunications, but much less so for water and roads.
23. Note that a major difference between the forecast and the past is that past investment levels include major rehabilitation requirements resulting from weak allocation of resources to O&M. In a sense, it could be argued that ex post O&M is "capitalized" and that the best approximation for it is the rehabilitation component of past investments. On the other hand, the forecast bets on a commitment to adequate O&M. This is why it is more useful to rely on the sum of investment and O&M to get a fuller sense of the resource needs of the sector.
24. DFID 2002.
25. Easterly and Servén 2003.
26. http://www.worldbank.org/infrastructure/files/iaPPublic.pdf.

7

Accelerating Human Development

The Millennium Development Goals related to human development—achievement of universal primary education; elimination of gender disparities in education; reduction of child and maternal mortality; control of major diseases such as HIV/AIDS, tuberculosis, and malaria—require a multidisciplinary and cross-sectoral approach if they are to be achieved. This is particularly so because a key factor in the success or failure of human development programs is improvement of governance—the policy and institutional framework governing public resource management, institutional capacities, control of corruption, community involvement, and empowerment of stakeholders. While substantial additional resources will be needed to finance expanded and improved access to education, health, and related services (requiring both stronger domestic resource mobilization and increased foreign support), the effectiveness of those investments in providing quality services, especially to the poor, will hinge on improvements in the underlying policy and governance regime.

Achieving the human development goals will require efforts on multiple fronts to deliver more and better services. Those efforts must address both supply- and demand-side constraints within each program. It is not enough to build more schools and clinics, for example, if the quality of service is so poor as to discourage their use, or if the poor do not have the resources to afford the service or lack the knowledge of its availability and value, or if the services are not properly funded and providers require "unofficial" payments. Moreover, those efforts must address the complex connection between progress in other development areas and human development programs.

Outcomes in education and health may be determined as much by what happens in other sectors as within these sectors. Do people have access to safe drinking water and basic sanitation? Do rural roads provide access to schools and clinics? Is there electricity to power those schools and clinics? Thus policies and programs need to be framed within an integrated country strategic framework that internalizes such linkages.

If current worldwide trends (reviewed in chapter 2) continue, the human development MDGs are unlikely to be achieved by the target dates. Progress *is* being made on the policy agenda. Investment in human capital in developing countries is on the rise, and the underlying policy framework bearing on its effectiveness is improving (see chapter 3 for ratings by multilateral institutions of social sector policies). Some countries are providing encouraging examples of successful innovation in service delivery to the poor. Overall, however, progress has been slow and uneven, and many gaps remain, particularly with respect to the institutional aspects of the agenda. The deficiencies are most serious in Sub-Saharan Africa and South Asia, but even in these regions individual countries (Cape Verde in education, health, and gender; Ghana in child mortality; and Ethiopia in primary enrollment) are making progress and are likely to meet at least some of the ambitious MDG targets.

The unreliability of information and wide gaps in data complicate the task of assessing progress toward the human development MDGs and of making policy to achieve them. Social sector data in many countries are particularly weak. Administrative data suffer from gaps and low quality, while survey data are available only periodically and capture only some characteristics. The need to monitor improvements and determine priorities for action increases the urgency of strengthening the information base.

To accelerate progress toward the goals, countries and their partners in the international community will need to scale up their efforts substantially. Priorities include:

- Expanding investment in human capital in low-income countries, while maximizing the impact of existing public spending by improving the targeting of public services in education, health, and social assistance
- Focusing on governance issues in service delivery to determine priority interventions to address service quality problems
- Piloting and evaluating empowerment options to strengthen the role of clients, especially poor people, in the design, scope, and delivery of key services.

Much recent and ongoing work analyzes aspects of the challenges posed by the human development MDGs:

- Working groups on education, gender, health, and major diseases of the United Nations' Millennium Project are reviewing recent findings and recommending directions for the international community.[1]
- The United Nations Development Programme (UNDP) is monitoring progress on the millennium goals; its latest *Human Development Report* assesses the prospects for attaining them.[2]
- The World Bank's 2004 *World Development Report* focuses on service delivery to the poor, paying considerable attention to education and health services.[3]

Drawing on those sources and others, this chapter reviews trends in the financing of human development programs, assesses the overall effectiveness of those programs, and finally, sets out an agenda for accelerating progress toward the human development MDGs.

Trends in Spending for Human Development

Available data show that spending on education, health, and other human development activities in developing countries has risen over the past decade, although it remains low relative to needs in many countries, especially the low-income ones.[4] The rising trend signifies a growing commitment on the part of governments to human development goals. Analysis shows that further increases in spending on these sectors, along with spending on related priority infrastructure such as water and sanitation, will be necessary to achieve the MDGs. To that end, public spending will need to shift further toward those sectors; and the shift must be accompanied by measures to enhance efficiency and effectiveness. Higher spending alone will not deliver the desired results.

Rising Public Spending on Education and Health

Public spending on education in low-income countries rose from 4.3 percent of GDP in 1990 to 4.7 percent in 2000 (figure 7.1).

After dipping in the mid-1990s (to an average of 3.7 percent in 1995) it recovered later in the decade. Spending rose in all regions, though in some it is well below the low-income country average. In 2000 public spending on education relative to GDP was 3.8 percent in Europe and Central Asia and 4 percent in Sub-Saharan Africa and South Asia, implying the need for special efforts there. Spending also rose in middle-income countries, to reach an average of 5 percent of GDP in 2000. The biggest leap occurred in Latin America, where historical underspending in education has contributed to relatively high economic inequality and lagging productivity. Interestingly, middle-income Sub-Saharan African countries spent more on education, as a share of GDP, than any other region in both 1990 and 2000. In comparison to the numbers for the developing world, OECD countries spend an average of 5.0 to 5.5 percent of GDP on education.

Public spending on health also rose relative to GDP, but modestly, and mainly because of the increase in middle-income countries (see figure 7.1). Public spending on health in developing countries as a share of GDP remains at about half the average level in high-income countries. In some low-income countries, spending on health is particularly low. In 24 of the countries for which data are available, including 14 in Sub-Saharan Africa, public spending on health is less than $5 per capita.

The rise in education and health spending relative to GDP in developing countries has been supported by the allocation of a higher share of total government spending to these services (figure 7.2). In 2000, on average, developing countries allocated 15.6 percent of total public spending to education and 8 percent to health, up from 13 percent and 6.2 percent, respectively, in 1990.

Significant progress has been made in mobilizing international and domestic resources to combat HIV/AIDS, tuberculosis, malaria, and other major diseases, although financing gaps remain. Spending on HIV/AIDS in low- and middle-income countries in 2003 was approximately $4.7 billion, a 20 percent increase over 2002 and almost five times the level of spending in 1996. International spending in 2003 included a projected $1.6 billion in bilateral assistance. Bilateral assistance is enhanced by the U.S. Emergency Plan for AIDS Relief, an

FIGURE 7.1 Investment in human capital is up, but more is needed
Public spending on education and health, 1990–2000

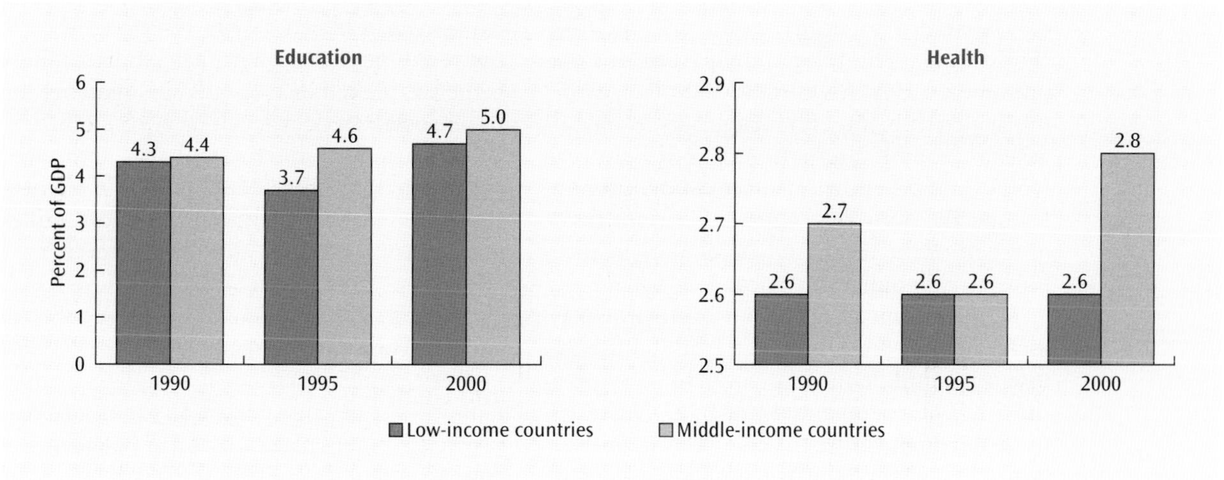

Education (Percent of GDP)

	Low-income countries	Middle-income countries
1990	4.3	4.4
1995	3.7	4.6
2000	4.7	5.0

Health

	Low-income countries	Middle-income countries
1990	2.6	2.7
1995	2.6	2.6
2000	2.6	2.8

Source: Compiled by IMF staff on the basis of country authorities' estimates.

FIGURE 7.2 Developing countries are allocating more public spending to human development

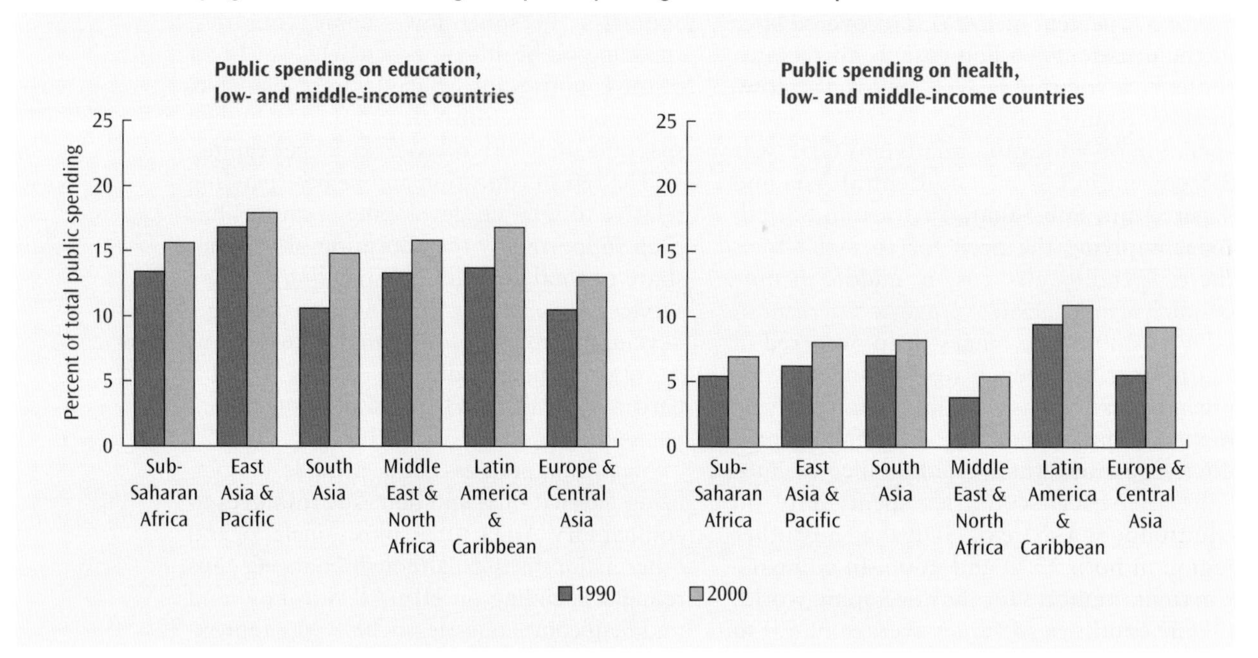

Source: Compiled by IMF staff on the basis of country authorities' estimates.

initiative that promises $10 billion over the next decade, with $2.4 billion approved for FY04. The sources of most multilateral funding, estimated at $600 million in 2003, are the Global Fund to Fight AIDS, Tuberculosis, and Malaria, a multidonor initiative launched to expedite the channeling of critical assistance to needy countries, and the World Bank. The Joint United Nations Programme on HIV/AIDS (UNAIDS) is providing leadership and financing for technical assistance and international coordination. UNDP and others are also providing funding for specific activities. Currently, more than one-half of the total international assistance flows to Sub-Saharan Africa.

Domestic spending on HIV/AIDS also is increasing, to an estimated $1 billion for 58 low- and middle-income countries—double the amount documented in 1999. This estimate is rough, however, as many countries lack adequate systems for tracking domestic spending on HIV/AIDS.

Private Supplements to Public Spending

Although greater public resources for education and health are helping to fill critical gaps in some countries, in most low-income countries, public revenues remain inadequate to provide the full range of needed services. Moreover, efficiency of resource use is uneven. One reflection of these shortcomings is the sizable reliance on private financing for basic social services, even in poor countries. In education, a study found that fees were common at all levels of schooling in 97 percent of countries, with unofficial (often illegal) fees charged in almost 40 percent of countries.[5] Some types of contributions exist, even in widely publicized no-fee countries such as Malawi and Uganda.

With public resources inadequate to provide access to quality education for all citizens, private spending plays a useful supplementary role. Community contributions can help supplement low teachers' salaries and support the cost of books, supplies, and basic maintenance.[6] The key is to ensure that public resources that do exist are sufficiently targeted to the poor and that private financing is mobilized from those with the ability to pay.

The same situation exists—and the same principles apply—in health care, where private expenditures often exceed public spending, especially at low levels of GDP per capita (figure 7.3). In India, for example, more than 80 percent of health spending is private. Much of private spending in the poorest countries is out-of-pocket payments to private providers, whereas in some middle-income countries insurance payments make up an important share of private spending.

Where services are "free" but not sufficiently funded by national or local government, informal side arrangements with providers tend to emerge. In the transition countries of Europe and Central Asia, where free services are "guaranteed" and the private sector is in nascent stages, and in South Asia, where the private sector is vibrant, under-the-table fees may finance up to 85 percent of all health spending. Since informal or illegal payments are common in many countries, official data can seriously underestimate the extent of reliance on private expenditures. In a study of seven Latin American countries, perceptions of informal payments were found to be the highest in Costa Rica, the country considered to have the broadest free system in the region.[7]

The poor tend to be affected more by such informal or illegal payments. As a proportion of household income, private expenditure on health is much higher for the poorer segment of the population in many countries (table 7.1).

Although governments around the world, and particularly in Africa, have committed themselves to strengthening public programs to combat HIV/AIDS and help those affected by it, much of the burden of paying for HIV/AIDS services continues to fall on individuals (box 7.1). Major gaps in the coverage of services translate into inequity in access

FIGURE 7.3 Public spending covers more of the cost of health care in high-income countries than in low-income countries
Public and private spending on health, developing versus developed countries

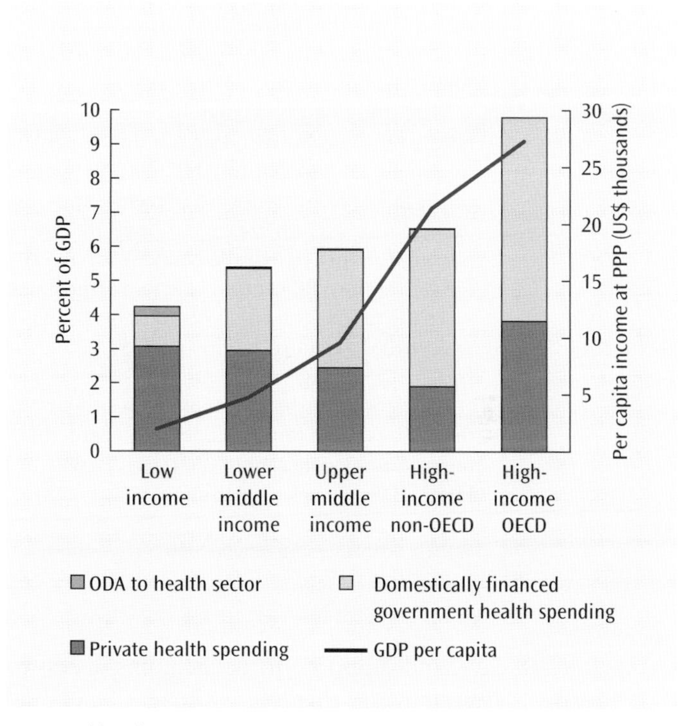

Source: World Bank 2004.

TABLE 7.1 Private health expenditure (as a percentage of annual household income)

Income level (quintiles)	Russia	South Africa	Brazil	Tanzania
Poorest	11.9	34.6	20.6	4.4
Second poorest	5.3	20.3	11.6	2.7
Middle	3.3	13.3	7.2	2.0
Second richest	2.1	9.2	4.1	1.3
Richest	0.8	3.2	1.2	0.5

Source: World Bank 2003c.

and financial ruin for poor households affected by the disease.

Despite the increased commitment of donor support, projected funding continues to fall short of what UNAIDS and others estimate is required for HIV/AIDS prevention,

BOX 7.1 Rwanda: HIV/AIDS and health expenditures

Recognizing the importance of documenting the overall flow of health funds—and funds related to HIV/AIDS—the Rwandan Ministry of Health reviewed the country's national health accounts. The analysis showed that the growing HIV/AIDS burden was a significant challenge in an already underfunded health system.

The study estimated that 40 percent of total per capita spending on health was funded by households. Of the total spending, about 10 percent was used for HIV/AIDS-related costs (prevention, treatment, and mitigation). HIV/AIDS expenditures were financed primarily by households (93 percent), followed by donors (6 percent), and government (1 percent). About 80 percent of HIV/AIDS expenditure was for treatment of related symptoms and infections in about 400,000 patients, 14 percent for antiretroviral treatment for a very small number of patients (202), and about 7 percent for prevention. Prevention was to a large extent financed by donor funds, whereas treatment costs were the financial burden of households. Thus, access to treatment of HIV/AIDS-related diseases was virtually defined by the patient's socioeconomic background and ability to pay the full cost of treatment, posing serious equity issues.

Few countries have completed a similar analysis. This makes it difficult to identify and address the serious fiscal implications of the epidemic, slowing consideration of future options, and clouding questions concerning the relative roles of households, government, and donors in developing HIV/AIDS policies and programs.

Source: Schneider and others 2000.

care, and support efforts, including access to antiretroviral therapies. Current spending represents less than half the $10.7 billion that UNAIDS estimates is required to finance a comprehensive health benefit package and less than a third of the $14.9 billion thought to be needed by 2007—a major challenge to mobilize additional resources, strengthen institutional implementation capacities, and scale up programs.

Social Safety Nets

Social assistance programs cushion the income of the poor from major shocks, such as an AIDS-related illness or a job lost in an economic crisis. Social assistance enables poor families to continue financing critical inputs, such as schooling and health clinic visits. The mounting HIV/AIDS orphan crisis in Africa is increasing the need for such assistance programs.

Wherever children contribute to household income, schooling has an opportunity cost. Social transfers can help poor families keep their children in school. Creative measures to compensate poor families through conditional cash transfers linked to schooling and health center visits (as in Brazil, Colombia, Mexico, and Nicaragua) have raised attendance at schools and induced a more regular use of preventive health care services.

Systematic information on the scale of social assistance programs is not available for many countries, but it appears that spending averages less than 1 percent of GDP in most regions other than Europe and Central Asia and Latin America. There is a great deal of variation among countries, not always related to national income (table 7.2). In Europe and Central Asia, the socialist legacy has left in place large social support programs that absorb significant public resources. For example, social assistance spending in Bulgaria and Serbia-Montenegro is estimated at 4.5 and 6.3 percent of GDP, respectively. Total spending on social protection, including social insurance, is typically much higher, averaging around 10 percent of GDP for the transition countries in the region for which data are available. By contrast, Pakistan and Malawi come in at the low end, spending only 0.1 and 0.2 percent of GDP, respectively, on social assistance. Typically, in poor countries, public resource constraints mean that spending on social assistance falls well short of the levels needed.

Quality and Effectiveness of Programs

The implication of the foregoing analysis is clear. Public spending on human development services, particularly in low-income countries, must rise if the development goals are to be achieved; and this rise must be supported in part by additional donor assistance. But increased spending will not deliver results if it is poorly directed and inefficiently implemented. A vital part of the agenda consists of actions to enhance the quality and effectiveness of spending at two levels:

- Allocation of resources must be better aligned with development priorities and better directed at target populations.
- The institutional framework through which resources pass must be improved to strengthen capacity for effective implementation and accountability for results.

In general, the policy and institutional regime in developing countries has been improving, both broadly and in the social sectors. This progress is confirmed by the World Bank and other MDB ratings reviewed in chapter 3. The improvements should enhance the effectiveness of programs. A recent study found that the elasticity of government spending in terms of its impact on desired outcomes rose with the score on the Country Policy and Institutional Assessments (CPIA). For example, at a CPIA score of 4 (a satisfactory rating), a 10 percent increase in public health and education spending was associated with a 7.2 percent decline in the maternal mortality rate.[8]

TABLE 7.2 Public spending on social protection for selected countries by region (percent of GDP)

Region	Social assistance	Social protection overall
Europe and Central Asia (21)	2.50	10.4
Latin America and Caribbean (18)	2.30	4.6
East Asia and Pacific (6)	0.70	2.3
Middle East and North Africa (5)	0.73	2.4
Sub-Saharan Africa (1)	0.24	1.9
South Asia (1)	0.90	1.9

Note: Numbers in parentheses indicate the number of countries for which data are available. Social protection includes social assistance plus social insurance (such as pensions, sickness and disability benefits, unemployment benefits).
Source: Blank, Grosh, and Weigand 2003.

Are Resources Reaching Targets?

A review of the delivery of human development services across countries shows, however, that there remains substantial scope for more effective use of resources. One key dimension of effectiveness is how well public programs are reaching and meeting the needs of the poor. Analysis of the incidence of public education and health spending in a range of developing countries shows that, contrary to the declared objectives of the programs, spending is often skewed toward better-off households and not the poor (figure 7.4).

In some countries, public subsidies on education and health do benefit low-income households disproportionately—for example, in Colombia, Costa Rica, Honduras, Jamaica, and Romania. But the overall pattern suggests considerable scope for improved targeting of subsidies. In education, for example, this would involve redirecting subsidies toward lower levels of education, which typically benefit the poor more, and improving service delivery to enhance the poor's effective access to and use of available services.

A commitment to spend does not necessarily translate into actual expenditures on service delivery. Recent evidence from several countries indicates that funds are not always reaching the front line (box 7.2) due to bureaucratic

FIGURE 7.4 Public spending on human development often benefits the rich more than the poor
Share of public spending for health and education that accrues to the richest and poorest quintiles, selected countries

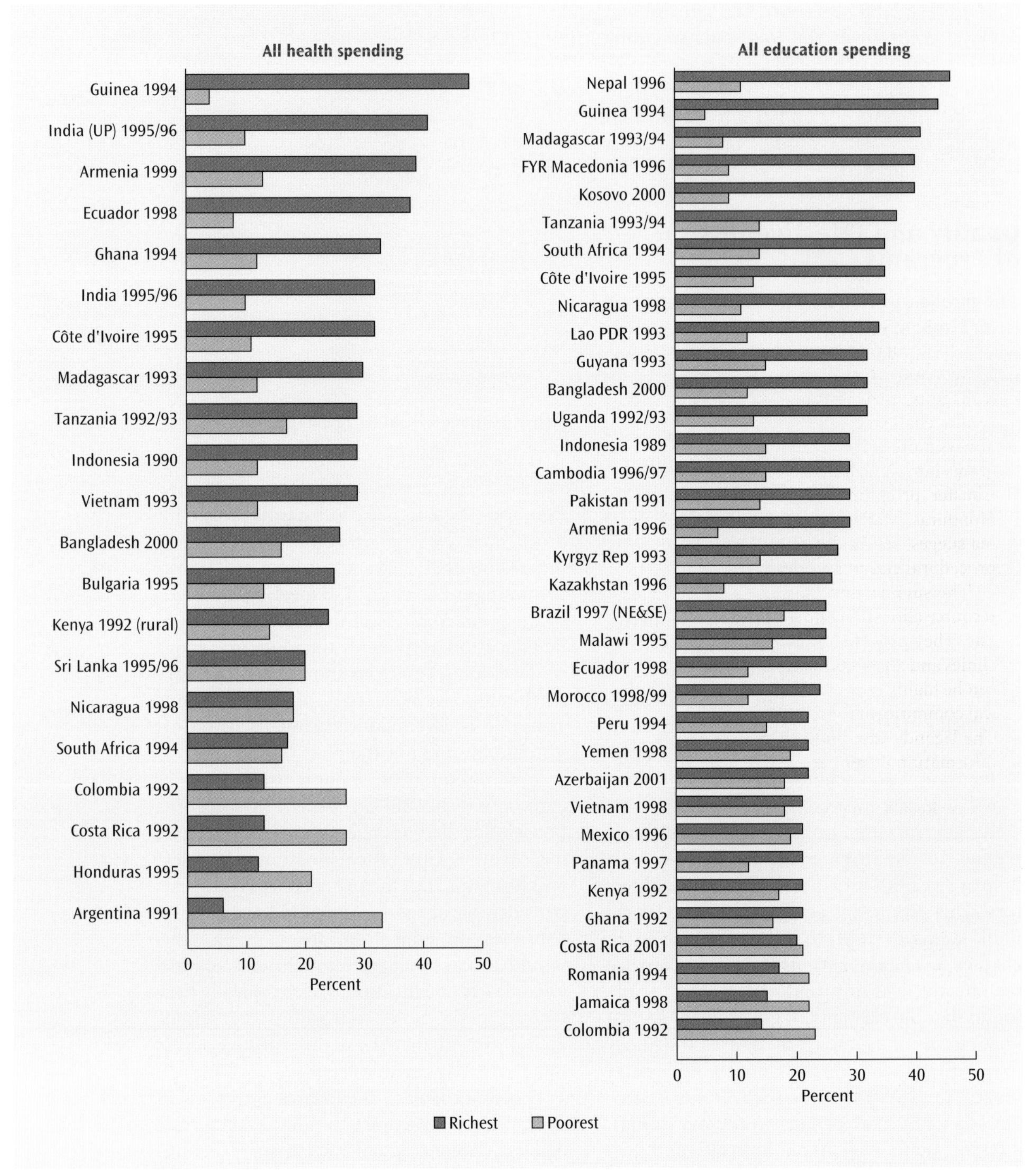

Source: World Bank 2003c.

BOX 7.2 The case of the missing money: monitoring public expenditure

In the early 1990s the Ugandan government dramatically increased spending on primary education. Yet school enrollments stagnated. Could it be that the money was not reaching schools? To answer the question, a public expenditure tracking survey started collecting data in 1996 on government transfers to schools. It found that 87 percent of the nonwage resources intended for the schools were diverted to other uses.

This information was made public, prompting a vigorous information campaign from the national government, which began publishing data on monthly transfers to local governments in newspapers. The central government also required primary schools and local administrations to post notices on receipt of funds. The information campaign brought large improvements: capture by interests along the way was reduced to less than 20 percent in 2001. Because poor people had been less able than others to claim their entitlement from the local officials before the information campaign, they benefited most from it.

Tracking surveys can find problems in unexpected places. A survey in Peru tracking a participatory food supplement program (Vaso de Leche, or "glass of milk") revealed that less than a third of each dollar transferred from the central government reached intended beneficiaries. Most of the leakage occurred below the municipal level—in the mothers' committees and households. The results challenged the belief underlying the program that local community organizations were always more accountable than public agencies. Authorities have decided to merge all nutrition programs into a social fund that will transform Vaso de Leche into a conditional, multipurpose, cash-transfer program with stronger accountability. These and other tracking surveys in Ghana, Honduras, Madagascar, Mozambique, Papua New Guinea, Rwanda, Senegal, Tanzania, and Zambia suggest several lessons. They confirm that budget execution is a major problem and show that procedural clarity and due process are often missing.

The surveys find that poor resource management is often a result of too much discretion in resource allocation under conditions of limited information, weak controls, and strong vested interests. They provide insights into the actual (rather than the formal) operation of schools and health clinics and allow comparisons of public, private, and nongovernmental providers. Tracking surveys can be highly cost-effective. But they need an authorizing environment: unless there is a solid political commitment for more transparency, government agencies may be reluctant to open their books. The Uganda case and a similar experience from neighboring Tanzania demonstrate the power of information in enhancing "client power" and ensuring the money will not go missing.

Source: Reinikka and Svensson 2004; Dehn, Reinikka, and Svensson 2003; World Bank 2003a.

bottlenecks, leakage, or lax management. Similarly, budgeted funds are not always available to be spent. In Pakistan, for example, because of poor public expenditure management, only 73 percent of the national health budget for 1999 was executed, whereas in Tanzania, spending reached 114 percent of the recurrent budget because of off-budget additions from user-fee revenue and donor transfers. In both cases, budget management becomes difficult, with unforeseen issues shifting the actual funding of public programs.

Issues in Education Quality

In education the quality of teaching is directly linked to the effectiveness of learning, but often quality is so low that the poor are deterred from attending school in the first place. One indicator of a problem is a high student-teacher ratio that reflects congestion in the classroom. It is no coincidence that the student-teacher ratio at the primary level in South Asia and Sub-Saharan Africa—the two regions with the weakest education outcomes—is the highest, more than twice the level in East Asia and Europe and Central Asia.[9]

One reason for the high student-teacher ratios is the relatively high salaries paid to teachers. Average annual teacher salaries in Africa are 4.5 times per capita GDP, whereas in East Asia the ratio is 1.5 and in Europe and Central Asia only slightly above 1. If the wage bill consumes the lion's share of the recurrent budget, little is left for textbooks and other instructional material. Evidence from Brazil and India shows that dollar-for-dollar spending on instructional materials is about 15 times more productive (in terms of increases in test scores) than spending on teacher salaries.[10] In Africa, most countries spend more than two-thirds of their recurrent education budget on salaries, with some reaching 90 percent or higher (figure 7.5). The problem is not limited to Africa.

But again, money does not guarantee service. Despite the high proportion of the budget devoted to teachers' salaries, absenteeism among teachers is high. Teacher absenteeism rates have been estimated at about 25 percent in India and Uganda. Within states of India, a study found absenteeism rates ranging from a low of 15 percent in Gujarat to a high of 39 percent in Bihar.[11] In Uttar Pradesh, India, surprise visits to 16 schools found a still higher rate of absenteeism—about two-thirds of teachers.[12]

Many governments provide education and health services in a top-down manner: the central government (with the help of donors) provides the financing, hires the teachers and doctors, and provides the complementary materials, such as textbooks and medicines. In too many cases, this system has failed to work for poor people—in part because they have little say in it. In a few cases where poor people have had a say—for example, by giving them a choice of service providers, involving parents in the running of the school, as in the El Salvador Education with the Participation of Communities program, or simply increasing the availability and transparency of information—the outcomes have been better. Possibly the biggest challenge in accelerating progress toward the MDGs—and also the biggest scope for reform—lies in strengthening the power and capacity of poor citizens to affect the delivery of services critical to their education and health.[13]

FIGURE 7.5 Teachers' salaries absorb most recurrent education spending
Percentage of recurrent education spending paid to teachers for selected Sub-Saharan African countries

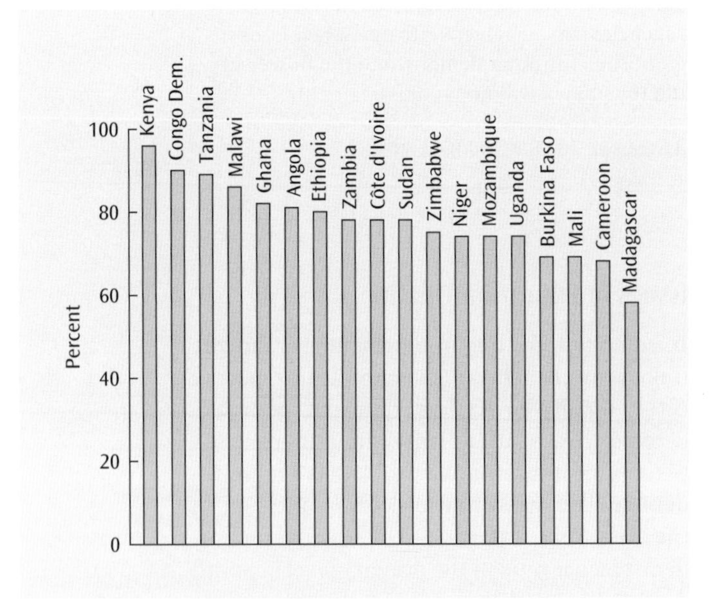

Source: Bruns, Mingat, and Rakatomalala 2003.

Gender, Education, and Women's Empowerment

Since the success of interventions to educate girls is fundamentally embedded in the sociocultural context of households and their decisionmaking processes, it is particularly important that family and community members be involved in the design and implementation of those interventions. Increasing girls' access to education facilities alone will not achieve the goal of reducing gender disparities in school attendance and achievement. Depending on the particular sociocultural context, other factors exert significant influence, such as the presence of female teaching staff, financial support to empower female students, school safety, gender-sensitivity of the curriculum, the availability of toilet facilities for girls, and information on the value of girls' education. Involving households and the community in the design of services would help in making them responsive to the particular needs of the female students.

By strengthening the ability of the student or client to influence the design of the service, choose among service providers, and monitor and discipline them, some countries have been able to accelerate progress toward increasing enrollment, improving education quality, and reducing gender disparities. A good example is Bangladesh's Female Secondary School Assistance Program (FSSAP), which gives schools a stipend based on the number of girls they enroll and which has been very effective is raising girls' attendance (box 7.3).

The empowerment of women of course calls for more than ensuring equal access to education opportunities. It also encompasses provision of adequate and equal access to health care, income-earning opportunities, and social and political rights. It requires that women have control over the resources they need, and the rights and voice to participate in decisions that affect them. Promoting gender equality and women's empowerment calls for a strong political commitment from governments to be responsive to the different service needs of men and women and to eliminate all forms of discrimination. Some progress has been made in this respect, but there is much more to do. Ratification of the U.N. Convention on the Elimination of All Forms of Discrimination against Women (CEDAW) and submission of regular reports on compliance is one indication of a country's commitment to ending gender inequalities in their laws and regulations and to creating institutions to protect women against discrimination. As of June 2002, all but four developing countries had ratified CEDAW, but only 71 percent had submitted at least one annual report.[14]

BOX 7.3 The Bangladesh Female Secondary School Assistance Program

Bangladesh's Female Secondary School Assistance Program (FSSAP) was launched in 1993. Its objective was to improve rural girls' enrollment and retention rates in secondary education.

The program cost of $88.4 million supported a package of interventions to increase the prospects that rural girls would enroll and remain in secondary school. A central component was the provision of cash stipends to girls. The stipend is transferred through the commercial banking system to individual bank accounts held in each girl's name. The program also transfers rural girls' tuition and examination fees directly to schools.

Complementary efforts to increase the proportion of female teachers, provide water and sanitation facilities, improve community engagement, and provide occupational skills make schools more attractive to girls and their families.

All unmarried girls of secondary school age who reside in rural areas were eligible to benefit from the program. Continuance in the program, however, required that girls attend school for at least 75 percent of the days in the school year, maintain their academic performance above a set minimum, and remain unmarried.

The program has been very successful in increasing rural girls' enrollment and retention rates. Stipend beneficiaries increased from 187,320 in 1994 to almost 900,000 in 2000. Girls now account for 54 percent of secondary enrollments in areas covered by FSSAP. Girls' attendance rates have improved significantly and at 91 percent, are above boys' 86 percent rate. The proportion of girls achieving pass marks in school examinations, at 89 percent, is now above the boys' rate of 81 percent. Girls' dropout rates from the program for noncompliance are low.

Source: Khandker, Pitt, and Fuwa 2003.

Health: A More Complex Agenda

A multiplicity of factors that affect health outcomes, and cross-sectoral links, make the attainment of health-related goals—reducing child and maternal mortality and combating major diseases—a still tougher challenge. Often policies focus narrowly on spending on health facilities and providers, but that is only one element of a broader and more complex agenda.

Female education and economic growth are the factors most closely correlated with low under-five mortality. Educated girls become better-informed women and mothers, who, in turn, are healthier, are better prepared when they have children, have fewer children, and care for them better. Unfortunately, progress in female education has been relatively slow, especially in primary completion rates and secondary and postsecondary enrollment rates. Gender gaps in education are largest in Sub-Saharan Africa, the Middle East, and South and West Asia. Efforts such as the Bangladesh FSSAP are encouraging, but unless they are scaled up, countries will find it difficult to achieve the MDG of reducing gender disparities in education. At the same time, the goal of reducing child mortality will become more difficult to achieve.

The second most important determinant of child survival is access to safe water and sanitation. (Challenges in developing this key infrastructure are discussed in chapter 6.) While overall access to safe water is increasing in most regions of the world, the distribution of safe water is quite unequal between rich and poor households. In many countries, almost everyone in the richest quintile of the population enjoys access to an improved water source, but fewer than half of households in the poorest quintile do. For example, in Ethiopia, only about 10 percent of the poorest households use an improved water source. Sanitation, too, is inequitably distributed. In Accra, Ghana, 70 percent of the households from the poorest quintile share toilets with 10 or more households; the comparable figure for households from the richest 20 percent is 10 percent. Since high child mortality is more prevalent among poor people, major progress in reducing it is unlikely without improved access to safe water and sanitation for the poorest households.

Lack of access to health services is often exacerbated by poor service delivery or information failures. It is not uncommon to find high levels of absenteeism in clinics and hospitals. Absenteeism rates of medical personnel in primary health facilities vary from 19 percent in Papua New Guinea to 43 percent in India. Within India, the rates are as high as 53 percent in the state of Bihar. The absenteeism rate among doctors in primary health facilities in Bangladesh is 73 percent.[15]

Lack of knowledge can be another constraint. For example, in Bolivia, many poor babies are not delivered by a trained attendant simply because mothers are unaware that they are eligible for free care. In India, where immunization is free, 60 percent of children have not been fully immunized. Asked why they had not immunized their child, 30 percent of mothers said it was because they were not aware of the benefits available, while another 30 percent said it was because they did not know where to go to have their child vaccinated.[16] Public action can play a significant role in disseminating information.

Maternal survival is strongly associated with the presence of a skilled attendant during birth. In general, the trend in attended births is positive, but the levels remain disturbingly low, especially for low-income countries in Africa and South Asia—Nepal and Pakistan especially (table 7.3). Even some middle-income countries, such as Morocco, have particularly low rates of attended births. Nonetheless, the rate of improvement in the frequency of attended births is highest for the poor, an encouraging finding.

A related measure of progress is the prevalence of contraception, which captures the possibility of birth spacing and other aspects of maternal health. Rates of contraception use are only about 27 percent on average in developing countries, and the rate for the

Table 7.3 Frequency of attended births by wealth and region, various years (percent)

Regional average	Level		Average annual change	
	Poorest quintile	Population average	Poorest quintile	Population average
East Asia and Pacific	28.8	59.3	—	—
Europe and Central Asia	88.4	95.1	2.3	0.5
Latin America and Caribbean	44.1	68.0	8.5	2.6
Middle East and North Africa	33.6	52.5	10.6	6.4
South Asia	7.0	21.5	11.6	7.7
Sub-Saharan Africa	24.6	46.5	1.1	–0.4

— Not available
Source: USAID, *Demographic and Health Survey* estimates, various years from 1995 to 2002.

poorest 20 percent of the population is about 19 percent. Furthermore, especially for the poor, the constraint may not necessarily be the availability of contraceptives. Often, power relationships within the household determine contraceptive use. About 70 percent of the women from the poorest 20 percent of the population in the Central African Republic, Côte d'Ivoire, Tanzania, and Uganda reported that their husbands did not approve of their contraceptive use. Similar findings have emerged in Central America.[17]

In the fight against HIV/AIDS and other major infectious diseases, financing issues are being addressed with the support of the international community. However, attention to the management and implementation capacity needed to make effective use of financing has lagged in many countries. Progress is being made on the institutional front. The Progress Report prepared for the U.N. General Assembly Special Session on HIV/AIDS noted that 90 percent of the 103 countries reporting had established national AIDS commissions or authorities, many of them structured to include representation from key stakeholder groups.[18] But in many cases such institution-building efforts are at an early stage.

Managing assistance to HIV/AIDS programs as "business as usual" will not work. Encouraging successes in Brazil, Thailand, Uganda, and some other countries point the way:

- First, governments need actively to mobilize nongovernmental organizations (NGOs) and community-based organizations (CBOs) to help overcome social and political obstacles to reaching target groups. Effective prevention and treatment of HIV/AIDS requires educating the public about the disease and promoting behavior change among population groups that are normally far beyond the reach of government.
- Second, to ease the burden on limited institutional capacities, governments, especially in severely affected countries, need to exploit opportunities to contract out services. While some progress is evident—for instance, Kenya's National AIDS Commission has hired a financial management agency that in turn has helped channel resources to more than 750 local CBOs and NGOs—the time required to establish new ways of doing business often conflicts with the urgent need for rapid and extensive action.
- Third, capacity building within government agencies should include the strengthening of monitoring and evaluation to assess performance and impact and inform the design and implementation of public and private programs.
- Fourth, with respect to the health system capacity, efforts need to focus on critical bottlenecks. Numerous NGOs in West Africa report that the binding constraint on expansion of the antiretroviral program

is a shortage of trained doctors, nurses, and laboratory technicians. They are being forced to recruit staff from existing health service delivery programs, exacerbating shortages there.

Social Assistance: Successes and Challenges

Finally, social assistance programs in several countries have been instrumental in improving and sustaining the access of the poor to basic education and health services. Piloted in some Latin American countries, programs providing transfers conditional on school attendance or regular health center visits have been scaled up nationally (for example, Mexico's *Progresa* program and Brazil's *Bolsa Escola*) and adopted in some other countries (for example, Bangladesh and Turkey).

Nonetheless, social assistance spending in many countries is fragmented, redundant, and poorly targeted. In Paraguay, for example, about 90 social assistance programs were being implemented recently by 22 agencies. In Argentina, 60 federal social protection programs have overlapping objectives and target groups. Bulgaria has 34 programs. Evaluation of these programs often is weak. A recent study of a sample of such programs found that just over 20 percent had well-developed evaluation arrangements.[19] Thus while there has been successful innovation in social assistance that merits scaling up, there is also scope for better targeting in existing social assistance spending.

Agenda for Accelerating Progress

Progress toward human development goals will require efforts on multiple fronts. More resources are needed to scale up programs in priority areas. But just as important, there is need to accelerate policy and governance reforms to make programs more effective. The reform agenda is multidimensional, spanning investment, policies, and governance. It is also multisectoral, with human development outcomes affected in important ways by improvements in other sectors, such as access to safe drinking water, basic sanitation, roads, and electricity.

Education

The challenges facing individual countries and the international community are well illustrated by developments relating to the primary education goal. While several analyses point out that this goal is attainable by 2015, public spending on education in low-income countries has risen slowly, constrained by limited resources, competing demands, and low institutional capacity. The allocation of spending, such as the funding bias toward secondary and higher education, typically benefits the nonpoor. In contrast, the quality of primary education is often so low (high student-teacher ratios, inadequate allocations to nonsalary expenditures, and frequent teacher absenteeism) as to discourage school attendance. The effective functioning of education services is underpinned by good governance—functioning civil service rules and processes, effective financial management, control of corruption, and direct participation of communities. Reforms in these areas are the key to progress, but they have lagged.

Community involvement in the design of education services is particularly important to the goal of reducing gender disparities in education. Girls' attendance at school can be influenced strongly by sociocultural factors, and community involvement can help ensure that services respond to those factors. Effective improvement in female access to education—and indeed to other services—requires that gender concerns be fully integrated into policy and service design.

Overall, while there has been progress, governments have been slow to undertake the policy and institutional reforms necessary to improve the coverage and quality of primary schooling, reflecting in part the political difficulty of some of the agenda. A stronger political commitment is required to deepen and accelerate reforms if the MDGs in education and gender are to be achieved.

Donors also need to improve the quality of their support. The record of the donor community has been mixed as well. Traditionally, donors have concentrated their aid on addressing supply constraints, such as building schools, rather than the underlying institutional impediments to effective delivery of primary education services.

Recognizing the limitations of the past approach, in terms of both providing adequate resources and supporting broader reforms in developing countries' education systems, donors coalesced around the Education for All–Fast Track Initiative, agreeing to provide additional support to primary education explicitly linked to countries' policy performance and increased accountability for results. The criteria for support emphasize adequacy and sustainability of domestic financing, service delivery standards consistent with education quality and efficient use of resources, and transparent monitoring of results through annual joint sector reviews. The initiative seeks to improve donor performance through concrete actions to harmonize aid.

While the EFA-FTI has been a positive force for spurring country action, donor programming and budgeting cycles have translated into slow disbursement, with only $6 million of the first $170 million committed actually disbursed as of January 2004. Also, the number of countries touched so far by the program has been small. At their meeting in Oslo in late 2003, donors agreed to mainstream the FTI approach, and 25 more countries are expected to join in 2004. World Bank projections suggest that as the FTI scales up to all low-income countries, at least $3.7 billion per year will be needed in external financing for primary education by 2005–06, compared with about $1 billion in 2002. How effectively the FTI contributes to accelerating progress toward the education MDGs will hinge on donor performance in actually delivering increased and more predictable financing in support of tangible country reforms and close monitoring of the achievement of results on the ground.[20]

Health

The goal of reducing child mortality is still more complex and difficult to attain. First, some of the public policies and actions that can make the greatest contribution lie outside the health sector (female education, clean water and sanitation) and so require greater cross-sectoral coordination. Second, actions within the health sector to improve the supply of services, such as access to health clinics or immunization, confront major challenges. These include underfunding, weak institutional capacities and governance undermining service quality, and limited availability of trained personnel (aggravated by incentive problems reflected in high absenteeism among doctors, especially in rural areas). Third, service provision often must also contend with challenges on the demand side, such as lack of money or knowledge, that limit poor people's effective access to or use of services.

Accelerating progress on child survival, therefore, requires a concerted effort in female education, provision of safe water and sanitation facilities, and expansion of access to effective health facilities complemented by incentives, governance arrangements, and accountability for better delivery of services. It also requires incentives and information to stimulate demand, especially for preventive services.

As with public actions in primary education, political factors work to slow the progress of actions to reduce child mortality. In most countries the share of public health spending that benefits the richest quintile exceeds that going to the poorest. While high child mortality is primarily a problem of poor people, ill health affects everybody. In countries without adequate health insurance markets (almost all low-income and many middle-income countries), public spending on health becomes a substitute for the insurance against catastrophic health expenditures that everybody needs.

Since they have greater political power, the rich are often able to capture public health expenditures to serve their needs. At the same time, the evidence is clear that if systems are set up exclusively for the poor, they tend to be less effective and of lower quality, because the poor lack the resources, clout, and voice of the middle or upper classes. Unless the power of communities to monitor and discipline service providers is enhanced—including possibly through co-payments—increasing public spending in health by itself is unlikely to have a significant impact on child mortality, or for that matter on maternal mortality.

Public resources in most countries are inadequate to provide free basic health or education to all citizens, and there is a clear role for private spending. Private out-of-pocket spending is part of health care financing everywhere—if not formally, then through informal or illegal payments, with the poor tending to bear the brunt of such payments. A more transparent and judicious use of fees can not only help alleviate the public resource constraints, but also contribute to improved quality of service by motivating greater stakeholder oversight of service delivery. It would also allow scarce public subsidies to be targeted more effectively to poor people.

As in primary education, the donor community has had a mixed record in strengthening public actions to reduce child mortality. On the one hand, sizable amounts of aid go toward fighting the diseases of children and supporting health expenditures in developing countries. On the other hand, most of that aid is provided for earmarked expenditures or for vertical programs that deliver a narrow package of interventions on a small scale, with insufficient attention to the incentives these create for undertaking the difficult public sector reforms that are needed to make a substantial dent in child mortality. Advocates for increasing foreign aid in health tend to focus almost exclusively on per capita spending on health by various countries—neglecting issues relating to the effectiveness of that spending or the fact that spending in other sectors may make a bigger difference to child-health outcomes. Aid would be more effective if the modalities of its provision were more flexible and supported broader reforms that include the institutional health-sector issues and intersectoral linkages that must be addressed in order to scale up impact.

The maternal mortality goal may be even harder to achieve than the child mortality goal. In addition to the resource and institutional constraints on the delivery of related health services, the outcomes depend greatly on underlying social, cultural, and behavioral factors. Progress in the longer term may hinge as much on efforts to broaden educational opportunities and raise awareness as on specific health service interventions. With respect to the latter, the intervention that seems to be most important (and most easily measured) is the presence of a skilled attendant during birth. Again, improving poor people's access to skilled attendants is more than a matter of resource availabilities, as it suffers from limited political support—the poor are the only segment of the population that relies on such paraprofessionals—and poorly functioning institutions.

Communicable diseases. Similarly, effectively combating the spread of major diseases—HIV/AIDS, tuberculosis, and malaria—requires action across a range of sectors and actors, including civil society and the private sector. The target of halting and beginning to reverse the spread of HIV/AIDS by 2015 is particularly challenging, given the long incubation period of this disease. Effectively combating this epidemic requires action at three levels (and this may also be similar for TB):

- Political—strong and explicit leadership and commitment at the highest political levels to help generate and sustain the kind of exceptional responses that the epidemic requires
- Strategic—a national HIV/AIDS strategy to guide the evolution of a multisectoral response by multiple actors
- Implementational—translation of the strategy into action at the necessary scale through mobilization of resources, domestic and foreign, and building of institutional capacities.

The progress made in these respects so far has been modest compared with the scale of the challenge.

The GFATM has focused on raising resources to contain the spread of HIV/AIDS, TB, and malaria. While substantial commitments have been made to the fund, implementation has been slow, as evidenced by the delays in signing grant agreements for approved projects and the limited volume of disbursements. Out of $3.4 billion in pledges, roughly $1.1 billion had been committed and only $236 million disbursed as of January 2004. In addition to slow follow-up at the donor end, implementation capacities of recipient governments have been a constraint. Problems stem partly from the fund's operational model, with its insufficient appraisal of financial issues, donor coordination, and institutional capacity prior to grant approval. The focus of country proposal reviews has tended to be on technical issues rather than implementation constraints—capacity of responsible agencies, service delivery networks, fiduciary environment. There is a need to find ways to better align programs and capacity, to build capacity simultaneously with the allocation of additional resources, and to better coordinate donor support to expedite implementation.

Scaling up on the basis of successful models. Well-designed social assistance programs targeted to the poor and linked to school attendance and health center visits can play an important role in enhancing the poor's effective access to and use of critical human development services, as well as cushioning the poor against major income shocks. Innovative conditional cash transfer programs successfully implemented in some Latin American countries provide models that can be considered for scaling up and replication elsewhere. At the same time, to make room for effective interventions such as these, countries need to review their overall social assistance frameworks, which often suffer from poor targeting, fragmentation, and fiscal unsustainability.

Notes

1. Papers produced by these working groups are available at the project Web site: www.unmillenniumproject.org.
2. UNDP 2003.
3. World Bank 2003c.
4. Data on public spending allocated to human development suffer from many gaps and are not available for all countries. The analysis presented here draws on two sets of data: data compiled by IMF staff, on the basis of country authorities' estimates, that provide information on the composition of public spending for low- and middle-income developing countries; and data assembled from various World Bank country Public Expenditure Reviews and joint IMF-World Bank expenditure tracking work relating to PRSPs and HIPC programs. Improved data on the level and composition of social sector spending are a priority area in the strengthening of statistics in developing countries.
5. Kattan 2003.
6. Indeed, fees, for those who can pay, could offer incentives to providers, which can serve to enhance service quality (such as lower teacher absenteeism), contribute to more flexible funding for schools and health centers, and help combat corruption by reducing the incidence of informal/illegal payments. Fees could also motivate service users to become more involved in monitoring and disciplining service providers. For some country evidence, see Lewis (2000).
7. Di Tella and Savedoff 2000; Lewis 2000.
8. World Bank 2004.
9. World Bank 2003b.
10. Filmer and Pritchett 1999.
11. World Bank 2003c.
12. Dreze and Gazdar 1996.
13. World Bank 2003c.
14. For more information, see the Web site of the U.N. Division for the Advancement of Women (DAW) at http://www.un.org/women watch/daw/cedaw.
15. World Bank 2003c.
16. World Bank 2003c.
17. USAID various years.
18. UNAIDS 2003.
19. Rubio and Subbarao 2003.
20. For a fuller discussion of progress and issues relating to the EFA-FTI, see Development Committee 2004.

8

Promoting Environmental Sustainability

Improving environmental policies and mitigating the environmental impacts of sectoral policies are an integral element of the agenda for achieving the Millennium Development Goals. Goal 7—ensure environmental sustainability—aims to mainstream the environment in policy and programs, reverse the loss of environmental resources, and improve access to environment-related services. The importance of the environment to the MDGs is reinforced by its strong links to the rest of the goals. It is difficult to imagine reducing income-poverty in rural areas where land is degraded. Reductions in child mortality will be more likely if households have access to adequate water supply, sanitation facilities, and modern fuels. And climate change resulting from unchecked environmental degradation would favor the spread of vector-borne diseases and increase the likelihood of natural disasters—disasters that, in turn, reduce income and destroy the infrastructure for education and health. If environmental sustainability is not ensured, progress toward the other MDGs may be short-lived.

Progress on Environmental Policies

Environmental policies are more difficult to monitor than most because data are scarce. Data directly measuring specific environment policies—pricing, regulations, institutions—on a cross-country basis are not available with any consistency. One source of information on policies is the World Bank's Country Policy and Institutional Assessment, which includes an assessment of countries' overall environmental management. The CPIA ratings show that environmental management is a policy area where the bulk of the agenda in developing countries is still to be addressed. The average country ratings are relatively low (figure 8.1). The ratings are improving, however, although they seem to have stalled in Asia and Latin America. The improvement in the past five years is particularly notable in Europe and Central Asia. The ratings rise with the income level; middle-income countries show appreciably better environmental management than low-income countries.

Monitoring Policies through Outcomes: Evidence of Limited Progress

Data are available on key environmental outcomes that indicate countries' progress toward environmental objectives, including the MDG related to the environment. Information on environmental outcomes, compiled

FIGURE 8.1 Environmental policy ratings are low but improving
Ratings of environmental management policies for developing countries by region and country income category, 1999 and 2003

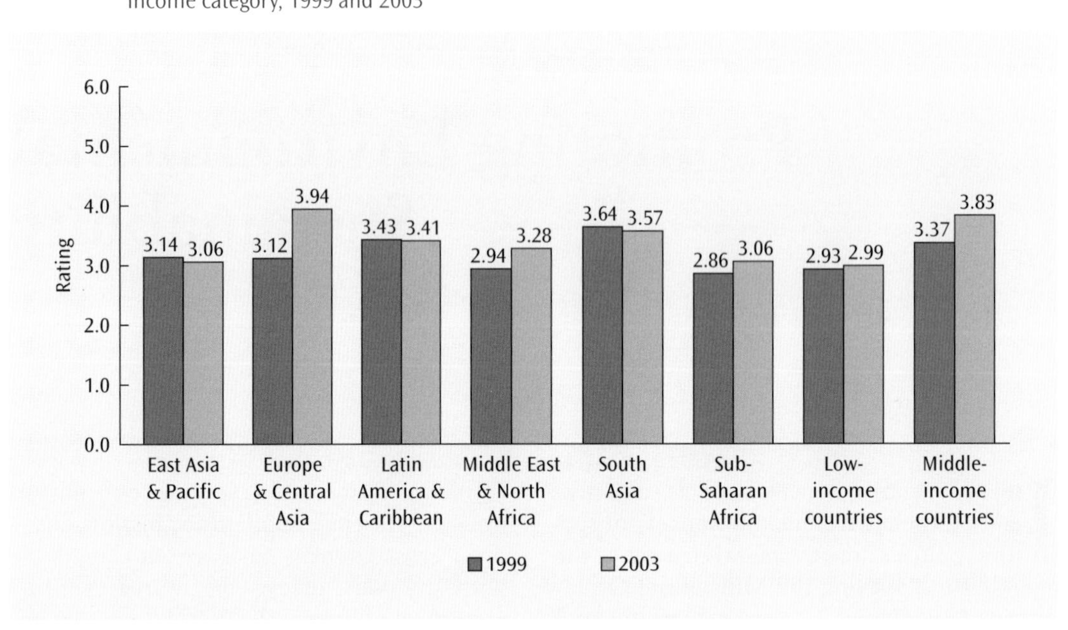

Note: World Bank CPIA ratings range from a low of 1 to a high of 6, with an increase denoting improvement.
Source: World Bank CPIA database.

from a variety of sources and published in *World Development Indicators,* includes land use (agricultural land, forests, protected areas), access to water and sanitation, water resources (available water resources, total withdrawal, agriculture withdrawal), energy (energy intensity, traditional fuel use, urban air pollution), and transport (passenger cars, fuel prices). But coverage and quality are mixed, as are the prospects of obtaining improved data. Although satellite technology is helping in some quantitative aspects (for example, in monitoring forest cover), information on environmental quality (water quality, land degradation) is hard to obtain. Even monitoring of an "easy" issue (urban air quality) has worsened since the GEMS/Air program closed.[1]

Environmental outcome indicators suggest that progress toward environmental sustainability is limited (table 8.1). For example, despite small gains in forest cover in Europe and Central Asia and the Middle East and North Africa during the 1990s, large losses were experienced in the rest of the developing world. As a consequence of economic and demographic growth, most developing regions are witnessing significant increases in carbon dioxide emissions—the impressive reductions in Europe and Central Asia are attributable largely to economic restructuring. Although generally decreasing across regions, the use of traditional (highly polluting) fuels remains extremely high in Sub-Saharan Africa, South Asia, and East Asia and the Pacific. The "adjusted net saving" measure, a useful indicator of sustainability, suggests that, based on current trends, welfare is likely to decline over time in Sub-Saharan Africa and the Middle East and North Africa, drawing attention to the need for improved economic, environmental, and resource policies in the countries of those regions.

TABLE 8.1 Selected outcome indicators of environmental sustainability by region and country income category

	Adjusted net saving[a] Percent of GNI		Deforestation Forest cover lost[b] 1990–2000		Carbon dioxide emissions Metric tons per capita		Solid biomass use in households[c] Percent of total energy use	
Region and country income category	2000	Increase 1990–2000[d]	Area (thousands of km)	Percent[e]	2000	Percent increase 1990–2000	2001	Percent increase 1994–2001
Region								
East Asia and Pacific	21.3	5.8	116	2.7	2.1	8.7	71.7	–0.9
Europe and Central Asia	—	—	–81	–0.9	6.5	–37.6	8.2	0.3
Latin America and Caribbean	4.4	0.5	459	4.6	2.6	19.7	37.6	–4.8
Middle East and North Africa	–10.0	0.9	–2	–1.4	4.1	33.1	12.5	–1.6
South Asia	11.3	1.6	9	1.1	0.9	31.8	84.1	–1.5
Sub-Saharan Africa	–3.3	1.3	530	7.6	0.7	–21.6	88.3	0.0
Income level								
Low	4.7	0.0	731	7.5	0.9	2.6	84.9	–1.9
Lower middle	13.1	6.0	–147	–0.8	3.0	–17.3	46.0	–0.3
Upper middle	6.9	1.9	151	5.9	6.2	9.4	23.4	1.9
High	12.8	2.5	–79	–1.0	12.4	4.7	5.7	–0.7
World	12.0	2.5	950	2.4	3.8	–6.9	37.6	0.1

— Not available.
a. A negative number indicates dissaving.
b. A negative number indicates that forest cover has increased.
c. Solid biomass is defined as any plant matter used directly as fuel or converted into fuels (such as charcoal) or electricity and/or heat. Included here are wood, vegetal waste (including wood waste and crops used for energy production), and animal materials and wastes.
d. Calculated as average for 1995–2000 minus average for 1985–90.
e. As percentage of 1990 forest cover.
Source: World Bank, *World Development Indicators;* World Bank staff.

Ensuring Environmental Sustainability and Achieving the MDGs: Need for Policy Integration

A desirable development outcome in itself, environmental sustainability also contributes to other outcomes such as economic growth, poverty alleviation, and better health. In particular, the environmental MDG has strong links with those related to poverty and health. For example, research in Zimbabwe shows that environmental resources make a significant contribution to rural incomes, representing some 40 percent of average income for poor households.[2] The World Health Organization estimates that 40 percent of under-five mortality is traceable to diseases strongly associated with environmental factors—among them diarrhea and acute respiratory infections.[3] But improving environmental conditions also will be important in achieving the education and gender goals. In many poor communities, women and girls spend vast amounts of time fetching water and collecting fuel wood, which prevents them from engaging in productive activities and attending school (box 8.1).

Because policy choices in different sectors—agriculture, water, energy, transport, trade, public finance—affect environmental sustainability, better integration of sectoral policies may be the fastest route to environmental sustainability, as highlighted by the United Nations Task Force on Environmental Sustainability (box 8.2). Effective environmental management means going beyond individual policy actions, such as implementing particular regulations, and ensuring that environmental concerns are fully integrated into development policymaking more broadly.

BOX 8.1 Multisectoral interventions to achieve the MDGs: lessons from child mortality in rural India

In 1999 some 10 million children under the age of five died in low-income countries—2.1 million in India alone. Using Indian health survey data, World Bank researchers have concluded that investments targeted at improving environmental conditions can substantially reduce child mortality. In particular, universal access to private piped water, electricity, and separate kitchens with clean cooking fuels would save the lives of 10.4, 5.5, and 33.6 children per 1,000 live births, respectively, in rural India. The analysis also shows that girls face a higher mortality risk than boys after the first month of birth (suggesting a significant gender bias in household resource allocation) and that child mortality is higher among those born to mothers with no education. Universal female primary education would reduce the under-five mortality rate from 99.9 to 77.0 deaths per 1,000 live births.

What does this mean? It means that environmental and human development goals are closely intertwined. In order to reduce child mortality, for example, developing countries need to mobilize contributions from multiple sectors—health, of course, but also education, energy, and water—and incorporate cross-cutting perspectives (environment, gender).

Source: van der Klaauw and Wang 2003.

BOX 8.2 The United Nations Task Force on Environmental Sustainability

The U.N. Task Force on Environmental Sustainability is one of 10 task forces making up the U.N. Millennium Project. Its preliminary findings conclude that progress toward environmental sustainability has been unsatisfactory, largely because environmental and biodiversity issues have been poorly integrated into mainstream thinking and policymaking. The task force places particular emphasis on the importance of biodiversity conservation and ecosystem integrity for environmental sustainability. Although a framework for action is still in progress—the final report is due in June 2005—the background paper suggests the main lines of action should be improving environmental awareness among policymakers and the general public, enhancing national capacity for ecosystem management, and consolidating international markets for global environmental services.

Source: United Nations Millennium Project 2003.

Priorities for Action

When establishing priorities for action to achieve environmental sustainability, one size does not fit all. OECD standards for environmental quality are not appropriate for many developing countries. In fact, the nature of environmental problems varies considerably by income level.

In middle-income countries, many environmental problems are the byproducts of growth—urban pollution, toxic emissions, and agricultural runoff. In low-income countries, the issues are closely tied to livelihoods, particularly soil quality and water availability, and to health outcomes (diarrheal disease and acute respiratory infections from dirty cooking fuels).

Because environmental issues are location specific, different clusters of countries have different priorities:

- In resource-rich countries, such as Indonesia, *governance issues* involving commercial resources
- In rapidly urbanizing countries and countries in transition, such as Thailand and Poland, *pollution management*
- In agriculture-dependent countries, such as Ethiopia, *natural resource management*
- In arid countries, such as Mali, *land and water management* and *adaptation to climate change*
- In diverse countries, such as Madagascar, *biodiversity conservation* and *tapping global finance* to help cover the opportunity costs of conservation
- In small island states and low-lying coastal countries, such as the Maldives or Bangladesh, *adaptation to climate change.*

The following elements that broadly define the environmental policy reform agenda in developing countries should therefore be adapted to income levels and particular country circumstances:

- Strengthening policy and institutional frameworks for environmental management
- Getting the prices right for energy, water, and agricultural inputs
- Facilitating access to basic services, such as improved water supply, sanitation, and clean energy sources.

Notes

1. The GEMS/Air program was funded and operated jointly by the United Nations Environment Programme, the World Health Organization, and the U.S. Environmental Protection Agency.
2. Cavendish 2000.
3. World Health Organization 2002.

III Developed-Country Policies

9

Fostering Growth and Stability

Macro-financial Policies

The overall prospects for economic growth and poverty reduction in the developing world depend critically on the maintenance of strong and balanced growth in the developed countries. Macroeconomic policies that promote such growth can thus contribute to progress toward the Millennium Development Goals and related outcomes in developing countries.[1] Good global economic conditions benefit developing countries in several ways, notably by boosting trade, foreign direct investment, and possibly official development assistance. Growth in developed countries can also benefit the rest of the world through its effects on labor migration and related phenomena such as flows of remittances from migrating workers.

Although the prospects for world economic activity appear to be reasonably bright for the next few years, sustaining a strong global economy will require the major countries to address some outstanding issues and imbalances. The challenges to be addressed include the orderly moderation of the U.S. current account deficit; the implementation of further structural reforms in several countries, especially in labor markets; and the fiscal impact of demographic changes building up in many developed countries. Disorderly adjustment in the largest economies could retard growth or leave global economic conditions vulnerable to exogenous shocks.

These challenges come at a time when many developing countries, struggling to recover from the recent slowdown in world trade, are facing uncertain prospects. In the next few years, the terms of trade are generally expected to disfavor most developing countries—particularly those exporting fuels. The outlook for private capital flows to developing countries, meanwhile, has brightened, but only the higher-rated emerging markets are likely to benefit from the improving conditions. The need for capital, particularly to finance infrastructure, continues to be large in developing countries as a whole, and can be partly met only by vigorous growth in remittances.

In addition, growth in middle-income countries, particularly emerging market economies, is highly susceptible to the negative effects of financial crises, which typically have the greatest impact on the poorest sections of the population. Improvements can be made in the international financial architecture to enhance prospects for stronger and more stable capital flows to developing countries and to reduce the likelihood, severity, and duration of financial crises. Rapid progress is being made in the use of collective action clauses (CACs), which should make debt workouts less costly and thus may make developing-country bonds more attractive to investors, but substantial work remains to improve practices in sovereign debt restructuring.

Macroeconomic Policies in Developed Countries: Trends and Prospects

In the United States, the current very accommodative stance of macroeconomic policy—with a rising budget deficit that is contributing to a record current account imbalance—is expected to be tightened in the longer term on the basis of a return of economic growth to rates of 3 to 4 percent (table 9.1 and figure 9.1). As economic growth in the United States gathers steam, an orderly tightening of monetary and fiscal policies would help restore balance.

In Europe, the substantial weakening of budgetary positions in recent years leaves little scope for fiscal stimulus. This adds urgency to the need to improve economic performance, which is being hampered by difficulties and delays in implementing needed structural reforms, especially in labor markets and social security systems. In the coming years, such reforms could help raise European growth to a sustainable range of 2 to 3 percent.

In Japan, the economic expansion is expected to continue in the near term. To sustain growth over the medium term, however, continued efforts will be needed to end deflation, to address the remaining weaknesses in the financial and corporate sectors, and to stabilize public sector debt.

Risks to the global economy. Alongside this improving scenario, substantial risks remain. In particular, the world economy could be hit by a worsening of political and security conditions, notably in the Middle East. The most significant risk on a global scale, however, continues to be a possible abrupt adjustment in the U.S. current account position. From 1998 to 2002, the current account deficit more than doubled to $480 billion, and in 2003 it rose further to more than $540 billion. Such large external imbalances are difficult to sustain for a long period, and most observers now anticipate an adjustment. Difficulties in financing the U.S. external position could lead to a sharp decline in the dollar,

TABLE 9.1 Macroeconomic indicators for advanced economies, 1993–2008

Indicator	1993–97	1998–2002	2003 estimated	2004–08 projected
Inflation (average, percent)				
United States	2.7	2.3	2.3	2.1
European Union	2.7	1.8	2.0	1.8
Japan	0.7	–0.4	–0.2	0.7
Advanced economies	2.5	1.7	1.8	1.8
Current account balance, percent of GDP				
United States	–1.5	–3.6	–5.0	–4.6
European Union	0.6	0.2	0.4	0.6
Japan	2.3	2.6	3.2	3.2
Advanced economies	0.2	–0.6	–0.8	–0.7
Fiscal balance, percent of GDP				
United States	–2.9	–0.1	–4.9	–3.6
European Union	–4.8	–0.9	–2.6	–1.8
Japan	–3.9	–6.8	–8.0	–6.8
Advanced economies	–3.6	–1.2	–4.1	–3.0
Real GDP growth, in percent				
United States	3.5	3.0	3.1	3.7
European Union	1.8	2.5	0.8	2.5
Japan	1.7	0.4	2.7	1.8
Advanced economies	2.8	2.6	2.1	3.1

Source: IMF *World Economic Outlook* database and IMF staff calculations.

FIGURE 9.1 A robust global economy requires orderly resolution of the large external and fiscal imbalances
Current account and fiscal balances, United States and all advanced economies, 1993–2003

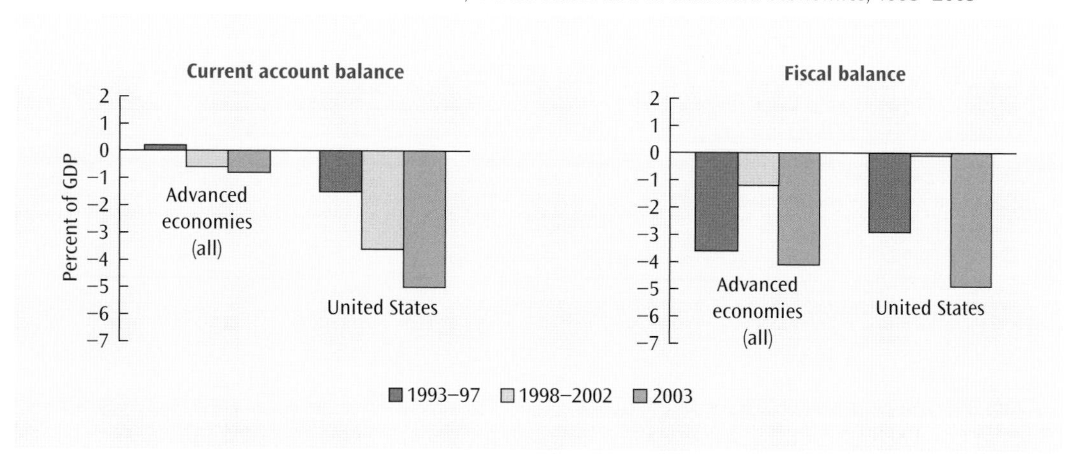

Source: IMF *World Economic Outlook* database.

however, with possible negative repercussions on the relatively highly indebted U.S. household and corporate sectors—for example, if the Federal Reserve were to raise interest rates to prop up the currency.

Given the size of the financing needs arising from the U.S. deficit, the moderation of its external imbalance could free up substantial financing for other countries, including developing countries. The degree of substitutability between finance for developing countries and the United States is no doubt limited, but to the extent that some crowding out is taking place, emerging market economies could benefit from lower needs for external financing in the U.S. economy.

Implications for Developing Countries

An improved global outlook presents an opportunity for higher growth in developing countries. More robust income growth in the developed countries is expected to stimulate activity in developing countries through trade, especially higher export volumes. Developing countries suffered from the slowdown in world trade in 2002, chiefly because of weak demand in developed countries. Over the medium term, however, the pickup in global activity that began in 2003 should translate into stronger and more sustained export growth for developing countries as a group (table 9.2). This could be helped further if progress is made in reducing trade barriers through a successful outcome to the Doha Round (see chapter 10). Stronger growth in world trade is particularly relevant for developing countries, such as those in East Asia, that trade intensively with developed countries. Although the terms of trade for developing countries are expected to fall in 2004–08, the decline should be limited mostly to fuel exporters; nonfuel primary commodity prices are projected to remain broadly constant. Although oil markets continue to be subject to great uncertainty, prices are expected to stabilize once production fully resumes in Iraq.

Private Capital Flows

Private capital flows can be an important source of growth in developing countries, especially if they take the form of foreign direct investment (FDI), which can raise investment, provide a vehicle for the transfer of knowledge to the host country, and enhance the human capital of the host country's work force. FDI is also desirable as a source of finance because it is less volatile than debt and because it provides better risk sharing between originating and recipient countries.

TABLE 9.2 Global economic environment and developing countries (annual average percentage changes, except as noted)

Indicator	1993–97	1998–2002	2003 (estimated)	2004–08 (projected)
World trade	7.9	5.2	4.1	6.5
Developing countries				
Volume of exports of goods/services	9.9	6.8	8.6	7.7
Terms of trade	0.8	0.2	0.3	–0.4
Fuel exporters	1.7	7.8	2.8	–2.4
Nonfuel exporters	0.8	–0.8	–0.2	–0.1
Private capital inflows net (billions of dollars)	234	175	200	—

— Not available.
Source: IMF *World Economic Outlook* database and IMF staff calculations; private capital flows are from World Bank *Global Development Finance* database.

FDI continues to supply the largest amount of external financing to developing countries. Although FDI drifted lower in 2003, it is expected to recover in 2004–05, in line with the global economic recovery.[2] While prospects for FDI flows to developing countries continue to be favorable, their destinations remain highly concentrated. Ten countries captured about 69 percent of North-South FDI in 2003 (down from a high of 78 percent in 2000). Nine of the 10 countries were middle-income countries. The share of middle-income countries in total FDI to developing countries is about 90 percent. The size of FDI flows relative to GDP is twice as large in middle-income countries as in low-income countries (figure 9.2). Only a small portion of FDI—$9 billion out of $135 billion in 2003—goes to Sub-Saharan Africa, which is the region most in need of investment if it is to achieve its development goals. Half the FDI flows to this region were received by three oil exporters. The challenge is to raise the capacity of African countries to attract and to make good use of FDI, which in turn will require improvements in education, infrastructure, and governance. Once a country has a strong enough business climate to attract FDI, inflows can fuel a virtuous circle of growth and further investment.[3] The availability of risk insurance against a broad range of political risk through private and official agencies could aid FDI flows to poorer countries in Africa and elsewhere.[4]

Although private debt flows[5] represent a transfer of savings from developed to developing countries, they can be a mixed blessing. Because private debt flows depend largely on investor confidence, they are not a very reliable source of financing, as the availability and cost of financing can change suddenly and with little warning (figure 9.3).[6] In particular, portfolio holdings are relatively easy for investors to sell on secondary markets, especially for those emerging market countries in which secondary markets are well developed. Countries that have benefited from substantial portfolio inflows may therefore be hit suddenly by a sharp increase in the cost of capital, or a loss of access, or both.

The challenge is to sustain the cyclical recovery in private debt flows over the medium term by maintaining investor confidence, while taking steps to lower the vulnerability of developing countries to sharp reversals in flows and to widen the set of countries enjoying access to financing. Moreover, discrimination by investors—signs of which have appeared in the wake of the recent experience with defaults and debt restructurings in emerging markets—can only improve the stability of private financial flows.

FIGURE 9.2 **Low-income countries receive little foreign direct investment**
Distribution of FDI to developing countries, by region and income category, 2003

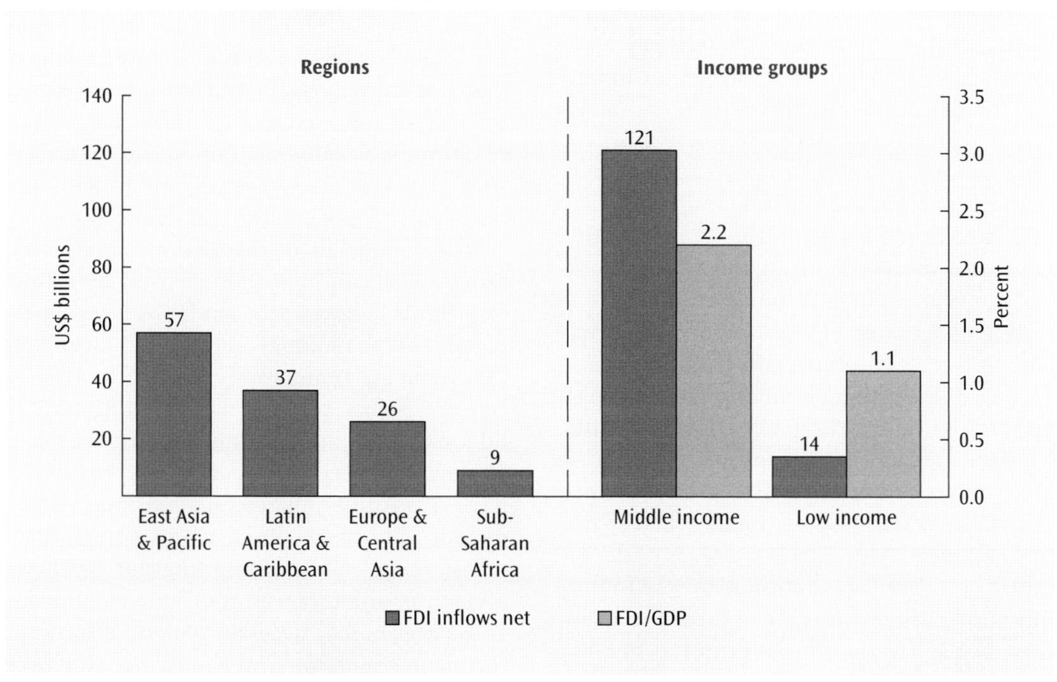

Source: World Bank *Global Development Finance* database.

More and better market information, combined with greater experience with emerging markets, translates into more appropriate pricing of investment opportunities and lower risk of contagion.

Developing countries have substantial infrastructure gaps that must be filled if they are to attain the MDGs, as discussed in chapter 6. Although private sector financing is important to achieving such long-term investment needs, financing for infrastructure has trended downward—led by the financial crises of the late 1990s and a weakening of the global infrastructure industry. Global capital markets are potentially well suited to finance large infrastructure requirements, but considerable institutional and regulatory changes in developing countries will be needed to attract these flows, including a strong institutional framework for the protection of creditors' rights. A greater availability in global markets of political risk insurance for project financing could assist infrastructure flows.

FIGURE 9.3 **Private capital flows to developing countries are recovering, led by debt flows**
Net private capital flows to developing countries, 1990–2003

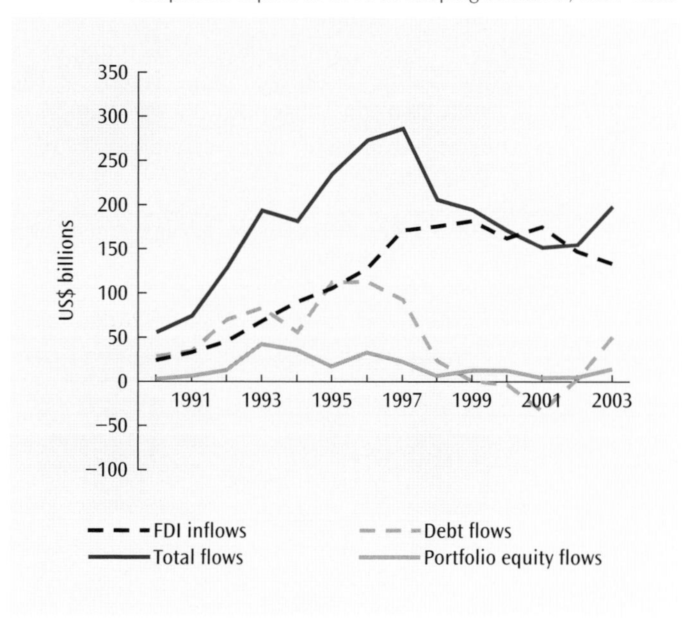

Source: World Bank *Global Development Finance* database.

Workers' Remittances

In contrast to official aid and private debt flows, workers' remittances have been a relatively stable and growing source of financing for development. Developing countries received an estimated $93 billion in workers' remittances in 2003, an increase of more than 20 percent from 2001 and more than 200 percent from 1990 (table 9.3).[7] Following steady increases during the 1990s, workers' remittances to developing countries now rank second after FDI as a source of external finance.[8] The especially sharp surge in recorded remittances since 2001 in part appears to reflect three new developments. Vigorous efforts to curb money laundering and thwart terrorist financing have helped divert remittance flows from informal to formal channels. Also, increased fears of deportation or other legal action prompted many migrant workers to remit a larger share of their savings to their home country. In addition, the growing importance of remittances has resulted in better reporting of data in many developing countries.

Remittances share some characteristics with capital flows but are also distinguished by important differences (box 9.1). The main source of remittances continues to be the United States, where the rise in remittances coincided with the economic boom of the 1990s and the liberalization of temporary migration (especially in the technology sector).[9] Latin America and the Caribbean continued to be the top recipient of remittances, absorbing nearly a third of total flows to developing countries.[10] Remittances to South Asia rose by more than one-third in 2001–03; Pakistan accounted for half of the increase. At about $4 billion, remittances to Sub-Saharan Africa were relatively flat. The region receives only a small fraction, under 5 percent, of total remittances.

The financial infrastructure supporting remittances can impose high costs on remitting funds. These costs can be as large as 20 percent of the remitted amount. It is estimated that reducing transaction fees by 5 to 10 percentage points could yield an additional $5 billion to $9 billion in annual remittance flows to developing countries. Policies that could have a positive impact on remittance flows include improving competition among money transfer banks, increasing migrant workers' access to banking services in source countries and households' access to such services in recipient countries, and removing exchange restrictions on remittances.

Strengthening the Environment for Emerging Markets

Since the Asian crisis of 1997–98, many steps have been taken to strengthen the global policy environment and financial architecture to make financial crises less likely in emerging market countries—and to resolve them quickly when they do occur.

TABLE 9.3 Remittances to developing countries, by region, 2001–03 (US$ billions)

Region	1990	1995	2001	2002	2003	Percentage increase 2001–03
East Asia and Pacific	3.0	9.9	13.7	17.0	17.6	28.9
Europe and Central Asia	3.2	5.6	10.2	10.3	10.4	1.9
Latin America and Caribbean	5.7	12.9	22.9	26.8	29.6	29.3
Middle East and North Africa	11.4	10.0	13.2	13.0	13.0	–1.2
South Asia	5.6	10.0	13.1	16.9	18.2	38.7
Sub-Saharan Africa	1.5	2.7	3.9	4.1	4.1	3.5
Total	30.4	51.2	77.1	88.1	93.0	20.7

Source: IMF *Balance of Payments Yearbook* and World Bank staff estimates.

BOX 9.1 Differences between remittances and capital flows

Remittances differ from private capital flows in several ways. Remittances are unilateral transfers that do not have to be paid back, whereas capital flows create liabilities that must result in outward flows—of income, interest, or principal. Remittances are sent by emigrants to their families; private capital flows are bound by no such ties. Because the motivation for remittances is largely altruistic—to help recipients pay for education, medical care, housing, food, or clothing—they tend to be stable over time and may even rise in times of economic difficulty in the recipient country. Other private capital flows, driven by expectations of financial return, tend to be more volatile, rising and falling "procyclically" with conditions in the recipient economy. Finally, remittances are made by individuals, whereas capital flows for the most part involve institutional investors, companies, and governments.

Some factors affect remittances and capital flows in a similar manner. Both types of flows are positively affected by the growth cycle in the source country, although capital flows tend to be more sensitive than remittances. Both are similarly affected by the prevailing investment climate (especially the exchange-rate regime) in the recipient country. During 1996–2000, average remittance receipts as a share of GDP were 0.5 percent in countries with a higher-than-median level of corruption (as indicated by the International Country Risk Guide index) compared with 1.9 percent in lower-than-median corruption countries. Similarly, remittances were nearly twice as high (1.5 percent of GDP) in countries with relatively even income distribution (represented by a lower Gini index) than in other countries (0.9 percent). Countries that were more open (in terms of trade/GDP ratio) or more financially developed (in terms of M2/GDP ratio) also received larger remittances.

It is useful also to distinguish remittances from official aid flows. Sometimes it is argued, for example in comparing the aid efforts of rich countries, that a smaller aid effort is compensated by a larger amount of outward remittance flows that may result from a more liberal immigration policy. A significant part of official development assistance, like remittances, represents unilateral transfers to developing countries. But the similarity between aid and remittances ends there. Aid is financed by governments using taxpayers' money. Remittances, on the other hand, are personal flows, paid by migrants from incomes earned in exchange for providing many essential services to the host nation—legal migrants also pay taxes, and hence, indirectly also contribute to the government's aid effort. Aid is essential for meeting the MDGs in many countries. Sub-Saharan Africa receives about five times more net ODA than remittances. Even if border barriers were sharply reduced, there is no guarantee that (migrants would come from and) remittances would flow to the countries that most need financial and technical assistance.

Source: Ratha 2003.

Rapid progress has been made in promoting the use of CACs in international sovereign bond issuances.[11] Following the first Mexican issue containing CACs in New York in March 2003, there has been a clear shift toward their use in international sovereign bonds. Belize, Brazil, Guatemala, the Republic of Korea, the Philippines, South Africa, and Turkey have followed Mexico in issuing sovereign bonds with CACs under New York law. Many of these issues were heavily oversubscribed and showed little evidence of carrying a premium associated with the use of CACs. Collective action clauses also were included in bonds issued by Uruguay in the context of the country's recent debt exchange. Several developed countries have taken steps to introduce CACs in their international sovereign bonds.

Discussions have continued on a voluntary Code of Conduct to encourage uniform adoption of best practices in sovereign debt restructuring and so speed up resolution of sovereign debt crises. These discussions by the international community on the potential benefits of a voluntary code have highlighted a range of views on the central issues. The main challenge has been to achieve a balance between flexibility (to accommodate diverse country circumstances) and concreteness (to enhance predictability).

International standards and codes also appear to be playing an important role in strengthening the functioning of international markets. The goal of the standards and codes initiative launched by the IMF and the World Bank is to encourage countries to adopt good practices, identify potential weaknesses in policies and institutions, and enhance transparency. The initiative covers 12 areas including data dissemination, fiscal transparency, and monetary and financial transparency. An IMF and World Bank report finds that major market participants appear to be using information on countries' observance of standards in making investment decisions.[12]

In response to the challenges created by financial market developments, the Basel Committee on Banking Supervision proposed a new capital adequacy framework. It is expected to be finalized by mid-2004 and implemented by the end of 2006.[13] The Basel II accord is based on three "mutually reinforcing pillars":[14]

- Minimum capital requirements of at least 8 percent of risk-weighted assets, with a more sensitive weighting of the riskiness of different assets
- More stringent supervisory review of capital adequacy—some banks may be required to have a capital ratio above the minimum 8 percent level
- Public disclosure—to enable stronger market discipline through enhanced public disclosure and transparency.

Basel II is designed to enhance the soundness of the banking industry by measuring the true financial risks in banks' portfolios and by aligning capital requirements with those risks.[15] But even as it strengthens the global banking industry, the accord could discourage lending to developing countries. It may increase the cost of capital for some borrowers—especially lower-rated borrowers—in part by undervaluing diversification (and thus overstating the risk of lending to developing countries) and by causing bank lending to move more tightly with the business cycle.

Notes

1. Simple regression analysis using data from 1971 to 2000 indicates that a 1 percent change in real GDP growth in developed countries is associated with a 0.4 percent change in GDP growth in developing countries. The strength of the correlation, however, is much weaker for primary commodity exporters (IMF 2001).

2. The downturn in FDI flows to developing countries in 2003 largely reflects the sharp decline in investment flows in a small number of middle-income countries that suffered a continuing weakening in privatization and cross-border merger and acquisition activities. By contrast, FDI to low-income countries remained stable.

3. The impact of FDI on growth has been difficult to verify empirically. Positive effects may kick in only when the absorptive capacity of the host country is above a certain threshold, measured in terms of education levels, capital infrastructure, or similar indicators (Borensztein, De Gregorio, and Lee 1998).

4. The demand for political risk insurance has been rising. Private risk insurers comprise 50–60 percent of the market. National export agencies and the Multilateral Investment Guarantee Agency account for the rest. Most industrialized countries have investment guarantee programs, but there are differences in the amount of such guarantees provided.

5. Debt flows display a geographical dispersion similar to that of FDI, with the most going to Latin America and East Asia and the least to Sub-Saharan Africa.

6. Most of the increase in private debt flows in 2003 has gone to countries in Europe and Central Asia, Latin America and the Caribbean, and East Asia and Pacific.

7. Official data underestimate the actual size of remittance flows. Officials in major fund transfer agencies argue, based on the size of the funds that flow through their system, that unrecorded remittances may be larger than recorded remittances.

8. World Bank 2004. For data on remittances and migration flows, see also Adams 2003. In low-income countries, remittances exceed FDI inflows

(net). The geographical movement (temporary or permanent) of unskilled migrant workers from developing countries, where unskilled labor is abundant, to developed countries, where productivity is higher, is likely to benefit both sending and receiving economies. However, immigration policies in developed countries favor highly skilled workers. The effects of this bias on the human capital endowment in the home country can be significantly negative, particularly if highly skilled workers never return (Skeldon 1997). The transfer of knowledge from the new immigrants back to the home country and the incentive effects on educational achievements in the home country only partially offset the negative effects of this brain drain (Faini 2003).

9. Remittances from the United States exceeded $31 billion in 2002. Those from Saudi Arabia, which is the second largest source of remittances, were about $16 billion.

10. In Mexico, remittances surpassed FDI in the second quarter of 2003. In Ecuador, remittances are second only to oil exports as a source of external finance. In Sri Lanka, remittances are larger than tea exports.

11. Collective action clauses are designed to facilitate coordination among creditors and lower the cost of debt restructuring. Early evidence suggests that the benefits of CACs in lowering the expected cost of restructuring outweigh the costs, such as weakening creditor leverage or raising the likelihood of a default (Eichengreen, Kletzer, and Mody 2003). While CACs address the creditor coordination problem for individual bond issues, they do not solve the problem of cross-issue creditor coordination (the so-called aggregation problem) or the problem of creditor coordination for the existing stock of debt (the so-called transition problem) (Chuhan and Sturzenegger 2004).

12. Based on a survey of large, internationally active financial institutions, the report found that 58 percent of survey respondents used Reports on the Observance of Standards and Codes (IMF–World Bank 2003).

13. See also the section on the financial sector in chapter 4.

14. Basel Committee on Banking Supervision 2003.

15. Claessens, Underhill, and Zhang 2003; Heid 2003.

10

Dismantling Barriers to Trade

Expanding opportunities for international trade can be a powerful engine for spurring growth and accelerating progress toward poverty reduction and the other MDGs. Reducing trade protection will produce large benefits, not only for developing countries but for developed countries as well.

While the actions needed to enhance the ability of developing countries to use trade as an instrument of growth and poverty reduction are primarily their own, developed countries can do much to help. Estimates of the overall trade restrictiveness of policies affecting merchandise trade reveal that some OECD countries effectively discriminate against low-income developing countries. Correcting trade-distorting agricultural support policies is particularly important, but the agenda is broader. In manufacturing, tariff peaks and escalation that hurt exports from developing countries are a key issue. Lower barriers to services exports, both cross-border and those requiring the temporary movement of service suppliers, could also produce sizable gains. Liberalization by OECD countries not only would have a direct beneficial effect, but the indirect effect may be even more important: helping governments pursue desirable domestic reforms.

Putting the Doha Round back on track is a critical priority. The alternatives, bilateral and regional agreements, will give rise to trade diversion and discrimination and most likely will exclude the more difficult areas of reform—sectors such as agriculture and policies such as antidumping. There is huge scope for reducing barriers to access to markets for both goods and services. A refocused effort centered on market access could help realize the development promise of the Doha Round.

The effort to dismantle barriers to market access should be complemented by three principles:

- Enhanced transparency of trade policy. OECD countries continue to use trade policy instruments whose effects are difficult to quantify and compare. An example is the use of specific tariffs (a tax per unit of quantity). These often imply very high ad valorem equivalents that are not transparent to consumers. Moreover, high specific tariffs impose a heavier burden on exporters from developing countries because they produce lower-quality (cheaper) products. Data on key trade-related policies, especially those relating to services trade, are limited and incomplete.
- Increased predictability of trade policy. Uncertainty about the conditions of market access can be reduced through stronger disciplines on the use of contingent

protection and simplification of regulatory requirements.[1]

- International agreement on targets for trade policy to help ensure that trade can, to the fullest extent possible, contribute to achieving the MDGs. Such focal points could include: (a) complete elimination by high-income OECD countries of tariffs on manufactured products by a target date; (b) complete elimination of agricultural export subsidies and complete decoupling of all domestic agricultural subsidies from production, and reduction of agricultural tariffs to, say, no more than 10 percent, by a target date; and (c) commitments to ensure free cross-border trade in services delivered through telecommunications networks, complemented by actions to liberalize the temporary movement of service suppliers from developing countries.

A major question confronting OECD countries is whether the political commitment can be mobilized to pursue a meaningful market access–driven agenda that removes the existing bias against poor countries. The answer depends in part on the willingness of industries in OECD countries to devote the required resources to support deep reforms in agricultural policies and elimination of tariff peaks and nontariff barriers that are biased against low-income countries. Equally important will be credible commitments to ensure that social policies are in place to assist workers and communities to adjust to a more competitive environment.

Growth, Poverty Reduction, and the Doha Development Agenda

The attainment of Goal 8 of the MDGs—a global partnership for development—requires increased effort by the developed countries to open up market access for goods and services produced in developing countries. This is particularly the case in agriculture, textiles and clothing, and labor-intensive services—sectors where developing countries typically have a comparative advantage. Further liberalization of trade can generate substantial increases in real incomes, by up to $500 billion or more if account is taken of the likely dynamic benefits of greater trade.[2] Insofar as such trade expansion is realized, it has the potential to substantially reduce poverty beyond baseline projections—140 million fewer poor people in 2015, a decline of 8 percent (figure 10.1). Such income and poverty reduction gains are not automatic, however. Much depends on complementary policies and the investment response to changed incentives. For Sub-Saharan Africa in particular, analysis suggests that trade can do much to help attain the income poverty MDG, but much more than open access to markets will be required. The outcome will depend greatly on improved trade capacity, a function of the investment climate. Aid has an important supportive role to play in helping countries enhance their trade capacity.

The 2001 WTO Doha Declaration represented the first time that the needs of developing countries were placed at the top of the multilateral trade agenda. In the context of the Doha Development Agenda, and subsequently in Monterrey in March 2002 at the U.N. Financing for Development Conference, high-income countries reiterated their commitments to improve market access for agricultural and industrial products, especially for developing countries.[3]

The trade policy environment through August 2003 benefited from the momentum generated in the run-up to the WTO's Cancún Ministerial Conference in September. The European Union announced a reform of its Common Agricultural Policy (CAP) in June, and agreement was reached in August on the implementation of the public health provisions of the WTO's Trade-Related Intellectual Property Rights (TRIPs) Agreement. However, the Cancún Ministerial failed to move the substantive agenda forward. Differences over agriculture, as well as disagreements in other areas—including multilateral frameworks for investment, competition, government procurement, and trade facilitation, the so-called Singapore issues—proved impossible to bridge.

FIGURE 10.1 Potential income gains from trade reforms are large and can help reduce poverty

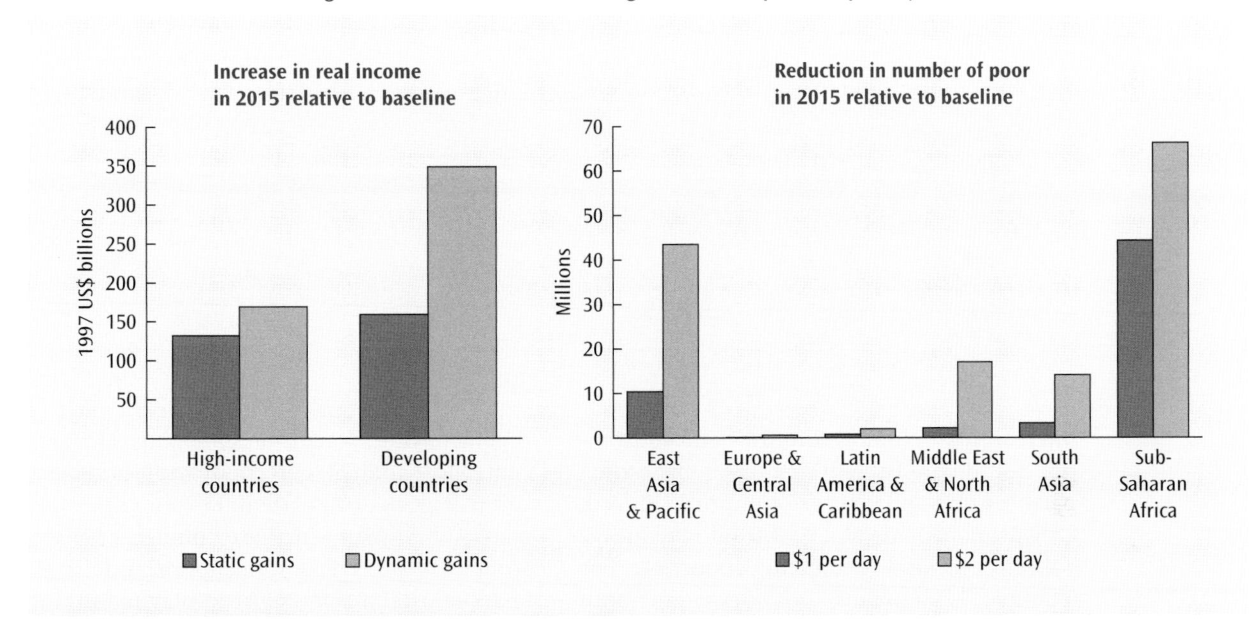

Source: World Bank staff simulations.

Recent proposals by the United States and the European Union to get the Doha Round back on track, which include the suggestion of abandoning negotiations on investment and competition policies and seek to break the impasse on agriculture, have improved the medium-term prospects for the Round.

Several risks are associated with continuing delays in the multilateral talks. The perception of failure can strengthen the hand of protectionists. High-profile trade disputes, held in check in order not to disturb the multilateral trade talks, could reemerge and damage the trading system, hurting smaller and poorer countries the most. The Cancún outcome may add momentum to strategies for regional and bilateral trade integration. This could prove to be a growing distraction from the Doha Round and alter the balance of interests in the multilateral talks. A shift toward greater discrimination in world trade, while possibly beneficial for countries that obtain preferred access, does not bode well for excluded nations. The majority of the world's poor live in countries such as China, India, Pakistan, and Indonesia that are not likely to be part of regional trade agreements (RTAs) with the major developed countries. Also, RTAs are unlikely to achieve significant progress in areas such as agriculture that matter most to the poor. It is important that RTAs minimize discrimination against nonmembers and not divert attention away from the multilateral WTO process.

Tariffs and Nontariff Barriers

Average most-favored-nation (MFN) tariffs applied by developed countries are substantially lower than those in developing countries.[4] In high-income OECD countries they average around 6 percent (table 10.1). On a trade-weighted basis, these tariffs are lower, averaging around 3 percent. Average collected tariffs, which are calculated by dividing total tariff revenue by the value of total imports, are even lower. One explanation for this difference is the impact of widespread membership in preferential trade agreements and various programs offering trade preferences to developing countries. The value of this "applied" average tariff is generally less than 2 percent. However, this average masks a significant bias against products of export

TABLE 10.1 MFN tariffs, developed countries, 1990 and 2002 (percent)

Group or country	Simple average 1990	Simple average 2002	Trade-weighted average 2002	Applied average tariff, 1990[a]	Applied average tariff, 2002[a]
High-income OECD, of which:	7.0	5.2	2.6	2.4	1.4
Canada	8.8	4.2	3.4	2.8	0.9
European Union	8.7	4.7	3.1	2.8	1.5
Japan	6.3	4.9	2.4	2.4	1.9
United States	6.4	5.2	3.1	3.3	1.7

a. Total collected tariff revenues as a share of total value of imports.
Source: WTO; IMF; European Commission budget.

interest to developing countries and substantial discrimination between different trading partners for similar types of imports. Indeed, a disproportionate share of total revenues is collected from low-income countries. For example, Mongolians and Norwegians both paid the United States about $23 million in tariffs in 2002. Mongolia exported $143 million; Norway $5.2 billion—or 40 times as much. In effect, Mongolians pay sixteen cents to sell the United States one dollar's worth of sweaters and suits, while the Norwegians paid half a penny to sell the United States one dollar's worth of gourmet smoked salmon, jet engine parts, and North Sea crude oil.[5]

A universally accepted definition of a tariff peak does not exist. Instead, two criteria are widely used to indicate the dispersion of tariffs. The first is the number of tariff lines above a threshold of 15 percent. The second is the number of tariff lines above a threshold defined as three times the national average. Developed countries have a low number of tariff lines that exceed 15 percent. Conversely, given the dispersion of their tariff profiles, they tend to have a higher number of lines that satisfy the second criterion. The frequency of peaks in the tariffs of developed countries is problematic for developing countries, since the high tariffs are typically on products of export interest to them, especially more processed products, causing what is called tariff escalation (figure 10.2).

In the Quad countries (Canada, European Union, Japan, United States), between 4 and 8 percent of the tariff lines are above 15 percent. More than 60 percent of imports subject to tariff peaks originate in developing countries. While many of these countries benefit from tariff preferences, many others do not.

Nontariff barrier (NTB) coverage ratios for high-income countries are in the 15 percent range, similar to that observed for middle-income countries (table 10.2). The use of NTBs has declined significantly since the late 1980s, due in part to WTO agreements to refrain from the use of voluntary export restrictions and to gradually phase out a regime of quantitative import restrictions imposed on textile and apparel products produced in developing countries—the Multifiber Arrangement (MFA). Under the WTO Agreement on Textiles and Clothing, quotas are to be phased out progressively over a 10-year period. The next-to-last stage in eliminating quotas was implemented on January 2002, when a further 15 percent of restrictive quotas were eliminated. On January 1, 2005, all remaining quotas (amounting to about 80 percent of originally restrictive quotas) are to be eliminated.

Although core NTBs have become less prevalent in OECD countries, the use of technical product regulations and mandatory standards has been increasing. At least one-third of all imports into the European Union, Japan, and the United States are subject to mandatory product standards. In most cases the standards involved are applied on a nondiscriminatory basis, and in principle they also apply to

FIGURE 10.2 Escalating tariff rates discourage development

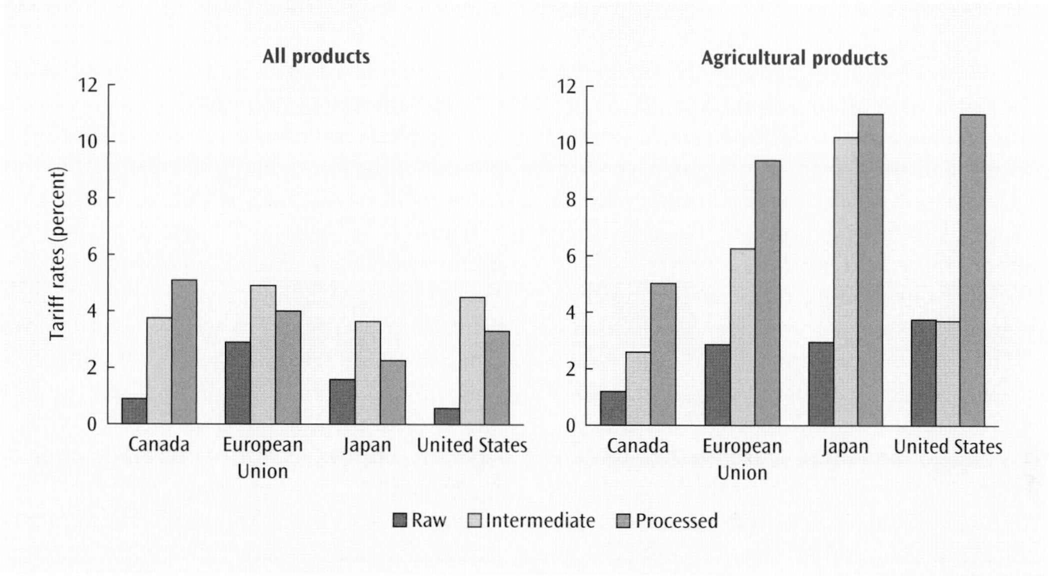

Source: WTO.

TABLE 10.2 Simple average NTB coverage ratios, 2001 (percent)

Group	Share of value of imports subject to technical regulations	Share of value of imports subject to core NTBs	Share of tariff lines subject to technical regulations	Share of tariff lines subject to core NTBs
High-income OECD, of which:	15[a]	14	12[a]	14
Canada	11	8	2	28
European Union	1[a]	15	1[a]	23
Japan	33	14	29	13
United States	34	19	21	14
Country-weighted average:				
High-income OECD	14	16	9	19

a. These numbers are a lower bound due to underreporting for the EU, reflecting the fact that regulations imposed by individual member states are not taken into account in the TRAINS database.
Source: UNCTAD TRAINS database.

domestic production. Thus they are not analogous to core NTBs, although research suggests they may have a disproportionate impact on exporters located in developing countries.

Agriculture

The agricultural policies of developed countries affect developing countries by distorting world prices and restricting access to markets. There are several methods for measuring agricultural support and the distortions produced by it. Each has shortcomings and strengths. The ones most often used are measures calculated by the OECD: the producer support estimate (PSE) and the total support estimate (TSE).[6] These indicators do not consider the economic inefficiencies (distortions) caused by the underlying policies and thus underestimate their true cost.

The need for overall measures of agricultural support arises because the instruments to support agriculture in OECD countries are manifold and complex. The two major types of intervention are market price support—policies that artificially raise domestic prices—and fiscal transfers to farmers. Border protection (such as tariffs) is an example of price-supporting policies. Because such support raises prices to both producers and consumers, it is more trade distorting than are direct payments to farmers.[7]

The share of the support that is provided through border measures versus direct payments varies substantially across OECD countries and commodities. During 2000–02, the average annual TSE in all OECD countries was $315 billion, or 47 percent of the value of OECD's agricultural production (table 10.3). The peak level of TSE was attained in 1999, when it stood at $356 billion. Compared with the base period used in the Uruguay Round negotiations (1986–88), the TSE has trended slightly upward in absolute amount, while the PSE has shown little change. The latter averaged $235 billion in 2000–02, or 35 percent of the value of OECD's agricultural production. Market price support has fallen from 77 percent of the PSE in 1986–88 to 63 percent in 2000–02, as many countries have moved to pay producers directly rather than use border measures. Some, but not all, of this shift indicates progress in decoupling payments from production, making support less trade distorting. The amount of decoupled payments based on historical entitlements is still small (only 4.6 percent of the total), but in the base period this category of payments was virtually zero.

During the Uruguay Round, disciplines on agricultural trade policy were substantially strengthened. A ban was imposed on quantitative restrictions, NTBs were converted into tariffs, minimum market access commitments were implemented through tariff rate quotas, and export subsidies and an aggregate measure of support (AMS) were made subject to reduction commitments. Despite these achievements, the PSE and TSE numbers reveal that agricultural protection remains high. Moreover, recent policy developments in the United States have implied an increase in support to farmers (the 2002 Farm Bill increased total potential payments to farmers by some 70 percent, or almost $75 billion over 10 years). In the European Union, efforts to reform the Common Agricultural Policy are moving toward less trade distortion by decoupling farm payments from production. However, such decoupling was only partially attained, and border protection was not

TABLE 10.3 Agricultural support, 1986–88 and 2000–02

	United States		European Union		Japan		OECD	
Type of support	1986–88	2000–02	1986–88	2000–02	1986–88	2000–02	1986–88	2000–02
Total support estimate ($ billions)	69	94	110	104	58	60	302	315
(% of agricultural production)	44	48	49	46	77	79	52	47
of which:								
Producer support estimate (PSE)								
($ billions)	42	47	94	93	49	48	248	235
(% of agricultural production)	27	24	42	41	65	63	43	35
Share of PSE from consumers								
(price support, %)	46	35	86	57	90	90	77	63
Share of PSE from taxpayers								
(fiscal transfers, %)	54	65	14	43	10	10	23	37
Per full-time farmer ($)	—	19,000	—	16,000	—	23,000	—	11,000

— Not available
Source: OECD.

BOX 10.1 The EU's Common Agricultural Policy reform

On June 26, 2003, European agriculture ministers reached an agreement on reform of the Common Agricultural Policy, or CAP. This reform constitutes a substantially watered-down version of the initial proposals. The scope for decoupling subsidies from production is more limited in key sectors, cuts in intervention prices are smaller, and the reform will be implemented later than initially envisaged.

The key elements of the agreement are:

- *Partial decoupling of subsidies from production* will be implemented differently by member states. In particular, member states retain the right to link up to 25 and 40 percent of subsidies to production in the case of cereals and beef, respectively, and are allowed to invoke regional exceptions if considered necessary to avoid the abandonment of production.
- *Progress was made on market policy,* although reform is limited. Plans to cut intervention prices for cereals have been abandoned, and price cuts in the dairy sector will be phased in over three to four years.
- *Direct payments to large farms will be reduced* in order to finance a new rural development policy, broadly in line with the January 2003 proposals.
- *Ministers agreed on a mechanism to enforce financial discipline* to ensure that the farm budget ceiling set for the period 2007–13 is not overshot.
- *The reform will enter into force later than originally proposed.* Although most of the reforms are to be implemented in 2005, member states can request a transitional period until 2007.
- *Other CAP reforms were not covered* and are scheduled for the future. The review of Mediterranean Products (olive oil, tobacco, and cotton sectors) started in September 2003. Other sectors, in particular sugar and wine, are scheduled for review in 2004.

Source: IMF staff.

reduced at all (box 10.1). This illustrates the importance of the WTO and the current Doha Round in attaining further reductions in trade-distorting support.

The Uruguay Round Agreement on Agriculture (URAA) classified domestic support into three "boxes":

- *Amber Box.* Trade-distorting support measures that are subject to reduction commitments, including market price support, as well as some product- and nonproduct-specific budgetary outlays.
- *Blue Box.* Payments based on fixed area and yields, number of heads for livestock, and base level of production. The mechanisms are supposed to constrain production, but the real motivation was a political need to exempt some key European and U.S. policies. The amount of Blue Box support was included in the baseline AMS, but was not subject to reduction commitments.
- *Green Box.* Support measures that are non- or minimally trade distorting and that are not subject to reduction commitments. They include general government services (such as research, disease control, infrastructure, and food security stockholding), certain forms of "production-decoupled" income support, structural adjustment assistance, direct payments under environmental programs, and regional assistance programs.

Reduction commitments in the URAA were made based on the AMS. This corresponds to Amber Box measures, but with exemptions for de minimis support, defined as support not exceeding 5 percent (developed countries) and 10 percent (developing countries) of the value of production of individual products or, in the case of non-product-specific support, the value of total agricultural production. Each industrial country's total AMS was supposed to be reduced by 20 percent (and two-thirds of this amount for developing countries) from a 1986–88 base over a six-year period (1995–2000). Due to the artificially inflated baseline levels, countries have in general been able to exceed their reduction commitments, with the result that most countries in recent years have been well below their ceiling for AMS. Deep reductions in the ceilings are required for the Doha Round to achieve significant reduction in trade-distorting support.

Trade-distorting agricultural support policies in OECD countries have a significant detrimental effect on developing countries. For example, OECD protection rates for sugar are frequently above 200 percent, and producers receive more than double the world market price.[8] OECD support to sugar producers of $6.4 billion a year roughly equals the value of developing country exports. U.S. subsidies to cotton growers totaled $3.6 billion in 2001–02, twice the amount of U.S. foreign aid to Africa. These subsidies depress world cotton prices by some 10 percent. In West Africa, where cotton is a critical cash crop for many small farmers, annual income losses for cotton growers are about $250 million a year.[9] In the European Union, producer support for beef reaches 84 percent of the value of domestic production.[10]

TABLE 10.4 Trade shares of products affected by agricultural subsidies (1995–98 average, in percent)

	Domestic support		Export subsidies	
Country category	Exports	Imports	Exports	Imports
All (143)	3.6	3.7	4.4	4.4
Developed countries (23)	3.1	3.3	4.0	3.9
Developing countries (90)	4.2	4.2	5.0	5.0
Least developed countries (30)	17.8	8.9	16.7	13.1

Note: 1995–98 is the most recent period for which detailed data were reported to the WTO. Numbers in parentheses indicate the number of countries.
Source: Hoekman, Ng, and Olarreaga 2004.

Although the major agricultural exporting economies will themselves benefit most from global agricultural reform, the least developed countries also stand to gain significantly. On average, some 18 percent of the total exports of least developed countries comprise goods that are subsidized in at least one WTO member country, compared with 3 to 4 percent for other countries (table 10.4). However, a similar observation holds for imports—9 percent of all least developed country imports involve products that are subsidized, compared with 3 to 4 percent for other countries. Given that OECD support tends to depress world prices of the affected commodities, reform could entail adjustment costs associated with possible increases in the world price of key food imports. Complementary financial support from the development community will be needed to assist developing countries that are negatively affected by an increase in world prices.

From the perspective of farmers in developing countries, the key issue is the impact of agricultural support policies on the prices they receive (or pay) for their products. This depends primarily on the extent to which output is increased and consumption decreased by policies in other countries. Research undertaken at the OECD and World Bank suggests that what matters most is market price support, that is, market access.[11] The research finds that the impact on world prices of reducing border barriers (tariffs) is likely to be much larger than the impact of reducing domestic subsidies, by a factor of 5 to 10, depending on products and countries. One reason for this difference is that tariffs are often very high for subsidized products, frequently taking the form of nontransparent specific duties. While minimum market access commitments negotiated during the Uruguay Round—implemented through tariff rate quotas (TRQs)—ensure some access, in many cases the TRQs are small, and the effect of the tariffs is to support high domestic price levels.

This does not imply that domestic support policies should be ignored—far from it.

Substantial reduction in production-linked OECD agricultural support policies is important for developing countries in its own right, but is also critical from a political economy perspective. OECD subsidy reforms are necessary to help developing countries pursue their own liberalization, an essential step in maximizing gains. Without action by OECD countries to decouple support from production, it is much harder for developing-country governments to pursue and sustain their own reforms.

Manufactures and Contingent Protection

Trade policies affecting developing-country exports of nonagricultural products are generally more liberal than policies affecting agriculture. As noted previously, in the majority of cases MFN tariffs are low. The exceptions pertain to certain labor-intensive sectors, such as clothing (apparel), for which import duties are much higher—particularly in Canada, Japan, and the United States, where tariff peaks average 16 to 17 percent and significant tariff escalation poses an impediment to poor countries trying to move their products up the value chain.[12] The textiles and clothing sector has also been ridden with quantitative restrictions on trade in recent decades. The 1995 WTO Agreement on Textiles and Clothing requires the abolition of all textile quotas by January 1, 2005. A challenge that will likely confront exporters after that date will be the threat of contingent protection (safeguards and, especially, antidumping). Antidumping is a frequently used instrument in developed countries against labor-intensive manufactures exported by developing countries (table 10.5), as well as more capital-intensive industries in which developing countries have built a comparative advantage—such as chemicals and steel. These instruments are also used to manage imports of agricultural products—examples include imports of catfish and shrimp in the United States—but are primarily applied to manufactures.

The existence of the antidumping instrument creates substantial uncertainty regarding the conditions of market access facing exporters. Antidumping investigations have a chilling effect on imports (they signal importers to diversify away from targeted suppliers). This has been of long-standing concern to East Asian countries in particular, especially China and Japan. China now faces the highest incidence of investigations and the highest average level of duties in the United States (table 10.6).[13] A similar conclusion applies to the other Quad members. Thus China is also the most often targeted country in EU antidumping, accounting for some 20 percent of all investigations in recent years, with average duties of 40 percent and in specific cases duties above 100 percent.[14]

TABLE 10.5 Antidumping investigations by selected OECD members, 1995–2002

	Against all economies	
Country/economy initiating	Number of antidumping initiations	Initiations per dollar of imports (Index United States = 100)
New Zealand	35	900
Australia	142	741
Canada	106	171
European Union	255	107
Japan	2	2
United States	279	100

Note: Annual data on a July–June reporting basis.
Source: World Bank staff calculations based on notifications to the WTO Antidumping Committee.

Overall Trade Restrictiveness Index

As noted in chapter 4 for developing-country policies, it is not possible to compare the various trade policy instruments just discussed across countries. Thus, an overall trade restrictiveness index (OTRI) was estimated that incorporates MFN tariffs (both ad valorem and ad valorem equivalents of specific tariffs), core NTBs, and domestic agricultural support.[15] In addition, in calculating the OTRI vis-à-vis low-income and least developed countries, trade preferences granted to developing countries

TABLE 10.6 Average tariff imposed in final U.S. antidumping duty determinations (percent)

Investigations	Total	Developing countries: Lower-income	Developing countries: Upper income	Developing countries: China	Developed countries: Japan	Developed countries: Other
1979–98 all cases	46	53	30	95	60	31
1989–98 cases only	58	66	36	116	74	34

Source: Bown, Hoekman, and Ozden 2003.

TABLE 10.7 Overall trade restrictiveness and import shares, high-income OECD and Quad, 2001 (percent)

Country	OTRI	OTRI toward low-income countries	OTRI toward least-developed countries	Share of total low-income country exports taken	Share of low-income countries in total imports from all developing countries
High-income OECD, of which:	6.3	4.9	4.2	69.6	4.6
Canada	5.6	7.7	0.1	1.2	4.2
European Union	6.6	3.9	0.6	21.1	3.2
Japan	3.9	1.5	1.1	11.2	10.8
United States	4.6	6.3	8.2	20.3	6.4

Source: World Bank staff estimates based on World Integrated Trade Solution and U.N. Comtrade database.

(both unilaterally and through major trade agreements) were included in the estimation.

The simple average OTRI for high-income OECD members was 6.3 percent in 2001 (table 10.7). Of the Quad economies, the European Union has the highest OTRI, at 6.6 percent. As a result of trade preference programs, the OTRI against low-income countries is lower than the overall OTRI (3.9 percent), and that against least developed countries is lower still (0.6 percent). This pattern of lower OTRIs against poorer countries does not apply uniformly. In the case of Canada, trade barriers discriminate significantly against low-income countries that do not fall into the least developed category, whereas in the case of the United States, barriers are higher both for all low-income countries and for least developed countries than for richer countries. Indeed, the OTRI is highest against least developed countries. Reasons for this include relatively high protection of apparel and other labor-intensive "sensitive" sectors, and the fact that some of the countries that face the highest OTRI on exports to the United States do not have significant preferences for their main exports. Note, however, that U.S. imports from low-income countries, as a share of total imports from developing countries, are higher than for the European Union.

OTRI estimates for agricultural products are generally a multiple of those for manufactures, reflecting the higher levels of protection of agriculture (figure 10.3). For high-income OECD countries, the OTRI is 25.6 percent for agriculture, compared to 3.6 percent for manufacturing. Only Australia and New Zealand

FIGURE 10.3 Protection in agriculture is high—a multiple of that in manufacturing
Ratio of agriculture OTRI to manufacturing OTRI in high-income OECD countries, 2001

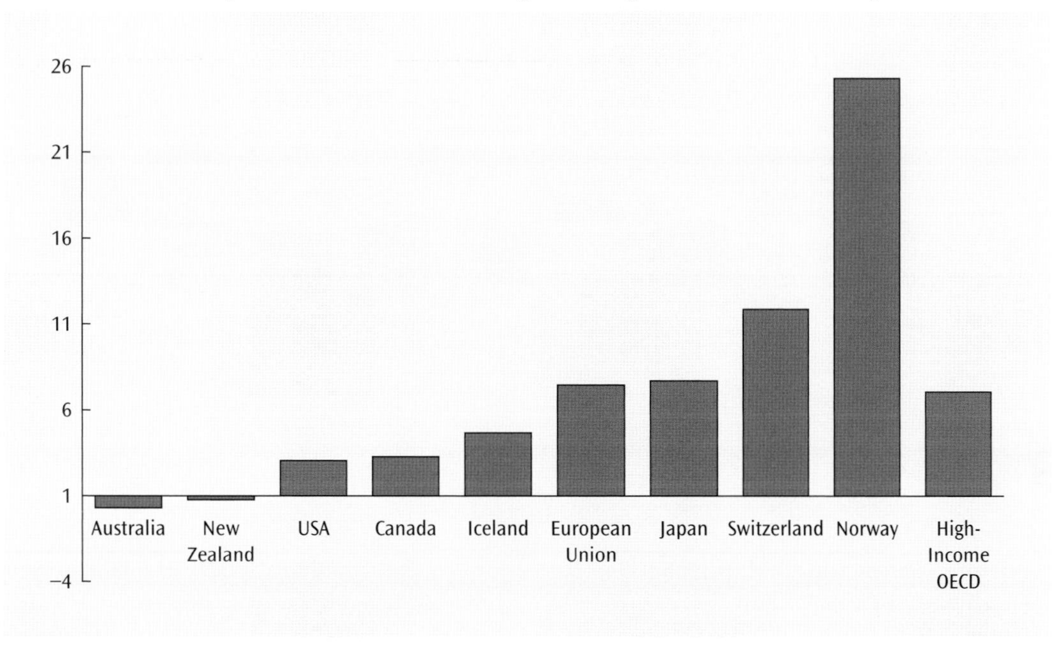

Source: World Bank staff estimates.

have a lower OTRI in agriculture than in manufacturing. Norway has the highest agriculture OTRI among OECD countries (42 percent), 25 times greater than its manufacturing OTRI. Norway is followed by Switzerland (35 percent) and the European Union (28 percent).[16] The high rates for Norway and Switzerland mainly reflect high ad valorem equivalents of specific tariffs on agricultural imports.[17]

Figure 10.4 plots, for high-income OECD members, the difference between their OTRIs for trade with low-income countries and their OTRIs for trade with all countries. A positive number indicates that the importing country imposes higher trade barriers on imports from low-income countries than on those from the rest of the world. Several OECD countries, including the United States, have a more restrictive trade policy vis-à-vis low-income countries relative to their overall trade policy stance.[18]

The OTRI estimates are in part a function of the estimates of the ad valorem equivalents (AVEs) of the NTBs that are included. The above numbers include the AVEs of specific tariffs, core NTBs, and agricultural producer subsidies. They do not include technical product regulations because of incomplete reporting of related data by countries. The exclusion of technical regulations in the estimation of the AVEs of NTBs is likely to bias downward the OTRI against low-income countries. If the existing, incomplete data on technical regulations are included, the OTRI estimates for all trade do not change much, but those against low-income countries increase. In the case of Japan, the OTRI against low-income countries rises toward the overall level of the OTRI. That is, the effect of any preference programs is eliminated. In the case of the United States, the OTRI against lower-income countries also rises.

The estimates of the OTRI vis-à-vis low-income countries are also biased downward by the assumption made in the estimation that major trade preference programs such as the African Growth Opportunity Act (AGOA) of

FIGURE 10.4 Is overall trade policy pro development? Mixed picture
Difference between OTRI applied to low-income countries and OTRI for all trade, 2001

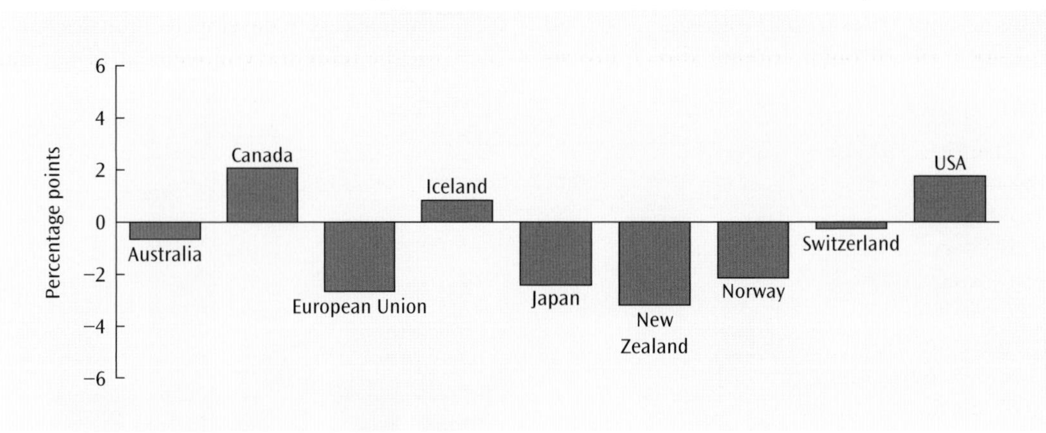

Source: World Bank staff estimates.

the United States and the European Union's Everything-but-Arms Initiative (EBA) are fully effective (that is, are fully utilized by recipients). Strict rules of origin may substantially reduce or even nullify the value of preferences for manufactured products. Moreover, part of the rents created by preferences, if any, accrue to importers, not the exporters. Taking these factors into account will increase the estimates of the OTRI against low-income countries. If it is assumed that utilization rates are only 50 percent, that is, only half of imports from least developed countries enter duty free, the OTRI against these countries is roughly the same as that applying to all trade: around 6 percent, with the United States having the highest barriers (12.6 percent). The potential importance of preferences for least developed countries is illustrated by the fact that without any preferences, they would confront an average OTRI of about 10 percent in high-income OECD countries—more than two times higher than the restrictions currently applied.[19]

The sensitivity of these results to assumptions regarding the effectiveness of preferences and to the coverage of NTBs in national trade policy databases points to the need for better data collection and reporting. This is most important for technical regulations, which the foregoing analysis was forced to ignore for comparability reasons. Recent research has shown how important it is for firms in developing countries to be able to satisfy technical product standards.[20] A concerted effort by the relevant international agencies (WTO, United Nations Conference for Trade and Development, or UNCTAD) to improve the coverage of data on technical regulations, ad valorem equivalents of specific tariffs (both bound and applied rates), and (bilateral) utilization of trade preferences by developing countries is important from a global monitoring perspective. The weakness in both trade policy data and information on services trade policies and international transactions greatly constrains efforts both to determine the overall trade policy stance and to monitor changes in it over time.

Trade in Services

Data constraints prevent the inclusion of policies affecting trade and investment in services in the OTRI. Services are the fastest-growing component of world trade. Developing countries have expanded exports of services nearly fourfold in the last decade (a faster rate than goods exports), and increased their share of the global marketplace for services to 18 percent, up from 14 percent in the early 1990s.

In large part this increase reflects growth in business process outsourcing (BPO) services. This activity arises from the outsourcing (and out-location through foreign direct investment) of noncore business processes throughout the value chain of both manufacturing and services industries. Within BPO activities, the more advanced developing countries are moving from providing only low-end back-office services (such as data entry) to more integrated and higher-end service bundles in fields such as customer care, human resource management, and product development. For example, Barbados is increasingly prominent in data processing; the Philippines, India, and China are actively exporting computer software; and South Africa is exporting telecommunications services.

Exports of BPO services are an example of one of four possible ways in which services can be traded: cross-border through telecommunications networks. The other three "modes of supply" involve either the movement of the consumer to the location of the service providers (as with international tourism) or the movement of the providers. The latter may be long term and involve foreign direct investment ("Mode 3" in the terminology of the WTO's General Agreement on Trade in Services, or GATS) or be temporary and involve the movement of individual service suppliers such as workers (Mode 4). Of these four modes of trading services, Mode 3 (commercial presence through FDI) is currently the largest in world trade, accounting for an estimated $2 trillion, followed by Mode 1 (cross-border supply, $1 trillion), Mode 2 (travel and tourism, $500 billion), and Mode 4 ($50 billion).[21]

The potential gains from successful liberalization of trade in services are huge. The U.S. banking industry alone is estimated to have saved more than $8 billion over the last four years, and the cost savings for the world's top 100 financial institutions could be as high as $138 billion annually. Analysis suggests that the real income gains associated with procompetitive reforms that increase the variety and quality of services and lower their costs could be a multiple of the potential gains resulting from liberalization of trade in goods.[22]

Greater access to developed countries' markets for the temporary movement of natural service providers and commitments to maintain liberal policies toward cross-border trade through telecommunications networks would both be valuable in themselves and assist developing-country governments in pursuing beneficial domestic reforms. Currently, Mode 1 faces few explicit restrictions in OECD countries. However, the well-publicized creation of jobs in developing countries' service industries has created concerns that may translate into protectionism. Although only a small fraction of the work force in the developed world is employed in agriculture and textiles, two areas that have seen significant protectionist pressure, more than two-thirds of the work force is employed in the services sector and many more have services-type jobs within manufacturing enterprises. The out-location of even a fraction of such jobs could provoke powerful protectionist pressures—signs of which are already visible. In several U.S. states, and more recently at the federal level, legislation is pending that would restrict outsourcing on government contracts. In Europe legal norms designed to protect workers in outsourcing deals, known as TUPE (Transfer of Undertakings and Protection of Employees), as well as recent privacy directives, could have an inhibiting effect on trade. Addressing the question of securing liberal cross-border trade in services should be high on the agenda of the international community.

The same is true for temporary movement of service suppliers (Mode 4). Many developing countries export services that are "embodied" in people. Although much of the associated movement of persons is long term, a substantial share of cross-border movements involves service industry workers who return to their home countries at some point. Remittance flows associated with migration are now a major source of external funding for developing countries. Remittances received by developing countries are estimated at $93 billion in 2003, up more than 20 percent from 2001 and approximately three times the level of 1990. Latin America and the Caribbean, with $30 billion in remittance receipts, accounts for nearly one-third of the developing-country total.[23]

There is little doubt that despite the dramatic developments in technologies for electronic delivery of services (Mode 1), Mode 4 will remain important for a range of services. The movement of service-supplying personnel remains a crucial means of delivery even for the Indian software industry. Nearly half of Indian exports are still supplied through the temporary movement of programmers to the client's site overseas. Greater freedom for the temporary movement of service providers would enable developing countries to provide the labor component of construction, distribution, transport, and a range of other services. As their populations age and their average levels of training and education rise, developed countries will face an increasing scarcity of moderately and less skilled labor. Given that there is no substitute for human labor in some activities (for example, the caring occupations, personal services, and a range of professional services), the demand for Mode 4 is likely to increase over time.

Most countries impose a range of barriers against Mode 4–based transactions. The temporary movement of service providers invariably is affected by regulations imposed by multiple authorities, including immigration legislation and labor market policy. Visa formalities are in themselves a significant obstacle, and the conditions attached are often used to implement a range of restrictions. These include prohibitions and quotas either explicitly or through a variety of economic needs tests. Wage-parity conditions tend to erode the cost advantage of hiring foreigners and have the same restrictive impact as quotas. Discriminatory treatment is implemented through a variety of fiscal and regulatory means. Nonrecognition of professional qualifications poses a particular challenge because of the difficulty in distinguishing between legitimate and protectionist denial of recognition.

Temporary movement of service providers potentially offers a way to realize the gains from trade while averting social and political costs in host countries, as well as avoiding negative brain drain effects for poor home countries. Recent research finds that if OECD countries were to allow temporary access to foreign service providers equal to just an additional 3 percent of their labor force, the gains to all countries would exceed $150 billion (figure 10.5).[24]

To date, only limited progress has been made in liberalizing international services transactions.[25] At Cancún, trade in services was not an area of disagreement. The Draft Ministerial Text recognized the progress made in the negotiations, which so far consists of a large number of confidential but reportedly ambitious requests that members (including several developing countries) have made to each other for greater market access, as well as reportedly disappointing offers of improved access submitted by 30 or so members (including some developing countries). Developing-country engagement in the negotiations has been inhibited by these countries' perception that the "assessment" of trade in services—mandated by the GATS as a condition for the new round of negotiations—has not been adequately conducted; that their domestic regulatory institutions are ill-equipped to deal with the demands of a liberalized market; and that there is little prospect of meaningful liberalization in areas in which they have an export interest.

For developing countries, what matters most in terms of what developed countries can do on trade in services—as in goods—is improved market access. This implies that negotiating modalities are needed that give particular attention to the removal of barriers to trade on those services and modes of supply in which developing countries have an export interest. Given that the rapid spread of information technology and telecommunications infrastructure is allowing service firms located in developing countries to contest markets in richer countries, binding commitments to impose no restrictions on such trade would be valuable. Specific commitments to open markets through liberalization of temporary movement of natural service suppliers would also be very valuable, although more difficult to achieve.

The Singapore Issues and Special and Differential Treatment

As tariffs were gradually reduced, governments in high-income countries increasingly sought to cooperate in disciplining the use of NTBs and trade-distorting domestic policies. They also began to use trade agreements as instruments for harmonization of domestic policies that have an impact on trade. The Agreement on Trade-Related Aspects of Intellectual Property Rights is the major example in the WTO. At the 1997 WTO Ministerial in Singapore, four new issues were put forward for negotiation: trade facilitation, competition policy, investment policy, and transparency in government procurement.

Many developing countries have come to question the development payoffs associated with regulatory harmonization enforced through the WTO.[26] The Cancún Ministerial illustrated the difficulty of expanding the coverage of the WTO to new regulatory areas. Poor countries expressed concerns that new multilateral rules might not be in their interest, would do little to promote progress on key issues such as agriculture, and could give rise to additional implementation burdens. A basic question now confronting the international development community is how to build in flexibility in rules that takes into account substantial differences in priorities and capacity across countries. An example of such flexibility is the mid-2003 agreement clarifying that the TRIPS agreements allow low-income countries without domestic pharmaceutical capacity to license imports of needed drugs on a compulsory basis.

A fundamental challenge confronting the WTO is ensuring that its rules support development. Traditionally, "special and differential treatment" (SDT) has been a means of increasing the development relevance of the trading system, as reflected in preferential market access for developing countries to developed-country markets and greater flexibility for them to use trade policies than is otherwise permitted by WTO rules. Efforts to date to agree on ways to strengthen and operationalize such provisions, however, have been divisive and unsuccessful.

FIGURE 10.5 Potential gains from liberalization of services, especially migration, are large
Welfare gains from a 3 percent increase in developed countries' temporary labor quota

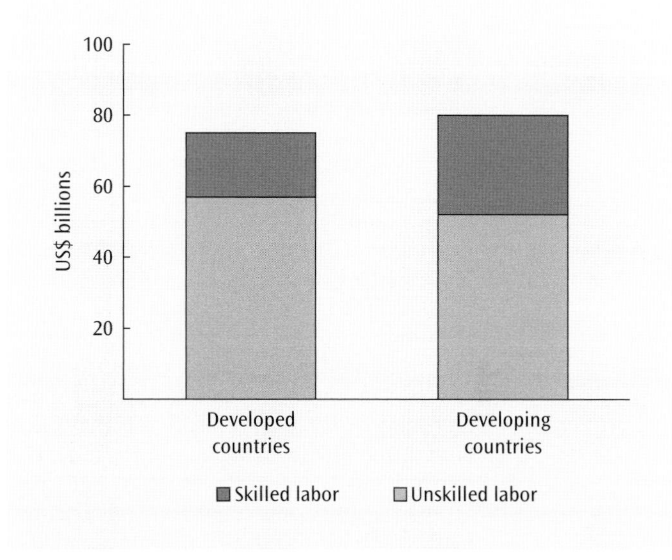

Source: Walmsley and Winters 2002.

A good understanding of the costs and benefits of specific proposals and rules requires engagement by developing-country stakeholders—a big challenge in many countries, given prevailing capacity constraints. One way of recognizing these constraints would be through SDT provisions that allowed for greater differentiation among developing countries in determining the reach of WTO rules. The need for differentiation is greatest for disciplines that require significant complementary legal, administrative, and institutional investments or capacity to implement, and for those that may give rise to large net transfers from low-income developing countries (as under the TRIPS agreement). The basic rationale for differentiation is that

BOX 10.2 Lessons from Integrated Framework diagnostic trade integration studies

Given the typically small domestic markets in the poorest countries, international trade can play a key role in achieving sustained growth and poverty reduction. The Integrated Framework for Trade-Related Technical Assistance to Least-Developed Countries (IF) is an international initiative combining the efforts of the IMF, ITC, UNCTAD, UNDP, World Bank, and WTO, in partnership with bilateral donors and recipient countries, to identify and respond to the trade development needs of the LDCs. The main elements of the IF process are: (a) preparation of a comprehensive *diagnostic trade integration study*, which documents constraints to trade in both the domestic economy and overseas and develops a plan of action to address the major constraints; (b) integration of the *action plan* into the country's poverty reduction strategy program; and (c) facilitation of interaction between the agencies, donors, and recipient governments in the *implementation* of the recommendations through technical assistance, capacity building, and investments.

Although specific conditions vary across countries, a clear message has emerged from the 13 diagnostic studies completed as of the end of 2003 (for Burundi, Cambodia, Djibouti, Ethiopia, Guinea, Lesotho, Madagascar, Malawi, Mali, Mauritania, Nepal, Senegal, and Yemen): success in reforming formal trade policies is not sufficient to ensure that trade can play its role in stimulating growth and poverty reduction. A range of barriers at home (including weak institutions, poor governance, and deficient infrastructure) and abroad (including trade barriers in key markets and instability in neighboring countries) constrain the ability of these countries to contest international markets. As long as these constraints persist, the positive impact on the poor of the trade liberalization that these countries have undertaken will remain muted.

Improving *domestic* market integration is essential if the potential benefits of trade are to be extended to the poorer segments of the population. The studies of Malawi and Nepal show that reduction of domestic transportation costs would bring strong welfare gains for farming households. Among these households, the poorest would benefit disproportionately because transportation costs make up a larger percentage of their expenditures. Case studies in Ethiopia and Guinea

certain agreements or rules simply may not be immediate development priorities or may require that other conditions be satisfied before implementation can be beneficial. The specifics of a new approach to SDT require considerable further thought and discussion. What matters is that such a debate be initiated. That would help make "development relevance" more than a slogan.

Trade Capacity, Technology Development, and Trade-Related Assistance

A major constraint limiting export growth in many low-income countries is a lack of supply capacity and a high-cost business environment. Firms in these countries may also find it difficult to deal with ever more stringent regulatory requirements, such as health and safety standards, that apply in export markets. Development assistance can play an important role in helping to build the capacity needed to benefit from increased trade and better access to markets. Commitments for trade-related technical assistance and capacity building have been rising and were equivalent to 4.8 percent of total official development assistance in 2001–02. Despite this expanding "trade-for-aid," such support needs to be substantially strengthened.

Aid can help address trade-related policy, institutional, and investment priorities; facilitate adjustment to a reduction in trade preferences following further nondiscriminatory trade liberalization; and assist in dealing with the potential detrimental effects of a significant increase in world food prices should that reveal that many of the poor would be left behind if there were overall trade reform but no improvements in markets within the country.

Transport costs are a major component of total costs for exporters. The studies show how a multitude of negative factors can contribute to extremely high transportation costs. These factors include deficient infrastructure, poor conditions of the vehicle fleet, lack of security, numerous formal and informal checkpoints, absence or nonenforcement of transit agreements, and lack of competition. In poor countries, especially those that are landlocked, the conjunction of these factors poses daunting challenges to domestic producers, seriously undermining the competitiveness of their exports. In Mali transport costs represent on average 30 percent of the value of traded goods (this ratio stands at some 18 percent for other Western Africa countries; in developed countries, it is typically around 5 percent). In Malawi, transport infrastructure is reasonably well developed, but high prices due to lack of competition in transport services add nearly 50 percent to sugar production costs.

Another major bottleneck clearly identified in the studies is inefficiency in customs clearance. Some countries have managed to reduce clearance times—for example, from an average of three to four weeks in Senegal to less than one week—but they still have a way to go to match more advanced developing countries, where customs clearance is usually achieved within a matter of hours. Customs procedures generally suffer from a lack of transparency and the prevalence of discretionary measures.

Although all the countries studied are eligible for trade preferences in developed-country markets, the impact of these schemes has been very uneven. For example, while Lesotho has significantly expanded its garment exports under the U.S. African Growth and Opportunity Act, other countries, such as Ethiopia and some West African countries, have largely failed to do so. EU preferences on sugar and tobacco for exporters in Malawi have been substantial, but the wider economic impact is less apparent. For most countries trade preferences have done little to mitigate the impact of the high transportation and transaction costs that they face compared with other trading countries and to stimulate trade volumes and diversification into a wider range of products.

Source: World Bank, Integrated Framework diagnostic trade integration studies.

materialize. At the September 2003 WTO Ministerial meeting, the IMF and the World Bank announced their readiness to help countries benefit from better market access opportunities and to undertake trade-related reforms and complementary actions. The IMF will provide financial support in the context of new or existing IMF-supported programs to countries that may face a net negative impact on their balance of payments from trade-related adjustments in other countries. The World Bank has been enhancing its lending and technical assistance portfolio in the trade area and strengthening learning programs and partnerships. New lending for trade capacity building doubled from $132 million in 1998–2000 to $267 million in 2001–03. Through the Integrated Framework for Trade-Related Technical Assistance, a program supported jointly by several bilateral donors and multilateral agencies, progress is being made in integrating trade policy more closely into country development strategies and addressing the related "behind-the-border" agenda (box 10.2).

Facilitation of technology transfer also would help enhance the capacities of developing countries to benefit from integration into the world economy. Developed countries could promote technology transfer in several ways. Examples include helping to build capacity in intellectual property rights and technical regulations and standards, establishing public and public-private research facilities, facilitating technology-related services trade, and supporting training programs in the functioning of modern technology markets. Many governments in high-income countries offer incentives to firms to locate in or provide technologies to lower-income areas within their own countries. One option is for governments to offer similar incentives to firms transferring technologies to low-income countries. They could also offer the same incentives for research and development performed in poor countries as for R&D conducted at home.

Notes

1. A simple rule that would move in this direction would be to forbid any WTO member from imposing tariffs at the tariff-line level that are higher than three times its average tariff. Predictability could also be enhanced through full binding by all WTO members of their tariff lines. For example, of the 41 African WTO members, only 9 have bound all their manufacturing tariff lines, while 15 have bound less than 10 percent of their tariffs.

2. These estimates correspond to the pro-poor scenario analyzed in chapter 1 of *Global Economic Prospects 2004* (World Bank 2003). They assume the elimination of agricultural export subsidies and domestic support, a tariff ceiling of 10 percent for agricultural products and 5 percent for manufacturing in OECD countries, and a tariff ceiling of 15 percent for agricultural products and 10 percent for manufacturing in developing countries.

3. WTO 2001, paragraphs 13 and 16.

4. Countries can apply a number of different tariffs on imports, depending on the country of origin of those imports. The MFN tariff is the highest tariff rate that is applicable to all imports, although, as is becoming increasingly common, this rate can be reduced on imports originating from certain countries. Such preferential rates can be either reciprocal or nonreciprocal in nature. Applied tariffs, whether they are preferential or MFN, also need to be distinguished from bound tariffs, which are negotiated ceilings on the value of a tariff. These ceilings, or bindings, are notified to the WTO and are applicable to the MFN tariff of a WTO Member.

5. WTO 2002.

6. The PSE incorporates the effect of trade policies by measuring the difference between the world price of a product at the border of the country and the domestic producer price. This difference is multiplied by domestic production to derive the "market price support" (MPS) for each product. Direct payments to producers—classified according to the basis on which the payments are made—are added to the MPS to derive the PSE. To derive the TSE, an estimate of expenditures on General Services Support (spending on collective services, such as research, agricultural education, inspection, infrastructure, marketing, and public stockholding) is added to the aggregate PSE, as are government transfers to consumers (such as food stamps).

7. Thus, for example, a 10 percent increase in producer price support (a form of direct payment) has only the production-increasing effect, while a 10 percent tariff raises the producer price to the same degree, which has the same production effect but also reduces consumption. The tariff has a "double-barrel" impact on imports. See, for example, Anderson (2003); Messerlin (2002); and Hoekman, Ng, and Olarreaga (2004) for a detailed discussion.

8. Mitchell 2004.

9. Baffes 2003.

10. Messerlin 2002.

11. Beghin, Roland-Holst, and van der Mensbrugghe 2002; World Bank 2003; Hoekman, Ng, and Olarreaga 2004.

12. The European Union has no tariffs above 15 percent for textiles and clothing. In the United States and Canada, most tariff peaks affect industrial products (over 85 percent), whereas in the EU and Japan most peaks affect agricultural products (91 and 77 percent, respectively). See Hoekman, Ng, and Olarreaga (2002).

13. Bown, Hoekman, and Ozden (2003) note that the number of cases against developing countries is much higher than their share in U.S. imports. The average duty on developed countries (excluding Japan) was 31 percent, compared with 53 percent for developing countries. Similar conclusions hold for other major users of antidumping.

14. Liu and Van den Bussche 2003.

15. OTRIs are computed bilaterally for every importing country and then aggregated across partner countries. See chapter 4 for a description of the methodology.

16. Note that the economic significance for low-income countries of very high trade protection in Norway or Switzerland can be smaller than that of more moderate levels of protection in much larger markets, such as the European Union.

17. Agriculture is more highly protected in both developed and developing countries. However, relative to manufactures, agricultural protection is higher in richer countries.

18. The bilateral OTRI estimates indicate that trade policies in the Quad are most restrictive toward lower-middle-income countries with GDP per capita in the $1,500 to $5,000 range.

19. Preference utilization by developing countries is generally quite low. According to a WTO document (WT/COMTD/LDC/W/31, 29th September 2003), the GSP (Generalized System of Preferences) utilization rates for preferences granted by Canada, the European Union, Japan, and the United States are 61, 31, 46, and 67 percent, respectively. In the case of Canada, duty-free access for LDCs was implemented as of January 1, 2003.

20. Otsuki, Wilson, and Sewadeh 2001; Wilson and Abiola 2003.

21. These numbers are very rough estimates based on balance of payments statistics and the very incomplete information reported on the services sales by affiliates of foreign-owned firms in host countries; see Karsenty 2002. Statistics on trade in services are very weak and do not allow a straightforward mapping between recorded foreign exchange flows and the four modes of supply.

22. Stern (2002) surveys the literature.

23. World Bank 2004.

24. This conclusion is conditional on the model used; relative orders of magnitude may differ using an alternative global model. See Walmsley and Winters 2002.

25. Schiff and Winters 2003; Mattoo 2003.

26. There has been a substantial amount of research on the economics of the Singapore issues. This research generally concludes that these issues are important from a development perspective—all relate to the investment climate—but expresses doubts regarding the appropriateness of dealing with them in the WTO. See, for example, World Bank (2003).

11

Providing More and Better Aid

While trade policy reform, as discussed in chapter 10, would expand opportunities for growth in developing countries, adequate foreign aid would be important in enhancing their capacities to exploit those opportunities. That is especially so for low-income countries, for which aid is the largest source of external financing. The Monterrey Consensus recognized the need for substantial additional external resources if low-income countries are to achieve the MDGs, and donors have committed themselves to a 7 percent annual increase in real terms up to 2006. If these commitments are realized, official development assistance would rise by about $18.5 billion by 2006 from the 2002 level of about $58 billion. While encouraging, the indicated increase in aid is well short of what is needed and can be productively used by developing countries. Moreover, a much higher proportion of aid will need to be provided in the form of cash, and in flexible ways, so that it can be deployed in accordance with country priorities to finance the costs of meeting the MDGs.

Equally important is the need to raise the quality of aid. It is widely accepted that aid is most effective in countries with sound policies and institutions. As reviewed in part II of this report, developing countries in general are improving their policies and institutions and creating conditions that are more conducive to the effective use of resources—domestic and foreign. Recent evidence supports a growing trend among donors toward aid selectivity, with more aid allocated to countries with better policies. Yet there is considerable variation in the selectivity focus of donors, reflecting their multiple objectives. The largest donors are not particularly selective, and the scope for improving the allocation of aid is substantial.

There is also much scope for increasing the effectiveness of aid by better aligning aid with recipients' development priorities—as manifested in country-owned and -led poverty reduction strategies and other development frameworks—and by harmonizing donor policies and practices. The Rome High-Level Forum of early 2003 has given a welcome impetus to the alignment and harmonization agenda. Consistent follow-through on that agenda will be important

The Heavily Indebted Poor Countries (HIPC) Initiative has contributed to lowering the debt burden of these countries and freeing domestic resources for growth and poverty reduction. Despite these achievements, maintaining debt sustainability is becoming an increasingly important issue for these and some other low-income countries, given their need for large increases in external financing to meet the MDGs. In some countries, financing the MDGs with new concessional borrowing could lead to an unsustainably large debt burden. Additional aid will need to have an appropriate mix of grant financing and new credits.

Aid Flows: Recent Trends, Prospects, and Requirements

Trends in Aid Volume: A Mixed Picture

After falling substantially in the second half of the 1990s, aid volumes rose in 2002. Net ODA flows, as estimated by the OECD's Development Assistance Committee, rose from $52.3 billion in 2001 to $58.3 billion in 2002. The ratio of ODA to donors' GNI, which fell from 0.34 percent in the early 1990s to 0.22 percent in 2001, rose to 0.23 percent. Preliminary OECD DAC estimates indicate that net ODA rose to $68.5 billion in 2003; the increase in real terms was much smaller—to $60.5 billion (at 2002 prices and exchange rates).[1] Aid volumes are set to rise further as DAC members start delivering on their Monterrey commitments. If the commitments made by donors at or since the Monterrey Conference of March 2002 are realized, total ODA would increase by about $18.5 billion over the 2002 level (32 percent in real terms), that is, from $58 billion to $77 billion (figure 11.1).[2] That would raise the ODA-to-GNI ratio to 0.29 percent in 2006. The aid effort and new commitments vary widely across donors (table 11.1).

The increase in development assistance is encouraging, but there is concern that a large part of it may not be directed to financing the incremental costs of meeting the MDGs. Of the roughly $6 billion nominal increase in net ODA by DAC donors in 2002 (the increase in real terms was about $4 billion), debt relief accounted for $2.9 billion, technical cooperation $1.9 billion, and emergency and disaster relief and food aid $0.7 billion (figure 11.2). Moreover, the increase in bilateral net ODA was concentrated in a few countries: Serbia and Montenegro ($1.3 billion), Mozambique ($0.9 billion), and Côte d'Ivoire ($0.7 billion), with the additional aid mostly reflecting debt

FIGURE 11.1 Aid is rising but is well short of what is needed
Net ODA from DAC donors

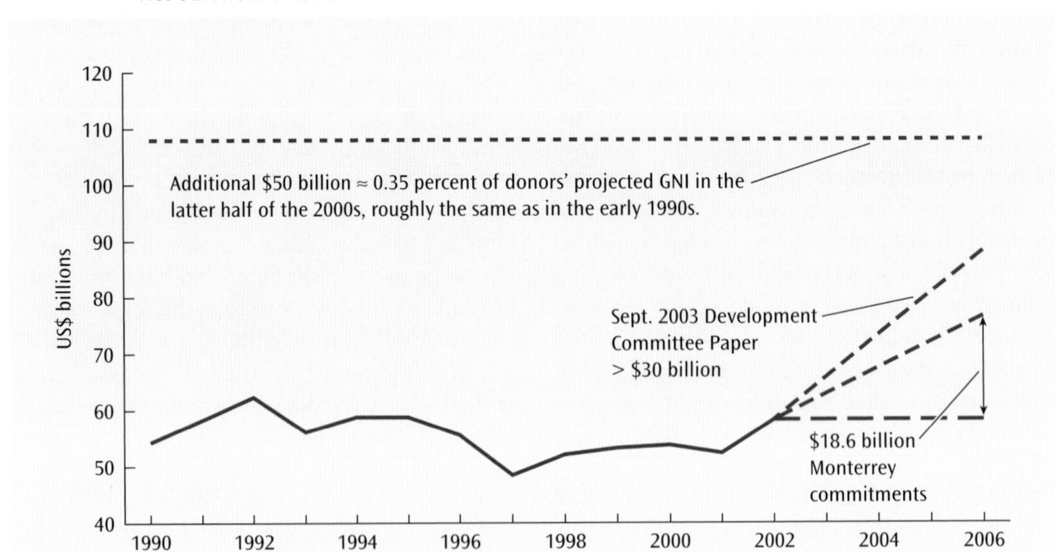

Note: The Development Committee paper estimated, on a conservative basis, that developing countries could effectively absorb at least $30 billion in additional aid annually (Development Committee 2003b).
Source: OECD 2004a; Development Committee 2003b.

TABLE 11.1 Actual ODA and post-Monterrey commitments (DAC donors), 2002 and 2006

	Net ODA in 2002	ODA/GNI in 2002	Net ODA In 2006	ODA/GNI in 2006	Real change in ODA in 2006 compared with 2002	
Donor	US$ billions	Percent	2002 US$ billions	Percent	2002 US$ billions	Percent
Five largest donors (by aid effort)						
Denmark	1.64	0.96	1.53	0.83	–0.11	–7
Norway	1.70	0.89	2.07	1.00	0.37	22
Sweden	1.99	0.83	2.25	0.87	0.26	13
Netherlands	3.34	0.81	3.57	0.80	0.23	7
Luxembourg	0.15	0.77	0.21	1.00	0.06	41
Five largest donors (by amount)						
United States	13.29	0.13	19.54	0.17	6.23	47
Japan	9.28	0.23	10.50	0.26	1.22	13
France	5.49	0.38	7.38	0.47	1.89	34
Germany	5.32	0.27	7.10	0.33	1.78	33
United Kingdom	4.92	0.31	6.91	0.40	1.98	40
Total (DAC Members)	58.27	0.23	76.85	0.29	18.58	32
Total (EU Members)	29.95	0.35	39.63	0.42	9.68	32

Note: Data for 2006 are projections based on announced commitments.
Source: OECD 2004a.

forgiveness; and in frontline states in the war on terror, such as Afghanistan ($0.7 billion). Looking ahead, there is some concern that additional aid flows could be significantly influenced by donors' strategic agendas, such as the war on terrorism and conflict and reconstruction in Afghanistan and Iraq.[3] It will be important to ensure that such strategic objectives do not crowd out development aid.

Non-DAC donors' ODA, which has averaged around 2 percent of DAC ODA in recent years, was also up in 2002. At $3.2 billion, these flows were at their highest level in more than 10 years. The increase was led by Arab aid, especially development assistance from Saudi Arabia, which rose by more than 400 percent (mainly humanitarian assistance to neighboring countries and an increase in development lending). In the 1990s, Arab aid fell as oil prices fell, but it has rebounded in tandem with the recent increase in oil prices. The favorable trend in non-DAC aid appears to reflect some of the same factors motivating DAC donors—a renewed focus on development spurred by the MDGs and the Monterrey Compact, as well as strategic considerations.

FIGURE 11.2 **The increase in ODA in 2002 was concentrated in special-purpose grants**
Breakdown of the $6 billion nominal increase in net ODA by DAC donors in 2002

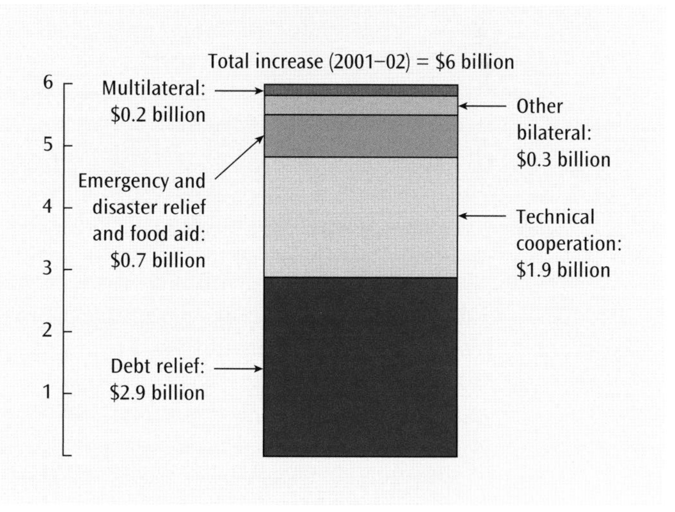

Source: OECD DAC database.

The rise in ODA has occurred in an environment of lower overall flows to developing countries. Official flows to these countries have declined sharply, mostly due to a fall in net nonconcessional lending from multilateral sources. Less nonconcessional borrowing from the IMF, repayments on past crisis financing packages, and substantial prepayments of loans to the World Bank are behind this decline. Concessional lending by multilaterals has also edged lower. As reviewed in chapter 9, private flows have begun to recover, but foreign direct investment to developing countries has declined.

At about $9 billion, private grants by nongovernmental organizations (using their own resources) are becoming an important source of finance for ODA recipients.[4] Private grants have expanded rapidly, experiencing a near 70 percent increase during 1997–2002, and now account for 0.03 percent of DAC members' GNI. The growth in private donor funds reflects the success that NGOs have had in influencing a broad array of development issues, from reducing debt burdens of the poorest countries to environmental, health, and governance issues.[5]

Aid Commitments Lag Countries' Absorptive Capacity and Needs

While the international community generally agrees on the need for substantially more resources if the MDGs are to be realized, there is a concern that countries may not be able to effectively absorb large increases in resource transfers. One reason is that large inflows of aid could complicate macroeconomic management because of the well-known "Dutch disease" phenomenon.[6] Another reason is that aid flows could undermine government institutions when these institutions are weak. In countries with weak governance, the elite can capture resource transfers and keep the benefits from flowing to the poor. Large amounts of aid could also overwhelm local capacity to use funds well.[7] Complex donor procedures and practices may add to the problems of absorptive capacity.

While the ability of poor countries to productively absorb increases in external resources is crucial to aid effectiveness, it is important to note that ODA increases in line with post-Monterrey commitments (see table 11.1) would leave the size of ODA relative to recipients' GNI below the level of the early 1990s.[8] Recent and ongoing reforms in many developing countries have improved the setting for effective use of aid.[9] A recent World Bank study found that countries with relatively good policies and institutions could effectively utilize a substantial increase in aid to boost progress toward reaching the MDGs.[10] It estimated that a doubling of flows could be productively used in the large Asian low-income countries, including Bangladesh, India, Indonesia, Pakistan, and Vietnam. These countries have prospects of continued good policies, a large gap with respect to MDG targets, and relatively low aid dependence. Sub-Saharan African countries with relatively good policies could on average effectively absorb increases in aid on the order of 60 percent. Of course, differences across countries are substantial. The study concluded that, as a conservative estimate, an initial increment of at least $30 billion annually could be effectively used by recipient countries. As countries improve their policies and governance over time and upgrade their capacities, the amount of aid that can be used effectively would rise into the range of $50 billion plus per year, the amount that most estimates suggest is likely to be necessary to support adequate progress toward the MDGs (box 11.1).

Modalities for Mobilizing Additional Aid

Apart from efforts to increase the amount of aid, the time frame of the MDGs—to 2015—has encouraged consideration of ways to "frontload" future aid commitments. The most fully developed of such approaches is the United Kingdom's proposal for an International Finance Facility (IFF). As a way to frontload significant aid flows toward achieving the MDGs, the IFF appears technically feasible—legally binding donor pledges could be used to back AAA-rated market borrowings by a treasury vehicle. Key requirements

BOX 11.1 Estimating the cost of the MDGs

The costs of achieving the MDGs are hard to estimate. There are several reasons for this. For one thing, putting a price tag on achieving these goals requires distinguishing between average and marginal cost. In education, for example, the marginal cost of enrolling a child could be higher than the average cost because children who are not in school might be harder to induce to attend school, or they may be in more scattered populations. For another thing, progress on one goal contributes to progress on other goals. Thus, safe drinking water and good sanitation promote better health. The interdependence of goals implies that costing each goal separately could result in double counting. There are multiple determinants for each goal, and they cut across many sectors. Measuring the multisectoral dimensions is difficult. The task of measuring the costs of attaining the MDGs is also complicated by the fact that the effectiveness of additional expenditure depends on appropriate changes in policies and institutions.

Studies on costing the MDGs fall into two broad categories: global costing exercises and country-level estimates. Global elasticities and average costs guide the former, while the latter use country-level information to scale up to the global level. Neither type of study effectively incorporates the multisectoral dimensions of MDGs.

Global costing exercises. The two well-known global studies are a report prepared for the United Nations by the High-Level Panel on Financing for Development led by Ernesto Zedillo (United Nations 2001) and a study at the World Bank by Devarajan, Miller, and Swanson (2002). Both studies assume that developing countries implement necessary reforms. The U.N. report estimated that roughly $50 billion a year in additional ODA would be required to achieve the MDGs. The cost of halving the proportion of people living in extreme poverty was estimated at $20 billion more in aid; and an additional $30 billion in ODA was estimated for the service goals. The report cautioned about the difficulties of estimation and noted that a firmer, more comprehensive estimate would need to be based on individual country estimates. Devarajan, Miller, and Swanson used two different approaches. One approach estimated the MDG resource needs by calculating the economic growth rate, and in turn the investment, required to achieve the goals. The second approach separately estimated the costs of achieving the individual goals. Both approaches yield comparable estimates—$40 billion to $60 billion a year in additional ODA. Another World Bank study (Development Committee 2003a) estimated that $30 billion in additional aid would be required to achieve selected targets within the service delivery MDGs. The study noted that this estimate did not include certain costs, notably that of complementary infrastructure.

Country-level costing. A World Bank study prepared for the September 2003 Development Committee meeting (Development Committee 2003b) estimated how much additional aid recipient countries could productively use to accelerate progress toward the MDGs. The approach linked aid requirements to countries' initial conditions, the soundness of their policies, and their capacity to make effective use of additional resources. The study analyzed 18 low-income countries with relatively good policies. Reflecting the different country characteristics, estimates of the additional aid that countries could effectively utilize vary greatly, from a range of 20 to 100 percent or more. Based on this analysis, the study concluded that developing countries could effectively absorb at least $30 billion in additional aid annually—a conservative estimate that does not fully take into account all costs, especially the costs of infrastructure investments needed to accelerate growth and improve service delivery and the costs of global public goods (such as combating infectious diseases and addressing environmental concerns).

A study by the United Nations Millennium Project (2004) took a different approach. It asked what it would cost to achieve the MDGs, with the cost estimate relatively unconstrained by absorptive capacity limitations of recipient countries. The study identified the full range of inputs and actions considered necessary to reach the goals, including costing detailed interventions in 14 sectors or categories. Preliminary results for five countries—Bangladesh, Cambodia, Ghana, Tanzania, and Uganda—for 2005–15 show that these countries would need substantial increases in external development assistance, with their requirements estimated at $44 to $57 per capita per year, which translates into a range of $7.5 billion annually for Bangladesh to about $1 billion annually for Cambodia. Scaling up from these country-level results, the study concluded the total ODA would need to rise substantially from current levels, but the total requirements would be less than the ODA target of 0.7 percent of rich countries' national income.

for the IFF to be feasible in practice would include breadth and strength of political backing for the obligations being undertaken, and resolution of issues on the treatment of pledges from a fiscal viewpoint by national authorities. Consideration could also be given to alternative structures based on the same principles.

Recent discussions of official financing for development have broadened the range of modalities under consideration beyond traditional aid. As a result, there is a need for more systematic analysis and comparison of a menu of approaches that might provide additionality, greater efficiency of aid, or both. The whole spectrum of concessionality needs to be examined from three points of view. First is the case for extending concessionality beyond its traditional country-defined boundaries to focus on MDG investments within countries not usually eligible for concessional lending. Second is the use of tailored concessionality to make more flexible financing available to poor countries, particularly when they face debt distress or exogenous shocks. Third is whether added concessionality is an appropriate means to address global and regional externalities such as public health. Work is under way on this menu of issues, from different perspectives, within the World Bank and the IMF. As this work progresses over the coming months, more defined options and proposals will emerge.[11]

The Changing Composition of Aid

Rising Share of Technical Cooperation

In addition to adequacy of amount, aid needs to be provided in forms that are responsive to recipients' needs. A significant feature of change in the composition of aid has been the rising share of technical cooperation and other special-purpose assistance. Technical cooperation now accounts for nearly a third of gross bilateral ODA. Technical cooperation is of course useful, as it transfers much-needed skills and knowledge. Often, however, it is associated with high-cost expatriate consultants and with absorbing local expertise in projects without building sustainable local capacity. Although technical assistance is not included in official statistics on aid tying, it can essentially be considered as a form of tied aid. Consequently, estimates of progress on aid untying should be interpreted cautiously. According to DAC estimates, the proportion of untied aid has increased from 60 to 80 percent in the past two decades (for those countries that report). These numbers exclude technical cooperation, administrative costs, and ODA by members that do not report the tying status of their aid.[12]

Tying is costly for recipients. A recent study of several projects in Ghana found that 11 to 25 percent of resources could have been saved if aid had been untied.[13] An earlier study found the costs to be in a similar range: 15 to 30 percent.[14] With DAC members agreeing in 2001 to untie all financial aid to the least developed countries, more progress on untying aid is likely. Efforts should also be made to evaluate the effectiveness of technical cooperation.

Need for More Flexible Forms of Aid

More aid needs to be provided in forms that can finance the incremental costs of achieving the MDGs. Of the total ODA, assistance provided through bilateral channels accounts for about 70 percent. Of the total bilateral assistance, currently only about 30 percent is available for project and program expenditures in recipient countries.[15] The rest is allocated to special-purpose grants such as technical cooperation, debt relief, emergency and disaster relief, food aid, and cost of aid administration. The proportion of bilateral ODA net of special-purpose grants has been declining steadily. The current proportion of 30 percent compares with a high of about 60 percent in the early 1980s (figure 11.3). This trend needs to be reversed. A much higher proportion of additional aid will need to be provided in more fungible resources—cash transfers—that countries can deploy in line with their priorities to finance the costs of meeting the MDGs.

Aid delivery needs to be more flexible, with aid provided in forms that reflect recipients' needs and circumstances.[16] As countries' public financial management systems improve, more aid can be provided through budget support or sectorwide programs. Depending on recipients' circumstances, part of the assistance provided through these means should be available to finance recurrent costs—much of the increase in costs associated with the improvement of education and health programs that are crucial to progress toward the MDGs is recurrent. Such flexible provision of aid would be appropriate in countries with sound budget frameworks, for example, Uganda and Burkina Faso. Where budget frameworks are at an early stage of reform, as for example in Madagascar, financing for recurrent expenditures could be provided through investment projects.

FIGURE 11.3 The proportion of aid provided in cash and more flexible forms should be rising, not falling
Total bilateral ODA minus special-purpose grants

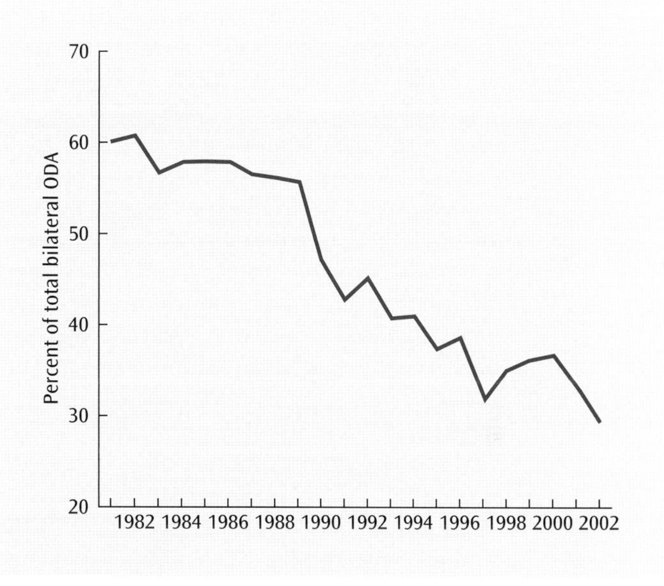

Source: OECD DAC database.

Quality and Effectiveness of Aid

The achievement of the MDGs requires both more and better aid. Issues relating to the quality and effectiveness of aid are receiving increasing attention. There is broad recognition that by complementing improved policies in recipient countries, better donor policies and practices can contribute significantly to enhancing the impact of aid. The agenda spans several key dimensions of the quality of aid: selectivity (allocation of aid across countries), alignment (consistency with recipients' development priorities), and harmonization (streamlining and coordination of donor procedures and practices and harmonizing them with those of the recipients). Related aspects include the reduction of aid volatility and fragmentation.

FIGURE 11.4 Institutions and policies matter for aid effectiveness
The relationship between the quantity of aid, the quality of policies, and GDP growth

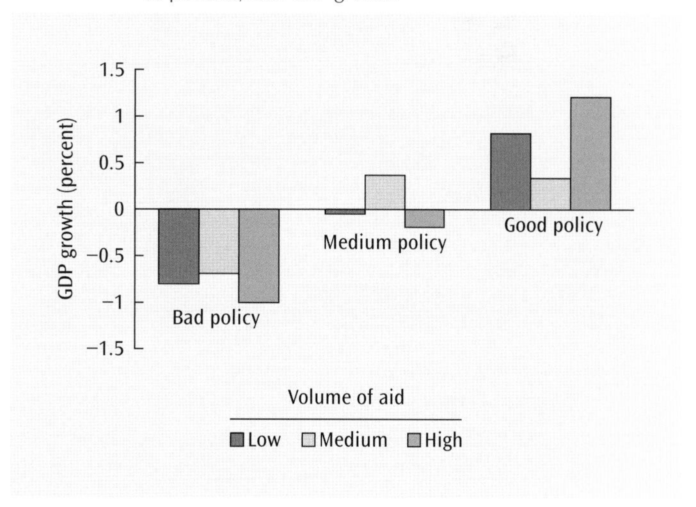

Source: Dollar and Levin 2004.

Aid Effectiveness and Selectivity

Aid has a greater impact on growth if it is targeted to countries with better policies and institutions (figure 11.4). The impact depends on the interaction between aid and policy. With bad policies, aid has little effect on growth; if anything, the relationship may be negative. With good policies, the effect of aid is positive and is stronger if aid is given in sufficiently large amounts. There is now general acceptance that policies and institutions matter for aid effectiveness, which is reflected in a trend toward increased selectivity in the allocation of aid.[17]

Recent research finds a significant relationship between donor assistance and the quality of recipients' policies.[18] About three-fourths of the donors exhibit a positive relationship between their aid allocations and the soundness of recipients' policies and institutions. Moreover, donors today are in general more selective than a decade ago. Selectivity has also increased with respect to poverty, with more aid being allocated to poorer countries, given the quality of policies. However, variation among donors is wide. On average, multilateral assistance is much more selective than bilateral assistance. Among bilateral donors, the largest ones (in terms of the absolute amount of aid provided) are less selective (box 11.2). This means that the typical donor is more selective than the typical aid dollar. Actions being taken by some of these donors, such as the establishment by the United States of the Millennium Challenge Account (MCA), are expected to increase the selectivity of their aid. The MCA aims to improve aid effectiveness by tying increased assistance to performance.

FIGURE 11.5 More selective donors provide more aid per capita to countries with stronger policies and institutions
Aid per bilateral donor country's capita to low-income countries, average for 1999–2002 ($ per capita)

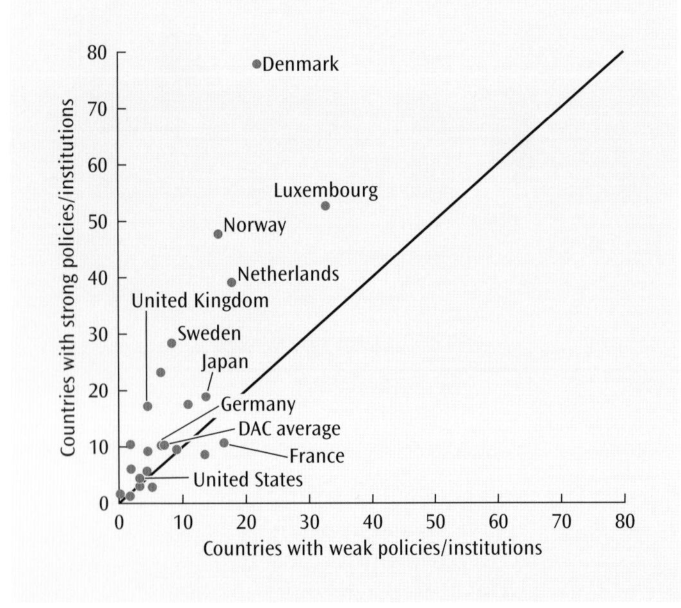

Source: Dollar and Levin 2004.

The more selective donors also provide much more aid per donor country's citizen (figure 11.5). The top providers of assistance per donor country citizen to low-income countries with better policies and institutions during 1999–2002 were Denmark (providing $78 per Danish citizen a year on average during this period), Luxembourg ($53), Norway ($48), and the Netherlands ($39).[19] Corresponding figures for some of the largest donors in absolute size are quite low (for example, $4.5 for the United States), with the result that aid provided to low-income countries with good policies and institutions per donor country citizen averaged a relatively modest $10.3 for DAC members as a whole during this period.

Even as donors move to target aid better, they need to take account of the special needs of the conflict-affected and other low-income countries under stress (LICUS). The challenge is to balance issues of weak policies and institutions with the need to maintain critical engagement. Appropriately timed and directed aid, sensitive to local efforts to rebuild and to institutional capacity constraints, can play a very useful role. There is no set pattern of aid interventions targeted to LICUS countries. They can include meeting humanitarian needs, improving basic service delivery, and preventing or responding to conflict. There is also wide variation among the LICUS in their capacity to absorb aid: for example, postconflict countries may be better able to absorb larger amounts of aid effectively than are other LICUS.[20] Bosnia, Rwanda, and Timor Leste have demonstrated the potential for aid-supported recovery and progress toward the MDGs. The new DAC initiative on difficult partnerships should help to shape more effective ways of providing aid to help countries under stress.[21]

Recent research shows that well-timed aid can also be quite productive following adverse exogenous shocks, helping to limit the diversion of development resources into short-term relief efforts.[22] Low-income countries are particularly vulnerable to natural

BOX 11.2 Measuring aid selectivity

Dollar and Levin (2004) develop two indexes to measure the selectivity of aid. A policy selectivity index measures the elasticity of aid with respect to the quality of recipients' policies and institutions (controlling for recipients' per capita income and population). A poverty selectivity index measures the elasticity of aid with respect to the recipients' per capita income level (controlling for their policy and institutional quality and population). An overall index is computed as an average of the two—average of the policy elasticity and the (negative of) the poverty elasticity—to measure how selective donors are in terms of focusing assistance on low-income countries with better policies and institutions.

The results show that in 2002, a 100 percent increase in the quality of recipients' policies was on average associated with 176 percent more aid. The relationship is much stronger for multilateral assistance (elasticity of 2.57) than for bilateral assistance (elasticity of 0.63). However, policy elasticity varies considerably among bilateral donors. The Nordic countries, the Netherlands, and the United Kingdom show high policy selectivity (elasticity of 2.5 or higher). Broadly similar results are obtained for poverty elasticity.

Some of the largest donors in absolute amount are less selective. France and the United States do not appear to have been particularly selective along either the policy or poverty dimension. Japan appears to be selective on policy but not on poverty, reducing the overall selectivity of its aid.

The authors test the robustness of their analysis to the choice of the measure for recipients' policies and institutions. The results reported in the table use the World Bank CPIA as the measure. Using two other measures of institutional quality that are available for a large number of countries—the International Country Risk Guide rule-of-law index and the Freedom House democracy index—the authors find that the rankings of aid selectivity are quite similar. Thus, whichever measure of the quality of policies and institutions is used, the same donors appear to be more or less selective. The authors also test the sensitivity of their analysis to different definitions of aid flows—ODA including loans and debt relief and grants only—and find that they do not significantly alter the results.

It should be noted that the selectivity index captures only one, albeit important, dimension of the quality and effectiveness of aid—its allocation across countries. Other dimensions of the quality of aid discussed elsewhere in this chapter include the form and composition of aid, its predictability, and alignment and harmonization. Moreover, the policy selectivity index needs to be interpreted cautiously. Some aid can be effective in situations where policies and institutions are still weak, such as in certain post-conflict and post-shock situations. This is an area where more research would be useful.

There is substantial scope for improving the allocation of aid
Aid selectivity index, 2002

Indicator	Policy selectivity	Poverty selectivity	Overall selectivity
Total aid	1.76*	–0.49*	1.12
Bilateral aid	0.63	–0.38*	0.50
Multilateral aid	2.57*	–0.83*	1.70
Five largest donors (by amount)			
United States	0.66	–0.76*	0.71
Japan	1.90	0.01	0.94
France	–0.07	–0.28	0.10
Germany	2.06*	–0.47*	1.27
United Kingdom	3.66*	–1.06*	2.36
Good practice examples			
Denmark (bilaterals)	4.77*	–1.11*	2.94
IDA (multilaterals)	4.23*	–4.20*	4.22

* Elasticity different from zero at 10 percent significance level.
Note: The last column is an average of the first two. Emergency and disaster relief are excluded from these calculations.
Source: Dollar and Levin 2004.

disasters, terms-of-trade shocks, and other adverse shocks, and those with inadequate cushions of external reserves or fiscal resources are likely to suffer especially severe effects on growth and poverty. The main policy challenges here are to accelerate the international response to such shocks, increase the amount of assistance, and make more use of grants rather than lending for this purpose.[23]

About a third of all ODA goes to middle-income countries. Many of these countries either have met or are on track to meet several of the MDGs well before 2015. The bulk of the resources needed to achieve the development goals in these countries will have to come from domestic sources, and their external financing needs will be met primarily from private or nonconcessional flows—especially in the upper-middle-income countries. Aid, however, can play an important role in the middle-income countries: as a catalyst for reform; as a reinforcer of domestic efforts to tackle large pockets of poverty (middle-income countries remain home to 280 million people who live on less than $1 a day and 870 million who live on less than $2 a day); and as a provider of countercyclical support to reduce vulnerability to financial shocks and help deal with their consequences. Over time, as income levels rise further in these countries and their domestic resource availabilities and access to private capital markets expand, their use of ODA should decline.

FIGURE 11.6 **Aid fragmentation is high**
Donor fragmentation index, 1975–2002

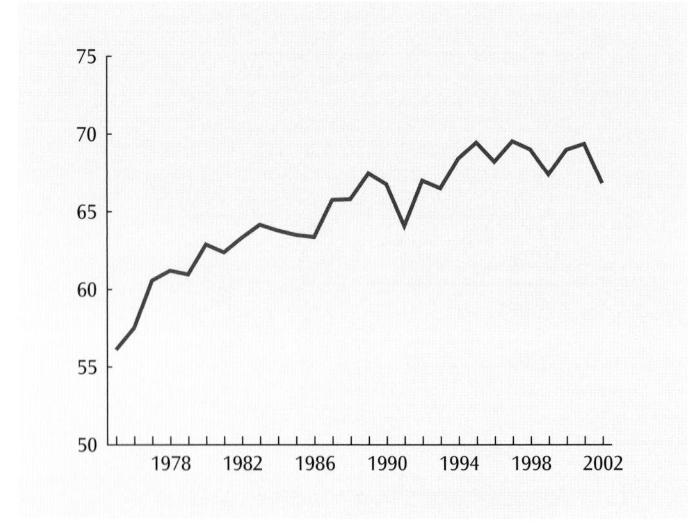

Source: OECD DAC database and World Bank staff estimates.

Donor Fragmentation

Bilateral aid is highly fragmented, with possible negative implications for aid quality. The argument against aid fragmentation is that if each donor has only a small share in a recipient country's total aid, then the donor's stake might be more narrowly focused on the success of the donor's own projects and less on the country's overall development. Another possible consequence is that if a project's fixed costs are high and there are returns to scale, then too many individual projects may impair efficiency. Fragmentation may also impose high transaction costs on recipients, as more time is taken up by donor requirements. Donors such as Canada, Finland, the Netherlands, and the United States (through the Millennium Challenge Account) are proposing to reverse the trend toward dispersion by concentrating more aid in fewer recipient countries.

A donor fragmentation index constructed from the shares of individual donors in annual aid disbursements shows that fragmentation has been rising (figure 11.6).[24] The index ranges from 0 to 100, with higher values implying more fragmentation. The index is 0 if one donor accounts for all of a recipient's aid. The degree of fragmentation rises as the number of donors rises, as their aid shares become more equal, or both. The issue of donor fragmentation is of course more serious in some countries than others. For Tanzania, for example, the fragmentation index in 2002 was a high 93 (compared to an average of 67). Egypt, in contrast, has an index value of 62. The degree of fragmentation is moderately correlated with the size of ODA in recipients' GNI, suggesting that greater aid dependency is associated with a higher degree of fragmentation.

Volatility in Aid Flows

Volatility in aid flows can put much stress on the ability of recipient countries to plan and use resources well and thereby hurt aid effectiveness. In many countries, aid tends to be more volatile than fiscal revenues.[25] This is especially a problem for countries with high aid dependency; these countries tend to experience more volatility and possess the least options for coping with it (figure 11.7).[26] Faced with uncertain aid flows, poor countries have, in principle, three options. They can try to apply a flexible fiscal framework in which taxes and expenditures are adjusted in response to aid receipts. They can try to smooth out aid fluctuations by allowing the level of international reserves to fluctuate. And they can use domestic nonmonetary financing to fill the gaps in aid levels. All three options present serious difficulties for such countries. Aid shortfalls are mostly absorbed by reductions in spending, and sometimes by increases in taxes.[27]

As countries build a track record of policy performance, their efforts should be supported with timely, more predictable, and longer-term aid commitments. Progress toward the MDGs is necessarily a long-term process and requires sustained reform of policies and institutions. Commitment to sustained reforms, especially in countries with a higher dependence on aid, is difficult without a reasonable degree of assurance about the aid flows and the circumstances under which they are likely to materialize.

FIGURE 11.7 Aid flows are typically more volatile than fiscal revenues in aid-dependent countries

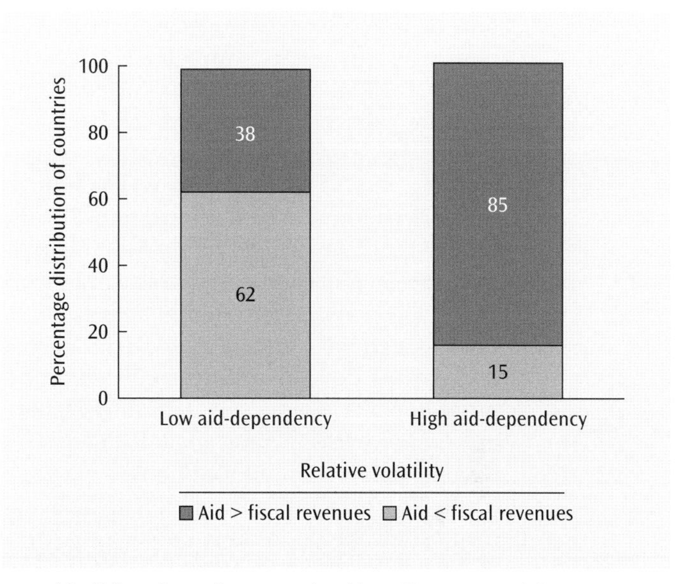

Note: High aid-dependency refers to countries with an aid-to-revenue ratio larger than 50 percent; low aid-dependency refers to countries with an aid-to-revenue ratio between 10 and 50 percent.
Source: Bulir and Hamann 2003.

Alignment and Harmonization

Alongside improvements in the allocation of aid across countries, two other factors are key to enhancing development effectiveness: (a) alignment of aid with partner country development strategy and priorities, and (b) harmonization of donor policies and practices around strengthened partner country systems. Improving alignment and harmonization is now an active item on the agenda of the international community, reflecting the development lessons of the past decade that underscore the importance of country ownership and leadership of the development program for its effectiveness. There is also recognition that the wide variety of donor requirements and processes for delivering aid in the past were generating high and unproductive transaction costs for partner countries and drawing down their limited institutional capacities.

Donors are beginning to anchor their support in country-owned and -led strategies. In low-income countries, the Poverty Reduction Strategy Paper (PRSP) provides the central framework for strategic alignment of international aid with national development priorities and for achieving better coherence and coordination in donor support activities. Finding effective ways of aligning aid with the PRSP and harmonizing donor policies and practices around it constitute the core of the alignment and harmonization agenda in low-income countries.

The strengthened focus on, and high-level political commitment to, the alignment and harmonization agenda was evident at the Rome High-Level Forum in early 2003. The Forum imparted a strong impetus to this reform agenda that is now being actively followed up. A new institutional architecture has emerged to take this work forward.

A new institutional architecture. The follow-up work to Rome is being coordinated by the OECD DAC Working Party on Aid Effectiveness and Donor Practices established in May 2003. The work, carried out in active collaboration with bilateral and multilateral donors and partner countries, aims to develop proposals for action in several areas important to aid effectiveness. These include alignment and harmonization, public financial management, procurement, managing for development results, and untying of aid.[28]

Task teams have been set up for each of these areas. The work on alignment and harmonization is focused on facilitating the implementation of the Rome agenda through dissemination and exchange of experience; tracking progress on more effective aid delivery; and improving existing mechanisms for exercising peer pressure (including using the peer review mechanism to monitor broader issues of policy coherence). Work in the area of public financial management is focused on developing a performance measurement framework for public financial management; increasing the predictability of aid; better integrating aid flows in recipient country budgets; aligning budget support with PRSP processes; and developing an accounting standard for aid. The work on procurement aims at mainstreaming good procurement practices and supporting capacity building in partner countries. The work on results aims to articulate a core set of principles of good practice in managing for development results, drawing on the emerging practices in different institutions. And the work on untying aid supports the 2001 DAC agreement to move toward untying aid to all least developed countries and to explore how to broaden their recommendation.

The Working Party plans to report on progress on its work to the DAC's Senior-Level Meeting in late 2004 and to the Second High-Level Forum scheduled to be held in March 2005 in Paris.

Monitoring progress on alignment and harmonization. To enable systematic monitoring of progress on the alignment and harmonization agenda, a preliminary set of indicators has been drawn up that is now being field-tested. The indicators cover the key dimensions of ownership, alignment, streamlining, and improvement of practices (table 11.2). A survey will be carried out in 14 developing countries to capture progress on alignment and harmonization at the country level. Data collected from this exercise will be used to report to the Second High-Level Forum in 2005.

Emphasis on country-level implementation. In the effort to improve alignment and harmonization, emphasis is being placed on country-level implementation, to test initiatives and assess their effectiveness. This process is increasingly being led by recipient countries, with the support of local-level donors. A number of countries have stepped forward as participants in country-level efforts to advance and mainstream harmonization.[29] The experience of Vietnam, one of the frontier harmonization countries, offers some concrete examples of implementation progress (box 11.3).[30]

Partner countries and donors are also increasingly looking to harmonize and align at the sector level, through the application of sectorwide approaches, or SWAps. In SWAps donors support government programs based on agreed sector strategies. Wherever possible, they use the country's systems for procurement, financial management, environmental assessment, and monitoring and reporting, and pool their funds to provide harmonized support. In the health sector, for example, about 20 countries currently receive support through SWAps.

In sum, an encouraging consensus has emerged in the international community on the need to better align and harmonize aid,

TABLE 11.2 Framework of indicators on progress on harmonization and alignment (provisional)
Rome Commitments on Harmonization and Alignment

	Commitments	Indicators
1. Ownership	**Partner countries coordinate development assistance**	
	1. Partner countries assume leadership roles in the coordination of development assistance (*3) 2. Partner countries, when necessary, reform their systems and procedures and adopt international principles and good practices (*3) 3. Donors increasingly support partner countries' capacity to manage development assistance effectively (*3)	1. Percentage of partner countries where partners and donors have agreed on an agenda for greater harmonization. 2. Percentage of partner countries that lead local coordination processes, including organizing and chairing consultative groups or roundtables. 3. *Comment: The Joint Venture on Public Financial Management is currently elaborating a framework on public financial management. A decision will be made on whether this might provide the basis for an appropriate indicator.* 4. Percentage of partner countries where partners and donors have agreed to an action plan and have committed resources to build institutional capacity to manage development assistance.
2. Alignment	**Donors align aid with partner country priorities and systems**	
	4. Development assistance is increasingly delivered in accordance with partner countries' priorities (*5.1) 5. Donors rely increasingly on partner country systems and procedures (*5)	5. Percentage of donors within a country whose country assistance strategies are consistent with PRSs or equivalent national frameworks. 6. Percentage of donors within a country whose development assistance is aligned with budget cycle. 7. Percentage of donors within partner country relying on (a) supreme audit institution to audit donor funds and (b) partner countries' procurement systems.
3. Streamlining	**Donors streamline aid delivery**	
	6. Donors implement common arrangements for planning, managing, and delivering aid (*6) 7. Donors reduce missions, reviews, and reports where appropriate (*5.2; *5.7) 8. Donors are transparent about their activities (*6)	8. Percentage of donors within a country that rely on a common conditionality framework consistent with PRSs or equivalent national frameworks. 9. Percentage of SWAps where funding, reporting, and monitoring are guided by a common framework. 10. Number of agreements on delegated cooperation. 11. Number of donor missions per partner country, of which joint donor missions. 12. Number of financial reports per country prepared by the Ministry of Finance and sector ministries solely for donors. 13. Percentage of donors within a partner country that disclose information on (a) planned aid flows and (b) country analytic work.
4. Practices	**Policies, procedures, practices, and incentives foster harmonization**	
	9. Donors review key policies and procedures to support harmonization (*5.2) 10. Global and regional programs increasingly promote and support harmonized approaches (*5.7; *5.9)	14. *Comment: These dimensions will be captured in the peer review reports and reports to the DAC SLM Level Forum.*

Note: Number in parentheses indicates number of the paragraph that refers to the specific commitment in the Rome Declaration. Paragraph 7 of the Rome Declaration on Harmonization called for tracking and refining indicators of progress on harmonization. This list of commitments and the accompanying list of indicators of effective partnerships address that undertaking.
Source: OECD 2003.

BOX 11.3 Vietnam's comprehensive government-led harmonization program

In Vietnam, a pioneer of harmonization, and a European Union harmonization pilot, donors have been supporting the implementation of the government's harmonization priorities, with progress in several areas.

At the strategic level. The Vietnamese government has taken the lead to develop a clear harmonization program and utilized its poverty reduction strategy for ODA planning and to ensure sector policy coherence.

Budget alignment. The Poverty Reduction Support Credit (PRSC) and other budget support will be aligned on an interim basis starting in 2004 and regularized in 2005.

Joint analytic work. The Asian Development Bank and the World Bank jointly undertook procurement and financial management diagnostics. The IMF, UNDP, Denmark, the Netherlands, the United Kingdom, and the World Bank jointly conducted a public expenditure review.

Harmonized financial management. The AsDB, Agence Française de Developpement (AFD), Japan, Kreditanstalt fur Wiederaufbau (KfW), and the World Bank have agreed on a common reporting format for selected ongoing and new projects; common assessments of implementing agency financial management arrangements; common content, format, and frequency of reports required by the donors; and common auditor acceptability criteria, with a shared list of acceptable firms, common audit terms of reference, and an agreed follow-up approach to audit findings including sanctions.

Harmonized procurement. Agreement has been reached among the AsDB, AFD, Japan, KfW, and the World Bank on common bidding documents, common upper-limit thresholds for International Competitive Bidding/National Competitive Bidding, common assessment of thresholds for prior/post reviews, and eligibility of dependent state-owned enterprises.

Environmental assessment. Harmonization efforts among the AsDB, AFD, Japan, KfW, and the World Bank are moving toward agreement on environmental assessment (EA) coverage, consultation through sharing of EA documentation, mitigation measures, management plans, and EA disclosure and timing.

Joint portfolio reviews. This is an ongoing collaborative effort by AsDB, Japan Bank for International Cooperation, and the World Bank, which has more recently been joined by AFD and KfW.

Capacity building. The Like-Minded Donor Group, constituting seven to nine bilateral donors, has teamed up with the government and other donors in a $10 million multidonor trust fund to strengthen government capacity related to procurement, project management, financial management, and budget support.

Source: World Bank, Operations Policy and Country Services Vice Presidency.

and the main elements of the agenda have crystallized in the past year. What is needed now is consistent implementation of these efforts and concerted monitoring to keep track of progress and ensure learning and cross-fertilization.

Progress on the HIPC Initiative

For the heavily indebted poor countries, debt relief is crucial to create the fiscal space for much-needed increases in spending to promote growth and reduce poverty. Overall, substantial progress has been made in the implementation of the HIPC Initiative. As of April 2004, 27 HIPCs—or more than two-thirds of the 38 countries that potentially qualify for assistance under the initiative—have reached the decision point and are receiving debt relief. In net present value (NPV) terms, these 27 countries account for 85 percent of the total expected relief for the 34 HIPCs for which data are available. Thirteen HIPCs have also reached the completion point—when creditors provide the full debt relief committed at the decision point on an irrevocable basis.

The process of reaching the completion point has generally taken longer than earlier envisaged. The delay is attributable to the challenges of achieving and maintaining macroeconomic stability and preparing and implementing poverty reduction strategies. Most of the countries in this situation, however, either have adopted the necessary macroeconomic policy changes or are making efforts to do so. Similarly, while the preparation of PRSPs has taken longer than expected, most countries that are in the interim period have finalized their strategies and are not expected to be constrained by the requirement for one-year satisfactory implementation. Progress has also been made in most cases on social and structural completion point triggers.

Challenges remain for countries that have not yet reached the decision point. Domestic conflict, unsettled postconflict situations, and protracted arrears continue to impede countries from reaching the decision point. The issue thus arises as to whether a number of countries could be left behind when the HIPC Initiative expires. The initiative is open to all eligible countries that establish a performance track record leading to the decision point before the end of 2004, when the sunset clause of the HIPC Initiative will take effect. Staffs of the Bank and Fund will present options for extension of the sunset clause to their respective Boards by September 2004.

HIPC relief is projected to substantially lower debt stocks and debt service ratios for most HIPCs that have reached the decision point. NPV debt stocks in the 27 HIPCs that reached the decision point by July 2003 are projected to decline by about two-thirds once they reach their respective completion points. HIPCs in the interim period have benefited from Paris Club debt relief as well as from relief from several multilateral creditors under the HIPC Initiative. The ratio of debt service to exports for the 27 decision-point countries declined from 16.9 percent in 1998 to an estimated 9.8 percent in 2003 and is projected to fall to 7.9 percent by 2006 (table 11.3).[31]

Poverty-reducing expenditures have risen in the countries that have reached the decision point. For these 27 countries, such expenditures in 2003 were estimated to be about three and a half times the amount of debt-service payments.[32] Annual debt service is projected to be about 24 percent lower during 2001–06 than it was in 1998–99, a reduction averaging

TABLE 11.3 Debt service and poverty-reducing expenditure by the 27 HIPCs that have reached the decision point (in US$ millions, unless otherwise indicated)

	Actual					Estimate	Projected		
Expenditure	1998	1999	2000	2001	2002	2003	2004	2005	2006
Debt service	3,696	3,179	3,131	2,451	2,419	2,729	2,711	2,534	2,794
Debt service/exports (%)[a]	16.9	14.5	13.9	10.4	10.0	9.8	8.7	7.6	7.9
Debt service/government revenue (%)[a]	25.2	21.8	21.8	16.5	14.9	14.6	12.8	10.9	11.0
Debt service/GDP (%)[a]	3.9	3.4	3.4	2.5	2.4	2.4	2.2	1.9	1.9
Poverty-reducing expenditure		6,067	5,934	6,712	7,581	9,104	10,832	11,521	12,465
Poverty-reducing expenditure/ government revenue (%)[a]		40.9	41.4	45.2	46.8	48.6	51.0	49.7	49.0
Poverty-reducing expenditure/GDP (%)[a]		6.4	6.4	7.0	7.5	8.0	8.7	8.6	8.7

Note: Debt service figures for 1998 and 1999 reflect debt relief already provided to Bolivia, Guyana, Mozambique, and Uganda under the original framework. Debt service figures do not include the impact of the "topping off" granted to Ethiopia and Niger in April 2004. Data on poverty-reducing expenditures are not available for all countries, particularly for 2003–06. In aggregate, the last available period was used for future years, thus understating the likely level of poverty-reducing spending.
a. Weighted averages.
Source: HIPC country documents and IMF staff estimates.

about $830 million a year. Poverty-reducing spending, meanwhile, increased from about $6.1 billion in 1999 to $9.1 billion in 2003 and is projected to increase to about $12.5 billion in 2006 (see table 11.3).[33]

Debt relief to HIPCs provided by traditional mechanisms, through the HIPC Initiative, and on a voluntary basis together generally reduces the ratio of HIPC net present value debt to exports to the average level of other low-income countries. Continued measures are needed by HIPCs and by creditors to ensure that debt sustainability is maintained after the completion point, just as similar measures are needed for other low-income countries. Bank and Fund staff have therefore proposed a debt sustainability framework for low-income countries to address this issue. The Executive Boards have endorsed the key elements of the framework, and work is continuing toward making the framework fully operational.[34]

This framework is intended to provide guidance on several issues related to the financing strategies for low-income countries, including the range of indicators for assessing debt sustainability, the role of policies in determining appropriate debt thresholds, the importance of including domestic debt in such assessments, and the appropriate mix of grants and new credits. These issues are becoming increasingly important in light of the need for large increases in external financing to meet the MDGs. In some countries, financing the MDGs with new concessional borrowing could lead to an unsustainably large debt burden. In April 2004, Ethiopia and Niger were granted additional "topping up" assistance under the HIPC Initiative, on an exceptional basis on account of exogenous factors that had adversely affected their debt sustainability. It needs to be stressed, however, that debt sustainability is not only a resource-flow issue. It also depends on increasing growth, diversifying exports, increasing access to global markets, and adequately mitigating the effects of exogenous shocks.

Although creditor participation has improved under the Initiative, some non–Paris Club bilateral and commercial creditors have persisted in not committing to provide HIPC relief. Most of the costs attributable to bilateral creditors continue to be borne by members of the Paris Club. Commercial creditors represent less than 5 percent of the NPV cost of relief, in part because of measures by the Debt Reduction Facility for IDA-only countries, which has reduced the stock of commercial debt in HIPCs. Moral suasion, however, remains the principal measure for encouraging participation and discouraging litigation by remaining commercial creditors. With respect to multilateral debt, 23 of the 31 multilateral creditors have indicated their intent to participate in the Initiative, representing more than 99 percent of the total debt relief required.

A key premise of the HIPC Initiative is that debt relief should be additional to other forms of external financing assistance. An important issue is whether countries receiving debt relief are also receiving additional resources or whether debt relief crowds out other aid flows. Merely observing the size of flows does not provide conclusive evidence of additionality, because the amount of aid these countries would have received without the HIPC Initiative is not known. There are also substantial difficulties in measurement because different donors account for debt relief in different ways. Debt relief is sometimes explicit, such as through grants for debt relief, or implicit, such as through debt service reductions.

The September 2003 HIPC Status of Implementation Report found, based on a review of balance of payments data, that gross and net flows of official external resources to the 27 countries that have reached the decision point increased substantially during 1999–2002.[35] Net flows (that is, the difference between gross resource inflows and debt service payments) increased from $4.5 billion in 1999, before provision of debt relief under the enhanced initiative in 2000, to $7.3 billion in 2002 once the enhanced initiative got under way. Although it is difficult to determine what resource flows would have been without HIPC in 1999–2002, the data do suggest that debt relief has been additional to other forms of external financing. The September report noted, however, that official external financing flows to the 27 decision-point countries declined substantially in the mid-1990s (as they did to other low-income countries).

Notes

1. OECD 2004b.

2. OECD 2004a. Amounts are at 2002 prices and exchange rates.

3. At the October 2003 International Donors Conference for the Reconstruction of Iraq, donors pledged more than $33 billion in assistance—loans, grants, and export credits—over four years. There is uncertainty as to when these pledges will be realized and whether over time they will represent an increase in total aid, as most of the initial announcements indicate, or a reallocation of aid from other countries.

4. The contribution of NGOs to development is difficult to quantify in dollars, for a number of reasons. First, many of their staff work on a voluntary basis and so the value of their labor is never quantified in money terms. Second, even when they are paid, as for example volunteers working as teachers or community workers in developing countries, the value of this compensation may be considerably less than the market value of their services. Third, many of the activities undertaken by NGOs are not strictly developmental in aim, but may promote cultural or recreational activities.

5. While NGOs have been successful in raising their own funds and in channeling official flows (about 7 percent of ODA supports NGO activity), they do face the challenge of continuing to be effective as they grow in size.

6. A recent study by Prati, Sahay, and Tressel (2003) suggests that the adverse trade effect may not be very large, and even a doubling of aid flows from 10 to 20 percent of recipients' GDP is estimated to lead to a real appreciation of only 6 percent.

7. Knack and Rahman 2004.

8. With a 7 percent annual increase in real terms for ODA and projected medium-term real growth for low-income countries of 4.8 percent a year, the ODA-to-GNI ratio would rise from around 2.7 percent to more than 3 percent. Aid dependence varies widely across low-income countries: for example, aid in 2001 was 0.4 percent of income in India and 28 percent in Mozambique.

9. See Goldin, Rogers, and Stern (2002) for a review of evidence on the increased productivity of aid.

10. Development Committee 2003b. The results are based on an analysis of 18 low-income countries with relatively good policies.

11. Development Committee 2004.

12. DAC members' reporting of tying status is uneven. For example, the United States does not report tying data. Tying statistics cover only about 40 percent of total bilateral ODA.

13. Aryeetey, Osei, and Quartey 2003.

14. Jepma 1991.

15. About 30 percent of total ODA takes the form of contributions to multilateral institutions. Of the total aid provided in turn by the multilateral institutions, close to 30 percent also is in the form of special-purpose grants (mainly from U.N. agencies).

16. Also see Development Committee 2003b.

17. Dollar and Levin 2004. Figure 11.4 draws on this paper and plots the unexplained (residual) component of growth, aid, and policies. The paper also refers to studies that find different results on the relationship between the quality of policies and institutions and the effectiveness of aid and provides an assessment.

18. Dollar and Levin 2004. Other recent studies of aid selectivity include Birdsall, Claessens, and Diwan (2003) and Roodman (2003).

19. For this calculation, low-income recipient countries are divided into those with strong policies and institutions and those with weak policies and institutions, where the latter is the bottom half of low-income countries on the CPIA ranking. This binary distribution has its limitations of course as it does not capture the relative position of recipients in terms of the CPIA score within the two categories. In the figure, the selectivity of a given donor is indicated by the angle of the line connecting the dot point to the origin relative to the 45-degree line.

20. Collier and Hoeffler 2002.

21. Development Committee 2003b; OECD 2004a.

22. Collier and Dehn 2001.

23. In this regard, the IMF is examining whether responses to shock-induced financing

needs can be made more consistent in the context of programs supported by the Poverty Reduction and Growth Facility (PRGF), and whether the terms of the Fund's instruments targeted to shock financing can be made more appropriate for low-income countries.

24. The methodology for computing the donor fragmentation index is from Knack and Rahman 2004.

25. Bulir and Hamann 2001, 2003.

26. Bulir and Lane (2002) find that aid flows on average are procyclical, so that countries receive more aid when economic activity is stronger.

27. Gemmell and McGillivray 1998.

28. See OECD 2004a for a detailed discussion of the work of the Working Party.

29. Sixteen countries or country groups stepped forward before or in Rome to expand or mainstream country-level efforts to streamline donor procedures and practices: Bangladesh, Bolivia, Cambodia, Ethiopia, Honduras, Jamaica, Kenya, Kyrgyz Republic, Morocco, Nicaragua, Niger, the Pacific Island group, the Philippines, Senegal, Vietnam, and Zambia.

30. Other examples of harmonization activities at the country level are listed in the Country Implementation Tracking Tool, at http://www.aidharmonization.org.

31. See IMF–World Bank 2004b.

32. The definition of poverty-reducing expenditures varies across countries. Commonly included are primary education, basic health services, and rural development.

33. Country authorities are putting in place public expenditure management systems that would ensure the efficiency of poverty-reducing expenditures. See IMF–World Bank 2003b.

34. IMF–World Bank 2004a. Also see IMF 2004.

35. IMF–World Bank 2003a.

12

Fulfilling Responsibilities for Global Public Goods

Developed countries need to step up action in support of key global public goods and areas for global collective action related to the millennium goals. Given their weight in the global system, developed countries bear a special responsibility with respect to the global public goods agenda. Developing countries, of course, also need to play their part in this effort.

Six areas surface in most discussions of global public goods: health, environment, financial stability, peace, trade, and knowledge.[1] Of course not all issues in these areas are of a public good nature. Only those that transcend national boundaries and are either regional or global in nature are relevant in this context. So the relevant actions include those aimed at preventing adverse health and environmental spillovers, preserving international financial stability and peace, and promoting the gains from international trade and the spread of knowledge. Together, these actions constitute an important contribution to the attainment and sustainability of development.

Some global public goods have been delivered more successfully than others, reflecting the special circumstances of each good and the mechanism chosen for its delivery. Ranked from relative success to relative failure, the following examples are often mentioned: aviation safety, postal systems, the Internet, eradication of smallpox, protection of the ozone layer, prevention of global warming, safety of the oceans (including pollution control), and sustainable use of natural resources such as fisheries.

Effective delivery of global public goods raises important institutional and financing issues. Institutional approaches could take the form of using existing institutions to assume responsibility for a specific global public good program, usually with a governance framework that ensures involvement and oversight by donors and other affected countries. Examples are the Consultative Group on International Agricultural Research (CGIAR) and the River Blindness Control Program within the World Bank, and peacekeeping programs of the United Nations. At the other extreme, some programs have involved setting up new institutional delivery mechanisms. An example is the Global Fund to Fight AIDS, Tuberculosis, and Malaria (GFATM). Some critics have voiced concern about the proliferation of such funds and institutions. Between these poles lie some innovative arrangements, such as the Global Environment Facility (GEF), which has an independent governance framework but relies fully on existing institutions for implementation. Networks and coalitions are increasingly common, particularly in the areas of standard setting for communication, commerce, and trade. Important lessons can be learned from networks with a long and successful experience, such as those for civil aviation, traffic safety, and postal services.

Appropriate models for financing global public goods have received considerable scrutiny recently. In addition to questions of externalities, free riders, and scarcity of funds, the need to finance complementary programs at the national level must be taken into account. Official development assistance is a large source of public funding for global public goods. Many multilateral and bilateral programs directly finance global public goods or channel resources to trust funds and specialized institutions. Each year approximately $5 billion in official development assistance is devoted to global public goods.[2] In recent years, private sources—foundations, companies, individuals—have become important in financing global public goods, usually in partnership with official sources. CGIAR and the River Blindness Control Program were early examples of mixed private-public funding. The Global Alliance for Vaccines and Immunization (GAVI), GFATM, and the Prototype Carbon Fund are prominent recent examples. Some of these partnerships are designed to create markets by providing up-front support and incentives for private companies to invest in the creation and delivery of key global public goods. Global public goods dealing with activities that fall predominantly in the commercial sphere—financial sector, telecommunications, air transportation—are financed largely on a private basis through appropriate industry cooperative arrangements and fees.

Global public goods recently have received much greater attention, a reflection of the trend toward globalization and the associated shrinking of the world. One manifestation of the increased attention is the International Task Force on Global Public Goods, established last year by France and Sweden to look into recent work and initiatives on the topic and to identify priorities for action (box 12.1). Another manifestation is the increased attention to global public goods and related programs at multilateral institutions, as set out in chapter 13.

Economic theory suggests that global public goods typically will be undersupplied, as countries fail to adequately take into account the implications of their policies and actions for people living in other countries;[3] hence, the importance of monitoring country performance in meeting commitments under international agreements and in signing onto such agreements in the first place.

BOX 12.1 International Task Force on Global Public Goods

The mandate of the International Task Force on Global Public Goods, chaired by Ernesto Zedillo (former president of Mexico) and Tidjane Thiam (former Minister of Planning, Development, and Coordination, Côte d'Ivoire), is to encourage the provision of international public goods, global and regional, that are of critical importance for eliminating poverty and achieving the MDGs.

The task force is to systematically assess and clarify the notion of global and regional public goods, to identify those public goods that contribute most directly to reducing poverty and meeting the other MDGs, and to make recommendations to policymakers and other stakeholders on how to provide and finance those goods. The task force is also to propose responsibility for follow-up, including monitoring of effectiveness and results.

Meeting for the first time in September 2003 at Yale University in New Haven, Connecticut, the task force agreed on areas for further work, to be discussed at its next meeting in Istanbul in early March. The task force's final report is due in 2005. Before then, a wide consultation is planned, to promote broad understanding of and consensus around the report's recommendations for action.

Note: For more information on the task force, visit http://www.gpgtaskforce.org/bazment.aspx.

For developed countries, it is worthwhile to organize the assessment of their policies and actions with respect to global public goods into three blocks: their participation in international agreements and institutions that commits them to act in a certain way; their support for capacity building and other programs (bilateral, multilateral, philanthropic) that help developing countries take critical actions; and their voluntary actions (if any) taken solo or in networks with like-minded partners.

This framework is used below to analyze certain issues relating to environmental sustainability—a key global public good. Future global monitoring reports will address other global public goods as well. In the meantime, financial stability, trade (including some issues relating to knowledge and technology transfers), and health are treated in the context of other chapters of this report.

Developed-Country Impact on the Global Commons: Limited Progress

Developed countries shoulder the predominant responsibility for preserving the global environmental commons and helping developing countries pursue environmentally sustainable development, both because of their larger contributions to global environmental degradation and their greater financial and technological resources for prevention and mitigation.

Policies aimed at improving environmental performance in and by the developed countries can be divided between those that will improve local environmental conditions and those aimed at reducing negative impacts on the global commons. An analysis of developed-country policies affecting their local environment is beyond the scope of this report, but the experience of the OECD with environmental performance reviews offers valuable lessons for developing countries (box 12.2).

The environmental performance of developed countries in relation to the state of the global commons is mixed. The ratification of international environmental conventions—with some notable exceptions—indicates a high degree of commitment to global environmental issues (box 12.3). The process of global environmental governance has witnessed some resounding successes, most prominently the Montreal Protocol, an international agreement to protect the ozone layer. The success of the protocol was facilitated by the existence of cost-effective alternatives to ozone-depleting substances, the availability of adequate funding for developing countries,[4] and the fact that

BOX 12.2 Progress toward environmental sustainability through performance review and peer pressure

Since 1991, the OECD has carried out environmental performance reviews (EPRs) of its member countries. Each EPR report is peer reviewed and approved by the OECD Working Party on Environmental Performance. Progress is assessed by establishing baseline conditions and examining policy commitments, institutional arrangements, and routine capabilities for carrying out national evaluations. Along with the traditional benefits of country analytic work, the peer review process promotes environmental improvement and continuous dialogue through benchmarking (the sharing of information on the policies, approaches, and experiences of the reviewed countries) and peer pressure.

The EPR process can be successfully replicated in developing countries. Indeed, since 1993 the United Nations Economic Commission for Europe (UNECE) has been carrying out EPRs on countries in Europe and Central Asia that are not members of the OECD.

Source: OECD and UNECE Web sites; World Bank staff.

BOX 12.3 International environmental agreements: toward global cooperation, with some notable exceptions

The last 20 years have seen the birth of six major international environmental agreements, the ratification of which reflects a solid consensus on the importance of multilateral efforts to tackle global environmental problems. Between 150 and 190 countries have ratified the Montreal Protocol to the Vienna Convention for the Protection of the Ozone Layer (1987), the Basel Convention on the Transboundary Movement of Hazardous Wastes and Their Disposal (1989), the Convention on Biological Diversity (1992), the Framework Convention on Climate Change (1992), and the Convention to Combat Desertification (1994). Of the 151 signatories to the most recent agreement, the Stockholm Convention on Persistent Organic Pollutants (2001), 41 have already ratified it. (It will enter into force with the 50th ratification.)

A notable exception to these positive results is the Kyoto Protocol to the Framework Convention on Climate Change (1997). To enter into force, the protocol must be ratified by 55 parties that together account for at least 55 percent of global greenhouse gas emissions, but the 120 parties that have ratified represent only 44.2 percent of emissions. Six so-called Annex I parties (developed and transition economies) have not yet ratified the protocol: Australia, Croatia, Liechtenstein, Monaco, Russia, and the United States (though Russia has recently indicated that it will). The United States has announced that it will not ratify the Kyoto protocol. It has not ratified the Basel or the Biodiversity conventions.

Source: Convention Web sites; World Bank staff.

inaction would exact high costs in the near future. But most global environmental problems do not share those characteristics, resulting in slower progress to resolve them.

Sectoral policies in developed countries make or break progress toward global environmental sustainability. The maintenance of high subsidies to fisheries and the failure of energy policies to forcefully reduce greenhouse emissions are just two vivid illustrations of the lack of rapid overall progress. More than a quarter of the world's fisheries are overexploited or depleted, as overfishing by local communities is aggravated by fishing fleets from developed countries. Global subsidies for fishing, meanwhile, conservatively estimated at $10 billion to 15 billion a year (about a quarter of the annual $56 billion trade in fish), are driving unrestricted and highly advanced fish harvesting.

The MDGs call for a reduction of greenhouse gas emissions. The 1997 Kyoto Protocol places most of the burden for reducing greenhouse gas emissions on rich countries, home to just 16 percent of the world's population but the source of more than half such emissions. Kyoto calls on developed countries as a group to reduce carbon dioxide emissions by at least 5 percent of 1990 levels by 2008–12. Overall, progress to date has been disappointing (figure 12.1). Within the European Union only two countries, Sweden and the United Kingdom, are on track to meet their targets. The overall EU target is to cut greenhouse gas emissions by 8 percent before 2010, but with existing policies only a 0.5 percent cut will be achieved. The United States, which produces 25 percent of global greenhouse gas emissions, has explicitly declined to ratify the protocol and contributes growing emissions.

Aid for the Environment: Long Stagnant

Official development finance for environmental concerns has followed the stagnant path of overall development financing in

1990–2000. A slight increase in official bilateral aid for environmental purposes followed the 1992 Rio Convention, but commitments peaked in 1996 and the increase was reversed by the end of the decade. A slightly different pattern emerges in multilateral commitments. After declining sharply in 1993, with total aid commitments, they rebounded in 1994 only to resume a declining trend. Commitments to environmental concerns averaged 3 percent of total bilateral aid and 5 percent of total multilateral aid, bringing total environmental aid to $2 billion per year—far from the commitments made at Rio (table 12.1).

Commitments to environmental funds set up to confront global issues are no exception. The Global Environment Facility was established in 1991 to help developing countries fund projects and programs that protect the global environment, initially in the fields of biodiversity, climate change, ozone depletion, and international waters. Since the 1994 restructuring, new funding for the GEF has remained stagnant. The first replenishment, covering 1994–98, saw pledges of $2.02 billion. New commitments were $1.99 billion for 1998–02 and $2.2 billion for 2002–06. Despite expansion to cover new environmental issues, such as land degradation and persistent organic pollutants, GEF funding has actually declined by almost 10 percent as a share of the combined GDP of the 38 contributing nations.

FIGURE 12.1 MDGs and Kyoto Protocol call for reduction of greenhouse emissions, but results tell a different story
Carbon dioxide emissions, 1990 and 2000

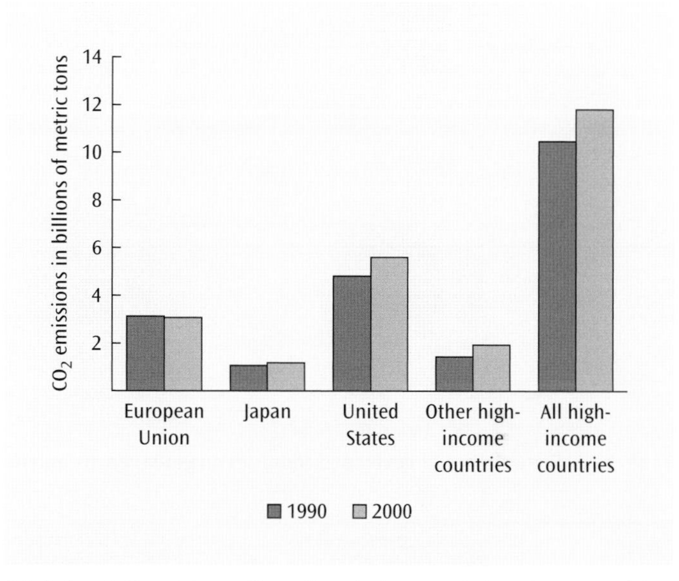

Note: Carbon dioxide emissions are the most important component of greenhouse gas emissions.
Source: World Bank, *World Development Indicators.*

Developed Countries and Global Environmental Sustainability: Widely Varying Performance

The performance of developed countries on global environmental sustainability is far from homogeneous. MDG 7 aims to "reverse the loss of environmental resources." Table 12.2 assesses developed country efforts to this end on three dimensions: depletion of the global commons through carbon dioxide (CO_2) emissions (an MDG indicator); provision of global public goods through participation in multilateral environmental agreements; and assistance, through environmental aid, to poor countries in their quest to halt and reverse environmental degradation. Sweden and Switzerland emerge as exemplary global citizens, whereas Australia and the United States tail the group of developed countries (table 12.2).

The contributions of developed countries to carbon dioxide emissions and climate change vary widely. In per capita terms, Australia, Luxembourg, and the United States emit more than three times the amount of Sweden and Switzerland. Nor is the participation of developed countries in environmental agreements homogeneous. While 15 countries have ratified the Kyoto Protocol, the Beijing Amendment, and the Biodiversity Convention, Australia and the United States have each ratified just one. And developed countries commit remarkably different amounts of aid for environmental sustainability. Denmark, the Netherlands, Norway, Sweden, and Switzerland commit around 0.02 percent of their GDP to environmental aid. Ireland and Italy give less than 0.001 percent—more than a 20-fold difference.

TABLE 12.1 Aid for the environment, 1990–2000
(US$ millions)

Aid	1990	1991	1992	1993	1994	1995	1996	1997	1998	1999	2000
Bilateral	1,033	652	921	737	806	1,083	1,822	1,526	1,012	1,394	984
Multilateral	657	604	1,683	368	1,942	822	744	812	1,439	590	962
Total	1,690	1,256	2,604	1,105	2,748	1,905	2,566	2,338	2,451	1,984	1,946
Total (% of bilateral donors' combined GDP)	0.010	0.007	0.014	0.006	0.013	0.008	0.011	0.011	0.011	0.008	0.008

Note: The table uses the World Bank definition of environmental aid, as applied in Pagiola and others (2002). Alternative definitions generate different levels of aid for environment but similar trends.
Source: Adapted from Pagiola and others 2002.

Table 12.2 Performance of developed countries on global environmental sustainability

	Depletion of the global commons	Ratification of multilateral environmental agreements[a]			Aid for environment
Country	Carbon dioxide emissions (metric tons per capita, 2000)	Kyoto Protocol	Beijing Amendment to Montreal Protocol	Biodiversity Convention	Bilateral aid for environment (% of GDP)[b,c]
Australia	18.0	No	No	Yes	0.0054
Austria	7.5	Yes	No	Yes	0.0078
Belgium	10.0	Yes	Yes	Yes	0.0012
Canada	14.2	Yes	Yes	Yes	0.0031
Denmark	8.4	Yes	Yes	Yes	0.0193
Finland	10.3	Yes	Yes	Yes	0.0060
France	6.2	Yes	Yes	Yes	0.0025
Germany	9.6	Yes	Yes	Yes	0.0070
Greece	8.5	Yes	No	Yes	..
Iceland	7.7	Yes	No	Yes	..
Ireland	11.1	Yes	No	Yes	0.0007
Italy	7.4	Yes	No	Yes	0.0004
Japan	9.3	Yes	Yes	Yes	0.0070
Luxembourg	19.4	Yes	Yes	Yes	..
Netherlands	8.7	Yes	Yes	Yes	0.0222
New Zealand	8.4	Yes	Yes	Yes	..
Norway	11.1	Yes	Yes	Yes	0.0230
Portugal	6.0	Yes	No	Yes	0.0003
Spain	7.0	Yes	Yes	Yes	0.0041
Sweden	5.3	Yes	Yes	Yes	0.0145
Switzerland	5.4	Yes	Yes	Yes	0.0216
United Kingdom	9.7	Yes	Yes	Yes	0.0064
United States	19.8	No	Yes	No	0.0021

.. Negligible or not available.
a. "Yes" indicates ratification or equivalent (acceptance, accession, approval).
b. Calculated using the World Bank definition of environmental aid; see Pagiola and others (2002) for details.
c. Average of 1998, 1999, and 2000; except Ireland (2000) and Portugal (1999 and 2000).
Source: World Bank, *World Development Indicators*; convention Web sites; World Bank staff.

Priorities for Action

The case for greater efforts by developed countries in supporting and financing global public environmental goods is a strong one. Rich nations bear a special responsibility for the environmental commons. Conservation, particularly the protection of biodiversity, is another important responsibility. That responsibility is partly a question of ability to pay. But it is also a question of *willingness* to pay—many citizens of developed countries are highly motivated to conserve nature where it is most at risk in developing countries. Tapping that willingness to finance conservation in poor nations will be essential in preserving resources at risk.

Without diminishing the importance of other needed policy changes, such as reducing fisheries subsidies, priorities for action in rich countries include:

- Increasing aid for environmental sustainability to help developing countries establish adequate frameworks for environmental management. This includes financing biodiversity conservation through mechanisms such as the GEF and actions aimed at improving natural resource management and reducing the burden of environment-related diseases in developing countries.
- Controlling greenhouse gas emissions in developed countries.
- Buying offsets or reductions in greenhouse gas emissions from developing countries.
- Assisting developing countries to adapt to climate change and increased climatic variability.

Notes

1. Ferroni and Mody 2002; Kaul, le Goulven, and Mendoza 2003. See also Development Committee 2000, 2001 and African Development Bank 2002.

2. World Bank 2001.

3. This conclusion follows from the growing literature on global public goods, whose origins most observers trace back to the seminal work by Paul Samuelson (1954) on the pure theory of public goods. That work formalized earlier thinking on the provision of public goods and for many years was used as the starting point for discussions of local public goods and public finance. With the more recent focus on global public goods, it has been used to understand those issues as well. Under the theory, a pure public good has two attributes: "nonrivalry" (that is, my consumption of the good in no way reduces your ability to consume it) and "nonexcludability" (that is, no one in the immediate vicinity can be prevented from consuming the good). Also under the theory, pure public goods are chronically undersupplied because those who pay for them do not reap the full gains they generate.

4. Since 1994 some $150 million a year has been made available through the multilateral fund associated with the protocol.

Role of International Financial Institutions

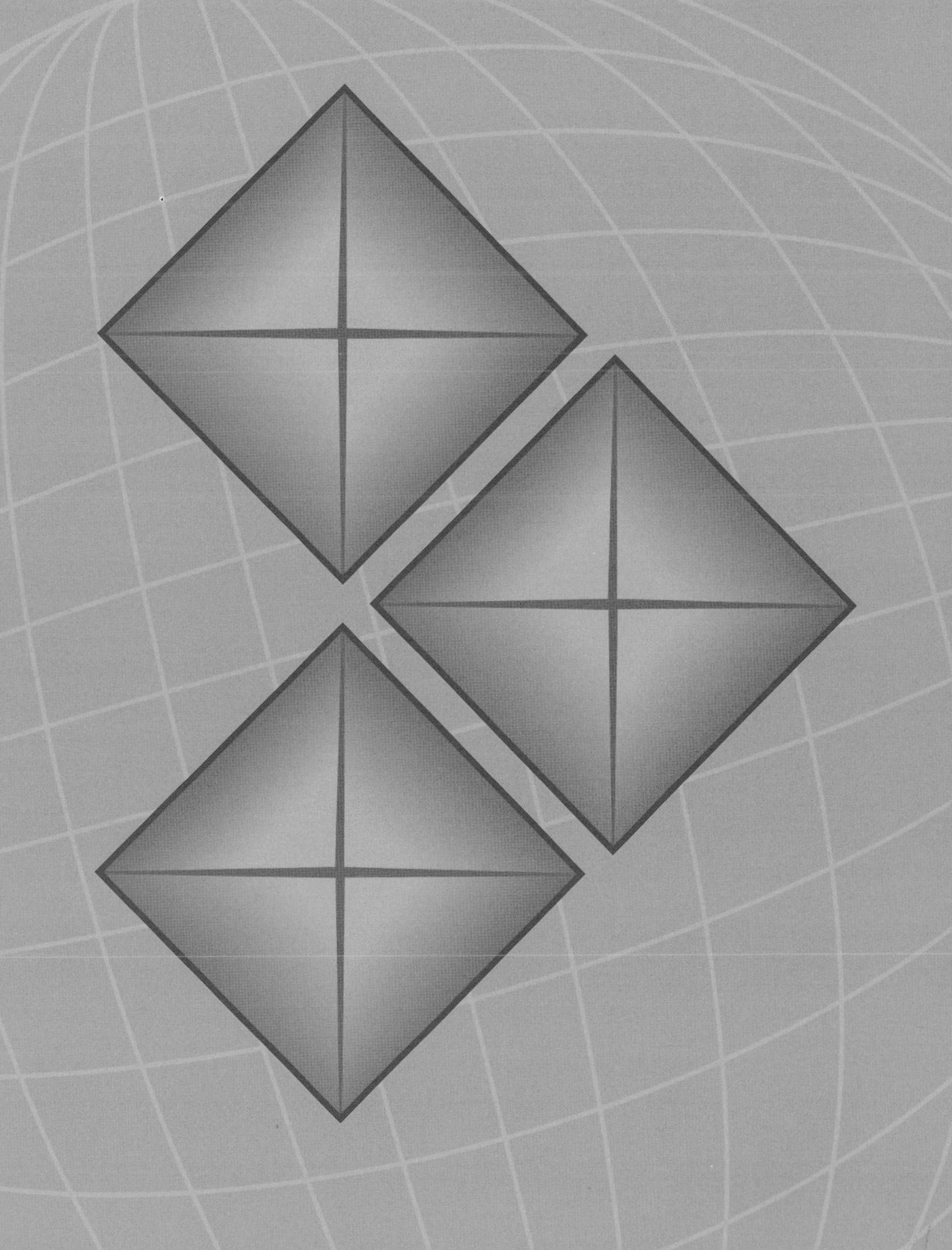

13

Monitoring the IFIs' Contribution

How well are the international financial institutions contributing to the achievement of the MDGs and related development outcomes? This chapter takes a modest first step toward answering that question, focusing on the International Monetary Fund, the World Bank, and the major regional development banks—the African Development Bank, the Asian Development Bank, the European Bank for Reconstruction and Development, and the Inter-American Development Bank—and drawing primarily on the self- and independent evaluations carried out by the international financial institutions themselves. Future efforts will extend and deepen the framework developed herein, including by bringing in the findings of external evaluations and surveys more explicitly,[1] and by broadening the framework to include the issue of developing-country voice in institutional governance, where the different ownership structures of the various IFIs can provide a useful platform for comparative analysis.

In this context, the chapter finds evidence that the IFIs are generally becoming more country focused, more collaborative, and more results oriented, while respecting their distinctive mandates and modalities for providing support for country, regional, and global programs. But it is inconclusive on the critical questions of comparative performance and whether the whole of the IFI contribution is larger (or smaller) than the sum of the IFI parts. Going forward, greater availability and comparability of independent and self-evaluation data from all IFIs should help improve comparative monitoring exercises such as this one and, in turn, reporting to the taxpaying public in all countries. The joint work program on results endorsed by the multilateral development banks at the Roundtable on Managing for Development Results held in Marrakech in February 2004 should provide a vehicle for progress on this key issue.[2]

The chapter is structured as follows. It first summarizes the framework used for considering the contribution of the IFIs individually and in the aggregate. It then applies the framework in turn to the IMF, the World Bank, and the major regional development banks. Next it looks at the trends in systemic coherence and whether the contribution of the IFIs is larger or smaller than the sum of the individual contributions. The last section draws out conclusions and implications for action.

Framework for Monitoring IFI Contribution

IFIs do not achieve development outcomes directly through their individual actions, but they can contribute to those outcomes. For IFIs and other agencies, success depends on effectively deploying assistance in high-quality ways in countries and programs that deliver, and on influencing country policies and programs—often at a distance. This complicates the job of assessing the IFI contribution to the achievement of the MDGs and related outcomes, but no more than it complicates the job of designing IFI programs to maximize that impact. An underlying theme of the chapter is the need for coherence between ex ante program appraisal and ex post evaluation. Assessing an institution's contribution *after* the fact is complex, but it is rendered more so if it is not anticipated *before* the fact, and incorporated into operational design.

What are the channels of influence through which the IFIs affect the attainment of the MDGs and related development goals, and how can they be measured? Simply counting the number of projects or volume of lending for MDGs is clearly not the answer, although numbers on IFI inputs may constitute part of the evidentiary picture. Rather, it is the IFIs' catalytic role that matters the most in the achievement of development outcomes—both by supporting policy and institutional development and by directing that support to those countries and sectors where the payoff to growth and poverty reduction is likely to be the largest. Significant IFI impact may come just as easily through a partnership on a global program, the policy dialogue on a piece of analytic work, or support to strengthen country capacity to design a fully owned reform program, as through a traditional lending operation. In such a setting, the measurement challenge is to discern the IFI influence on the global and regional context and the country policies and actions in the critical areas identified in the preceding chapters. Meeting this challenge is best pursued through a thoughtful and transparent results-chain analysis that links final outcomes to the specific inputs (including the level and distribution of IFI financing across countries) and outputs needed to produce them, and that can be evaluated upon program completion.

The framework for considering the IFI contribution is structured around four themes: country programs, global programs, partnership, and results. These themes are used to examine the IFIs individually and then collectively (box 13.1). The first two themes reflect the fact that increasingly the IFIs have two major product lines that are relevant to the achievement of the MDGs and related outcomes: their country programs and their global programs. Of course, the balance between the two—as well as the corre-

BOX 13.1 Framework for assessing IFI contributions

Country programs
- Alignment with countries' priorities for poverty reduction and other MDGs
- Relevance and selectivity in program design

Global programs
- Support for capacity building for regional and global public goods
- Anchor in international system for global public goods

Partnership
- Harmonization of institutional policies and practices
- Coordination of country support programs

Quality and results
- Results orientation, including monitoring, evaluation, and reporting systems
- Findings on quality and results of strategies and operations

sponding instruments of support—varies across the individual IFIs, in line with their distinctive mandates and comparative advantages, as elaborated in the sections below. For example, the IMF's country program focus is on macroeconomic and fiscal sustainability, which is essential for sustainable growth and poverty reduction. Its global program focus is on international financial stability, in line with its role as the institutional anchor of the international financial system. The World Bank's country program focus is broader, covering the full range of social and structural issues important for the achievement of poverty reduction and the MDGs. Its global focus is on partnership and capacity-building programs designed to benefit developing countries. Focusing on countries in their respective regions, the regional banks also have broad development mandates. The exception is the European Bank for Reconstruction and Development, whose mandate is more narrowly focused on transition. All the regional banks have substantial programs for regional public goods.

Partnership has been singled out in the analysis for special attention, given its central importance to the IFIs' joint and individual effectiveness in helping countries achieve their development goals. The lessons of experience (and common sense) suggest that where many donors are involved in a country or global program, it is essential that they harmonize their rules and reporting requirements to avoid overtaxing scarce country capacity. In addition, where there is a Poverty Reduction Strategy Paper, donors should synchronize the timing of their own country business strategies with it, so that the country can know the resources it is likely to have available when it is doing its programming and budgeting. But maximizing the gains from partnership requires going beyond harmonization and synchronization. It also requires strategic alignment, with agencies being coordinated and strategically selective in their support programs in line with country priorities and their distinctive comparative advantage vis-à-vis other agencies. Such action will also help to ensure that the whole of IFI and donor support adds up to more than the sum of the individual parts.

Finally, the critical bottom line is results. Here the chapter zeroes in on two topics: (a) the systems the IFIs have in place for assessing their results, and (b) the emerging picture of what those systems suggest about the IFI contribution. As the main tool for demonstrating results, evaluation is fundamental to this work—both self-evaluation undertaken by the management of programs and independent evaluations undertaken on behalf of governance bodies that oversee management, such as the board of directors.[3]

Activities of Individual IFIs

This section looks in turn at the activities of the IMF, the World Bank, and the regional development banks, using the organizing structure outlined above.

International Monetary Fund

The IMF contributes to the achievement of the MDGs through several important, if indirect, channels primarily related to the macroeconomic policy environment. These channels include the Fund's work on the global economic and financial system and industrial country surveillance; its financing to member countries; and its policy advice and technical assistance to developing countries. Given the nature of these contributions and the fact that they draw on many aspects of the IMF's work, there is no simple yardstick for assessing effectiveness. Information from a variety of sources must thus be brought to bear in making such an assessment.

COUNTRY PROGRAMS

A key responsibility of the IMF is to provide financing to member countries so that they can address external imbalances without resorting to measures destructive of national or international prosperity. This financing is provided on the strength of a program of policies designed to address the underlying imbalances that necessitated the financing. For low-income countries facing temporary shocks and for middle-income countries facing capital account crises, the IMF's financing alleviates the burden of immediate adjustment that could otherwise set back those countries' efforts to achieve the MDGs.

Beyond the direct benefits of its financing, the Fund provides advice to its member countries, in the context of financial arrangements (where its advice is linked to program conditionality) and of its regular surveillance of all member countries. From the perspective of achieving the MDGs and related development objectives, the IMF's role in providing advice is particularly important. The primary orientation of the IMF's advice is toward the achievement and maintenance of macroeconomic stability over the medium term, given its importance for growth and poverty reduction. Moreover, country experience is replete with episodes in which macroeconomic disturbances have derailed progress toward growth and prosperity. In emerging-market countries, crisis prevention and management are a central focus of the IMF's work, which takes stock of lessons from crises in Asia, Latin America, and elsewhere.[4]

A major challenge for the IMF's policy advice is to ensure not just that the advice is correct—itself a major area of controversy—but that members are helped to implement appropriate policies. This challenge involves issues of capacity and ownership. Capacity issues should be taken into account in designing programs. Capacity can also be strengthened through technical assistance (TA), which the IMF provides in a range of areas related to its responsibilities, including fiscal issues, the monetary and financial sector, and statistics. The IMF recently stepped up its provision of TA through the establishment of two African technical assistance centers (AFRITACs). There are also plans to establish a center in the Middle East. The most recent review of the IMF's TA, undertaken in 2004, focused on strengthening effectiveness and management with a view to addressing the institution-building needs of members, particularly low-income countries. It found that, while clear progress has been made, attention still needs to be given to these areas and to developing a clear strategic direction for TA in the future.[5]

Country ownership is an element that has been examined in connection with the IMF's conditionality review during 2000–02.[6] The focus on ownership reflects concerns that in many cases IMF-supported programs may not be adequately aligned with member countries' own priorities and that this gap may be reflected in weak implementation. Research suggests that program implementation depends mainly on domestic factors rather than the efforts of IMF staff. The conditionality guidelines approved in September 2002 stress that ownership is an essential foundation of an IMF-supported program. The implementation of these guidelines will be reviewed periodically, beginning in mid-2004.[7]

In low-income countries, the PRSP is a vital tool for building ownership and orienting policies toward the MDGs. The PRSP provides a framework in which a country can formulate its strategy for poverty reduction on the basis of a domestic consultative process. It also therefore provides a basis for donors and IFIs to align the conditions for their financial support with the country's own strategy. A review of the PRSP process undertaken jointly by the World Bank and the IMF in 2002 found that the PRSP was widely seen as useful, but that the consultative processes used to prepare the PRSP needed to be strengthened.[8] A key issue is the alignment of the PRSP and a program supported by a Poverty Reducation and Growth Facility (PRGF) financial arrangement. The former should provide a road map to the MDGs, while the latter must be based on realistic projections of macroeconomic developments and external financing, even if those projections fall short of what is needed. The main challenge is to use the tension between the country's needs on the one hand and its available resources and capacity on the other to elicit more action from donors to provide the financing and from the country authorities to undertake the reforms needed to bring reality into line with aspirations.[9] As a related issue, extensive evidence suggests that the growth projections underlying IMF-supported programs have tended to be biased toward overoptimism. This points to a need to strengthen the analytical framework in which IMF-supported programs are designed.

The IMF's financial arrangements have come to play a longer-term role in low-income countries, typically providing financing on concessional terms through successive PRGF arrangements. A long-term engagement with low-income countries helps to ensure that the Fund's financing and policy advice are appropriately directed at helping these countries achieve their development goals. The nature of the Fund's engagement, however, may change as the country's situation changes. Some low-income countries have episodic financing needs associated primarily with temporary macroeconomic imbalances to be addressed through policy corrections; providing such financing is a natural role for the Fund. In contrast, for others, financing is required on a more continuous basis to facilitate the institutional reforms and investments in human capital and infrastructure needed to achieve development goals.[10] In the latter context, the Fund has tended to remain engaged and to continue to provide financing, but typically as a relatively small part of overall financing flows from other international financial institutions and donors. In such cases, a financial arrangement is, to a considerable extent, a vehicle for policy advice and monitoring, and the IMF's involvement is a signal of the country's macroeconomic management to other providers of official financing. Associated with this signaling role is the risk that the IMF could be drawn into prolonged program relationships that may not be justified on the basis of financing need and the quality of policies—pointing to the need to consider alternative, nonprogram, modes of IMF engagement. The policy on assessment letters enables the IMF to provide a more authoritative assessment of policies, either in or outside the context of a program relationship.

GLOBAL PROGRAMS

Within the international system, the IMF is tasked with promoting a stable and open global economic and financial environment, which is essential for the achievement of the MDGs and related development outcomes. The Fund contributes to such an environment first of all through the surveillance of systemically important countries. The Fund's Article IV consultations with industrial countries are a vehicle for promoting appropriate policies, such as curbing domestic imbalances that may pose risks for the global economy. Multilateral surveillance, in the context of the *World Economic Outlook* and the *Global Financial Stability Report,* can highlight both global macroeconomic and financial risks and urge changes in policies by the major countries. In these and other contexts, the Fund is an advocate for increased foreign aid to achieve the MDGs and for increased market access for developing countries' exports. The effectiveness of the IMF's surveillance will next be reviewed later in 2004.[11]

PARTNERSHIP

In carrying out its mission and mandate in contributing to the achievement of the MDGs, the IMF works with partner agencies, especially the World Bank but also with other multilateral and bilateral providers of aid and financing.

The IMF's engagement in low-income countries puts it in a position to facilitate and possibly to catalyze other financing. In many cases, the approval or successful review of an IMF arrangement is itself a signal to other international institutions and donors that policies are sufficiently sound that it is prudent to provide their financing. The IMF recently took steps to address concerns that these signals were not as clear as they should be. Notably, it clarified the use of assessment letters to convey the institution's views for both on- and off-track programs. The IMF also plays a more direct role in facilitating other official financing through its participation in donor meetings.

It is increasingly recognized that macroeconomic stability and growth depend heavily on structural and institutional factors.[12]

Providing advice on many of these issues is primarily the responsibility of the World Bank and other development agencies. Coordination with the World Bank is therefore critical. Due in part to concerns that weaknesses in coordination had contributed to an expansion of IMF policy conditionality, new guidelines for Bank-Fund coordination in program design and conditionality were approved in May 2002.[13] The most recent review of Bank-Fund collaboration in relation to these guidelines indicates that collaboration appears to be improving, but that there is room for further improvement. At the same time, collaboration has some natural limits, due to the different mandates and time frames of the two institutions and their different organizational structures. The review highlights efforts that have been made to strengthen collaboration in particular areas, such as in the work on low-income countries and in public expenditure management issues.[14]

QUALITY AND RESULTS

The IMF has long had internal systems for ensuring the quality of its advice and programs, in the form of management controls and oversight by the Executive Board. Also, periodic reviews by staff have taken stock of emerging results and lessons learned, feeding this information back into the design of new programs and instructions to staff. Notably, the review of conditionality that will be undertaken in 2004 will examine the objectives and outcomes of Fund-supported programs and the design of the policy framework, in addition to reviewing the application of the 2002 conditionality guidelines. These reviews have been supplemented by independent external reviews on key topics, such as the external evaluation of the Enhanced Structural Adjustment Facility (ESAF) in 1998.[15]

The creation in 2002 of the Independent Evaluation Office (IEO)—which reports directly to the IMF's Executive Board, not through management—complements these efforts.[16] To date, three reports have been prepared, discussed by the Board, and then published. The first report examined the prolonged use of Fund resources, documenting the number of member countries with long periods of program engagement and examining case studies.[17] The report raised concerns that long-term engagement could undermine the revolving nature of the IMF's financial resources for balance of payments adjustment; that in some cases, prolonged engagement reflects persistent weaknesses in program design and implementation; that the use of an IMF financial arrangement as a signal to donors may distort decisions on IMF financing; and that the presence of the IMF may inhibit the development of domestic decisionmaking processes. In discussing this report, the Executive Board noted that in many instances—particularly in low-income countries—prolonged program engagement may play a constructive role in tackling deep structural problems whose solution requires protracted effort. The Board initiated procedures for *ex post* assessments of members with longer-term program engagement and for semiannual factual reports on the incidence of such engagements. The report also gave added impetus to work assessing program design and strengthening surveillance in program countries.

The IEO's second report examined the role of the IMF in three recent capital account crises: Indonesia in 1997–98, Korea in 1997–98, and Brazil in 1998–99.[18] It noted that IMF surveillance was more successful in identifying macroeconomic vulnerabilities than in recognizing and analyzing the risks arising from financial sector and corporate balance-sheet weaknesses. Insufficient candor and transparency also limited the effectiveness of surveillance on policies. With regard to the design and implementation of IMF-supported programs in response to these crises, the report noted that macroeconomic outcomes turned out to be very different from program projections and that in a number of respects the policies incorporated in the programs could, with the benefit of hindsight, have been improved. The report noted that, in response to these crises, reforms have been undertaken to strengthen the IMF's capacity to anticipate and help avert crises as well as to better manage the crises that do occur.

The third IEO report examined the experience with fiscal adjustment in IMF-supported programs.[19] This report found that the Fund does not follow a one-size-fits-all approach in its programs, as claimed by some critics. But it found that Fund staff could improve the presentation in staff reports of the rationale for their fiscal policy advice. The report also made recommendations for anchoring fiscal adjustment and reforms in a medium-term framework, both in the context of IMF-supported programs and surveillance. Steps are now under way to implement a number of these recommendations.

During 2004 the IEO will undertake assessments of the PRSP process and the PRGF (jointly with the World Bank's Operations Evaluation Department), the IMF's technical assistance activities, and the IMF's role in Argentina.

World Bank

The World Bank contributes to the achievement of the MDGs and related development outcomes in a number of ways. Its most tangible contribution is the support it provides to development programs in low- and middle-income countries. Closely related is the support the Bank provides for global and regional programs, where considerable expansion has taken place in recent years. The Bank's country and global program work is carried out with developing- and developed-country partners—as well as with partners in other international institutions—and is increasingly focused on results.

Against this background, this section looks at the evidence on what the Bank is doing in its country and global programs, how it behaves as a partner, and by what yardsticks it measures its contribution to development results. The analysis draws on the extensive assessment and evaluation material available on World Bank activities, both self-assessments carried out by central units within the Bank and independent evaluations carried out by the Bank's Operations Evaluation Department (OED). These documents are prepared periodically, providing a series of snapshots on the Bank's contribution and institutional performance in critical areas. For the most part, they show an institution whose performance has been improving in recent years, but with a number of specific areas still needing further work.

This picture is broadly consistent with recent survey evidence. In the global poll of world opinion leaders in late 2002 to early 2003 that the Bank commissioned,[20] most respondents reported a generally positive view of the Bank, with many saying that the Bank has been doing a better job in the past few years in a number of areas, especially poverty reduction. But a number of criticisms also were expressed, especially with respect to how respondents saw the Bank's effectiveness in fighting corruption, the social impact of the policy reforms it supports, and the arrogance and bureaucracy with which it is perceived to operate. Similarly, in the survey of country authorities carried out for the recent review of Bank-Fund collaboration, reform programs supported by the Bank were reported to be largely or fully owned by the country in 88 percent of cases, and a similar majority pointed to Bank participation widening ownership of the authorities' development strategy. [21] But 11 percent of the respondents reported only partial ownership.

COUNTRY PROGRAMS

The World Bank's approach to country programs recognizes that one size does not fit all, and that the Bank's support must be tailored to country conditions and grounded in national strategies setting out countries' development vision, objectives, and priorities.[22] As the Bank's central operational document for each country program, the Country Assistance Strategy (CAS) is a key place to start in assessing the Bank's contribution. The CAS summarizes the diagnosis of country conditions, the lessons learned from previous external support, and the forward program. It is prepared by the country team in cooperation with the authorities and partners, approved by senior management, and discussed by the Executive Board. In presenting the Bank's prospective program, the CAS is meant to explain what is proposed as well as why, in terms of the particular value added and additionality that the Bank can bring to the table. For most low-income countries, the PRSP is the vehicle setting out the national strategy that the Bank helps countries to formulate and that serves as the foundation for the CAS. For middle-income countries, there is not an agreed format like the PRSP for setting out the national strategy, and the Bank relies on a wide variety of country-specific vehicles as a basis for the CAS.

Alignment with Country Priorities. In practice, how well do Bank CASs align with country priorities? According to a series of retrospectives prepared by Bank management and OED reviews, most CASs do provide fairly full coverage of the country's development program, describing the government's development objectives and the key elements of the development strategy—highlighting strengths and weaknesses.[23] The most recent CAS retrospective judged the treatment of the national development program and priorities to be substantial in 86 percent of the 39 CASs and CAS Progress Reports in its review cohort. This represents a significant increase from the levels reported in the previous retrospectives (60 percent in the first and 80 percent in the second). However, it must be noted that the CASs in the review cohort were discussed by the Board before the end of 2000. As the period since then has seen enhanced focus on country ownership and national strategies, through the PRSP in the case of low-income countries and country-specific processes in the case of middle-income countries, these trends are likely to have intensified. Informal reviews of more recent CASs do point to a further step-up in country focus, and the expectation is that this finding will be validated in the next CAS retrospective.

In part, this expectation is based on parallel developments with respect to PRSPs, which had been prepared for 37 countries as of the end of March 2004. Only two CASs in the retrospective review cohort were based on full PRSPs (Burkina Faso and Uganda), and the treatment of the national strategy was strong in both. Also, the CASs for Albania, Guyana, Mauritania, Vietnam, and Yemen, which were prepared on the basis of full PRSPs (albeit after the closure of the cohort for the last retrospective), were similarly strong, with analysis clearly linked to the PRSP, providing a firm basis for consideration of the CAS diagnostic and programming options. CASs also will benefit from ongoing improvements in the PRSPs themselves. A recent Bank-Fund staff review of PRSPs reports evidence of progress as more recent PRSPs build on the experience of earlier ones, and countries more advanced in the process gain implementation experience.[24] But the review also identified a number of challenges that affect the PRSP's usefulness in underpinning the CAS. These include the importance of (a) bringing in the MDGs and articulating expected outcomes more explicitly; (b) striking the right balance between ambition and realism in setting PRSP targets; (c) identifying reliable indicators of progress and outcomes; and (d) ensuring appropriate prioritization across PRSP targets. Going forward, Bank management has suggested—and clients appear receptive to the proposal—that it is important for countries to strengthen the results focus of PRSPs and highlight the links with the longer-term MDG targets and the associated policy and institutional reforms and domestic and foreign financing requirements.

These findings are broadly in line with OED's conclusions, which are drawn from its Country Assistance Evaluations (CAEs) and other evaluations, such as the multidonor review of the Comprehensive Development Framework (CDF)[25] and the ongoing PRSP assessment that OED is conducting in partnership with the IMF's IEO. OED has consistently stressed the importance of more realistic targets in PRSPs—cautioning that many countries and regions will not achieve the MDGs by 2015—as well as greater attention to monitoring and evaluation, which it noted is particularly important given the different time frames for PRSPs (typically 3 years) and the MDGs (typically 10–15 years).[26] Relatedly, OED has urged the Bank to identify the objectives and targets of its CASs with greater specificity and to implement internal changes to foster the design and implementation of the multisectoral strategies and operations that will be essential for achieving the MDGs. Also highly relevant for the PRSP-CAS nexus, OED finds evidence of the PRSP process contributing to the development of country ownership, especially when a highly inclusive participatory process is conducted through the country's normal political processes and institutions; OED further points to the need to lessen the tension between the PRSP's role as a process for building domestic consensus and ownership and the role that it plays with regard to debt relief and access to aid resources.[27]

The CAS model applies equally to the middle-income countries (MICs), for which Bank management has just completed a major review of its program and strategy.[28] A key finding of this review is that despite many examples of successful Bank engagement in individual MICs—for example, Brazil, China, Mexico, and Turkey—trends in Bank lending are not in line with the objective of scaling up support to MICs, given the vast numbers of poor people living there. In large part, the disconnect reflects a secular decline in Bank infrastructure lending to MICs, as well as reduced lending to countries that have gained access to financial markets. However, some other multilateral development banks have maintained or even increased their lending over the same time period, suggesting that internal Bank factors related to the cost of doing business may be partly to blame. Going forward, the Bank is adopting a back-to-basics approach, cutting red tape by relying more on MICs' stronger policy development and systems for fiduciary and environmental safeguards, proactively engaging in value-adding operations in infrastructure and service delivery, and promoting the use of IBRD risk-management instruments—all grounded in high-quality economic and sector work (ESW). The approach is designed to reinvigorate the Bank's engagement with this critical set of clients and help them promote sustainable, equitable, job-creating growth; raise living standards; and reduce poverty.

Relevance and Strategic Selectivity. Strategic selectivity involves systematically examining the tradeoffs among possible Bank Group activities, assessing their relative impact, and establishing priorities while taking resource constraints into account. It requires looking at the potential magnitude of impact, the likelihood of successful country action—including, importantly, through policy reforms—and the possible availability of alternative sources of support as a way to assess the expected value-added of the Bank's contribution. Getting this part of the CAS right is essential for maximizing the Bank's impact. It goes to the heart of ensuring that the Bank is doing the right things—in addition to doing them right. Ensuring the relevance of Bank support is a key objective of the Bank's agenda on managing for results and is the driving force in the development of the results-based CAS, currently being piloted (box 13.2).

The last CAS retrospective found an improvement in selectivity, with more than 70 percent of CASs rated satisfactory or better, compared with only 50 percent in the previous retrospective. However, when the retrospective raised the bar on selectivity to include discussion of tradeoffs and the rationale for instrument choice, fewer than 60 percent of the cohort CASs were rated satisfactory or better. Clearly, as Bank management has stressed, there is ample scope for improvement in this important area, especially along three dimensions: (a) the specific channels through which the proposed Bank

BOX 13.2 Results-based CAS

The results-based Country Assistance Strategy is designed to improve the strategic relevance and selectivity of Bank country programs and provide greater support for strengthening country capacity to manage for results, thereby increasing the Bank's contribution to country outcomes. The concept of a results-based CAS was first elaborated in 2002 as a central element of the Bank's action plan on managing for results.

The results-based methodology involves a change in mindset and approach to formulating the CAS—from starting with programming inputs and then analyzing their likely impacts, to starting with desired outcomes and then identifying what inputs and actions (by the Bank and others) are needed to achieve them. Supporting and complementing this change in mindset, the results-based CAS introduces a framework for articulating expected outcomes and identifying indicators for tracking implementation progress and evaluating outcomes at program completion. Strengthened monitoring and evaluation at the CAS level is critical to success, including introduction of a CAS Completion Report, or self-assessment, of progress under the previous CAS and review of this report by OED.

Interim guidelines on results-based CASs have been issued,[a] and a pilot phase of preparing results-based CASs is under way. Five results-based CASs were presented to the Board in 2003—Brazil, Cameroon, Mozambique, Sri Lanka, and Ukraine. More pilots are being completed in fiscal 2004, and other country teams are beginning to apply the results-based methodology to CAS design. Further work includes implementing regional plans to support country teams in preparing results-based CASs, evaluating the pilot phase for results-based CASs in late fiscal 2004, issuing a revised operational policy and a good-practice note for results-based CASs, and mainstreaming the results-based CAS in fiscal 2005.

a. See (http://opcs/CAS/cs-g.html).
Source: World Bank 2004d.

program was expected to work—in other words "the results chain"; (b) the analysis of the Bank's comparative advantage vis-à-vis its partners to explain the CAS's strategic selectivity; and (c) the specific implications of the lessons learned from past country and Bank implementation experience for the design of the strategy.

Strategic relevance and selectivity are also central themes of OED's CAEs and other country program evaluations, which have been carried out in more than 60 countries since the first such evaluations, for the Argentina and Ghana programs, in fiscal 1995.[29] As OED notes: "While each project proposed in the CAS may individually be consistent with CAS objectives, it is not always clear that the summation of Bank lending in the CAS is the best way to achieve CAS objectives."[30] In several country evaluations, OED has rated overall country program outcomes as unsatisfactory even though the large majority of the individual project outcomes earned a satisfactory rating. In other words, the Bank did things right at the project level but did not necessarily do the right things to achieve stated CAS objectives.

GLOBAL PROGRAMS

A critical part of the World Bank effort to support country development is the analytic and advocacy work it does in the global arena, especially with respect to the policies and actions of developed countries on trade, aid, and debt relief, given their importance in achieving the MDGs, as discussed in earlier chapters. In addition, as noted there, the Bank is monitoring international scaling-up efforts in four priority areas for the service delivery MDGs—Education for All, HIV/AIDS, health, and water and sanitation. It is also directly providing support in these and other areas through its country and global programs. One example is its support for the Global Fund to Fight AIDS, Tuberculosis, and Malaria, for which the Bank is trustee.

Bank support for global programs began three decades ago, with the establishment of the Consultative Group on International Agricultural Research (CGIAR), for which the Bank is a convener and donor to the system, as well as a lender to developing countries for complementary activities.[31] New global programs were gradually added over time, with a major step-up in global partnerships and associated program support activities commencing in the late 1990s, reflecting the rapid pace of globalization, the sharply increased attention to global policy issues in the development community, and the Bank's increased partnership orientation. In September 2000 the Development Committee endorsed the Bank's priorities in supporting global public goods, focusing on five areas—public health, protection of global commons, financial stability, trade, and knowledge.[32]

Global programs are now reflected in Bank corporate strategy papers and operational activities, with about 50 programs (managed by either the Bank or external recipients) receiving grants from the Development Grant Facility. In these programs, the Bank is working in capacity-building and support programs with countries, to help them meet their requirements under international agreements, and in partnership programs focused on the delivery of global and regional public goods, including by providing seed money for new such programs.[33]

The assessment framework for global programs—both within the Bank and in other agencies—is at a much earlier stage of development than it is for country programs, reflecting the more recent vintage of most global programs. Within the Bank, the self-assessment framework is still being developed—as is the ex ante appraisal framework—while on independent evaluation, OED has recently completed its Phase I review of the Bank's global programs and is in the final stages of the analysis of Phase II. As a general matter, OED concluded that the Bank has played a useful role in these programs by providing a platform for learning, advocacy, and collaborative action to address key global challenges. With notable exceptions, including large and high-profile programs such as the Global Environment Facility (GEF) and CGIAR, for the most part OED found the programs to be undermanaged, especially relative to country programs, with too little attention to formal appraisal and evaluation criteria, too little policy content, and unclear accountabilities.[34]

Building on the work of a high-level internal review team, Bank management has generally endorsed OED's recommendations and is paying increased attention to strategic focus, country alignment (with any implementation at the country level included in the CAS program), developing country voice, business planning and resource management, and risk management and quality assurance in the Bank's global programs.[35] Its enhanced efforts in these areas aim to build on a series of measures adopted in recent years to improve the governance and oversight of the Bank's global programs and partnerships through new processes for screening proposed programs and ensuring their strategic focus, better systems for tracking implementation, and enhanced attention to independent and self-evaluation on program completion.

PARTNERSHIP

The World Bank's policy is to operate jointly with partners when addressing major development issues. This policy applies equally to Bank country and global program activities, broadly as follows. First, the Bank works closely with the IMF, the MDBs, the United Nations and U.N. agencies, OECD-DAC, the European Union and bilateral donors, WTO, and other partners in its country and global work. Second, as a global development institution with broad coverage across countries and issues, the Bank often plays a strategic role in providing what smaller and more specialized agencies cannot because of their size or narrower mandate—a role that underpins the way strategic selectivity manifests itself in Bank CASs, as discussed earlier, and that shapes the particular Bank contribution to global and regional partnerships and programs. Third, in carrying out its partnership activities, the Bank wears different hats as befits the occasion—leader, follower, adviser, helper, and so on. It need not and does not play the lead role in every instance. This point warrants emphasis both internally in guiding staff behavior and externally, especially in light of the findings of the Bank's global poll with respect to perceptions of institutional and staff arrogance.[36]

Underpinning the Bank's partnership policy is its extensive work on harmonization—designed to better align its processes and procedures with those of clients and with those of other agencies. In turn, such alignment reduces the transaction costs of development assistance. To this end, the Bank is intensifying its collaboration with interested clients and partners to extend and deepen the increasing number of country-level harmonization activities. Many of these were begun before the Rome Harmonization Forum in February 2003 and several have been initiated over the past year.[37] The Bank is currently pursuing the harmonization agenda in a number of countries, playing either leadership or supportive roles as the occasion and circumstances warrant. These countries include the seven associated with the Rome Declaration, as well as a growing number of others in which harmonization programs and activities have just started or are being broadened or deepened.[38] This work, of course, relates closely to the Bank's ongoing support for country-led partnerships for the implementation of national development strategies, whether in the context of PRSPs for low-income countries or of country-specific vehicles in the case of middle-income countries. And, for all countries, Bank management is using internal review processes (including the Operations Committee) for CASs and lending operations, to proactively identify opportunities for further country-level harmonization. The World Bank is also playing leadership and supportive roles in the context of the DAC Working Party on Aid Effectiveness, which was established after the Rome forum to support and facilitate harmonization efforts.[39]

Supporting and complementing these country-level efforts, the Bank has taken several important steps in recent years to modernize the fiduciary framework governing its lending operations. These steps have helped to set the stage for Bank participation in harmonization with country and partner systems. New financial management guidelines allow borrowers to submit project reports based on their own financial reporting systems.[40] New fiduciary processes permit the Bank to participate in pooled financing arrangements in sectorwide approaches (commonly known as SWAps) characterized by common arrangements for financial reporting, auditing, procurement, and disbursement. The Bank's audit policies have been aligned with international auditing standards and good practice, allowing for adaptations of audit scope to assessed project risk.[41] A new loan administration platform is being designed to facilitate harmonization of disbursement procedures with country procedures and those of other lenders. Finally, major investments have been made in the Bank's financial management diagnostic work, especially on the country financial accountability assessment, to upgrade quality, work jointly with MDB and other partners, and inform the country policy dialogue on financial management systems. These investments complement joint work with the IMF, the European Commission, and bilateral donors on the Public Expenditure and Financial Accountability (PEFA) initiative and the OECD-DAC harmonization process to help clients strengthen their public financial management systems.

The Bank has taken complementary steps on procurement procedures to improve the scope for harmonization with country systems and with MDB (and other) partners and to upgrade their capacity building and learning content. To these ends, the Bank has introduced higher prior-review thresholds when client capacity warrants and clarified when local procurement laws and practices—including for e-procurement—can be used in Bank-financed (and cofinanced) projects. As with financial management, the Bank has also taken steps to transform the country procurement assessment into a diagnostic tool for the policy dialogue, with country procurement assessments now carried out jointly with clients and MDB and other partners. The Bank is also working with the OECD-DAC on an initiative for helping countries strengthen their procurement systems, which also will lead to stronger in-country systems around which donors can harmonize their support. Finally, based on the master documents produced and agreed by the MDB Procurement Harmonization Group, the Bank has issued new documents on the procurement of civil works and goods. In November 2003, the Board approved adjustments to the Bank's Procurement Guidelines that reflected these and other changes.

QUALITY AND RESULTS

The bottom-line measures of the Bank's contribution are the quality and results of its operational products and services. This section looks at Bank systems for measuring and monitoring quality and results and then summarizes what those systems suggest about the Bank's contribution to development outcomes and its institutional performance.

Monitoring Systems. Historically, the Bank measured its operational performance primarily by lending commitments—both dollars lent and projects approved. Building on the findings of and the follow-up to the Wapenhans Task Force Report,[42] the quality dimension was added in 1996 as a second primary indicator of operational performance. Adding the quality of lending and analytic and advisory services as an indicator served to focus Bank management attention on that dimension, and, after the investment of much time, resources, and commitment— including the creation of the Quality Assurance Group (QAG), with a major program and the full support of top management—the Bank's performance on quality improved substantially. Adding results as a third indicator was a logical next step, taken in 2002 to further improve the Bank's effectiveness by subjecting this important measure to more systematic management scrutiny. In the context of this decision, the Bank adopted an ambitious plan to better measure, monitor, and manage for results; the Development Committee endorsed this plan in September 2002.[43]

Since then, there has been significant progress in designing and piloting the necessary changes in Bank systems to implement the results agenda. Central to the agenda are effective monitoring and evaluation systems. This is true not only for investment lending, for which there is a long tradition of monitoring and evaluation, although implementation performance needs to be improved, but also for the CAS, adjustment lending, and non-lending services, for which monitoring and evaluation is a more recent development. In all these areas, work is under way to see how best to apply, adapt, and improve existing approaches, building on the lessons learned from recent monitoring and evaluation pilots and OED reviews. As noted earlier (see box 13.2), country teams are piloting results-based CASs that identify country outcomes (from the PRSP or other national strategy) to which the Bank will contribute, along with intermediate indicators linked to the particular products and services that the Bank will provide. With respect to the Bank's lending and non-lending products and services, operational policies and processes are being reviewed with the aim of expediting implementation and the achievement of results, while documentation requirements are being reviewed with the aim of increased transparency in the reporting of results objectives and achievements.

Consistent with the above, OED's most recent assessment of Bank systems concluded that the framework for self-evaluation by Bank management, and independent evaluation by OED, is strongest at the project level.[44] At the country level, OED found that the framework for independent evaluation, comprising OED CAEs, was well established, and it welcomed the recent introduction of CAS Completion Reports, which it saw as responding to its long-standing recommendation and closing an important gap in self-evaluation at the country level. But OED also stressed the importance of the remaining weaknesses in independent evaluation of sector strategies and global programs and of gaps in self-evaluation of sector strategies, nonlending operations, trust funds, and knowledge initiatives, while also acknowledging that new initiatives are under way on self-evaluation of global programs. On the latter, the first annual Sector Strategy Implementation Update will provide a basis for improved monitoring and self-assessment of sector strategy implementation, including through the development of strengthened monitoring indicators.

Meanwhile, in response to a request from the IDA Deputies, a two-tiered Results Measurement System has been developed to measure progress on selected country outcomes across IDA countries and to measure IDA's performance at the institutional level in contributing to development outcomes (box 13.3).[45] The results-based CAS framework is expected to provide the necessary inputs in the medium term, but in the meantime, Bank management expects to use IDA portfolio indicators derived from OED ratings for project outcomes and QAG quality assessments, which are leading indicators of success in achieving CAS outcomes. Although OED does not routinely conduct impact evaluations, some increase in such activities may be warranted, in view of their relevance to the results agenda, and to the overall framework for assessing the Bank's contribution. For example, a recent impact evaluation of the Bank's support to education in Ghana found—on the basis of a careful analysis of the results chain and examination of data collected specifically for the study—a very substantial positive impact on education outcomes.[46]

Effectiveness and Results. Looking beyond the systems to the actual outcomes of the Bank's assistance, what does the evidence show? Here the real issue is how to demonstrate Bank impact. OED considers that the Bank's country strategies have been on the whole fairly successful, based on what it sees as relatively high CAE outcome ratings—with 65 percent of all years assessed and 75 percent of the post-1998 years rated moderately satisfactory or better. Once the results-based CAS has been mainstreamed, the self-assessment framework for such judgments also would be available. CASs would be capable of being evaluated to start with, providing a basis for judging and comparing scores in achieving CAS outcomes. But in view of the considerable lead time required to have a large enough cohort for meaningful assessment, the leading indicators of CAS impact will need to be relied on until fiscal 2006 or fiscal 2007.

Overall, these indicators—OED and QAG scores—point to consistently improving portfolio quality from fiscal 1997 up to fiscal 2002, as the major steps that management was taking were being reflected in a step-up in quality. OED evaluations of projects exiting the portfolio each year confirm the positive trend. Fiscal 2002 marks the third consecutive year of project performance exceeding the Bank's Strategic Compact target of 75 percent satisfactory or better outcomes.[47] By number of projects, the score was 79 percent; weighted by value, it was 85 percent. More dramatic is the continued upward climb in sustainability ratings to similarly high levels from much lower starting points. However, for fiscal 2003 exits, early OED ratings point to a decline in outcome scores. Pending the completion of OED's analysis of the full cohort of projects completed in fiscal 2003, QAG has launched a special analysis of possible issues that may need to be addressed by management in ensuring the continued improvement in portfolio management and quality.

Both QAG and OED have emphasized the role of economic and sector work in the Bank's effectiveness. QAG findings point to the importance of ESW, and its increasing quality, as leading indicators of positive outcomes in Bank operations and country programs. Assessments by QAG confirm the continuing improvement in the quality of the Bank's country analytic work, reflecting the increased attention to it by senior Bank management in recent years. OED's findings are that in countries where recent outcomes of Bank assistance were evaluated as satisfactory, high quality, relevant, and timely, ESW generally made a substantial contribution. Where outcomes were not satisfactory, deficiencies of ESW in one or more of these dimensions were a contributing factor. CAEs report favorable outcomes when high-quality ESW was timed to precede Bank operations and country programs, and unfavorable outcomes when ESW was not timed in this way. Even when ESW was timely and of high quality, the relevance of Bank strategies was reduced when its findings were not used or used only selectively in programs and lending operations. ESW was found to be particularly important for first-time or renewed borrowers and for stop-go reformers.

Regional Development Banks

This section looks at the role and contribution of the four major regional development banks—African Development Bank, Asian Development Bank, European Bank for Reconstruction and Development, and Inter-American Development Bank—also using the organizational structure of box 13.1.[48]

COUNTRY PROGRAMS

Notwithstanding differences in mandates and instruments, each of the regional banks is focused on country issues. All have country strategy papers and are increasingly involved in the PRSP process, in line with the agreed MDB/IMF Protocol on Collaboration on the PRSP. The regional banks are increasingly focused on the MDGs, with the EBRD focused on transition impact. Their strategies in turn drive their country lending and nonlending programs. Their independent evaluation departments assess their strategies on program completion, thus affording opportunities to test and validate results and take stock of the lessons learned.

Work is under way in each of the four regional banks to adapt and improve existing approaches to country strategies, in line with the results agenda. The AfDB has aligned its country strategy papers more closely with PRSPs, deepening the analysis, based on poverty diagnostics, sectoral priorities, and outcome indicators articulated in country-owned PRSPs, and spelling out in the country strategy paper how the proposed AfDB lending and nonlending activities will contribute to poverty reduction. In the AsDB, there also has been progress in linking country strategy papers to PRSPs, and work is under way to design a results-based country strategy paper. In the EBRD, individual country strategies are results based as they are evaluated against the performance of the country portfolio of projects and against the sector reform and transition challenges tracked by the *Transition Report* and sector strategies. The IDB introduced new guidelines for its country strategies last year, requiring, *inter alia*: an explicit focus on results, with a "strategy matrix" articulating the link between the country's own development objectives and strategy and the development objectives and strategies of all donors, including the IDB; identification of the proposed IDB-assisted interventions together with performance indicators and targets of expected results; and reflection of the findings of the country program evaluations prepared by the IDB's independent evaluation office.

GLOBAL PROGRAMS

The regional banks are involved in global and regional programs covering financial stability, trade, environment, post-conflict assistance, and knowledge, with all but EBRD also involved in the control of infectious diseases.[49] In many cases the banks are focused on regional public goods (RPGs), or on regional

BOX 13.3 Proposed IDA14 results-measurement system

The proposed IDA14 results-measurement system is designed to reflect the priorities and processes of national poverty reduction strategies, be linked to the MDG framework, show aggregated results across IDA countries, and assess IDA's contribution to development results. It measures results on two levels:

Aggregate country outcomes. The first tier includes 17 possible indicators to measure the progress of IDA-eligible countries on core development outcomes (see table). The majority of these indicators were chosen to be consistent with country priorities articulated in national poverty reduction strategies, aligned with MDG indicators, and relevant to IDA's mandate and activities in borrowing countries. Indeed, most of the indicators are considered in PRSPs, either as specific targets or as subjects for discussion in the text. Ten are MDG indicators. The others are complementary, relating to growth for poverty reduction, and reflecting IDA's support for the economic growth, private sector development, and public sector management that are necessary to reduce poverty.

IDA's contribution to country outcomes. The second tier involves introducing a stronger focus on results and a self-assessment system in World Bank Country Assistance Strategies in IDA-eligible countries, and assessing the quality and outcomes of projects in the IDA portfolio, drawing on data from the Operations Evaluation Department and the Quality Assurance Group. The following indicators have been put forward to monitor progress in this tier: the number of countries that use a results-based CAS; CAS final outcome ratings as validated by OED through the CAS Completion Report review; project outcome ratings as validated by OED through the Implementation Completion Report review; and quality-at-entry indicators for IDA projects as assessed by QAG.

In April 2003 IDA Deputies reviewed this architecture and found it to be a sound basis for moving forward. At their first meeting of the IDA14 replenishment in February 2004, Deputies reemphasized the importance of measuring development effectiveness and results at the country level and identified this area as a key theme for further discussion and work during the replenishment. Over the coming months, IDA Deputies will face important decisions about the monitoring of aggregate country outcomes within the results-measurement system. They will need to reach consensus on a set of country outcome indicators, each with different merits. The 17 indicators proposed for consideration are those that—at this time—best meet the three criteria of relevance to key development outcomes, sensitivity to policy actions, and measurability in a sufficient number of IDA countries. However, to varying degrees, the ability to monitor these indicators on a regular basis—and the quality of the resulting information—are dependent on expanded coverage, increased periodicity, and standardization of questions within household surveys and other data-gathering mechanisms. The existence of reliable and relevant indicators to measure development progress will also depend on the inclusion of the issue of statistics and evidence-based policymaking in the policy dialogue with countries. The implications for the international community are twofold. First, a greater financial and technical commitment will be needed to strengthen statistical capacity and monitoring and evaluation systems in low-income countries and to reinforce international reporting systems. Second, expectations must remain realistic for improvements across a

aspects of global public goods, looking to the World Bank on the global aspects. They also are involved in helping their regional clients build country capacity to meet requirements under global agreements. For the AfDB, critical issues are post-conflict assistance and health, especially in the face of the HIV/AIDS epidemic. For the AsDB, key issues are the environment, health, and knowledge, with a particular focus on those issues where there are spillover effects within the region, or within the AsDB's subregional coverage. For the EBRD, nuclear safety is an area of special focus, where the Bank has the international lead in supporting transition countries in the decommissioning of capacity, along with the resolution of other environmental liabilities of the earlier era. Another is financial stability,

Outcome indicators under consideration for IDA14 results-measurement system

Indicator	PRSPs that include indicator %	PRSPs covering subject %	Availability in WDI database %	Typical frequency of reporting	Agency responsible for data compilation
1. Proportion of population below $1/day poverty line	13	100	72	Every 3–5 years	World Bank
2. Prevalence of underweight children under five years of age	44	63	97	3 years	UNICEF, WHO
3. Under-five mortality	72	97	100	3 years	UNICEF, WHO
4. Proportion of year-old children immunized against measles	9	72	100	Annual	UNICEF, WHO
5. HIV prevalence rate of pregnant women 15–24	3	69	91	Only 1999	UNAIDS, UNICEF
6. Proportion of births attended by skilled health personnel	59	72	84	3–5 years	UNICEF, WHO
7. Ratio of girls to boys in primary, secondary, and tertiary education	69	78	94	Annual	UNESCO
8. Primary school completion rate	31	100	100	Annual	UNESCO
9. Proportion of population with sustainable access to an improved water source	94	94	100	3 years	UNICEF, WHO
10. Fixed lines and mobile telephones per 1,000 inhabitants	25	34	97	Annual	ITU, World Bank
11. Formal cost of business registration	3	13	72	Annual	World Bank
12. Time for business registration	6	13	75	Annual	World Bank
13. Public expenditure management	0	100	—	TBD	World Bank
14. Agricultural value added	22	66	94	Annual	UNSD, World Bank
15. GDP per capita	41	100	94	Annual	UNSD, World Bank
16. Access of rural population to an all-season road	16	44	—	TBD	World Bank
17. Household electrification rate	34	59	—	3 years	World Bank

— Not available.
Note: TBD = to be determined.

range of indicators in countries with limited capacity. Thus, it is especially important to reach consensus on a small number of indicators that countries identify as highly relevant for managing their development processes.

Source: World Bank, Concessional Finance and Global Partnerships Vice Presidency.

especially the adoption of the standards and codes underpinning market economies. The IDB has five priority areas in the provision of regional and global public goods—financial sector assessments, regional integration, curbing of infectious diseases, promotion of environmental services, and support for research in agriculture and regional policy dialogue. It has prepared a new policy framework for its support for RPGs, including a financing facility geared to providing grant financing for what it calls "early stage RPGs," where dialogue among countries is needed; "later stage RPGs," where larger institutional resources to manage the emerging program are needed; and the initial stages of "club RPGs," which will likely be financially self-sustaining once they are up and running.[50]

PARTNERSHIP

For the regional banks, the partnership topic has two interrelated aspects. One, at the institutional level, is their role and participation in the harmonization effort; the other, at the country level, is their performance as partners. Reflecting their growing interest in both, the regional development banks are active participants in the DAC Working Party on Aid Effectiveness.

Working in partnership with the World Bank and others, the regional development banks are continuing their work on the unfinished institutional harmonization agenda and thematic areas of common concern. Central to the agenda is the focus on the harmonization of results reporting emerging from the Marrakech Roundtable. As noted there, developing countries have made significant progress on country ownership, strategic vision, and donor alignment through the poverty reduction strategy process, but many countries continue to struggle with the diversity of donor reporting requirements, especially with respect to project monitoring and evaluation—hence the urgency of action. Legal documentation and disbursement procedures are examples of issues that have recently become subjects of discussion and will be taken forward. Meanwhile, existing working groups have continued their work on institutional harmonization in tandem with their country-level work. The Financial Management Group, for example, has completed good-practice papers and continues to work with relevant professional bodies on an international accounting standard for development operations. In addition to its work on country-level capacity building, the Procurement Group has completed harmonized bidding documents for prequalification for civil works and civil works contracts and for selection of consultants. The Environmental Group has completed a common framework for environmental impact assessments, while focusing most of their efforts on country-level work. And the Evaluation Group has followed up on good-practice papers on public and private sector evaluations, through a benchmarking exercise, and put joint country evaluations on its agenda. The MDB Gender Group, operating in cooperation with U.N. and OECD-DAC gender groups, has recently co-sponsored a workshop on Gender and the MDGs.

For country-level activities, the partnership issue is typically less about partnerships between individual regional banks, because there is little overlap among them. Rather the issue is more often about partnerships with the World Bank, IMF, U.N. agencies, and bilateral agencies, with which the regional banks are linking up, together with governments interested in harmonization efforts at the country level. To a large extent, the issue here is one of country strategy and the selection of operational support vehicles taking into account what other partners are providing. But it may also involve harmonization in a specific lending context, especially where new sectorwide approaches are challenging previous methods of support for country development and co-financing arrangements. Concrete cases, such as the Bangladesh example (box 13.4), put the focus on where the really tough work on harmonization lies—reconciling differences in institutional guidelines for procurement and financial management within a particular country context in a real-time situation.

QUALITY AND RESULTS

The recent Marrakech Roundtable, sponsored by the MDBs in collaboration with the OECD-DAC, provided an important opportunity for the banks to take stock of where they are in their application of results-based approaches and the progress made since the first Roundtable in June 2002.[51]

Systems and Processes. The regional development banks have all been actively pursuing the results agenda in the context of their country assistance strategies, as discussed above, and in their business processes for assuring the quality and development effectiveness of their operations. To this end, all the banks are giving greater attention to the

BOX 13.4 Sectorwide approach to primary education development

The Bangladesh Second Primary Education Development Project is a concrete example of how the harmonization and alignment agenda can be implemented at the country level to improve aid effectiveness and support the MDGs. Investment in primary education is a key to reducing poverty, enhancing opportunity, and improving the quality of life. Bangladesh has made progress in primary education in the last two decades. Nonetheless, significant problems remain: in the quality divide between the rich and poor, and in access of the poor, especially of girls. Donors have responded to requests to assist—indeed so much so that 11 donors were funding 27 separate projects in primary education, all with their own separate donor-specific operating requirements. To try to achieve greater coordination, the government made a bold move. Supported by the local donor community, the government adopted and endorsed a Macro-Plan, and a sector strategy, which outlines the objectives for primary education over the next six years and sets out the policy framework and implementation plan for improving education quality, enhancing access to schooling, and ameliorating overall management and oversight of primary education. Rather than a series of projects, the government worked with donors, led by the Asian Development Bank, to develop the Second Primary Education Development Project as a coherent program (a sectorwide approach, or SWAp) in support of the strategy, which covers all public primary schools in the country.

While the program approach may stretch government capacity, the government and development partners have achieved a satisfactory congruence of goals and aspirations through the collaborative and participatory process, including agreement on results that can be monitored and quantified. The multidonor-supported program approach aims to reduce transaction costs for the government. Key aspects of the SWAp are to replace 27 different project structures with 1 overarching structure, with cofinanced funds from the AsDB, IDA, and six other partners disbursed through a pooled account, on which AsDB reports to other donors, and with 90 percent of procurement carried out by the government under a newly enacted law.

Source: World Bank, Operations Policy and Country Services Vice Presidency.

quality and impact of their operations through enhanced monitoring and evaluation and portfolio management. In previous years, the AfDB had taken a number of measures to improve project quality at entry, supervision, monitoring and evaluation, and portfolio management. These measures are now being extended and deepened in line with the results agenda, where the focus is on "higher level" interventions and evaluations at the country, sectoral, and regional levels. AsDB has significantly improved its portfolio management and monitoring of project implementation to make it more results focused. Project documentation throughout the project cycle has been refocused on development objectives, with lessons learned highlighted in project completion and audit reports. Special attention is also being paid to the quality and analytical content of AsDB's economic, technical, and sector work, as a basis for the policy dialogue with clients. Last year, the EBRD introduced a new Transition Impact Monitoring System, with periodic monitoring and reporting on project performance. The new system is designed to facilitate a portfolio approach to project monitoring. Progress reporting is done both on a project and on a portfolio basis to allow a comparison of the transition impact potential of the portfolio against other sources of project risks and returns, and other sector and country dimensions. The IDB has taken a number of important steps to upgrade project quality and management. Building on a pilot quality-at-entry assessment, improvements are being made to project design and evaluation, including the introduction of a structured self-evaluation system for use during project supervision, where reporting is being strengthened, and also on project completion, where the coverage by the independent evaluation unit is being expanded.

The regional banks also are using corporate reporting for informing shareholders and stakeholders about progress on the results and quality agenda, recognizing the critical role such reporting plays in sustaining management attention to the agenda and in turn institutional follow-through. The AfDB reports on results through three main channels. First, much operational reporting on quality, results, and evaluation takes place through the Board Committee on Development Effectiveness. Second, AfDB is piloting the Results Measurement Framework, which it provides to the African Development Fund Deputies, as part of the latter's oversight function. Finally, AfDB is beginning to implement a Corporate Balanced Scorecard in reporting to its Executive Board on strategic planning and budgeting.

The AsDB is reporting through the dialogue on results with the recently created Board Committee on Development Effectiveness and with the Asian Development Fund Deputies, including in the context of the design and implementation of the Asian Development Fund Results Measurement System. In addition to project-based results management, the EBRD uses results-based management for its own institutional performance and budgeting, with a focus on transition impact and financial indicators in its institutional scorecard, which it shares with its Executive Board. Both the transition impact and financial performance objectives are reviewed annually by the Board in the context of EBRD's Medium-Term Strategy Update and Strategic Portfolio Review; these reviews inform the EBRD's annual dialogue with its Board on the budgeting process. The IDB is also strengthening its corporate reporting, including to its Board Committee on Policy and Evaluation. At the 2004 Annual Meetings in Lima, Peru, the Committee of the Board of Governors discussed progress on IDB's development effectiveness reform efforts to date, and a Medium-Term Action Plan for enhancing IDB's development effectiveness and results orientation is currently under preparation.

Effectiveness and Results. The independent evaluation departments of the four regional banks fill broadly similar roles within their organizations, contributing to institutional learning and accountability. To some extent they also provide a basis for comparing performance across the institutions—although there are limits to comparability, as the measures used in the different banks are not exactly the same. Going forward, harmonization of evaluation criteria, both for individual operations and for aggregate institutional scores, would be worthwhile, building on the earlier effort by the Evaluation Cooperation Group to assess the differences across the MDBs and to produce a good-practice standard.[52]

In the meantime, the following profiles are illustrative of the situation across the regional development banks, based on publicly available material. The AfDB reports in its annual report that in general the latest annual evaluation review found that the overall performance rating for outcomes was satisfactory or better for more than two-thirds of projects; the percentage scores for institutional development and sustainability were appreciably lower.[53] According to AsDB's annual evaluation reports, 40 percent of completed projects and 100 percent of programs are selected for evaluation each year. In 2001, of the 17 projects and 3 programs evaluated, none were found to be unsuccessful, with 14 percent highly successful, 41 percent successful, and 45 percent partly successful. In 2002, of the 27 projects and 6 programs, none were unsuccessful, while 12 percent were highly successful and 18 percent only partly successful.

In the EBRD, which provides extensive and transparent information on its evaluation activities and findings, the focus is on transition impact, covering privatization, competition, and corporate governance, and on overall performance, which includes financial and environmental performance in addition to transition impact.[54] On overall performance, 52 percent of operations evaluated during 1996–2002 were given successful or highly successful ratings, while 74 percent were rated successful or highly successful on transition impact (the differences were largely attributable to low scores on financial performance). For IDB, 67 percent of operations reviewed in 2001 were found to have adequately defined output indicators, according to a report of the independent evaluation office, a finding that contributed to the adoption of some of the reforms mentioned earlier.[55]

Systemic Issues

There is evidence that the Bank, the Fund, and the MDBs are working better together, as well as with other partners, including the U.N. agencies, WTO, OECD-DAC, and EU and bilateral donors. This brings benefits to clients and partners alike, through the improved efficiency and effectiveness of the IFI system. But further progress is possible, which calls for continued attention to the issue.

Bank-Fund Collaboration

There has been progress on Bank-Fund collaboration in operational work in recent years, reflecting major investments by both institutions toward that end, involving staff, management, and the Executive Boards of the two institutions.[56]

The PRSP process provides a basis for coherent and consistent work of the Bank and the Fund, fully aligned with the country's development strategy. The Joint Staff Assessments (JSAs), which evaluate the soundness of the PRSPs, have proved instrumental in enabling staffs to develop common views. Reinforcing upstream engagement and coordination of the two institutions, using in particular the opportunity offered by the JSA process, would further efforts to promote synergies, better delineate responsibilities in support of the PRSPs, and reduce gaps and overlaps.

In middle-income countries, there is no explicit framework for country-led coordination as in the case of countries with PRSPs. The wide variety of development needs among MICs and difficult-to-predict shifts in country needs for balance-of-payments support lead to differences in the timing and nature of Bank and Fund support and in the content and scope of conditionality, making the implementation of collaboration more challenging.[57] Nevertheless, the principles for effective collaboration are similar, including early consultation on program design and conditionality, and division of responsibilities based on respective mandates and comparative advantage. Meanwhile, a key priority for many MICs, especially those with access to financial markets, relates to joint Bank-Fund work on the prevention and resolution of crises and the strengthening of member countries' financial and fiduciary systems.

Staff coordination is supported by two institutional coordination mechanisms: the Joint Implementation Committee (JIC) for cooperation on HIPC/PRSP countries, and the Financial Sector Liaison Committee (FSLC) for cooperation in financial sector work. The JIC, established in 2000, has provided a useful framework for institutional coordination on the work on low-income countries. Going forward, the JIC's role is being expanded to anchor monitoring of progress on overall Bank-Fund collaboration in an institutional framework. The mandate of the JIC is to address cross-cutting issues on Bank-Fund collaboration; monitor progress on implementation of the framework of collaboration on country programs and conditionality; and, when needed, provide an additional instrument to help country teams in the two institutions to reach agreement on priorities, thus ensuring coherence of policy advice and program design. This covers issues that arise in both the low- and middle-income country contexts. As such, the JIC will provide the institutional framework for monitoring progress on overall Bank-Fund collaboration.

The FSLC, established in 1998 for cooperation on financial sector work, continues to be useful as a forum through which staff exchange information, coordinate work programs, undertake joint missions, and provide consistent policy advice to country authorities, including for financial sector conditions in lending operations. These staff interactions are supported and complemented by broad-based and well-developed mechanisms of institutional coordination. Regular meetings between the Managing Director of the Fund and the President of the Bank, as well as between the Managing Directors of the Bank and the Deputy Managing Directors of the Fund, provide the foundations for a regular dialogue at the most senior level of both institutions. Area Department management in the Fund and Regional Vice-Presidencies in the Bank are also in close and regular contact; and so are respective central units on key policy issues of mutual interest, with a growing number of joint activities.

Finally, the Executive Boards of both institutions are engaged in monitoring Bank-Fund collaboration, with periodic reports on progress in key areas. Meanwhile, regular and transparent reporting in board documents of the views of each institution on reform priorities, program conditionality, and progress in implementation of the agreed program constitutes a crucial element for ensuring consistency of views, transparency, and staff accountability.[58] One mechanism, introduced in 2002,[59] for improved collaboration and communication with the respective Executive Boards, is the enhanced annexes on IMF and World Bank relations in program documents. Aside from keeping the Boards abreast of developments, these annexes are intended to help ensure upstream engagement between the staff of the two institutions, delineate the division of responsibilities, and provide an assessment of the country's reform efforts.

Multilateral Development Banks

Among the MDBs, cooperation also has continued to grow. As with the evolution of Bank-Fund collaboration, the progress reflects the response to the signals emanating from top management and from shareholders. The presidents of the MDBs meet at least twice a year to review substantive and strategic issues, including collaboration among their respective agencies. They also have issued joint statements on a number of common themes, and cosponsored important international events, the Marrakech Roundtable on Managing for Development Results being only the most recent. At their last meeting, the presidents also agreed to strengthen MDB cooperation on capacity building and infrastructure.

Operational vice presidents and their management teams from the World Bank and the respective regional development banks also meet regularly. These meetings include periodic consultations on Memoranda of Understanding (MoU), which have become strategic tools for setting out the division of labor in specific countries and sectors. These MoUs are now reviewed and updated regularly. A review of the MoU between the AfDB and the World Bank was completed in July 2002. In December 2003 a meeting was held in which an agreement was reached on a corresponding action plan for country, sector, and regional thematic cooperation under the MoU. A review of the MoU between the AsDB and the World Bank is scheduled for later this calendar year. The EBRD and the World Bank are cosignatories to three country- and issues-specific MoUs, each of which is reviewed on its own time line. The MoU between the IDB and the World Bank is currently under review.

The quality of MDB cooperation in their country work is the critical test for determining the benefits this partnership can bring to the clients. Notwithstanding occasional staff tensions on individual operational issues, there is evidence of an improved relationship in operations, and better strategic and thematic coherence is gradually showing up in specific operations. All MDBs are committed to supporting countries in preparing PRSPs, basing their assistance strategy on the PRSPs or other such country-owned strategies, and coordinating the strategy with the other

MDB(s) also involved with the country. Cooperation in support of the PRSP process is progressing, but there is recurring friction over the different roles of the World Bank (and IMF) and the regional banks, not least in relation to the preparation of the Joint Staff Assessments. After an uncertain start, coordination of World Bank and regional development bank country strategies is now becoming more accepted, with recent good examples from Honduras and Nicaragua. Discussions have taken place on closer coordination or even joint country strategies in Cambodia, Papua New Guinea, Mongolia, Sri Lanka, the Pacific Islands, and Uganda. The viability and relevance of such coordination, particularly in larger middle-income countries, are not uniformly accepted and will continue to be discussed. That said, government leadership is accepted as the norm to aim for in MDB support for country development in both low- and middle-income countries. Meanwhile, MDBs have continued to strengthen cooperation (with each other and other partners) on individual operational products, at times doing such work jointly and in other cases dividing the work between them. Joint portfolio reviews, public expenditure reviews, fiduciary assessments, and procurement assessments are examples of this type of cooperation, as are activities in support of PRSP preparation. Similarly, there is a growing number of examples of joint or coordinated lending or grant operations, in education, health, infrastructure, environment, and other areas.

IFIs and Beyond

Until now, this chapter has focused on IFI activities, both individually and collectively. But also of interest to the Development Committee and others is the question of how these activities fit into the evolving landscape for country and global development, including the activities of other multilateral agencies. A companion paper has been prepared on that topic,[60] building on the analysis developed in collaboration with staff in partner agencies last year and discussed with World Bank Executive Directors.[61]

That paper sets out a three-tiered architecture, governing the coherence, coordination, and cooperation among the various agencies, around which the detailing and assessment of specific actions will be structured.

- The first tier—where development actually takes place, and the MDGs will be met, or not—is at the country level. Here the consensus both in rhetoric and increasingly in reality is the centrality of national ownership, national policies, national systems, and national leadership for successful development. This principle is at the core of the CDF, the PRSP process, the World Bank's strategy for assisting middle-income countries, the United Nations Development Assistance Framework, the MDBs' country strategies and country strategy papers, and the various strategy documents of bilateral and other donor agencies. It was central to the discussions at Monterrey, Rome, and Marrakech, and as indicated in the paper, there has been much progress across agencies—the IFIs, U.N. agencies, the EU, and bilaterals—taking it forward.
- In the second tier are all the multilateral and bilateral support agencies, charged with helping countries achieve their development outcomes. Clearly these agencies must coordinate with each other in their country work. Increasingly they are doing so, under the leadership of the country itself, with each agency supporting country priorities according to their respective mandates and comparative advantage. But agency headquarters also need to coordinate to establish the scope (and policies) for their country representatives to support national activities; shape the strategic directions and future staffing profiles and skills mix of their respective agencies to ensure that, taken as a whole, the international capacity needed to support country development is in place; and share information and data for monitoring, to inform developing countries of how they are

doing vis-à-vis comparators and to tell global taxpayers how the development system is performing. An example of such cooperation is the inputs to the current *Global Monitoring Report* provided by OECD-DAC, U.N., and WTO staff and the inputs provided by Bank and Fund staff to the annual reports of the Secretary General to the General Assembly on the implementation of the Millennium Declaration.

- The third tier is in the realm of ideas and objectives, with the convergence of international thinking of recent years on the ends and means of development—capped by the MDGs and the Monterrey Consensus. As discussed in earlier chapters, there is broad agreement on the MDGs and related outcomes as the goals of development and on the responsibilities of developing and developed countries in terms of policies and actions for achieving them, with the focus increasingly on the implementation of those policies and actions and on specific measures for monitoring progress. In turn, this growing consensus and coherence on objectives have opened the way for greater specialization in agencies, grounded in their respective mandates, and complemented by increased cooperation with partner agencies to fill gaps in international support for country development.

Conclusions

Where does this leave us? First, the evidence presented above points to progress in individual IFIs on transparency, country focus, and results orientation. However, there clearly is no room for complacency; a key challenge will be to extend and deepen the progress that has been made so far. Important areas for further improvement include:

- For the IMF, the priority is to continue to refine its role in assisting low-income countries to confront the macroeconomic challenges of achieving sustained high levels of growth and poverty reduction. To that end the Fund is adapting its instruments of financial and technical support to the needs of its low-income members, with particular attention to how such support can be used to catalyze other donor assistance, deal with post-conflict situations, assist members in responding to exogenous shocks, and establish institutions that will enable low-income countries to gain increasing access to private sector financing. The Fund's work agenda also aims at strengthening the design of Fund-supported economic programs in low-income countries, while enhancing alignment with the PRSP. A third element of the Fund's ongoing work, together with the World Bank, is to develop an effective and flexible framework for assessing debt sustainability in low-income countries.
- The World Bank's country support priorities are to continue to work with partner agencies to support country efforts to deepen the PRSP process as a basis for the design of its assistance strategies in low-income countries; to adapt its approaches, instruments, and institutional processes to the evolving needs of middle-income countries; and to complete the major agenda the Bank has set out on managing for results, harmonization, and simplification. Supporting and complementing the deepening of country-led approaches in the Bank's assistance strategies is the strengthening of its analytic, knowledge, and advocacy work. A key priority for Bank-supported global and sectoral programs is the implementation of an effective framework for appraisal, monitoring, and evaluation that is every bit as strong as the framework for country programs.
- The regional development banks also have large agendas before them—in their country programs and their support for regional public goods. All need to complete their ongoing reforms associated with the results agenda, as they set out at the Marrakech Roundtable. In addition, like the World Bank, greater efforts are needed on the overall governance and accountability

framework for their regional and sectoral programs.

Second, looking across the IFIs, there also has been progress—both institutionally and in day-to-day work at the country level. Bank-Fund collaboration and coordination among the MDBs are smoother and more productive than they were as recently as five years ago. In tandem with the increase in partnership and coordination, there is a healthy trend toward greater specialization in line with institutional comparative advantage. This reverses the trend of the early 1990s when overlaps in agencies' capacities increased, as the consensus on the comprehensiveness of the development paradigm was beginning to grow. But the "gains from trade" between and among IFIs have not all been harvested yet. Opportunities include increased selectivity of agency programs in line with comparative advantage, harmonization of agency practices around national poverty reduction strategies and systems, and joint evaluations of their support.

Finally, it is none too early to begin thinking beyond the above agenda to the next phase of IFI reform, focused on dynamic comparative advantage. Small steps in that direction include proactive encouragement of cross-IFI secondments, the broadening of the professional networks from individual institutional networks into IFI networks, and the explicit consideration of the IFI dimension in sector strategy papers. Beyond these measures, it will be necessary for the IFIs to tackle strategic issues more directly and to take advantage of the enhanced partnerships across IFIs, so that they can organize and staff themselves effectively to support country, regional, and global development.

Notes

1. See, for example, Scott 2004 and World Bank 2003d.
2. Joint Marrakech Memorandum 2004.
3. OED 2003b.
4. Ghosh and others 2002; Collyns and Kincaid 2003.
5. IMF 2004b.
6. IMF 2001; Boughton and Mourmouras 2004.
7. IMF 2002b.
8. IMF 2002c; IMF–World Bank 2002b.
9. IMF 2003a. The forthcoming PRSP Progress Report will examine a related set of questions.
10. IMF 2003e.
11. For the most recent review, see IMF 2003b.
12. IMF 2003f, chapter III.
13. IMF-World Bank 2002c.
14. IMF-World Bank 2004.
15. IMF 1998.
16. For external assessments, see IMF 2004a, pp. 41-51.
17. IMF 2002a.
18. IMF 2003c.
19. IMF 2003d.
20. World Bank 2003d.
21. IMF–World Bank 2004.
22. Development Committee 2000b.
23. The latest retrospective report, issued in March 2003, examined the 28 CASs and 11 CAS Progress Reports discussed by the Executive Board in fiscal 2000 and the first half of fiscal 2001. It assessed the progress made in improving the quality of the different dimensions of the CAS since the previous retrospective, issued in May 2000. See World Bank 2000, 2003b.
24. Development Committee 2003.
25. OED 2003e.
26. OED 2003a.
27. OED 2004a.
28. World Bank 2004b.
29. OED 2003c.
30. OED 2003a.
31. OED 2003d.
32. Development Committee 2000a.
33. World Bank 2003c.
34. OED 2002.
35. World Bank 2003f.
36. World Bank 2003d.
37. World Bank 2003e.
38. Including Bangladesh, Bolivia, Brazil, Cambodia, Colombia, Dominican Republic, Egypt, Ethiopia, Fiji, Ghana, Honduras, India, Jamaica, Kenya, Kyrgyz Republic, Mexico, Mongolia, Morocco, Mozambique, Nicaragua, Niger, Pacific Islands, Rwanda, Senegal, Serbia, Sri Lanka, Tajikistan, Tanzania, Uganda, Vietnam, and Zambia.
39. See chapter 11.
40. This flexibility is being implemented in all new Bank-financed projects; Bank staff are working

with country authorities and other donors to agree on reporting formats.

41. The associated guidelines for staff and annual financial reporting and auditing for Bank-financed activities were issued in June 2003. The new policy applies to all projects appraised from July 1, 2003.

42. Wapenhans Task Force 1992.

43. Development Committee 2002.

44. OED 2003b.

45. IDA 2003.

46. OED 2004b.

47. OED 2003a.

48. This section is based on the progress reports the regional development banks prepared for Marrakech, as well as other sources as specifically noted. See www.managingfordevelopmentresults.org.

49. MDB Joint Liaison Group 2002.

50. IDB 2004.

51. World Bank 2004c.

52. MDB Evaluation Cooperation Group 2002.

53. AfDB 2002, p. 56.

54. EBRD 2003.

55. IDB 2003.

56. This section is based on IMF–World Bank 2004.

57. The considerations affecting Bank-Fund collaboration in MICs are discussed in IMF–World Bank 2001.

58. As indicated earlier in the chapter, in addition to reporting on country matters, Bank and Fund staff have been reporting jointly to their Executive Boards on a wide range of thematic and policy issues of joint relevance to the two institutions, such as public expenditure management, trade, FSAPs, and ROSCs.

59. IMF–World Bank 2002a.

60. World Bank 2004a.

61. World Bank 2003a.

References

The word *processed* describes informally reproduced works that may not be commonly available.

Chapter 1 Monitoring Framework

Asrey, Steven. 1996. "Water, Waste and Well-Being: A Multicountry Study." *American Journal of Epidemiology* 143(6): 606–23.

Barro, Robert. 2001. "Human Capital and Growth." *American Economic Review,* Papers and Proceedings 91(2): 12–17.

Behrman, Jere, Andrew D. Foster, Mark Richard Rosenzweig, and Prem Vashishtha. 1999. "Women's Schooling, Home Teaching, and Economic Growth." *Journal of Political Economy* 107(August): 682–714.

Berg, Andrew, and Anne Krueger. 2003. "Trade, Growth, and Poverty: A Selective Survey." IMF Working Paper WP/03/30. Washington, D.C.

Development Committee (Joint Ministerial Committee of the Boards of Governors of the World Bank and the International Monetary Fund on the Transfer of Real Resources to Developing Countries). 2002. *Development Committee Communiqué.* Washington, D.C. September 22.

———. 2003a. *Achieving the MDGs and Related Outcomes: A Framework for Monitoring Policies and Actions.* DC2003-0003. Washington, D.C. March 26.

———. 2003b. "Background Paper." DC2003-0003/Add.1. Washington, D.C. March 28.

———. 2003c. "Development Committee Communiqué." Washington, D.C. April 13.

———.2003d. "Poverty Reduction Strategy Papers: Progress in Implementation." DC2003-0011. Washington, D.C.

———. 2003e. "Supporting Sound Policies with Adequate and Appropriate Financing." DC2003-0016. Washington, D.C. September 13.

———. 2003f. "Global Monitoring of Policies and Actions for Achieving the MDGs and Related Outcomes: Implementation Report." DC2003-0013. Washington, D.C. September 15.

———. 2003g. "Development Committee Communiqué." Dubai. September 22.

Filmer, Deon, and Lant Pritchett. 1999. "The Impact of Public Spending on Health: Does Money Matter?" *Social Science and Medicine* 49.

Glewwe, Paul. 1999. "Why Does Mother's Schooling Raise Child Health in Developing Countries: Evidence from Morocco." *Journal of Human Resources* 34(1): 124–59.

Glewwe, Paul, and E. King. 2001. "The Impact of Early Childhood Nutritional Status on Cognitive Development." *World Bank Economic Review* 15(1): 81–113.

Goldin, Ian, Halsey Rogers, and Nicholas Stern. 2002. *The Role and Effectiveness of Development Assistance: Lessons from World Bank Experience.* Washington, D.C.: World Bank.

Harrison, Makiko, Eric Swanson, and Jeni Klugman. 2003. "Targets and Indicators for MDGs and PRSPs: What Countries Have Chosen to Monitor." World Bank. Processed.

IMF (International Monetary Fund). 2001. "How Do Fluctuations in the G-7 Countries Affect Developing Countries?" *World Economic Outlook* (October).

Klasen, Stephan. 2002. "Low Schooling for Girls, Slower Growth for All? Cross-Country Evidence on the Effect of Gender Inequality in Education on Economic Development." *World Bank Economic Review* 16: 345–73.

Miguel, Edward, and Michael Kremer. 2001. "Worms: Education and Health Externalities in Kenya." Working Paper 8481. National Bureau of Economic Research, Cambridge, Mass.

Pritchett, Lant, and Lawrence H. Summers. 1996. "Wealthier Is Healthier." *Journal of Human Resources* 31(4): 841–68.

Schultz, Paul. 1987. "School Expenditures and Enrollments, 1960–1980: The Effects of Income, Prices and Population Growth." In Gale Johnson and Ronald Lee, eds., *Population Growth and Economic Development.* Madison: University of Wisconsin Press.

Udry, Christopher. 1996. "Gender, Agricultural Production, and the Theory of the Household." *Journal of Political Economy* 104(5): 1010–46.

United Nations. 2000. "Millennium Declaration." A/RES/55/2. New York, September 18. www.un.org/documents/ga/res/55/a55r002.pdf.

———. 2001. "Road Map towards the Implementation of the United Nations Millennium Declaration: Report of the Secretary General." A/56/326. New York, September 6.

———. 2002a. *Outcome of the International Conference on Financing for Development, Monterrey Consensus.* A/57/344. New York.

———. 2002b. *Report of the World Summit on Sustainable Development.* Johannesburg.

———. 2003. "Implementation of the United Nations Millennium Declaration: Report of the Secretary General." A/58/323. New York. September 2.

Wagstaff, Adam. 2003. "Intersectoral Synergies and the Health MDGs: Preliminary Cross-Country Findings, Corroboration, and Policy Simulations." World Bank, DECRG/HDNHE, Washington, D.C. Processed.

WHO (World Health Organization). 2001. *Macroeconomics and Health: Investing in Health for Economic Development.* Report of the Commission on Macroeconomics and Health. Geneva.

———. 2002. *World Health Report 2002.* Geneva.

World Bank. 2003. *Global Economic Prospects 2003.* Washington, D.C.

WTO (World Trade Organization). 2001. "Ministerial Declaration, Adopted on 14 November, 2001, Doha." WT/MIN (01)DEC/1. Geneva.

Chapter 2 MDG Prospects: Reasons for Optimism, Grave Concerns

Adams, Richard. 2002. "Economic Growth, Inequality and Poverty: Findings from a New Data Set." Policy Research Paper 2972. World Bank, Washington, D.C.

Development Committee (Joint Ministerial Committee of the Boards of Governors of the World Bank and the International Monetary Fund on the Transfer of Real Resources to Developing Countries). 2003. "Supporting Sound Policies with Adequate and Appropriate Financing." DC2003-0016. Washington, D.C. September 13.

Dollar, David, and Aart Kraay. 2002. "Growth Is Good for the Poor." *Journal of Economic Growth* 7(3): 195–225.

Goldin, Ian, Halsey Rogers, and Nicholas Stern. 2002. *The Role and Effectiveness of Development Assistance: Lessons from World Bank Experience.* Washington, D.C.: World Bank.

OECD (Organisation for Economic Co-operation and Development). 2004. *Development Co-operation Report 2003.* Paris.

Preston, Samuel H. 1980. "Causes and Consequences of Mortality in Less Developed Countries during the Twentieth Century." In Richard Easterlin, ed., *Population and Economic Change in Developing Countries.* Cambridge, Mass.: National Bureau of Economic Research.

Ravallion, Martin. 1995. "Growth and Poverty: Evidence for Developing Countries in the 1990s." *Economic Letters* 48(3–4): 411–17.

———. 2001. "Growth, Inequality and Poverty: Looking Beyond Averages." Policy Research Working Paper 2558. World Bank, Development Research Group, Poverty and Human Resources, Washington, D.C.

Rokx, Claudia, Rae Galloway, and Lynn Brown. 2002. "Prospects for Improving Nutrition in Eastern Europe and Central Asia." Health, Nutrition, and Population series. World Bank, Human Development Network, Washington, D.C.

UNESCAP/UNDP (United Nations Economic and Social Commission for Asia and Pacific/United Nations Development Programme). 2003. "Promoting the Millennium Development Goals in Asia and the Pacific." Bangkok.

UNESCO (United Nations Educational, Scientific, and Cultural Organization). 2003. *Gender and Education for All—The Leap to Equality.* Paris.

UNICEF (United Nations Children's Fund). 2002. "End of Decade Databases: Child Mortality." www.childinfo.org/cmr/revis/db2.htm.

United Nations. 2003. *Implementation of the United Nations Millennium Declaration: Report of the Secretary General*. A/58/323. New York. September.

United Nations Millennium Project Task Force on Education and Gender Equality. 2004. "Interim Report: From Promises to Action. Recommendations for Gender Equality and the Empowerment of Women" (draft). www.unmillenniumproject.org/documents/tf3genderinterim.pdf. February.

World Bank. 2001a. *Engendering Development: Through Gender Equality in Rights, Resources, and Voice*. New York: Oxford University Press.

———. 2001b. *Global Economic Prospects 2002*. Washington, D.C.

———. 2002. *A Case for Aid: Building a Consensus for Development Assistance*. Washington, D.C.

———. 2003a. "East Asia and Pacific Regional Update." http://www.worldbank.org/eapupdate.

———. 2003b. "East Asia Update: From Cyclical Recovery to Long Run Growth." www.developmentgoals.org.

———. 2003c. *Global Economic Prospects 2004*. Washington, D.C.

———. 2003d. *World Development Report 2004: Making Services Work for Poor People*. Washington, D.C.

———. 2004. *The Millennium Development Goals for Health: Rising to the Challenges*. Washington, D.C.

Chapter 4 Improving Enabling Climate for Growth—Economic and Financial Policies

Alesina, Alberto, Silvia Ardagna, Guiseppe Nicoletti, and Fabio Schiantarelli. 2003. "Regulation and Investment." Working Paper 9560. National Bureau of Economic Research, Cambridge, Mass.

Anderson, James, and Peter Neary. 2003. "The Mercantilist Index of Trade Policy." *International Economic Review* 44(2): 627–49.

Aziz, Jahangir, Francesco Caramazza, and Ranil Salgado. 2000. "Currency Crises: In Search of Common Elements." IMF Working Paper WP/00/67. International Monetary Fund, Washington, D.C.

Barro, Robert J. 1997. "Determinants of Economic Growth: A Cross-Country Empirical Study." Lionel Rogers Lectures. Cambridge, Mass.: MIT Press.

Batra, Geeta. 2003. "Investment Climate Measurement: Pitfalls and Possibilities." Discussion Paper. World Bank, Investment Climate Department, Washington, D.C.

Berg, Andrew, and Anne Krueger. 2003. "Trade, Growth, and Poverty: A Selective Survey." IMF Working Paper WP/03/30. International Monetary Fund, Washington, D.C.

Dollar, David, Mary Hallward-Dreimeier, and T. Mengistae. 2003. "Investment Climate and Firm Performance in Developing Countries." World Bank, Washington, D.C. Processed.

Dollar, David, Mary Hallward-Dreimeier, Anqing Shi, Scott Wallsten, Shuilin Wang, and Lixin Colin Xu. 2003. "Improving the Investment Climate in China." Working Paper 26876. World Bank, Development Research Group, Investment Climate, Washington, D.C.

Fallon, Peter, and Robert Lucas. 2002. "The Impact of Financial Crises on Labor Markets, Household Incomes and Poverty: A Review of Evidence." *World Bank Research Observer* 17(1): 21–45.

Hallward-Dreimerier, Mary, Scott Wallsten, and Lixin Colin Xu. 2003. "The Investment Climate and the Firm: Firm-Level Evidence from China." Working Paper 3003. World Bank, Development Research Group, Investment Climate, Washington, D.C.

IMF (International Monetary Fund). 2003. *World Economic Outlook*. Washington, D.C. October.

Kee, Hiau Looi, Alessandro Nicita, and Marcelo Olarreaga. 2004. "Calculation of the Overall Trade Restrictiveness Index." World Bank, Development Research Group, Washington, D.C. Processed.

Maskus, Keith, and John S. Wilson, eds. 2002. "*Quantifying the Impact of Technical Barriers to Trade: Can It be Done?*" University of Michigan Press.

Mattoo, Aaditya, Randeep Rathindran, and Arvind Subramaniam. 2001. "Measuring Services Trade Liberalization and Its Impact on Economic Growth: An Illustration." Policy Research Working Paper 2655. World Bank, Development Research Group, Washington, D.C.

Scarpetta, Stefano, Philip Hemmings, Thierry Tressel, and Jaejoo Woo. 2002. "The Role of

Policy and Institutions for Productivity and Firm Dynamics: Evidence from Micro and Industry Data." OECD Economics Department Working Paper 329. Organisation for Economic Co-operation and Development, Paris. April.

Standard and Poor's. 2003. *Global Stock Markets Factbook*. New York.

Wilson, John S. 2002. "Liberalizing Trade in Agriculture: Developing Countries in Asia and the Post-Doha Agenda." Policy Research Working Paper 2804. World Bank, Policy Research Department, Washington, D.C.

World Bank. 2003. *Doing Business in 2004*. Washington, D.C.

Yaron, Jacob, McDonald Benjamin, and Gerda Piprek. 1997. *Rural Finance: Issues, Design, and Best Practices*. Washington, D.C.: World Bank.

Chapter 5 Upgrading Public Sector Governance

Beck, Thorsten, George Clarke, Alberto Groff, Philip Keefer, and Patrick Walsh. 2000. "New Tools and New Tests in Comparative Political Economy: The Database on Political Institutions." Policy Research Working Paper 2283. World Bank, Washington, D.C.

Bruno, Michael, Martin Ravallion, and Lyn Squire. 1998. "Equity and Growth in Developing Countries: Old and New Perspectives on the Policy Issues." In V. Tanzi and K. Chu, eds., *Income Distribution and High-Quality Growth*. Cambridge, Mass.: MIT Press.

Dollar, David, and Aart Kraay. 2002. "Growth Is Good for the Poor." *Journal of Economic Growth* 7(3): 195–225.

Evans, Peter B., and James E. Rauch. 1999. "Bureaucracy and Growth: A Cross-National Analysis of the Effects of 'Weberian' State Structures on Economic Growth." *American Sociological Review* 64: 748–65.

IMF (International Monetary Fund). 2003. "Growth and Institutions." *World Economic Outlook* (chapter 3). Washington, D.C. April.

IMF–World Bank. 2002. "Actions to Strengthen the Tracking of Poverty-Reducing Public Spending in Heavily Indebted Poor Countries (HIPCs)." Washington, D.C. March.

———. 2003. "Bank/Fund Collaboration on Public Expenditure Issues." Washington, D.C. February 14.

Kaufmann, Daniel, Aart Kraay, and Massimo Mastruzzi. 2003. "Governance Matters III: Governance Indicators for 1996–2002." Policy Research Working Paper 3106. World Bank, Washington, D.C.

Kaufmann, Daniel, Aart Kraay, and Pablo Zoido-Lobaton. 1999. "Governance Matters." Policy Research Working Paper 2196. World Bank, Washington, D.C.

Knack, Stephen, and Philip Keefer. 1995. "Institutions and Economic Performance: Cross-Country Tests Using Alternative Institutional Measures." *Economics and Politics* 7 (November): 207–27.

Knack, Stephen, Mark Kugler, and Nick Manning. 2003. "Second Generation Governance Indicators." *International Review of Administrative Sciences* 69(3): 345–64.

Lambsdorff, Johann Graf. 2003. "Framework Document 2003." Background Paper to the 2003 Corruption Perceptions Index. http://www.transparency.org/cpi/2003/dnld/framework.pdf.

Mauro, Paolo. 1995. "Corruption and Growth." *Quarterly Journal of Economics* 110: 681–712.

NEPAD (New Partnership for Africa's Development). 2003a. "African Peer Review Mechanism." Sixth Summit of the NEPAD Heads of State and Government Implementation Committee, Base Document. http:/www.touchtech.biz/nepad/files/documents/49.pdf.

———. 2003b. "Objectives, Standards, Criteria and Indicators for the African Peer Review Mechanism." http:/www.touchtech.biz/nepad/files/documents/110.pdf.

OECD (Organisation for Economic Co-operation and Development). 1994. *Taxation and Investment Flows: An Exchange of Experiences between the OECD and the Dynamic Asian Economies*. Paris.

Pritchett, Lant, and Lawrence H. Summers. 1996. "Wealthier Is Healthier." *Journal of Human Resources* 31(4): 841–68.

Tanzi, Vito, and Howell Zee. 2000. "Tax Policy for Emerging Markets: Developing Countries." *National Tax Journal* 53(2): 299–322.

UNECA (U.N. Economic Commission for Africa). Forthcoming. *African Governance Report*. Addis Ababa.

WHO (World Health Organization). 2002. "Mobilization of Domestic Resources for Health: Report of the Working Group 3 of the

Commission on Macroeconomics and Health." Geneva. August.

World Bank. 2003. "Lessons on Governance Reform from the 1990s. A Concept Note." World Bank, Public Sector Governance Group, Washington, D.C. November. Processed.

Chapter 6 Strengthening Infrastructure

Angel, Shlomo. 2000. *Housing Policy Matters: A Global Analysis.* New York: Oxford University Press.

APHRC (Africa Population and Health Research Center). 2002. *Population and Health Dynamics in Nairobi's Informal Settlements.* Nairobi.

Bacon, Robert. 1999. "A Scorecard for Energy Reform in Developing Countries." Public Policy for the Private Sector. Note 175. World Bank. April.

Caldéron, Cesar, William Easterly, and Luis Servén. 2003. "The Output Cost of Latin America's Infrastructure Gap." In William Easterly and Luis Servén, eds., *The Limits of Stabilization: Infrastructure, Public Deficits, and Growth in Latin America.* Palo Alto, Calif.: Stanford University Press.

Camdessus, Michel. 2003. "Financing Water for All." In James Winpenny, ed., *Report of the World Panel on Financing Water Infrastructure.* Marseilles: World Water Council.

Datt, Gaurav, and Martin Ravallion. 1998. "Why Have Some Indian States Done Better than Others at Reducing Poverty?" *Economica* 65(257): 17–38.

De la Fuente, Angel, and Antonio Estache. 2004. "A Survey of the Evidence on the Growth Effects of Infrastructure." World Bank, Infrastructure Vice Presidency, Washington, D.C. Processed.

Deininger, Klaus, and John Okidi. 2003. "Growth and Poverty Reduction in Uganda, 1999–2000: Panel Data Evidence." *Development Policy Review* 21(4): 481–509.

Development Committee (Joint Ministerial Committee of the Boards of Governors of the World Bank and the International Monetary Fund on the Transfer of Real Resources to Developing Countries). 2003. "Water Supply and Sanitation and the MDGs." DC2003-004/Add.3. Washington, D.C. April.

DFID (U.K. Department for International Development). 2002. "Making Connections: Infrastructure for Poverty Reduction." January. Processed. http://62.189.42.51/DFIDstage/FOI/dc/7mar02_making_connections.pdf.

Easterly, William, and Luis Servén, eds. 2003. *The Limits of Stabilization: Infrastructure, Public Deficits, and Growth in Latin America.* Palo Alto, Calif.: Stanford University Press.

Estache, Antonio, Vivien Foster, and Quentin Wodon. 2002. "Accounting for Poverty in Infrastructure Reform—Learning from Latin America's Experience." World Bank Institute Studies in Development Series, Washington, D.C.

Fan, Shenggen, Linxiu Zhang, and Xiaobo Zhang. 2002. "Growth, Inequality and Poverty in China: The Role of Public Investments." Research Report 123. International Food Policy Research Institute, Washington, D.C.

Fay, Marianne, and Tito Yepes. 2003. "Investing in Infrastructure: What Is Needed from 2000 to 2010?" Policy Research Paper 3102. World Bank, Infrastructure Vice Presidency, Washington, D.C. Processed.

Foster, Vivien, and Jean-Philippe Tre. 2000. "Measuring the Impact of Energy Interventions on the Poor: An Illustration from Guatemala." In *Infrastructure for Development: Private Solutions and the Poor.* Conference volume for Private Provision of Infrastructure Advisory Facility (PPIAF). London: Department for International Development (U.K.) and World Bank.

Global Water Partnership. 2000. *Towards Water Security: A Framework for Action.* Stockholm.

Jalan, Jyotsna, and Martin Ravallion. 2001. "Does Piped Water Reduce Diarrhea for Children in Rural India?" Policy Research Working Paper 2664. World Bank, Development Research Group, Washington, D.C. Processed.

Jayasuriya, Ruwan, and Quentin Wodon, eds. 2003. "Efficiency in Reaching the Millennium Development Goals." Working Paper 9. World Bank, Washington, D.C.

JMP (Joint Monitoring Programme for Water and Sanitation of WHO-UNICEF). 2000. Data for 2000. http://www.wssinfo.org.

Kingdom, William, and Nicola Tynan. 2002. "A Water Scorecard: Setting Performance Targets for Water Utilities." Viewpoint 242, Private Sector and Infrastructure Network, World Bank, Washington, D.C.

Leipziger, Danny, Marianne Fay, and Tito Yepes. 2003. "Achieving the Millennium Development Goals: The Role of Infrastructure." Policy Research Working Paper 3163. World Bank, Washington, D.C. Processed.

Qiang, Christine Zhing-Wen. 2004. "Regulatory Developments in ICT." World Bank CIT Department, INF Vice Presidency, Washington, D.C. Processed.

Ramirez, Maria Teresa, and Hadi Esfahani. 2000. "Infrastructure and Economic Growth." Bank of Colombia, Bogotá. Processed.

Roberts, Peter. 2003. "Transport Indicators." World Bank TWU Department, Washington, D.C. Processed.

Roja, F. K. 2003. "The Penalties of Inefficiency in Infrastructure." *Review of Development Economics* 7(1): 127–37.

United Nations Millennium Project Task Force on Water and Sanitation. 2003. "Achieving the MDG for Water and Sanitation: What Will It Take?" Interim Full Report. New York. December.

Winpenny, James, ed. 2003. *Report of the World Panel on Financing Water Infrastructure.* Marseilles: World Water Council.

World Bank. 1994. *World Development Report.* Washington, D.C.

———. 2000. World Business Environment Survey. http://info.worldbank.org/governance/wbes/.

———. 2002. "Water Sector Reform Scorecard: A Global Overview of Urban Water Supply and Sanitation Sector Reform." Washington, D.C. Processed.

World Economic Forum. 2003. *Global Competitiveness Report, 2002–03.* Cologny/Geneva.

Chapter 7 Accelerating Human Development

Blank, Lorraine, Margaret Grosh, and Christine Weigand. 2003. "Patterns in Social Protection Expenditures." World Bank, HDNSP, Washington, D.C.

Bruns, Barbara, Alain Mingat, and Ramahatra Rakotomalala. 2003. *Achieving Universal Primary Education by 2015: A Chance for Every Child.* Washington, D.C.: World Bank.

Dehn, Jan, Ritva Reinikka, and Jakob Svensson. 2003. "Survey Tools for Assessing Performance in Service Delivery." In Francois Bourguignon and Luiz Pereira da Silva, eds., *The Impact of Economic Policies on Poverty and Income Distribution: Evaluation Techniques and Tools.* New York: World Bank and Oxford University Press.

Development Committee (Joint Ministerial Committee of the Boards of Governors of the World Bank and the International Monetary Fund on the Transfer of Real Resources to Developing Countries). 2004. "Education for All (EFA)–Fast Track Initiative: Progress Report." DC2004-0002/1, Washington, D.C. March 26.

Di Tella, Raphael, and William Savedoff. 2000. *Diagnosis Corruption: Fraud in Latin America's Public Hospitals.* Latin America Research Network. Washington, D.C.: Inter-American Development Bank.

Dreze, Jean, and Haris Gazdar. 1996. "Uttar Pradesh: The Burden of Inertia." In Jean Dreze and Amartya Sen, eds., *Indian Development: Selected Regional Perspectives.* New Delhi: Oxford University Press.

Filmer, Deon, and Lant Pritchett. 1999. "The Impact of Public Spending on Health: Does Money Matter?" *Social Science and Medicine* 49: 1309–23.

Kattan. 2003. "User Fees in Primary Education." World Bank, Washington, D.C. January. Processed.

Khandker, Shahidur, Mark Pitt, and Nobuhiko Fuwa. 2003. "Subsidy to Promote Girls' Secondary Education: The Female Stipend Program in Bangladesh." World Bank, Washington, D.C. March. Processed.

Lewis, Maureen. 2000. "Who Is Paying for Health Care in Europe and Central Asia?" Eastern Europe and Central Asia Region Monograph. World Bank, Washington, D.C.

Reinikka, Ritva, and Jakob Svensson. 2004. "Local Capture: Evidence from a Central Government Transfer Program in Uganda." *The Quarterly Journal of Economics* 119(2).

Rubio, Gloria, and Kalanidhi Subbarao. 2003. "Impact Evaluation in Bank Projects: A Comparison of Fiscal 1998 and 1999." World Bank, Poverty Reduction and Economic Management (PREM) Network, Washington, D.C.

Schneider, Pia, A. K. Nandakumar, Denis Porignon, Manjiri Bhawalkar, Damascene Butera, and Courtney Barnett. 2000. "Rwanda National Health Accounts 1998." Technical Report 53. Partnerships for Health Reform Project. Bethesda, MD: Abt Associates Inc.

UNAIDS (Joint U.N. Programme on HIV/AIDS). 2003. "Progress Report on the Global Response to the HIV/AIDS Epidemic, 2003." Geneva.

UNDP (United Nations Development Programme). 2003. *Human Development Report.* New York.

USAID (United States Agency for International Development). Various years. *Demographic and Health Survey.* Washington, D.C.

World Bank. 2003a. *Restoring Fiscal Discipline for Poverty Reduction in Peru.* World Bank, Washington, D.C.

———. 2003b. *World Development Indicators 2003.* Washington, D.C.

———. 2003c. *World Development Report 2004: Making Services Work for Poor People.* Washington D.C.

———. 2004. *The Millennium Development Goals for Health: Rising to the Challenges.* Washington, D.C.

Chapter 8 Promoting Environmental Sustainability

Cavendish, William. 2000. "Empirical Regularities in the Poverty-Environment Relationship of Rural Households: Evidence from Zimbabwe." *World Development* 28(11): 1979–2003.

United Nations Millennium Project. 2003. "Background Paper of the Millennium Task Force on Environmental Sustainability." New York. Processed.

van der Klaauw, Bas, and Limin Wang. 2003. "Child Mortality in Rural India: Determinants and Policy Implications." World Bank, Washington, D.C. Processed.

WHO (World Health Organization). 2002. *World Health Report 2002.* Geneva.

Chapter 9 Fostering Growth and Stability: Macro-financial Policies

Adams, Richard, Jr. 2003. "International Migration, Remittances, and the Brain Drain: A Study of 24 Labor-Exporting Countries." Policy Research Working Paper 3069. World Bank, Washington, D.C.

Basel Committee on Banking Supervision. 2003. "The New Basel Accord, Consultative Document." Bank for International Settlements, Berne.

Borensztein, Eduardo, José De Gregorio, and Jong-Wha Lee. 1998. "How Does Foreign Investment Affect Growth?" *Journal of International Economics* 45(June): 115–35.

Chuhan, Punam, and Federico Sturzenegger. 2004. "Default Episodes in the 1980s and 1990s: What Have We Learned?" In Joshua Aizenman and Brian Pinto, eds., *Managing Volatility and Crisis: A Practioner's Guide.* World Bank, Washington, D.C. http:/www.wbweb.worldbank.org/prem/prmep/economicpolicy/mv/handbook.htm.

Claessens, Stijn, Geoffrey R. D. Underhill, and Xiaoke Zhang. 2003. "Basel II Capital Requirements and Developing Countries: A Political Economy Perspective." Paper presented at the workshop on Quantifying the Impact of Rich Countries' Policies on Poor Countries, October 23–24, organized by the Center for Global Development and the Global Development Network. World Bank, Washington, D.C.

Eichengreen, Barry, Kenneth Kletzer, and Ashoka Mody. 2003. "Crisis Resolution: Next Steps." IMF Working Paper WP/03/196. International Monetary Fund, Washington, D.C.

Faini, Ricardo. 2003. "Is the Brain Drain an Unmitigated Blessing?" Discussion Paper 2003/64. World Institute for Development Economics Research, Helsinki. September.

Heid, Frank. 2003. "Is Regulatory Capital Procyclical? A Macroeconomic Assessment of Basel II." Paper presented at Basel Committee Banca d'Italia Workshop, March 20–23. Rome.

IMF (International Monetary Fund). 2001. *World Economic Outlook.* Washington, D.C. October.

IMF–World Bank. 2003. "International Standards: Strengthening Surveillance, Domestic Institutions, and International Markets." Washington, D.C.

Ratha, Dilip. 2003. "Enhancing Workers' Remittances to Developing Countries." World Bank, Washington, D.C.

Skeldon, Ronald. 1997. *Migration and Development.* Harlow, England: Addison Wesley Longman.

World Bank. 2004. *Global Development Finance 2004.* Washington, D.C.

Chapter 10 Dismantling Barriers to Trade

Anderson, Kym. 2003. "How Can Agricultural Trade Reform Reduce Poverty?" Background Paper prepared for the United Nations Millennium Project Task Force on Trade. New York. Processed.

Baffes, John. 2003. "Cotton Market Policies: Issues and Facts." Policy Research Working Paper 3218. World Bank. Washington, D.C. Processed.

Beghin, John, David Roland-Holst, and Dominique van der Mensbrugghe. 2002. "How Will Agricultural Trade Reforms in High-Income Countries Affect the Trading Relationships of Developing Countries?" World Bank, Washington, D.C. Processed.

Bown, Chad, Bernard Hoekman, and Caglar Ozden. 2003. "Developing Countries and U.S. Antidumping: The Path from Initial Filing to WTO Dispute Settlement." *World Trade Review* 2(3): 349–71.

Hoekman, Bernold, Francis Ng, and Marcelo Olarreaga. 2002. "Eliminating Excessive Tariffs on Exports of Least Developed Countries." *World Bank Economic Review* 16(1): 1–21.

———. 2004. "Reducing Agricultural Tariffs versus Domestic Support: What's More Important for Developing Countries?" *World Bank Economic Review* 18(1).

Karsenty, Guy. 2002. "Trends in Services Trade under GATS: Recent Developments." Presentation to the WTO Symposium on Assessment of Trade Services, March 14–15. Geneva.

Liu, Xiang, and Hylke Van den Bussche 2003. "EU Antidumping Cases against China." Licos Discussion Papers 11902. Catholic University, Leuven, Belgium.

Mattoo, Aaditya. 2003. "Services in a Development Round." World Bank, Washington, D.C. Processed.

Messerlin, Patrick. 2002. "Agriculture in the Doha Agenda." Policy Research Working Paper 3009. World Bank, Washington, D.C.

Mitchell, Donald. 2004. "Sugar Policies: Opportunities for Change." Policy Research Working Paper 3222. World Bank, Washington, D.C.

Otsuki, Tsunehiro, John S. Wilson, and Mirvat Sewadeh. 2001. "Saving Two in a Billion: Quantifying the Trade Effect of European Food Safety Standards on African Exports." *Food Policy* 26(5): 495–514.

Schiff, Maurice, and L. Alan Winters. 2003. *Regionalism and Development.* New York: Oxford University Press and World Bank.

Stern, Robert. 2002. "Quantifying Barriers to Trade in Services." In Bernard Hoekman, Philip English, and Aaditya Mattoo, eds., *Development, Trade and the WTO: A Handbook.* Washington, D.C.: World Bank.

Walmsley, Terri, and L. Alan Winters. 2002. "Relaxing Restrictions on Temporary Movement of Natural Persons: A Simulation Analysis." University of Sussex, Economics Department. Brighton, U.K. Processed.

Wilson, John S., and Victor Abiola, eds. 2003. *Standards & Global Trade: A Voice for Africa.* Washington, D.C.: World Bank.

World Bank. 2003. *Global Economic Prospects and the Developing Countries 2004: Realizing the Development Promise of the Doha Agenda.* Washington, D.C.

———. 2004. *Global Development Finance, 2004.* Washington, D.C.

WTO (World Trade Organization). 2001. "Ministerial Declaration, Adopted on 14 November, 2001, Doha." WT/MIN (01)DEC/1. Geneva.

———. 2002. Speech by the Director General, April 12, Montreux.

Chapter 11 Providing More and Better Aid

Aryeetey, Ernest, Barfour Osei, and Peter Quartey. 2003. "Does Tying Aid Make It More Costly? A Ghanaian Case Study." Paper presented at the Workshop on Quantifying the Impact of Rich Countries' Policies on Poor Countries, Center for Global Development and the Global Development Network, Washington, D.C. October 23–24.

Birdsall, Nancy, Stijn Claessens, and Ishac Diwan. 2003. "Policy Selectivity Forgone: Debt and Donor Behavior in Africa." *The World Bank Economic Review* 17(3): 409–35.

Bulir, Ales, and A. Javier Hamann. 2001. "How Volatile and Unpredictable Are Aid Flows, and What Are the Policy Implications?" IMF Working Paper WP/01/167. International Monetary Fund, Washington, D.C.

———. 2003. "Aid Volatility: An Empirical Assessment." *IMF Staff Papers* 50(1): 64–89.

Bulir, Ales, and Timothy Lane. 2002. "Aid and Fiscal Management." IMF Working Paper WP/02/112. International Monetary Fund, Washington, D.C.

Burnside, Craig, and David Dollar. 2000. "Aid, Policies, and Growth." *American Economic Review* 90(4): 847–68.

———. 2004. "Aid, Policies, and Growth: Revisiting the Evidence." Policy Research Paper 0-2834. World Bank, Washington, D.C.

Collier, Paul, and Jan Dehn. 2001. "Aid, Shocks and Growth." Policy Research Working Paper 2688. World Bank, Washington, D.C.

Collier, Paul, and A. Hoeffler. 2002. "Aid, Policy and Growth in Post-Conflict Countries." Policy

Research Working Paper 2902. World Bank, Washington, D.C.
Devarajan, Shantayanan, Margaret J. Miller, and Eric V. Swanson. 2002. "Goals for Development: History, Prospects and Costs." Policy Research Working Paper 2819. World Bank, Human Development Network, Washington, D.C.
Development Committee (Joint Ministerial Committee of the Boards of Governors of the World Bank and the International Monetary Fund on the Transfer of Real Resources to Developing Countries). 2003a. "Progress Report and Critical Next Steps in Scaling Up: Education for All, Health, HIV/AIDS, Water and Sanitation—Synthesis Paper." DC2003-0004. Washington, D.C.
———. 2003b. "Supporting Sound Policies with Adequate and Appropriate Financing." DC2003-0016.Washington, D.C. September.
———. 2004. "Financing Modalities toward the Millennium Development Goals: Progress Note." DC2004-003. Washington, D.C. April 12.
Dollar, David, and Victoria Levin. 2004. "The Increasing Selectivity of Aid, 1984–2002." Policy Research Working Paper 3299. World Bank, Washington, D.C.
Gemmell, Norman, and Mark McGillivray. 1998. "Aid and Tax Instability and the Budget Constraint in Developing Countries." CREDIT Research Paper 98/1. University of Nottingham, Centre for Research in Economic Development and International Trade, U.K.
Goldin, Ian, Halsey Rogers, and Nicholas Stern. 2002. *The Role and Effectiveness of Development Assistance: Lessons from World Bank Experience.* Washington, D.C.: World Bank.
IMF (International Monetary Fund). 2004. "IMF Discusses Operational Framework for Debt Sustainability in Low-Income Countries." Public Information Notice 04/34. Washington, D.C. April 5. www.imf.org/external/np/sec/pn/2004/pn0434.htm.
IMF–World Bank. 2003a. "Heavily Indebted Poor Countries (HIPC) Initiative: Status of Implementation." IDA/SecM2003-0477/1. Washington, D.C. September.
———. 2003b. "Update on Implementation of Action Plans to Strengthen Capacity of HIPCs to Track Poverty-Reducing Spending." IDA/R2003-0043. Washington, D.C. March. www.imf.org/external/np/hipc/doc.htm. www.worldbank.org/publicsector/pe/HIPCUpdate.pdf.
———. 2004a. "Debt Sustainability in Low-Income Countries—Proposal for an Operational Framework and Policy Implications." Washington, D.C. February 3. www.imf.org/external/np/pdr/sustain/2004/020304.pdf.
———. 2004b. "Heavily Indebted Poor Countries (HIPC) Initiative: Statistical Update." IDA/SecM2004-0184. Washington, D.C. April.
Jepma, Catrinus J. 1991. "The Tying of Aid." Organisation for Economic Co-operation and Development, Development Centre Studies, Paris.
Knack, Stephen, and Aminur Rahman. 2004. "Donor Fragmentation and Bureaucratic Quality in Aid Recipients." Policy Research Working Paper 3186. World Bank, Washington, D.C.
OECD (Organisation for Economic Co-operation and Development). 2003. "OECD Questionnaire, Indicators of Progress in Harmonization and Alignment, Annex A, Explanatory Note" (first draft for discussion). Paris. December.
———. 2004a. *Development Cooperation Report 2003*. Paris.
———. 2004b. "ODA Statistics for 2003 and ODA Outlook." DCD/DAC(2004/22. Paris.
Prati, Alessandro, Ratna Sahay, and Thierry Tressel. 2003. "Is There a Case for Sterilizing Foreign Aid Flows?" IMF Seminar Series 2003-88. International Monetary Fund, Washington, D.C. June.
Roodman, David. 2003. "An Index of Donor Aid Performance." Center for Global Development. Washington, D.C.
United Nations. 2001. "Report of the High-Level Panel on Financing for Development." Presented to the General Assembly, June 28, New York.
United Nations Millennium Project. 2004. "Millennium Development Goals Needs Assessment." New York.
World Bank. 2002. *A Case for Aid: Building a Consensus for Development Assistance.* Washington, D.C.

Chapter 12 Fulfilling Responsibilities for Global Public Goods

African Development Bank. 2002. "MDB Support for Global Public Goods Provisions: Progress Report." Addis Ababa, Ethiopia.

Development Committee (Joint Ministerial Committee of the Boards of Governors of the World Bank and the International Monetary Fund on the Transfer of Real Resources to Developing Countries). 2000. "Poverty Reduction and Global Public Goods: Issues for the World Bank in Supporting Global Collective Action." World Bank Report to the Development Committee. Washington, D.C.

———. 2001. "Poverty Reduction and Global Public Goods: Progress Report." World Bank Report to the Development Committee. Washington, D.C.

Ferroni, Marco, and Ashoka Mody. 2002. *International Public Goods: Incentives, Measurement, and Financing*. Boston, Mass.: Kluwer Academic Publishers; Washington, D.C.: World Bank.

Kaul, Inge, Pedro le Goulven, and Ronald Mendoza. 2003. "Providing Global Public Goods: Managing Globalization." New York: Oxford University Press.

Pagiola Stefano, Roberto Martin-Hurtado, Priya Shyamsundar, Muthukumara Mani, and Patricio Silva. 2002. "Generating Public Sector Resources to Finance Sustainable Development." Technical Paper 538. World Bank, Environment Department, Washington, D.C.

Samuelson, Paul. 1954. "The Pure Theory of Public Expenditure." *Review of Economics and Statistics* 49(2): 257–81.

World Bank. 2001. *Global Development Finance 2001: Buildings Conditions for Effective Development Finance*. Washington, D.C.

Chapter 13 Monitoring the IFIs' Contribution

AfDB (African Development Bank). 2002. *Annual Report*. Addis Ababa, Ethiopia.

Boughton, James, and Alex Mourmouras. 2004. "Whose Programme Is It? Policy Ownership with Conditional Lending." In David Vines and Christopher Gilbert, eds., *The IMF and Its Critics: Reform of Global Financial Architecture*. Cambridge, U.K.: Cambridge University Press.

Burnside, Craig, and David Dollar. 2000. "Aid, Policies, and Growth." *American Economic Review* 90(4): 847–68.

Collyns, Charles, and Russell Kincaid, eds. 2003. *Managing Financial Crises—Recent Experience and Lessons for Latin America*. IMF Occasional Paper 217. International Monetary Fund, Washington, D.C.

Development Committee (Joint Ministerial Committee of the Boards of Governors of the World Bank and the International Monetary Fund on the Transfer of Real Resources to Developing Countries). 2000a. "Poverty Reduction and Global Public Goods: Issues for the World Bank in Supporting Global Collective Action." DC2000-16. Washington, D.C. September.

———. 2000b. "Supporting Country Development: World Bank Role and Instruments in Low- and Middle-Income Countries." DC2000-19. Washington, D.C.

———. 2002. "Better Measuring, Monitoring, and Managing for Development Results." DC2002-0018. Washington, D.C. September.

———. 2003. "Poverty Reduction Strategy Papers: Progress in Implementation." DC2003-0011. Washington, D.C. September.

EBRD (European Bank for Reconstruction and Development). 2003. *Annual Evaluation Overview Report*. http://www.ebrd.org/projects/eval/showcase/main.htm.

Ghosh, Atish, Timothy D. Lane, Ales Bilir, M. Schulze-Ghattos, and Alexandros T. Mourmouas. 2002. "IMF-Supported Programs in Capital Account Crises." IMF Occasional Paper 210. International Monetary Fund, Washington, D.C.

IDA (International Development Association). 2003. "IDA Results Measurement System: Update Note." IDA/R2003-0189. Washington, D.C. October.

IDB (Inter-American Development Bank). 2003. *Analysis of Project Evaluability Year 2001*. RE-275. Washington, D.C. January.

———. 2004. *Regional Public Goods: The Opportunity for an Expanded Bank Role*. Washington, D.C.

IMF (International Monetary Fund). 1998. *External Evaluation of the ESAF—Report by a Group of Independent Experts*. Washington, D.C.

———. 2001. "Strengthening Country Ownership of Fund-Supported Programs." Washington, D.C. December. http://www.imf.org/external/np/pdr/cond/2001/eng/strength/120501.htm.

———. 2002a. "Evaluation of the Prolonged Use of Fund Resources." SM/02/87. Washington, D.C. September.

———. 2002b. "Guidelines on Conditionality." IMF Executive Board Decision 12864-(02/102). Washington, D.C. September.
———. 2002c. "Review of the Poverty Reduction and Growth Facility." SM/02/51. Washington, D.C. February.
———. 2003a. "Alignment of the PRGF and the PRSP." SM/03/94. Washington, D.C.
———. 2003b. "Enhancing the Effectiveness of Surveillance: Operational Responses, the Agenda Ahead, and Next Steps." Public Information Notice 03/50. Washington, D.C. April 10.
———. 2003c. "Evaluation of the Role of the Fund in Recent Capital Account Crises—Report by the Independent Evaluation Office." SM/03/171. Washington, D.C. May.
———. 2003d. "Independent Evaluation Office—Evaluation of Fiscal Adjustment in IMF-Supported Programs." SM/03/291. Washington, D.C. August.
———. 2003e "Role of the Fund in Low-Income Member Countries over the Medium Term—Issues Paper for Discussion." SM/03/257. Washington, D.C. July.
———. 2003f. *World Economic Outlook* (April). Washington, D.C.
———. 2004a. *Finance and Development*. Washington, D.C. March (articles by Kenen, Lissakers, Milleron, and Welch).
———. 2004b. "Technical Assistance Evaluation Program—Findings of Evaluations and Updated Program." March 1. http://www.imf.org/external/np/ta/2004/eng/030104.htm.
IMF–World Bank. 2001. "Strengthening World Bank-IMF Collaboration on Country Programs and Conditionality." SecM2001-0461/1 and SM/01/219, Supplement 1, Revision 1. Washington, D.C. August.
———. 2002a. "Operationalizing Bank-Fund Collaboration in Country Programs and Conditionality." Staff Guidance Note. Washington, D.C.
———. 2002b. "Review of the Poverty Reduction Strategy Paper Approach." SM/02/53. Washington, D.C. February.
———. 2002c. "Strengthening IMF–World Bank Coordination on Country Programs and Conditionality—Progress Report." World Bank Document SecM2002-443 and IMF Document SM/02/271. Washington, D.C. August.
———. 2004. "Strengthening IMF–World Bank Collaboration on Country Programs and Conditionality—Progress Report." SecM2004-0072/1. Washington, D.C. March 26.
Joint Marrakech Memorandum. 2004. "Promoting a Harmonized Approach to Managing for Development Results: Core Principles; and Action Plan on Managing for Development Results." Presented to the Second Roundtable for Managing Results, February 4–5, sponsored by the World Bank and four regional development banks.
MDB (Multilateral Development Banks) Evaluation Cooperation Group. 2002. "Good Practice Standard on MDB-Supported Public Sector Evaluations." June.
MDB Joint Liaison Group. 2002. "The Role of the MDBs in the Provision of Global Public Goods." Washington, D.C.
OED (Operations Evaluation Department, World Bank). 2002. "The World Bank's Approach to Global Programs: An Independent Evaluation." Washington, D.C.
———. 2003a. "2002 Annual Review of Development Effectiveness—Achieving Development Outcomes: The Millennium Challenge." Washington, D.C.
———. 2003b. "2003 Annual Report on Operations Evaluation." Report 25861. Washington, D.C.
———. 2003c. "Approach Paper: Country Assistance Strategy Evaluation Retrospective." CODE2003-0071. Washington, D.C. November.
———. 2003d. "The CGIAR at 31: An Independent Meta-Evaluation of the Consultative Group on International Agricultural Research." Washington, D.C.
———. 2003e. "Multi-party Evaluation of the Comprehensive Development Framework." CODE2003-0034. Washington, D.C. May.
———. 2004a. "2003 Annual Review of Development Effectiveness—The Effectiveness of Bank Support for Policy Reform." Report 28290. Washington, D.C.
———. 2004b. "Books, Buildings, and Learning Outcomes: An Impact Evaluation of World Bank Support to Basic Education in Ghana." Report 28779. Washington, D.C.
Scott, Alison. 2004. "Assessing Multilateral Effectiveness." U.K. Department for International Development, London. February.

Wapenhans Task Force. 1992. "Report of the Portfolio Management Performance Task Force." World Bank, Washington, D.C.

World Bank. 1998. "Country Assistance Strategies: Retrospective and Outlook." SecM98-242. Washington, D.C. March.

———. 2000. "Country Assistance Strategies: Retrospective and Implications." R99-228/2. Washington, D.C. May.

———. 2003a. "Coherence, Coordination, and Cooperation among Multilateral Organizations." SecM2003-0112. March, and SecM2003-0380. August. Washington, D.C.

———. 2003b. "Country Assistance Strategies: Retrospective and Future Directions." Washington, D.C. March.

———. 2003c. "Delivering Global Public Goods Locally: Lessons Learned and Successful Approaches." Development Grant Facility Technical Note. Washington, D.C.

———. 2003d. "The Global Poll: Multinational Survey of Opinion Leaders 2002." Prepared for the World Bank by Princeton Survey Research Associates. May 2003. www.worldbank.org.

———. 2003e. "Harmonization Follow-up: Global Architecture and World Bank Activities." SecM2003-0387/1. Washington, D.C. November.

———. 2003f. "Update on Management of Global Programs and Partnerships." SecM2003-0095. Washington, D.C. March.

———. 2004a. "Coherence, Coordination, and Cooperation among Multilateral Organizations: Progress and Challenges." SecM2004-0152. Washington, D.C. April.

———. 2004b. "Enhancing World Bank Support to Middle-Income Countries." SecM2004-0071. February.

———. 2004c. "Managing for Development Results in the Multilateral Development Banks." Prepared with inputs from MDBs. Washington, D.C. February.

———. 2004d. "Managing for Development Results in the World Bank." Washington, D.C.